MW00712182

Macromedia Flash 5 Developer's Guide

P.S. Woods

Osborne/**McGraw-Hill**

New York Chicago San Francisco
Lisbon London Madrid Mexico City Milan
New Delhi San Juan Seoul Singapore Sydney Toronto

Osborne/**McGraw-Hill**
2600 Tenth Street
Berkeley, California 94710
U.S.A.

To arrange bulk purchase discounts for sales promotions, premiums, or fund-raisers, please contact Osborne/**McGraw-Hill** at the above address. For information on translations or book distributors outside the U.S.A., please see the International Contact Information page immediately following the index of this book.

Macromedia Flash 5 Developer's Guide

Copyright © 2001 by The McGraw-Hill Companies. All rights reserved. Printed in the United States of America. Except as permitted under the Copyright Act of 1976, no part of this publication may be reproduced or distributed in any form or by any means, or stored in a database or retrieval system, without the prior written permission of the publisher, with the exception that the program listings may be entered, stored, and executed in a computer system, but they may not be reproduced for publication.

1234567890 CUS CUS 01987654321

Book p/n 0-07-219240-2 and CD p/n 0-07-219239-9
parts of
ISBN 0-07-213121-7

Publisher	Brandon A. Nordin
Vice President & Associate Publisher	Scott Rogers
Acquisitions Editor	Jim Schachterle
Acquisitions Coordinator	Tim Madrid
Project Editor	Jenn Tust
Technical Editor	Jonathan Flanigan
Copy Editor	Judith Brown
Proofreader	Paul Medoff
Indexer	Jack Lewis
Computer Designers	George Toma Charbak, Elizabeth Jang, Roberta Steele
Illustrators	Lyssa Sieben-Wald, Micheal Mueller, Alex Putney
Series Designer	Roberta Steele
Cover Designer	Greg Scott
Series Illustrator	Eliot Bergman

This book was composed with Corel VENTURA™ Publisher.

Information has been obtained by Osborne/**McGraw-Hill** from sources believed to be reliable. However, because of the possibility of human or mechanical error by our sources, Osborne/**McGraw-Hill**, or others, Osborne/**McGraw-Hill** does not guarantee the accuracy, adequacy, or completeness of any information and is not responsible for any errors or omissions or the results obtained from use of such information.

For every Flasher who has participated in a constructive, intelligent conversation on a bulletin board or list. It is the conversation that makes Flash great.

About the Author

After struggling as a musician, P.S. Woods rose from an entry-level position to become the General Manager of an upscale hotel, during which time he also obtained a degree in Business Management. A longtime computer user and programming enthusiast, Woods continued to dabble in web media and programming until colleagues suggested that he pursue his interest full-time. He spent five years in hospitality before leaving the comfort of his river-view office and steady paycheck to become a full-time independent contractor. During his career as a freelance developer and consultant, he has contributed many articles and product reviews to the Flash community through the Web Developers' Virtual Library (www.wdvl.com). In his consulting career, he has been retained by clients as small as a storefront ISP in the Mojave Desert and as large as Price Waterhouse Coopers. Woods lives in the heart of New York wine country with his wife, Irene, and the World's Smartest Dog.

Contents

Acknowledgments

I would like to thank the academy…

Thanks first and foremost to the Flash community. Any developer worth his salt has learned an appreciable fraction of what he knows from colleagues.

Thanks to Osborne/McGraw-Hill for publishing this thing. I can't believe it's finally done! Thanks to Jim, Tim, and Jenn for all your help and patience. Especially patience. Thanks also to Judith Brown, the copyeditor, Paul Medoff, the proofreader, and the OMH production and illustration teams for all their hard work on this project.

Thanks to all the companies that sent me free stuff: Macromedia, Electric Rain, Strata, Electric Image, cyScape—and even the ones who sent me stuff I didn't like. I know it's just business; but I still appreciate it.

Thanks to Branden Hall for setting up and maintaining the best resource for Flash coders on the web, and for his tireless innovations, insights, and discoveries that he shares there. Thanks for replies to inquires, which seem to come back *instantly* at any time of the day or night. Don't you sleep? Ever?

A heartfelt "falcon and" to Jim Robblee for feedback, database advice, and generally entertaining correspondence. The book should be out by Febtober.

Introduction

This book is a resource for experienced Flash developers to dig deeper into their favorite tool. While the scope is immense—everything I can think of that is related to Flash—there are many detailed examples, including a vast number of code examples. The overarching concept behind the book, from cover to cover, is to give the reader exposure to all the different issues in Flash development.

Because I believe that the best way to learn is by reading a short description, deconstructing a simplified example, and then graduating to examples of increasing complexity, that is how I arranged each topic in each chapter.

Every introduction I can remember reading gives some kind of prescription for the order in which to read the text. However, I have never known two readers to approach an educational text with the same goals, so I won't make such a declaration. What I *can* do is give you a few hints about how the book is arranged.

Each section covers a huge slice of the spectrum of Flash development topics; and each chapter represents a specific subject. Within each chapter, the text and examples progress from general and simple to specific and more complex, such that you could probably pick up at the beginning of most chapters, given a solid background in some kind of scripting.

Nearly every concept in the book is illuminated in an example. A few of the examples are fun and silly; but the majority are stripped of context and focus on the concept they illustrate. The relevant code from each example is reproduced in the book within a contextual discussion, so that you can simultaneously view the output and code of a single example.

Who Should Read This Book

Macromedia Flash 5 Developer's Guide is for any novice to advanced Flash developer who wants to probe deeper into the tool and its scripting language. This book is not for beginners, as no discussion of basic skills is included. It picks up where the factory documentation leaves off. If you feel confident in basic skills like animation, drawing tools, importing media, etc., and want to learn more about advanced Flash techniques, this might be a good book for you.

If you are accustomed to organizing a Flash movie according to the timeline-based Flash 4 paradigm, but would like to learn more about controlling your Flash applications with ActionScript alone, this is a good transitional guide. The chapters in the first part, by necessity, use timeline-based organization. In the section on ActionScript, the examples graduate in sophistication until you are using a single frame and dynamically pulling Movie clips from the library, moving them, and removing them using scripting.

If you have mastered the basic visual skills in Flash, but lack experience in scripting, don't worry—the part on JavaScript serves as an introduction to both basic scripting concepts and ECMAScript (the standard on which both JavaScript and ActionScript are based).

What's in the Book

The book is arranged in six parts, representing the major divisions of Flash development as I see them. The parts are as follows.

Flash Components

Part I covers specific techniques and subtle aspects of the native, non-scripting related tools within the Flash development environment. Topics include animation, file size optimization, and a very general discussion of how digital audio works.

Flash and the Web Browser

Part II offers both an introduction to JavaScript and a range of HTML considerations concerning Flash. Two full chapters are devoted to JavaScript, which serve as a suitable introduction to ActionScript. So much space is devoted to JavaScript for two reasons. First, JavaScript by itself is useful to any developer who works in any close proximity to web output—Flash definitely qualifies there. Second, JavaScript is so similar to ActionScript, from core concepts to syntax, that many scripts can be ported from one to the other with no changes whatsoever. If you are new to the ActionScript—or even to the Flash 5 flavor of ActionScript—this is a good primer.

ActionScript

Part III is the largest section and the focal point of the book. Flash's native scripting language and its capabilities were greatly expanded in version 5 and now require a lot of attention, time, and energy to master. Topics range from simple flow control to building data-driven XML applications.

Connectivity and Server-Side Processing

Part IV focuses on free and open-source server-side tools that are useful to Flash developers. By the end of the section, you will be able to build data- and media-driven Flash applications using PHP, MySQL, XML, and Swift-Generator.

Much of the attention in this part is given to setting up a web server on your desktop machine that you use for Flash development. If you don't already have such a setup, it is well worth your time to go through this process. You will save as much time on your next data-based Flash project as you will spend setting up the server.

Flash Peripheral Issues & Getting the Most out of Flash

Part V includes a single chapter that gives a broad overview of 3D topics, along with an introduction to modeling in 3D using the free (and very cool) Strata 3D package. There are also examples of animation in Swift 3D with detailed discussions, and a rundown of the unique new tool Amorphium Pro.

And, to wrap up the book there's a chapter with general tips for organizing your Flash workspace and optimizing your workflow. Subjects range from how to save code snippets to basic tips and tricks with vector illustration tools.

Flash Components

OBJECTIVES:

- ► Gain an in-depth knowledge of Flash's native illustration tools

- ► Explore specific techniques for working with bitmap images

- ► Learn how to use shared libraries effectively

- ► Discover the benefits of using permanent libraries efficiently

- ► Deconstruct examples by using optimization techniques

- ► Learn the key to printing with the Flash Player

CHAPTER 1

Flash Native Tools

IN THIS CHAPTER:

Drawing and Illustration

Timeline-Based Animation

Working with Raster Images

This chapter is a review of some of the less obvious features in the Flash 5 drawing and animation toolset. You can think of it as a chance to bone up on the features you should have learned when you first got Flash (if you are a rambunctious visual learner like most of us), or as a casual review to skim for nuggets (if you are already confident in your basic skills). Think of it as the first day of a third-year course.

The tool with the most elusive subtleties is the Bézier tool. We will cover Flash's idiosyncratic implementation of path tools, including tracing examples, a demonstration video, and a history of the tool.

Developers from a graphic arts background will appreciate Flash's unique approach to combining paths. This chapter includes examples using these features, including a piece that uses repetition of a circle to create a snake.

The topics and examples focus on the visual aspects of Flash, both illustration and animation. We will focus first on the mechanical minutia of some of the more complex and harder-to-manage tools, then cover some specific techniques to achieve the best results. Finally, we will dive headlong into frame-based animation and break down an example.

Drawing and Illustration

The battery of illustration tools included in Flash 5 elicits strong reactions from experienced artists. The reviews range from "useless" to "the best thing that ever happened to vector graphics." I subscribe to the second category of opinions.

Tools

The first thing you have to understand about Flash's toolset, especially if you're migrating from another vector illustration tool, is what it was originally designed for and how that original vision has shaped its development.

Like its older brother Director, Flash was originally conceived using frame-based film as a model. At the time when Flash's progenitor FutureSplash was created, the closest tie that Web animators had to the past was traditional pen and ink animators. (We'll talk more about this later.) This is reflected in every aspect of Flash's native illustration tools. Instead of tools that create polygons and other geometric shapes, you have tools that focus primarily on creating and editing hand-drawn shapes, the dimensions of which need not concern the illustrator.

The legacy that we developers inherit from this central concept of Flash is twofold. On one hand, Flash's set of path-oriented tools—Bézier, subselection, ellipse, polygon (nonexistent)—clearly have a smaller scope than any professional-quality vector illustration tool like Illustrator, Freehand, or CorelDraw. On the other hand, Flash offers, hands down, the absolute best collection of free-form drawing tools in a vector tool, irrelevant of the medium. Besides the pencil and freehand tool that are a staple of cartoon-style drawing, you have an entire system of modifying shapes that is 100% intuitive. I have heard the Flash illustration system described as everything from "Bézier for dummies" to "electronic clay," and all of the flattering descriptions are absolutely true.

No other vector illustration tool provides a set of tools that is so powerful and so easy to learn and use. For a narrow range of illustration tasks—most notably cartoon-style hand-drawn graphics—Flash is the best thing going.

Bézier Tools

Version 5 marks Flash's induction into the world of serious multimedia development. The Bézier tool is one clear sign that Flash has arrived. While it does make a few serious and annoying departures from features that have become standard in other vector illustration tools, the Flash pen tool is still a tremendous boon to Flash developers. In order to gain perspective on how this amazing widget complements Flash's older set of free-form tools, we will begin with a brief inquiry into the history of the tool.

History of the Bézier Pen

The pen tool is also known as a Bézier tool, which was named after its inventor, Pierre Etienne Bézier. Bézier's tool has been used in every professional-quality visual design tool since the early days of engineers' computer drafting. Flash 5 now includes a simple implementation of this incredible, ingenious device.

The history of Bézier's invention is worth a short diversion in order to understand why the tool was designed and what it is best suited for. I hope to introduce you to his importance in modern art and graphic design (and it couldn't hurt my karma to give a shout out to someone who contributed so much).

When thinking about automobile design during the 20th century, several movements come to mind. There was the slow, fumbling metamorphosis from the horseless carriages. The original automobile was followed by the giant boats of the 1940s, the Buck Rogers, junior-high conception of a flying machine of the 1950s, and finally, in the late 1980s, the Ford Taurus.

The Taurus was positively stunning when Ford introduced it in 1985. It single-handedly saved the middle class from the design malaise that Detroit had inflicted upon the American public. (It was the most popular car in history. Hmm, could there be a lesson here?) There was something that every potential car buyer recognized in the Taurus but couldn't quite put a finger on it. The ideas "nice lines," or "it's aerodynamic," or "…the Taurus' *futuristic* (in 1985) design…" were among the buzz as top-rated queries into what made the Taurus such delicious eye candy.

This easily recognizable, hard-to-explain quality of the Taurus is called *organic* design, and the most useful, intuitive tool for creating organic design is the Bézier line. Before Pierre Bézier developed his interactive system of composing complex mathematical curves with a simple visual interface, engineers were limited to the kinds of tools your high school math teacher kept in a chalk-dusty box. I cannot overstate the impact of this technology.

Engineers were suddenly free from worrying about how to translate the smooth, expressive lines on the drafting board into something that could be understood by the metal-shaping machines. Now the drafting software could just remember the coordinates of the four points that determine a Bézier line and feed it to the other machines.

Today, auto design is just one of innumerable applications for this tool. Any good 3D modeling you see—from Saturday morning cartoons to the last Hollywood blockbuster you watched—uses Bézier curves as an intuitive interface to create natural, expressive 3D lines (called *splines* just to show you that 3D artists are hipper than you might think). If you are interested in the math behind the curve, there is a good explanation at http://www.cee.hw.ac.uk/~ian/hyper00/curvesurf/bezier.html.

Bézier developed his line-drafting system while working as a senior engineer at the Renault car company. After spending the better part of the 1960s developing computer drafting techniques, he went on to share his genius with engineering students at the Conservatoire National des Arts et Metiers. Today, Bézier is remembered at Renault, and there is a short bio of him on their corporate Web site.

Nuts and Bolts of the Bézier Tool
Bezier_Tool.mov

If you are already familiar with the pen tool in any mainstream image editing software, you can skip this section. Flash 5 implements a very basic, familiar Bézier toolset. This tool is easy and useful; however, it's often neglected by designers.

Two tools are included in Flash's Bézier toolset—the pen tool and the subselection tool. In general, you will use the pen tool to create your initial path, after which you will use the subselection tool to tweak your path into just the right shape.

Look at the video on the CD titled *Bezier_Tool.mov* to get a feel for how this toolset works. Figure 1-1 is a reference that supplements the video.

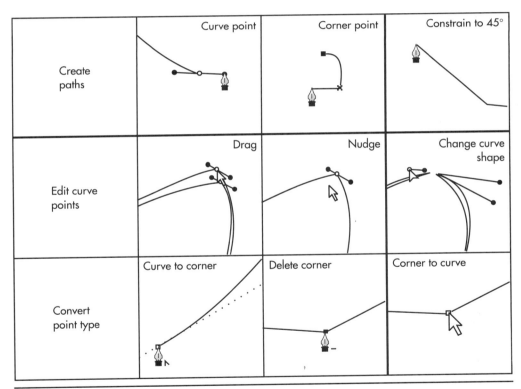

Figure 1.1   *Bézier tools operations*

Creating Paths with the Pen

As shown in Figure 1-1, there are three methods for creating a path with the pen tool.

▶   To draw a curve point (the end of one or two curved path segments), click and drag the pen tool.

▶   For a corner point (the end of one or two straight path segments), simply click with the pen tool.

▶   To constrain a point to a 45-degree angle relative to the previous point on the path, hold the SHIFT key as you draw a point.

Subselection Tool—Edit Curve Points

You will use the subselection tool (the white arrow) for most of your path editing.

▶   To move either type of point, simply drag it with this tool.

▶   You may also choose a point with the subselection tool and nudge it with the keyboard arrow keys.

▶   The bread and butter of Bézier curves is in using the tangent handles to change the shape of the curve.

Converting Point Type

Both the pen tool and the subselection tool are capable of converting the type of a point on the path.

▶   The most common operation is converting a curve point to a corner with the pen tool. Hold the pen nib over the point until you see the upside-down *v*; then click.

▶   Delete a corner point by holding the pen tool over it until the minus sign is visible; then click.

▶   Hold down the ALT key as you drag a corner point to make tangent handles appear. (Convert the corner point into a curve point.)

You can split the respective directions of the tangent handles on a curve point by holding down the ALT key as you drag one tangent handle with the subselection tool.

Miscellaneous Actions

► You may split a curve point into independent tangent handles by holding the ALT key when you drag the handle:

► You may add a point to a curve with the pen tool. Place the pen where you want to add a point and hold until the plus sign appears; then draw the point.

► To finish drawing a path, double-click the pen tool. Alternatively, you may close the path by single-clicking or dragging on the original point. (The pen cursor will show a circle to show that this option is ready.)

► If you want to undo the last point you made while the pen tool is still in drawing mode, just press DELETE (CTRL-Z will still work, too).

I have included an FLA file on the CD for you to practice some very common path operations that you will want to perform with the Bézier tool. This movie simply contains paths in a guide layer for you to copy and includes a play-by-numbers-style set of instructions. If you make it all the way through this exercise easily, you have officially begun your lifelong journey toward mastery of the traditional path tools. A good exercise to continue to achieve proficiency is to take images of pleasing organic objects and attempt to re-create their natural paths with a minimum of points. A good place to start is an AltaVista image search for the word "flower." After that, the shapes to trace include shapely animals like the ones you find in swap meet art—cats, dogs, horses, and dolphins.

CAUTION

There are two aspects of the current implementation of the pen tool that I consider hindrances to an efficient workflow. One is the annoying default fill when you switch to the pen tool—the fact that you can't adjust this default or use a hot key to turn off the fill. The other is a serious limitation on the ability to draw complex paths: Flash automatically adds points to your path while you are editing it with the direct selection tool. Not only that, but the Undo command fails to revert the path to the previous state. The circumstances that cause this are detailed in the example BézierPractice.fla.

Pencil

There isn't much to say about the pencil tool beyond the obvious, but there is one nuance that bears careful examination. As you are doubtless aware, there are three modifiers for the pencil tool (shown in the next image): Straighten, Smooth, and Ink. Just for review, here's a summary of what each of these modifiers does.

- ▶ **Straighten**   Same as smooth, except that it draws square corners
- ▶ **Smooth**   Summarizes the paths you draw with a pencil tool by eliminating small deviations from what it "thinks" you intended to draw and rounding out the corners
- ▶ **Ink**   Renders more or less exactly what you draw

Personally, I still haven't found a single application for the first two modifiers in my own drawing style. I can't imagine why you would want to give up control of what you're drawing. However, I get the impression from looking at work of novice Flashers that these modifiers are used a lot. The symptoms are everywhere: corners in unusual places, primitive drawings that are unusually smooth, and a generally inhuman lack of character in the shapes.

News flash: no amount of tricky algorithms is going to improve your skill at freehand drawing. The following is my personal approach to using the pencil tool, which I think is a little more sensible. These steps are shown in Figure 1-2.

1. Draw a shape freehand using the Ink modifier, not paying attention to minor defects. Use Undo as necessary to eradicate major disasters.

2. Use the eraser tool (flip your pen over on most drawing pad systems) to clean up any remaining unwanted or unnecessary lines.

3. Use the Optimize Curves function (Modify | Optimize or CTRL-ALT-SHIFT-C) to reduce the complexity of the paths. This step is a compromise between your taste and your desire to reduce the file size. We will talk about this more in Chapter 3.

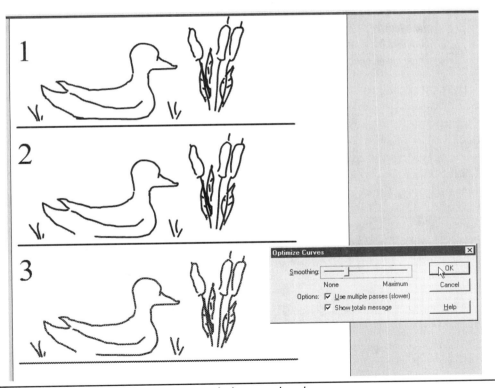

Figure 1.2   *Three stages of drawing with the pencil tool*

Brush
pencilToolDuckwBrushStrokes.fla, brushPortrait.fla

In my estimation, the brush tool is the centerpiece of the Flash illustration toolset. It has most of the positive features of the brush tools found in high-end illustration software and none of the negative features. For instance, you can naturally draw complex shapes with beautiful fidelity to pressure sensitivity, and you don't have to manually simplify the paths that make up the individual strokes—Flash does it automatically.

> ### NOTE
> *If you do any kind of drawing with the pencil and brush tools, a pressure-sensitive drawing pad is an absolute requisite. If you don't have one already, you can find a small, high-quality pad with minimal features at any large computer store for $50 to $80. I like Wacom drawing pads. I use the Intuos 9 × 12 for my home workstation and the scaled down Graphire pad for my notebook. Each of these pads includes a cordless mouse with features that exceed those of a standard fingerwheel mouse.*

To demonstrate this simple power of the brush tool, let's take another look at my duck drawing, (*pencilToolDuckwBrushStrokes.fla* on the CD). Following the model of traditional frame-based animation, we are going to take this drawing, originally conceived as heavily stroked outlines, and fill the outlined areas with color. The first step is to select modifier options for the brush tool. As you can see in the following illustration, I first chose the option for Use Pressure (the little swoosh), then chose Paint Fills from the drop-down menu. Using this option lets you get a little sloppy close to the lines, while still allowing you to overlap an area you have already painted. These options reflect Flash's roots in traditional animation, where animators would draw outlines, and another team of artists would trace the outlines in dark ink on one transparent layer and paint the fills on another transparent layer.

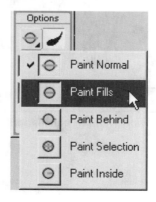

With these clever options employed, coloring the inked outline becomes short work. My final rendition, as seen in the following image, uses the product of nearly 30 seconds of earnest work and heartfelt artistic expression.

We are finally ready to start composing elements for Dr. Ezekiel's site. Open *brushPortrait.fla* on the CD and look at the image we will trace to make our "portrait." If you hide the layer with the photo, you will see that I have already traced the key lines and made that image, giving the impression of a hand-drawn portrait made with the charcoal pencil. This trick is as old as the American advertising industry.

Hide or delete the layer with my drawing and take a stab at tracing the photo with the brush tool. This tool is perfectly suited for jobs like this because it faithfully reproduces your brush strokes without bothering you with the paths that make up the shapes.

Mask

DrEzekielsBonaFide.fla

If you are new to the concept of a mask, don't worry about all the expanded definitions and nuances of masking in sophisticated image editing software. Flash is much easier than that. Flash implements masks to conform to the simplest definition.

A *mask* is an opaque layer that conceals what is below it. A typical mask has holes in it to reveal the layers below. It is as if a mask were a piece of opaque paper in a stack of transparent sheets, revealing the things below it through the shapes cut out of it.

The only additional concept you need in order to use masks in Flash is that the shape you draw on a mask layer is the hole that reveals what is below (not the opaque part). In other words, the *mask layer* is the *paper*, the *shape* (solid fills) you draw on it is the *hole* cut into it.

The central example for this chapter, *DrEzekielsBonaFide.fla*, uses a mask throughout the entire animation to establish a viewing area in the center of the movie and hide the slop that overflows this area (see the following image). As you can see, the symbol that contains the cowboy's body runs over the edge. That's because it's easier to draw when you are not worried about aligning perfectly with the border.

The mask also facilitates the fly-in effect later in the movie with the product photo (frame 200). Without a mask, it would be unwieldy to produce this effect.

Notice that in the image above, none of the layers under the mask—the ones with the purple diamond showing that they are "under" the mask—are locked. This is why you can see these layers beyond the scope of the mask. A common problem when working with a mask is the tension between needing to see the effect of the mask and needing to work on the layers under the mask.

TIP

When you want to work on objects that will appear under a mask, yet see the effect of the mask as you work, save converting the mask layer for the last step. While you work, use a path in the shape of the mask's outline to remind yourself where the mask will be. Then, when you are done working on the masked layers, fill your reference path and convert the layer to a mask.

Masks are a cheap and easy way to produce a variety of eye-pleasing and apparently complex visual effects. You can create animated masks, draggable masks, and gradient masks. If you are not already using them, you might want to spend some time experimenting to see what you have been missing.

Fill Modifier

gradientFillXformModifier.fla

The transform fill modifier is one of the things that makes it easy to see at a glance whether a Flash designer has started to dig down beneath the quick-start level of Flash's comprehensive visual toolset. After viewing a dozen or so Flash movies from a mediocre source, the most casual observer easily recognizes the default gradient fill pattern.

Creating subtle gradients is a good way to create texture in the very flat (by default—it doesn't have to be) world of vector graphics. The standard gradient fills don't look like much, but with a little care, they can give the impression of a barren desert and sky on a sunny day.

Take a look at the example *gradientFillXformModifier.fla*. This file contains only the background from our central example. If you select the paint bucket tool, then the transform fill modifier, as seen in the following image, you can click on either of the solid fills and transform them in any dimension you please.

Toggling between this tool and the fill palette, you can easily eyeball any gradient you can imagine. Although gradients are slightly less efficient than flat fills in terms of file size and processor demands, they are still much better than the alternative—bitmap images. With a little patience and a good eye, you can probably achieve any effect you are looking for.

Techniques

So far we have been talking mainly about the rudiments of some of the tools that have less than obvious meanings. In this part of the chapter, we are going to use primarily straightforward tools to complete advanced illustration techniques.

Circle Snake
circleSnake.fla

The next piece that needs to be added to the Snake Oil site is a snake. We are going to make the little critter you see in the lower-left corner, under the menu items. This example will refer to *circleSnake.fla* on the CD, and it demonstrates a common theme in Flash's native tools: trading sophistication for simplicity and speed. This illustration takes advantage of Flash's intelligent and automatic path combination behavior. In other words, it uses the default behavior of Flash to combine overlapping shapes as an illustration technique.

When you open this example, you will see the completed composite path on the locked guide layer and the elemental circle on the top, unlocked layer. Try to remake the snake without looking at the guide.

First, place three copies of the circle so that they overlap exactly at the vertical tangents. Next, delete the segments that you already know you don't want. You can see what your drawing should look like at this point in the following image. If you haven't done this kind of operation in a professional illustration package, you probably won't appreciate how powerful Flash is in this respect. Most vector drawing tools require you to select overlapping paths in exactly the right order, while making sure the correct one is in front, then select from a long list of path operators with confusing names. Flash does all of this for you in a way that a child can understand!

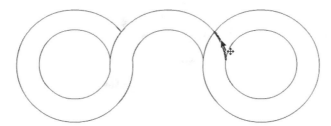

Next add a circle for the head. At this point you have a choice between negotiating giant circles to make up the bottom of the head and the top edge of the tail, or just using the pen tool. I chose the pen tool. You can see that the image is starting to look wiggly:

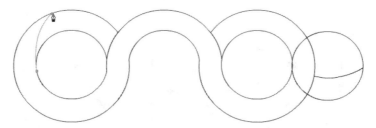

Finally, add a circle for the eye and two circles for the snake's tongue (see the following image). I used the same type of intersection for the tongue as I used for the body of the snake, except that I rotated it 30 degrees after I deleted the portions of the path I didn't want. An easy way to mark off sections of an open path, like the tongue circles, is to make a quick jot across the path with the pencil tool. That way, you only have to make one touch with your pen or mouse, which saves time.

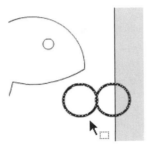

Nonrectangular Bitmap
cutOutBitmap.fla

By now every Flasher knows that you can fill a path with a bitmap instead of a flat color or gradient. We are going to approach this handy tool with a slightly different technique that *anyone* can put to good use.

Start by opening the next example, *cutOutBitmap.fla*. The first thing you will notice when you open the FLA is that one image—the one on the right—looks finished, slick, and well, *right*. The other is about par for the average implementation of bitmaps in Flash.

If you are observant, you will immediately put your finger on what is wrong with the one on the left. There is a bounding box marking the border between the bitmap and the movie stage. I did this intentionally by toning down the stage's white by 2% in order to make a point: bitmap borders are often visible and when they are, they degrade the Flash movie visually.

The reasons are many and vary in level of mystery; but you can be certain that you cannot rely on Flash to render numerically identical colors in bitmaps and vectors so that they look the same on every computer. It just isn't going to happen.

The solution is simple: instead of accepting your fate, shoulders hunched and feet shuffling, take charge and use a bitmap-filled path, like the one on the right. Here's how.

First fix the bitmap. It is necessary to manually override the screwy mystery defaults that Flash imposes on all bitmaps. You may have noticed that any bitmap you place in Flash—even a supercrisp magazine cover by a famous photographer—

shows up anti-aliased in the compiled output, as if the program thinks no bitmap is good enough to show on the Web. Not only that, but there is no way to override this annoyance in the symbol properties dialog. (There is a check box, but it hasn't worked in two consecutive versions.) To fix the bitmap, you have to do two things: first uncheck Allow Smoothing in the symbol properties dialog, as shown in the following image; then place the bitmap in a graphic symbol and break it apart (Modify | Break Apart or CTRL-B).

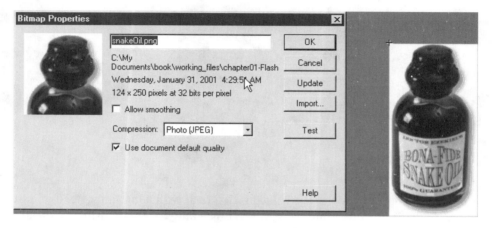

Now—and only now—will the bitmap appear as you worked so hard in Photoshop to make it appear. Since that part is out of the way, create a new layer in the graphic symbol containing the bitmap and draw a path with the pen tool. The purpose of the path is to make a selection around the area of the bitmap you want to show, just like some artists use the pen tool in Photoshop to make selections. The following image shows my initial pass as I started to edit it. Notice that I included the not-so-subtle drop shadow.

When you are happy with your path, cut it from the top layer and paste it in place (Edit | Paste in Place or CTRL-SHIFT-V) in the bitmap layer. Now you can just select any edge of the bitmap and delete it. You will also want to delete your path, so that you don't have a dark outline around your bitmap.

Voilá! You now have a bitmap that is the exact shape you want. Actually, you have a path with a bitmap fill. If you look at the bitmap (not the graphic symbol) in the library, you will see that the whole rectangle is still there.

I have adopted this method as my default treatment for all bitmaps with a flat-colored background. It is just not worth the frustration of trying to match colors, only to find out that the colors don't match on other machines.

Isometric 3D

IsoCube.fla, isoMap.fla

If you haven't noticed, there is at present a full-fledged design craze with the simple idea of isometric perspective at the center. This trend has permeated the Flash designers' community to the point that you are likely to see isolated isometric elements that have nothing to do with the rest of the design.

The interesting thing about isometric perspective is that it is a decidedly utilitarian design tool that has immigrated to artistic/commercial design. Whether you consciously recognize it or not, any shape rendered in this quasi-3D perspective elicits the imagery of technical diagrams, instructions for putting together prefab furniture, and other such mundane design jobs. The whole reason for the popularity of isometric rendering is given in the name: each of the three dimensional axes are proportional in the rendered image. This fact makes it easier for you to figure out which part is "Wing Hex Spinner Q7" when you try to put together your new CD rack. This whole subject is good fodder for after-dinner coffee conversation.

Flash is a good match for iso 3D because it implements a good basic array of transformation tools: rotate, scale, and skew. We are going to use an exercise in isometric 3D, *isoCube.fla*, to demonstrate a few not-so-obvious features of these tools of the transform palette.

The following image shows the orientation of the sides as we will refer to them in the subsequent steps. You can conceive of them any way you like—there is nothing absolute about this convention.

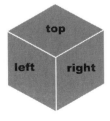

The first step is to draw the three sides of your 3D object that you want to show. There is a bit of a trick to this. You have to measure your sides so that they match; and the sides that will be touching in the final image are not all touching when you start, (remind you of studying for the SAT's?).

To avoid confusion, I use the construct you see in the first frame of the example. The top row contains the top quadrilateral of the final image. Because I find it most intuitive to think of it as an extension of the right side, I place it directly over the right side to begin with. Now it is easier to see if two of the three touching sides will match at a glance. The remaining touching sides, the left side of the top quadrilateral and the top side of the left quadrilateral, need to be measured. You can do this using the info palette. Don't worry if this doesn't make sense when you read the words the first time. Try the exercise and you will pick it up quickly.

Once you have your three sides (you can use the three instances of the square graphic symbol in the example FLA), follow these steps:

1. Place your objects on the stage.
2. Select the top side. Skew it 60° horizontally and 30° vertically.
3. Select the right side. Skew it −30° vertically.
4. Select the left side. Skew it 30° vertically.
5. Reposition the objects as desired.

You should now have a cube like the one in the second frame of the example. If not, lather, rinse, and repeat. If you made it that far, you are ready to try the next example and the next element in our Snake Oil Flash Web site, *isoMap.fla*.

This example is a little trickier. To start with, there are a few objects that have as a top an extension of the *left* side instead of the right. You will have to figure out how to adapt the instructions to mirror the transformations we used for the top side. Another challenge is rooftops drawn at odd (not multiples of 30 degree or 45 degree) angles. For these, I think it is easiest to simply copy the left side to where the back would be if visible, and then use the pen tool on a new layer to connect the dots and draw the top side. The final product can be found in frame 6.

NOTE

There are many different formulas for constructing isometric perspective. The formula discussed here is the one used to create true isometry; but there are plenty of good reasons for deviating from this pattern, including the appearance of the finished product and easier programmatic movement between tiled pieces (remember Q-Bert?).

In this example, we had the advantage of knowing the final transformation to be applied to each object in each direction; but this will not always be the case. If you use geometry to derive your own formula for an isometric perspective, you may want to rotate an object, skew it, and then rotate it again. The problem with this approach is that Flash retains all the previous information between transformations. For example, if you rotate a symbol 14.2° and then decide you need to rotate it another 17.9°, you can't just type in 17.9—that would result in a cumulative rotation of 17.9°. You have to add the numbers yourself. The other advantage is that we are transforming perfect squares, not oblong quadrilaterals, so you could conceivably make a mistake and still get the right result.

There are two possible solutions. The first is to simply use individual shapes instead of graphic symbols or movie clips. However, this is not optimal for many cases, such as in our *isoCube.fla* example, where each side of the cube is an instance of the square graphic symbol. Using shapes would literally triple the resources required for the cube.

A better solution is to use a *dummy* object on the stage. A dummy object is simply a shape or symbol that is used together with the symbol you really want to transform, then discarded. For example, you can rotate one of the squares in *isoCube.fla* by 14.2°, then SHIFT-select a dummy object—possibly another square—and add another 17.9° to the rotation by simply typing 17.9 into the rotate dialog in the transformation palette. Each time you select a unique group of objects, you get a new set of transformation parameters. When you are done, simply delete the dummy object.

Timeline-Based Animation

I should offer you, gentle reader, a personal note at this point in order to frame the following sections properly. I started drawing flipbook animations in junior high, just like about 20% of all boys. I took it a step further and found a weekly animation class at the nonlocal library about an hour away (and signed my mom up to drive me there every week—thanks, Mom). The class was taught by a professional animator/ illustrator who worked for a local ad agency. It was great. I learned about the illusions that make film possible, claymation, shooting animation on an 8mm-movie camera, animating characters (we traced our characters frame by frame on typing paper that we hole-punched ourselves), and even a little about illustration. I have loved animation ever since.

The other side of the coin is my earnest interest in seeing Flash become more closely aligned with the way things are done in grown-up Web development. That means paying attention to standards, adding value with interactivity (*not* passively viewed animation), complying with accepted usability practices, and generally building Flash applications that focus on delivering useful information quickly in ways that other vehicles like XHTML cannot. I fear that if these concerns do not gain importance and find real-world applications quickly, Flash will not survive. People are bound to get tired of second-rate television entertainment pumped through the Web sooner or later.

Frame-based animation has its place. Entertainment. Possibly education. This discussion is meant to give you some introduction and background in frame-based animation, but not necessarily to advocate its use in every Flash application you build. There is a standard criterion for traditional animation that I think applies when you are considering whether a Flash animation adds value to a project.

TIP

The storyline of an animation must stand on its own. No amount of clever drawing or good sound effects will shock a pulse into an uninspired narrative. Write the story first (as text); then make a storyboard; then start drawing frames. No story, no animation.

Frame by Frame

Onion skinning is one of those tools in the Flash native toolbox that most developers understand at least vaguely, but never completely learn or use. Its roots and its primary application are with hand-drawn animation for video or film; but once you learn to use onion skinning, you will find other applications for it. It is a valuable tool.

Onion Skinning Background

In order to use Flash effectively for animation, you need to understand the three main divisions of animation style available to you in the software. The most widely employed style by far is using tweening to move symbols, which are drawn once and then used over and over. The second method, which dates back about a hundred years, is drawing each frame individually. The third, and my preferred method, is using ActionScript to move objects on the stage because this gives you the most open-ended framework for creating interactivity in a small file. In this section, we are talking about drawing each frame individually.

The illusion of motion in both live action film (for example, *The Matrix*) and cartoon animation (for example, *Snow White*) is made possible by the natural phenomenon known as the *persistence of vision*, or the visual perception of things for longer than they are actually there. People learned that they could take advantage of this inaccuracy in human sensory processing by showing photographs taken in rapid succession to create the illusion of motion. You may have read accounts of the "first" motion picture, where a photographer used trip wires to capture the motion of racehorses. This was by no means the first inquiry into creating this illusion. It was, however, the first experiment witnessed by wealthy country club types, so that is what you find in the history books.

A definite first was Winsor McCay, creator of Gertie the Dinosaur. Gertie was, in cutting-edge turn-of-the-(20th)-century quasi-scientific jargon, a "brontosaurus." Gertie wowed audiences using the breakthrough technology known as *paper*. (McCay's early works were done on a chalkboard. He'd draw an image, snap a frame of film, erase the picture, draw the next frame, snap a frame, erase...) Gertie did a little dance against a static background that looked like a mountain path or maybe a limestone quarry. The weird thing about McCay's production model is that he retraced the same background in every single frame! This seems laughably ignorant today, but at the time, movie audiences were positively dazzled by the genius of McCay's animated sequences. It is unlikely that anyone at that time thought of advancement in animation in terms of production technique or medium.

Fast-forward to 1915. J. R. Bray patented the clear plastic animation cel in 1915, though a number of sources credit Bray's employee, Earl Hurd, with the invention of the process. Bray's approach had been to mechanically reproduce a large number of background images on translucent sheets of paper. Illustrating on the transparent celluloid allowed animators (at the price of Bray's royalties) to draw characters— or even parts of characters—separately from the background. The background was drawn once, then used over in each successive frame on the bottom layer. The process should be starting to sound familiar.

The process of animation continued to evolve along lines parallel to manufacturing industries, until the Hanna-Barbera team brought hand-drawn animation to its modern state of assembly-line, robotic, cold precision. Among the most notable concepts that have persisted from beginning to end (if you count Gertie as the beginning) are

▶ The illusion of a steady stream of vision is created by a rapid succession of static images.

▶ Translucent paper (or a visual equivalent in some medium) is used to see the frame or frames immediately preceding the one being drawn.

The latter of these apparently immutable laws of the cartoon world has been called *onion skinning* because of the resemblance of the translucent paper to onion skin. This term has been around long enough that its exact origin is unknown. For interested parties, there are tidbits galore about the people and the technical processes that brought animation from Gertie to *Toy Story* at http://www.animationhistory.com.

Onion Skinning in Flash
onionSkinning.fla

The visual environment in Flash is built around the metaphor of Bray's animation process, using a stage, frames, transparent layers, and *tweening* (a term dating back at least as far as "The Flintstones"). A lead animator draws the key frames—*keyframes* in Flash—leaving the team of animators to draw the frames in between. In Flash, a set of instructions and the logic in the Flash Player take over the role of the team of animators. Though frame-by-frame, hand-drawn animation is seldom incorporated in Web projects, Flash is a perfectly suitable environment for a talented animator to realize his or her vision.

The kind of onion skinning that most closely resembles the traditional method is shown in the following image. This is what onion skinning looks like without selecting any of the options. This image is taken from the next example, *onionSkinning.fla*.

You have a wide variety of options to display the neighboring areas of the timeline that you are not immediately concerned with. Following is a list of options, how to invoke them, and what they do.

▶ **Onion Skin Outlines**   If you want to see the surrounding frames as outlines (rather than translucent fills and outlines), you may select Onion Skin Outlines. Onion Skin and Onion Skin Outlines are mutually exclusive options.

▶ **Show Layers as Outlines**   If your scene is complex, this method of animation can quickly clutter your stage. Try using the Colored Outlines option in the timeline. This will make each object and shape in the effected layers show as an outline. This allows you to draw or place objects without getting confused by the clutter, while still having the other layers available for reference.

▶ **Anchor Onion**   If you want to use a static range of frames as reference as you draw the rest, select Anchor Onion from the options drop-down menu. This makes the in and out markers stay in their current position.

▶ **Edit Multiple Frames**   Suppose you have drawn several frames and you need to tweak the transition slightly between each frame. You will quickly find yourself switching back and forth between frames enough to wear out either the heel of your mouse hand or your right index and middle finger (< and >). Instead, use the Edit Multiple Frames option. This allows you to edit every frame simultaneously within the onion skin in and out markers. Each frame will show in its fully opaque colors.

Using Symbols in Frame-by-Frame Animation
onionSkinning.fla

It is an unavoidable axiom of Flash that the more you change elements on the stage from frame to frame, the larger the file will be. While our final movie is much closer to the bottom of the usability scale than the top in this respect, our current example, *onionSkinning.fla*, measures up well at only 6k, including MP3 audio. This is less than most GIF banner ads that just blink.

One reason for this is that the movie only describes the fundamental motions that are absolutely required to describe a convincing sneeze. For 22 frames of old-school animation at 12 fps, you really don't see that many keyframes on the timeline.

The other reason is that symbols are used for every little bit that either doesn't move or is repeated. The cowboy's head, shoulders, and hat never move, so they are all included in the bottom layer called *symbol*. The part of the cowboy that does move—the face—is redrawn for the frames that require movement. The facial expression that connotes the very beginning of the "y" sound and the whole "ch" sound, the clenched teeth, is repeated, so it is made into a symbol and merely pasted in place when needed. This kind of miserly frugality is required to build animations with any hope of being deployed over the Web.

One last thing to review in this example is the audio. You can drag the playhead at the top of the timeline, as seen in the following image, and hear where you are in the soundtrack. This is possible because the sound sync type has been set to stream. You use this feature to determine where you are in the soundtrack, which enables you to synchronize movements (like a sneeze) with specific sounds.

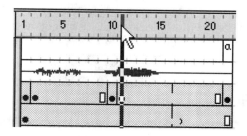

Tweening

You are doubtless already acquainted with standard motion tweening using keyframes. This section covers some of the finer points of the different types of tweening.

Motion Guide
motionGuide.fla

A *motion guide* allows you to create a motion tween with only two keyframes that follows a nonlinear path. You may have seen a demo of this feature and written it off as advanced or unreliable, but I consider it indispensable. Adding a motion guide to a motion tween can add much-needed character to the homogeneous mix of Flash hackery at a minimum of file size increase and redraw demand. The example we will use in this section is *motionGuide.fla*.

In order for a tweened object to lock to a motion path, its center must be directly under the path in the motion guide layer at each keyframe (the keyframes in the tweened object's layer—you should not have to create any keyframes manually for the motion guide). To make sure this is the case, turn on the snap option in the arrow tool's options box (the little magnet), and drag the bottle so that its center (the little plus sign) is directly under the path in each keyframe (first in frame 1, then in frame 12).

When you snap a tweened object to a motion guide in the first keyframe of the motion tween, you are telling the object to start at that point and follow that path.

If the object is not positioned on the same path in the next keyframe in the motion tween, it doesn't make sense to try to follow the path; hence the need to lock the object to the beginning keyframe *and* the end keyframe.

You also either have to grab the tweened object by the center (or close to the center) or grab the path by the endpoint with the selection tool, depending on which you want to move. This strikes me as being a little on the fussy side, but you get used to it. As a matter of fact, you *need* to get used to it to consider yourself proficient in Flash basic skills. If you don't feel 100% comfortable with this process, you should practice with geometric shapes until you do.

You will know when you have snapped to the motion guide because a small, heavily stroked outline of a circle will appear, accompanied by a more lightly stroked outline of the tweened object. This shows you where you can move the object along the path, such as in this image:

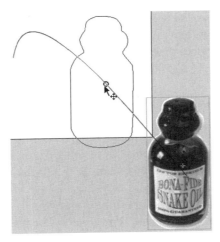

I love motion guides. I try to avoid linear, timeline-based tweens whenever possible. It just doesn't make sense to pass up the opportunity to add a little organic spice to an animation when the cost in file size and development time is so little.

TIP

If you have two or three nonconcurrent, consecutive tweens on a single layer in a single scene, you will probably save time, energy, and file size by using motion guides.

Shape Tweening
shapeTween.fla

Our next example is a tearjerker—literally. We are going to use shape tweening to produce the tear the cowboy makes after his horrendous sneeze. To get started, open *shapeTween.fla.*

Shape tweening allows you to create morph effects, changing smoothly from one image to another. It is effective primarily for creating the illusion of objects made from some liquid or ultraplastic material changing from one form to another, a lá *Terminator 2.* You can also use it to simulate organic movements that require a lot of random shapes, such as waves crashing on a beach.

This example simply morphs the beginning of a tear in the bottom of the cowboy's eye into a full tear that fills the lower half of his eye. To create this effect, I first drew the tear as it appears in frame 2. Next, I created a keyframe at frame 6 and reshaped the tear using the selection tool. (It's times like these that you really appreciate how easy it is to edit vector paths in Flash.) Finally, I drew frame 9, when the tear is just about to form a drop. The only thing left at this point was to select the beginning keyframes (2 and 6) and select Shape from the Tweening pull-down menu in the frame palette.

At first, it may seem like you could easily use simple motion tweening to do the same thing, but just try it. With motion tweening, you can scale, rotate, move, shear, and colorize an object, but you can't change the path that makes up the original shape.

Sometimes you will not be pleased with the choices Flash makes regarding which points in the first keyframe of a shape tween flow into the corresponding points in the second keyframe. This is when you use shape hints (Modify | Transform | Add Shape Hints or CTRL-SHIFT-H). A shape hint is shown as a little red circle, as in the following illustration, and is serialized with letters. (You can use as many as you want in a single shape tween.) It automatically appears in the second keyframe when you add it to the first. You place it on the path you are transforming. The point you signify in the first keyframe flows directly into the point you mark with the corresponding letter in the second keyframe.

Mixing Tweening Styles in a Flash Movie

If you develop Flash movies for any kind of electronic distribution, hand-drawn, frame-by-frame animation will not be the best solution for most situations. But you will need it for effect here and there. Check out the "Sex Slave Rebels" decalogue http://goultralightsgo.com/naoki/decalogue/decalogue.html to see a very compelling mixture of (mostly) object-based and (a little, here and there) frame-by-frame animation. (Check out *The Matrix* homage/parody in number 10 for some good frame-by-frame animation.)

Working with Raster Images

Not considering the "smoothing" annoyance we already discussed, there is really no excuse for poor handling of bitmap images in Flash. I have reduced my approach to handling bitmaps (not including color—that's a big subject) to the following dogma:

► You must use a high-quality image editor. This includes software like Photoshop, GIMP, PaintShop Pro, Photo-Paint, and Fireworks—generally anything with a lot of options for both color mode and output formats.

► When an image leaves your photo editing program bound for Flash, it must be uncompressed (no JPEG or LZW, etc.) and no larger in terms of dimensions than it will be in the Flash movie. Flash will apply JPEG compression to the images when it compiles the SWF output, but it currently can't downsample your images.

► Use paths to create bitmap fills (like we did in the *cutOutBitmap.fla* example) in favor of using extremely file-heavy transparency masks. Transparency is the equivalent of using two bitmaps when one of equal dimensions would work just as well.

► When you use a tween to move a bitmap or bitmap fill, that should be the only thing moving on the stage. Moving a bitmap is excruciating to the processor that must draw the SWF.

► Remember that Flash is a *vector* drawing and animation tool. If you can't live without bitmaps, maybe you should think about another medium as an outlet for those effects.

Formats: Strengths of Each

Following are my first preferences for incoming bitmap formats, along with the reasons these formats are advantageous. Flash 5 greatly expanded the number of supported import formats, which makes life a lot easier for many people.

▶ **PSD**   To know Photoshop is to love Photoshop. The best thing about being able to import this format is that you can work in Photoshop with all features enabled (layers, masks, channels—you name it) and see the results of any step *in SWF output* with three or four mouse clicks or hot keys.

▶ **PNG**   This format is nice from a workflow perspective. Often it is necessary to work in Photoshop on one scale, then downsample to the exact scale you will use in Flash. Instead of constantly resizing the PSD, you can use Export for Web and have a perfectly sized, uncompressed, true-to-the-original image ready for Flash in a few clicks. This format also has the advantage of typically being smaller than a native format like PSD or CPT.

▶ **TIF**   This puts you in touch with the print world. Occasionally, I have clients who can supply professional-quality photography or graphics to meet any specifications. TIF is typically the easiest bridge between such clients and Flash. I have never been so daring as to ask for the exact image size I think I might need, but I suppose you could.

What to Take Away from This Chapter

Flash has a powerful set of native tools for creating and animating your illustrations, but that toolset is focused. Knowing Flash's roots in the old-world animation metaphor, its strengths and weaknesses, and the mechanical minutiae of each tool is an absolute prerequisite to getting the most out of this amazing software.

Managing Elements with the Movie Explorer and Library

IN THIS CHAPTER:

The Flash Library

Movie Explorer

Every Flasher has seen the library palette and used its basic features since first opening the software. There are, however, many advanced features hidden in the unusual Options menu. You can easily miss some of them and, consequently, you'd miss out on cool functions and workflow enhancements. Some of these features are new, and others are just tucked away where you wouldn't find them unless you read the documentation.

The movie explorer palette is new in Flash 5. It applies the familiar Windows Explorer interface to the structure of your Flash movie. Its ease of use masks the awesome power of this clever tool, so we will cover its most useful applications in this chapter.

The Flash Library

Most of you probably know the Flash library as a repository of symbols that are reused within a movie; but this is a shallow definition of this important tool. The library is better described as a central terminal connecting elements in a Flash movie with the world outside the authoring environment—the source of the elements on one side and the published SWF output on the other.

In this part of the chapter, we will look at the powerful and timesaving features of the Library Options menu. Then I will show you an example of how to share library items across the Internet. Flash 5 has a very smart, mature approach to sharing movie elements, and the library is where you make this happen.

General Library Functions

Using the library with all of its features can really streamline the workflow for your Flash projects. In this section we'll look at methods for organizing, updating, and editing symbols in the library. If you have read and understood the Flash documentation thoroughly, these should all be familiar.

Viewing and Sorting
Albers_F4_ folders.fla, Albers_F4_ flat.fla

The library offers two methods for organizing the elements in your Flash movie. I can't decide which one I like better—it depends on the structure of the movie for me. The two basic choices are using folders and using the attribute columns in the library palette as shown next:

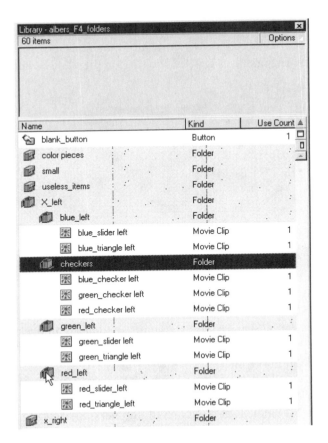

Folders should be a familiar concept, even if you haven't used them in Flash. You use folders, and folders within folders, to organize the elements in your movie the same way you would use them in just about any visual operating system to organize files on your hard drive. The hierarchy you create with folders in the library can be as shallow or as deep as you choose. Note that this example (*Albers_F4_folders.fla* in the Chapter 02\Examples folder on the CD) was originally composed in Flash 4; so you shouldn't rely on it for instruction in good modern ActionScript.

Grouping elements in a folder was definitely more of a necessity in Flash 4, but I still use it occasionally. I find it to be most useful in libraries that will be shared with other movies, such as permanent libraries and shared libraries, both of which we will cover later this chapter, and in SmartClips, which we will cover in Chapter 10. I use this approach because it allows me to have a Movie clip with a complex hierarchy at the root level of the library, while all of the nested elements remain in a folder. This helps reduce clutter in libraries that you don't use very often.

You can also sort elements in your Flash movie by their attributes. The Flash library expands from its default view to show all of the attributes that are common to all Flash elements. Expand the view by clicking on the wide window icon in the library palette:

This may seem relatively impotent compared with the folders method, but sorting by attribute columns can easily provide all the organization you need for movies with fewer than 40 elements. To see what I mean, open *Albers_F4_flat.fla* in the Chapter 02\Examples folder on the CD.

Expand the library palette, as shown in Figure 2-1. By clicking on the column header for each of the listed attributes, you can sort the library as you like. A bit of planning and careful element naming are all you need to organize your library effectively. This library shows what it looks like after I clicked the Name column first and the Kind column second.

Organizing elements in your library may not seem sexy, fun, or even worthwhile; but if you are not doing it, you are probably wasting a lot of time scrolling through your library looking for elements. Using the library should be automatic—more like finding your mouth with a toothbrush than finding your keys in the dark.

Properties

The properties dialog is accessible from the library palette. This dialog is the single most important tool you will use when optimizing movies containing bitmap images and audio. See Chapter 5 for more in-depth coverage of optimization.

Audio   In either of the example Flash files we have looked at so far, click on the audio element "mjay84" to highlight it. You can get at the Sound Properties dialog

Name	Kind	Use Count	Linkage	Date Modified
fashion	Bitmap	1		Tuesday, August 15, 2000 1:58:50 PM
blank_button	Button	1		Saturday, July 29, 2000 10:13:33 PM
button:flyout	Button	18		Saturday, July 29, 2000 8:34:16 PM
button:zoomer	Button	18		Saturday, July 29, 2000 8:34:16 PM
art:flyout	Graphic	9		Saturday, July 29, 2000 8:34:16 PM
blue_swatch	Graphic	2		Saturday, July 29, 2000 4:34:01 PM
green_swatch	Graphic	2		Saturday, July 29, 2000 4:36:19 PM
red_swatch	Graphic	2		Saturday, July 29, 2000 4:36:34 PM
white_swatch	Graphic	3		Saturday, July 29, 2000 9:21:34 PM
blue	Movie Clip	2		Saturday, July 29, 2000 9:33:08 PM
blue_checker	Movie Clip	1		Saturday, July 29, 2000 10:23:56 PM
blue_checker left	Movie Clip	1		Saturday, July 29, 2000 11:37:21 PM
blue_checker right	Movie Clip	1		Saturday, July 29, 2000 11:56:14 PM
blue_slider	Movie Clip	1		Saturday, July 29, 2000 9:34:42 PM
blue_slider left	Movie Clip	1		Sunday, July 30, 2000 12:29:52 AM
blue_slider right	Movie Clip	1		Sunday, July 30, 2000 12:27:27 AM
blue_triangle	Movie Clip	1		Saturday, July 29, 2000 11:30:47 PM
blue_triangle left	Movie Clip	1		Saturday, July 29, 2000 11:39:40 PM
blue_triangle right	Movie Clip	1		Saturday, July 29, 2000 11:57:10 PM
control:slider	Movie Clip	1		Saturday, July 29, 2000 9:09:30 PM
control:triangle	Movie Clip	1		Saturday, July 29, 2000 9:10:25 PM
green	Movie Clip	2		Saturday, July 29, 2000 8:28:04 PM
green_checker	Movie Clip	1		Saturday, July 29, 2000 10:24:21 PM
green_checker left	Movie Clip	1		Saturday, July 29, 2000 11:27:56 PM
green_checker right	Movie Clip	1		Saturday, July 29, 2000 11:54:26 PM
green_slider	Movie Clip	1		Saturday, July 29, 2000 9:32:09 PM
green_slider left	Movie Clip	1		Sunday, July 30, 2000 12:32:39 AM
green_slider right	Movie Clip	1		Sunday, July 30, 2000 12:30:35 AM

Library - albers_F4_flat
43 items   Options

Figure 2.1   *The expanded and sorted library palette*

either through the Options menu in the upper-right corner of the library palette or by right-clicking on a symbol and selecting Properties from the Context menu. Do one of these to bring up the properties dialog for "mjay84."

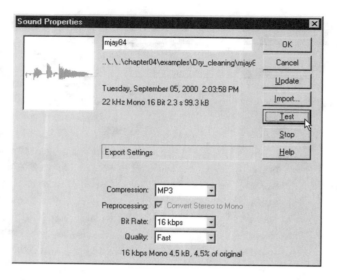

This dialog has volumes of useful information, as well as tools to update, replace, and optimize audio symbols with. You can even test the sound to see how it will fare when the movie is resampled and compressed upon publishing.

Bitmap The properties dialog for bitmap symbols is exactly analogous to audio. Open the properties dialog for the symbol "fashion." As shown next, this dialog gives you a similar range of options as with the audio symbol. Use this dialog to optimize your images individually before you publish your movie for distribution. Unfortunately, the Bitmap Properties dialog offers a relatively weak preview function. You have to test your movie (CTRL-ENTER) to see how the bitmap looks with the settings you choose here.

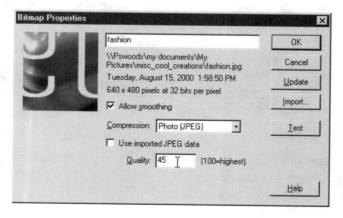

Edit With

Another library option exclusive to non-native Flash elements is Edit With, shown next. This option is available either by using the Context menu within the library palette or the Library Options menu. Edit With allows you to edit a bitmap or a sound in an external application. The Options and Context menus offer you the choice of using either the default application associated with the original file type or an application you choose by navigating to its executable.

If I had to make one criticism about the library palette, it would be that this option should put you in the Windows Start menu instead of the Program Files directory. Either that, or you should be able to make additional associations within Flash, as you can in Dreamweaver. Because of this weakness, it is probably best to change your global Windows file associations so that the program you most often use will appear in the Context menu. To do this in Windows, go to Start | Settings | Folder Options | File Types. Alternatively, almost any modern application will provide the option to change file associations to point to itself.

If you haven't already used this feature, the benefits may not be obvious; so here's an example. If it's not already open, navigate to the previous example and import a bitmap image from your hard drive. Right-click on the bitmap symbol you just imported. Use one of the Edit With options to open the symbol in Photoshop or the image editing software of your choice.

Add a small line of text somewhere on the image, as shown next. Now if this process were as slick as possible and could save an image or sound to a temporary file or some such scheme, you could simply click Save and be done with it. It's almost that good.

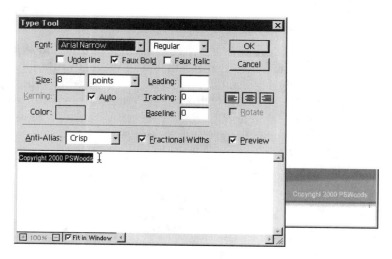

Instead, try to save your file. Look at that! You are in the directory from which you imported your image. Flash remembers where this image came from so that you can decide whether to overwrite it or to save it as a new version. This is probably done in the interest of preserving a progressive history for your images or sounds.

Choosing whether to overwrite the file or save as a new version makes little difference in your Flash workflow. Make a decision based on whether you think you will want to come back to the original file. If you are sure that you will never regret the change, overwrite the file. Otherwise, use a sequential file-naming scheme and save your change as a new version. A good way to get the best of both worlds is to use Photoshop to edit all your bitmap images and use layers to abstract your changes. This way, you can overwrite files and use the handy update feature, while still saving your image in various states.

Update

Now that we have added text to the image in an external editor, we are ready to update the results in Flash. In Flash, locate your bitmap object in the library and open its properties dialog.

If you replaced your original file with the edited version, just click the update button to update the bitmap symbol in Flash. When you use update, you have to click the check box for each image you want to update and then click Update, as seen in the next image. If you saved the edited version to a new file, click import and select the new file. With either method, you keep your workflows centered in Flash.

If you decide to edit multiple bitmaps, such as when you change the color scheme of an entire Web site, you can update all your bitmaps at once. Sort your library by type, so that you have all your bitmaps together. SHIFT-select all the bitmaps and right-click. You have the option to update multiple bitmaps, as shown next. You must select the check box for each image you want to update.

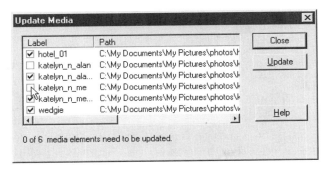

Finding Unused Symbols

If you have a large number of symbols in your library—especially if you use Flash's native tools to compose images—you may end up with unused symbols when you're ready to publish your movie. This really doesn't hurt anything except your storage medium, and possibly the amount of RAM necessary to open and manipulate the Flash file. Flash knows not to publish items that never get used in a movie.

The first requirement if you want to find unused symbols is to tell Flash to start counting how many times each symbol is used. In the Library Options menu, select Keep Use Counts Updated. This populates the column for Use Count in the expanded view of the library palette.

Next, go back to the Options menu and select Select Unused Items. This highlights Flash Movie clips, graphics, and buttons but not imported items like graphics and sounds. If you want to catch imported elements in your net as you look for unused items, switch to the movie explorer palette to see items nested in unused Movie clips. If you want a quick and easy way to clean out your Flash file, you can use this feature to flush out symbols that never appear on the stage or work area. Remember, this has no impact whatsoever on the size of the exported SWF.

Shared Libraries

Shared libraries are a new and much needed feature in Flash 5. They enable you to save components of a Flash site in the user's cache. Instead of saving the information for a sound, graphic, or font over and over in each Flash movie, you can now share library assets across the Internet. In fact, your Flash movies and the libraries they use don't even have to be on the same server.

There are just a few caveats and pitfalls you should know about before we start:

▶ When a Flash movie calls an item from a remote library, it stops and loads the entire library. Therefore, you should include only the items that are sure to be used in the shared library.

▶ You need to define a URL for the shared library. This works just like URLs in every other medium. If the library and the movie that uses it are not in the same directory, you have to specify the URL. Otherwise, you can just name the library *shared_library.swf*, for example.

▶ This sharing method is a huge advantage for sites with multiple movies that share assets, but it does require that you make multiple trips to the server and load multiple libraries. For this reason, it is not advisable to use shared libraries unless you think a user might load multiple movies with redundant elements, including fonts.

Posting a Library to a URL
shared_library.fla

The first step in using shared libraries is to define the assets to be shared. Open and look at *shared_library.fla* from the Chapter04\Examples\Shared Libraries folder on the CD. There's not much there, and we're not going to add much to it. This is how it usually is with shared libraries.

Font Symbol

The first thing we're going to do is add a font symbol. A font symbol allows you to cache embedded fonts on the user's machine by repeatedly calling it from a shared library. From the Options menu on the library palette, select New Font. You will see the Font Symbol Properties dialog:

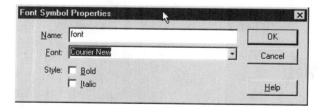

If you select Bold or Italic, you will be able to use those styles in the font, but at the expense of additional file size. Click OK and then right-click on the new font symbol in the library. Select Linkage from the Context menu.

All you have to do to make this a shared library item is to click Export This Symbol and name it. The name is absolutely arbitrary; you won't even have to remember it. Do the same thing for the bitmap symbol: open the Linkage dialog, click Export This Symbol, and name it.

You don't quite have a shared library yet. The library actually resides inside an SWF, so you have to publish the movie to be able to use the shared library. Go ahead and publish the movie. Note that you will have to save it to a directory on your hard drive in order to publish to a place where you can find it.

Linking to a Shared Library
shared_library.fla

Close *shared_library.fla* and create a new Flash movie in the same directory. We are going to pretend that this directory is a folder on your Web server. In fact, keeping all of your SWFs in one directory is a good scheme for a small site. You can at least keep all of your shared libraries in a single directory to make it easy on your memory and anyone else who uses the libraries.

From the File menu in your new Flash movie, select Open As Shared Library and open *shared_library.fla*. You should now be looking at a new library palette containing the shared elements from *shared_library.fla*. Drag both of the items from the library palette onto the stage in your new FLA. You now have shared library assets in your movie. Close the library palette so that you don't get confused between the shared library and the library native to this Flash movie.

To see proof that the library items are being dynamically loaded, put some (embedded) text on the stage in the font contained in your font symbol. Test your movie. You should see a big bitmap, an embedded font, and a file size of 0KB.

If you look at the linkage properties in the new movie, as shown next in the Symbol Linkage Properties dialog, you can see that Flash assumes the published movies are in the same directory because the URL of the shared library is a relative path. If you wanted to have a shared library in a different directory, you would change this to a more descriptive URL.

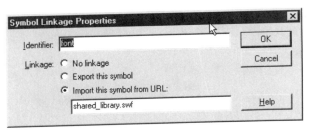

Permanent Libraries

The subject of permanent libraries is going to come up again twice later in the book: in the ActionScript section and in the optimizing your work environment section. Permanent libraries in Flash are analogous to script snippets in hacker legends like Note Tab Pro and 1ˢᵗPage2000. They are tremendous timesavers, and you should start using them if you haven't already.

Permanent libraries are the Flash movies that were included with your installation of Flash 5. They reside in the Program Files folder for Flash. The next image shows the default libraries on my machine. Access permanent libraries in the Flash authoring environment by going to Window | Common Libraries.

Name	Size	Type	Modified
Learning Interactions UIs		File Folder	10/2/00 8:32 AM
Buttons	425KB	Flash Movie	7/13/00 11:29 PM
Graphics	218KB	Flash Movie	7/13/00 11:34 PM
Learning Interactions	414KB	Flash Movie	8/3/00 7:07 PM
Movie Clips	138KB	Flash Movie	7/13/00 11:18 PM
Smart Clips	55KB	Flash Movie	8/3/00 5:38 PM
Sounds	1,269KB	Flash Movie	7/13/00 11:29 PM

You can easily add to or delete from these libraries by opening up the FLAs in the Flash Program Files folder. You can add new categories by adding FLAs to this folder. By using the simple directory scheme, you can develop your own custom library of reusable Flash elements. This is not restricted to graphic elements. You can save Movie clips that only contain ActionScript. This feature is so powerful that I can hardly believe there's anyone who doesn't use it. If you have ever typed identical blocks of ActionScript more than once, or if you have navigated to FLAs on your hard drive, you have already lost out by not using permanent libraries.

Take the example of a scrolling text field. You have a text field—no big deal. Then you have graphics, which could be anything from a font arrow to a complex Movie clip. Then you have the ActionScript, which will be complex if it provides smooth scrolling. Now compare the time it takes to compose and align all of the elements, debug the ActionScript, and test the entire thing to the time it takes to drag a Movie clip to the stage. That's how sharp the contrast is between using permanent libraries and being a hack. Don't be a hack.

Movie Explorer

The movie explorer became my new best friend when I got Flash 5. It reminds me a lot of track view in 3D Studio Max. The only way they could improve it would be to expand it to include editable fields for every attribute of every object.

Navigation and Debugging

The movie explorer is most useful for navigation and debugging. It lays out an entire movie in hierarchical form so you can see how everything fits together. It also allows you to jump between Movie clips and different elements without digging for them on the stage or through the library.

Showing Elements

The most obvious and mundane of explorer functions is an important one nonetheless. When you opened the first example in this chapter, for instance, you probably had no idea what you were looking at. I find the easiest way to get a grip on the structure of someone else's movie is to glance at the published output first then go straight to the movie explorer.

By looking at the movie explorer in any complicated FLA, you can immediately begin to get a feel for what is going on. Figure 2-2 shows you how the slider control works without mucking around in multiple embedded Movie clips.

Customize the items you want to show in the movie explorer with the buttons at the top of the palette. I personally use the button on the far right a lot, which offers a complete listing of all available elements in a single box.

Selecting Elements

You can also use the explorer to navigate between Movie clips. Since you can see everything at a glance, you can select buttons, Movie clips, ActionScripts, or any other element simply by clicking it in the movie explorer.

Displaying Panels for Selected Elements

The next in the logical progression of features for the movie explorer is the ability to pop up relevant panels for any selected element. This may or may not be more

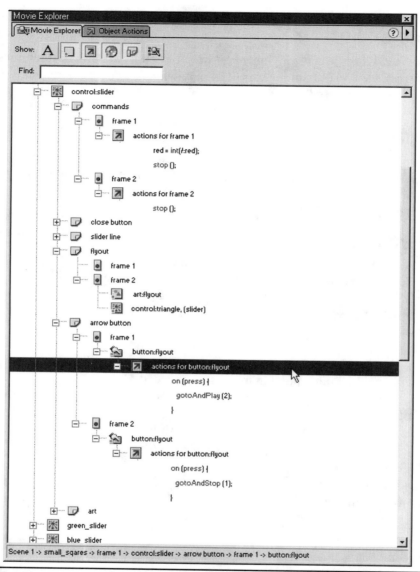

Figure 2.2   *How to manipulate the slider controls easily*

convenient than the hot keys you assign to individual panels. To access this feature, click the pop-up menu in the movie explorer palette. If your ActionScript window is expanded to nearly full screen like mine usually is, it will open in the front and block your view of the other panels. You can easily correct this by sizing your ActionScript panel so that it doesn't overlap the others.

Viewing the ActionScript

This is where the movie explorer earns its keep. When you are looking through a complex movie trying to find where your perfectly conceived script went wrong, the more you can see at once, the better.

I like to separate the ActionScript palette and the movie explorer into different windows, as shown in Figure 2-3. (They are grouped together by default.) That way, you can see other bits of ActionScript while you work on one.

Printing the Visible Navigation Tree

If you like to have the hard copy of your code, or if you just want to see the structure of the movie, the printed output from the movie explorer can't be beat. The Print option is at the bottom of the pop-up menu for the movie explorer. This prints all the elements visible in the explorer at the time that you select Print.

Searching for Elements

Movie explorer provides another feature aimed at giant movies with a lot of elements. If you lose track of a Movie clip, or if you just want to get to it without scrolling, type its name in the Find box. This also works for frame numbers, font names, ActionScript strings, and Generator objects.

As shown in the next image, I typed **tell** in the Find box in order to find instances of the "tell" target action in the example. This action is depreciated in Flash 5, so it's generally best to convert it to modern parlance. See Chapter 9 for more on target paths.

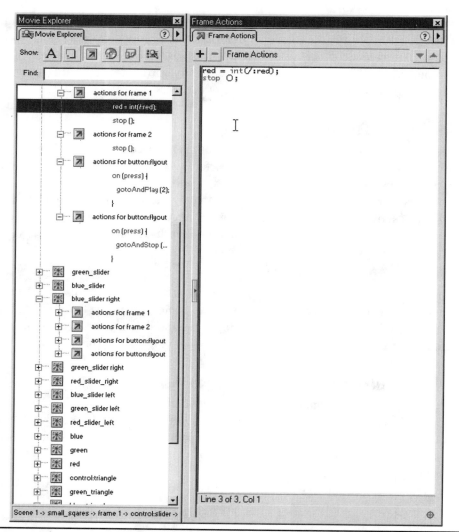

Figure 2.3   *The ActionScript (Frame Actions) palette and the movie explorer, each in its own window*

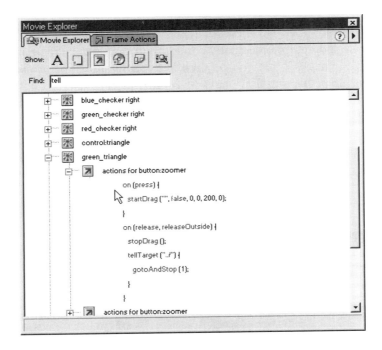

Proofing

Some unfortunate people (like the authors of books) are meant to suffer—poring over text, agonizing over the style of punctuation and minutia like whether the meaning of a sentence is clear. The most exciting thing these people can hope for is to be chosen as the one to apply fonts to the text. Flash provides valuable tools to do this.

Read All Text

The movie explorer allows you to read all of a movie's text in a single window without having to navigate. You simply filter every nontext element out of view. At this point you can print the output if you like.

Copy to Clipboard

The Copy to Clipboard option actually copies all of the text visible in movie explorer. The downside is that you get a lot of extra data that you probably don't want. The up side is that you don't have to go digging for the text.

Replacing Fonts

As you can see in Figure 2-4, changing fonts for multiple text blocks becomes ridiculously easy. Just SHIFT-select the elements you want to change, use your Open Panels option to get the character palette, and select the font you want.

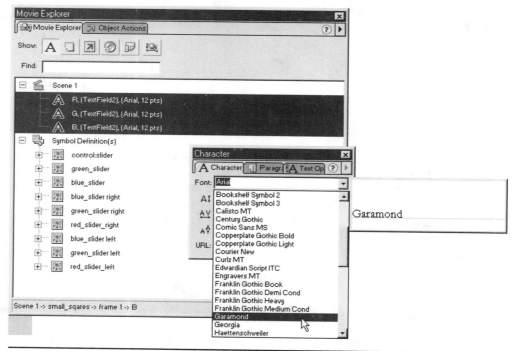

Figure 2.4 *Changing fonts for multiple text blocks*

What to Take Away from This Chapter

The interface for the Flash developer is a little bit different from anything else; and it should be. After all, Flash *is* a different medium. If you are not careful, you can miss some simple and powerful features in the authoring environment. If you haven't done so already, take an afternoon to learn every little thing about the mundane tools in Flash that you use every day.

Optimizing Flash Movies

IN THIS CHAPTER:

Bitmaps

Flash Native Elements

Audio

Streaming Tricks and Techniques

One key factor that determines the success of any online medium is its ability to load quickly. This does not necessarily mean small file size. For instance, you may watch a streaming QuickTime movie on Ifilm.com that takes up 20MB on the server, but it may only take a few seconds to start playing. You may stream a 15-minute discussion from Wired News.com in MP3 format that starts even faster.

Users expect Web pages to load and play within a few seconds. If you start with a "loading" Movie clip, you will probably never have a chance to show your talent, and the user will move on.

Equally important is how much processing power your Flash movie requires. It is possible to create a movie that loads instantly, has a small file size, but skips and jumps when viewed on a slower machine. While file-size-saving features like tweening and MP3 encoding schemes are helpful to deliver a movie quickly, they send a stream of instructions to the user's computer that can be overwhelming if abused.

This chapter is dedicated to streamlining your Flash movies to get the best possible file size and streaming scenario. It covers specific techniques for optimizing bitmap images as you bring them into Flash, then moves on to general considerations when planning your movie and putting it together. A video tracing project is included to show Flash's amazing capability for visual complexity when all elements are optimized. Finally, everything comes together in one project, including optimized audio and a few tricks to avoid the deadly "loading" trap.

Bitmaps

With the combined power of Flash and professional vector illustration tools like Illustrator and Freehand, artists possess a dazzling array of tools to represent or express their vision. A talent that can appreciate these tools does not feel suffocated by the limitations of vector art. As Flash is designed as a vector medium, it should implement primarily vector art. However, there are certain tasks for which bitmap images remain ideal, if not necessary.

▶ Bitmaps are ideal for conveying texture. Adobe's SWF-producing application, LiveMotion, has a sophisticated approach to this aspect of the vector/bitmap relationship. LiveMotion lets you apply a (bitmap) texture to vector shapes. Flash 4 and 5 are very close to this goal and allow you to paint or fill with a bitmap.

▶ Bitmaps display an image that end users will accept as a factual representation or an objective record of physical objects, like a photograph. For some reason, people will accept a photograph as "real," but not images composed in other media.

Compressing Raster Images Within Flash

As an example, let's suppose that you import a compressed bitmap image (JPEG, for instance) into Flash and use it in a movie. Afterward, you export an SWF file and accept the default conservative JPEG compression setting. If you have tried this, you know that the result is distortion. The image is being compressed *twice*: once when it is converted into the JPEG format and again in Flash.

A better approach is to save your image to a *lossless* (no pixels are lost) format and import it into Flash. In this scenario, you control the compression of the image from a central location: the Flash Symbol Properties dialog. You will find that this gives you the sharpest output.

With Flash 4, the best option for importing bitmaps in a lossless format is PNG24. Flash 5 adds the ability to import more file types, including Photoshop PSD files and TIF. You must have QuickTime 4 installed on your machine to use this option. Unfortunately, Flash doesn't support Photoshop layers, except that it renders the final image using the correct layer stack order. If you need to separate the layers in your PSD images within a SWF, investigate Adobe's LiveMotion. If you use raster images in a lot of your Flash work, you should have LM in your toolbox.

If you have a workflow that employs a lot of traditional graphic design elements, the ability to import PSD is a huge benefit. The need for exporting images to a Flash-readable format is eliminated. This is especially handy if you have to go back to Photoshop to edit an image and update it in Flash. On the other hand, PNG24 remains valuable because it is the only bitmap format you can bring into Flash with a transparency mask.

Scaling Bitmap Images Before Importing

 glamour_shot.swf, glamour_shot_sm.swf

When you increase the size of a bitmap image inside Flash, each pixel translates into several pixels, making the image look chunky and distorted. On the other hand, you can get good visual results by scaling a bitmap down in Flash, but at the cost of unnecessarily increased file size. The only reasonable solution is to scale your image in Photoshop (or an alternative image editing program) and subsequently update the image in Flash.

Look at the sample Flash movies named *glamour_shot.swf* and *glamour_shot_sm.swf* in the Chapter 5 directory on the CD for an illustration of this phenomenon.

Glamour_ shot.swf uses a PNG24 image scaled to half size inside Flash. *Glamour-shot-sm.swf* uses the same image, except that it was sized to its proper dimensions in Photoshop. The difference in file size is nothing short of dramatic: 32KB versus 12KB. You should not be able to discern any difference between them visually.

It may seem like a limit or an inconvenience to rule out scaling an image inside the Flash development environment. However, it should not slow down the organized developer who uses Flash's Update option (shown next). Simply keep the current version of the bitmap in a directory of working files. (See Chapter 21 for more on organizing your hard drive.) When you need to change the size, export the image from your image editing software to overwrite the file and select Update in Flash. This is found in the context menu for the image library item or in the Object Properties dialog.

There are just a couple of other considerations for this subject. First, remember the scaling ability of the Flash movie itself. You can set the movie to disallow scaling in the HTML export options. Second, there actually is a time and place for scaling a bitmap image to a larger size. If you are having trouble getting a movie to stream because of the extra weight of bitmaps, try importing them at three-quarter size and scaling them up. This greatly reduces file size; in my experience, about a third of the time the visual output is acceptable, so it's worth a shot. Scaling up a bitmap should be the last resort in optimization.

Project—Deb's Dance Dojo

debs_photo.swf

This project is an example contrived to illustrate a number of optimization techniques. In this phase, a photograph is edited to apply a transparency that can be imported into Flash. Later in the chapter we will add (simulated) video, sound, and navigation elements. The assignment is to create an all-Flash Web site for a dance school called Deb's Dance Dojo. Imagine that the client has communicated a wish for a stage theme, including a photograph of herself in which she holds up another photograph of herself, some plain text information about the school, and a short video clip.

This project makes use of Adobe Photoshop (5.5 or above), but any professional image editing software will also work. This will be a short exercise to illustrate the value of scaling bitmaps prior to import, along with how to apply a transparency hat endures the import into Flash.

Look at the finished product for this phase of the project to visualize the goal. Open *debs_photo.swf* from the CD's Chaper05\Examples folder and run through it once.

Photoshop Elements

deb.psd, Deb_xparent.png

Open *deb.psd* from the CD's Chaper05\Examples folder. Use your preferred selection tools to select the black background from the picture. The goal is to create a transparency in the foreground around Deb, so that the letters can appear behind her. In the next image, you see how I am using the wand tool to select the background. I used a high wand tolerance (40), since the contrast is sharp between the foreground and background.

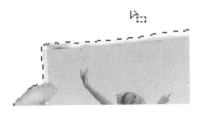

The combination of the wand tool and quick mask is great if you have good detailed motor skills and a decent drawing pad. You can get an almost-good-enough selection instantly with the wand, and then come back and clean up nearly as quickly with a hard-edged paintbrush. The following image shows cleaning up the border with the quick mask tool.

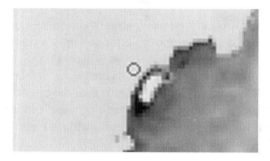

Once the background selection looks good, choose Layer | Add Layer Mask | Hide Selection from the Layer menu. Now the background portion is transparent. Notice that there is a lot of space where the background used to be that is now transparent. None of this will show in the Flash movie, but it will make the file large by adding useless information. Crop out the unnecessary portion as shown here:

Magnified portion to be cleaned up

The image is ready to export to PNG format. Open the Save for Web dialog (CTRL-ALT-SHIFT-S) and save the image as PNG24. Don't forget to check the Transparency option in the export dialog. Save it as *Deb_xparent.png*.

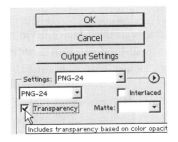

Flash Elements
debs_photo_start.fla

Open *debs_photo_start.fla* from the CD's Chaper05\Examples folder. Import Deb's image into its designated layer and place it in the lower-right corner. Now test the movie. The transparency works, and the images look sharp. To change the dimensions of the movie to 400 × 300px, you use the idea of having a stage in the center of the movie and the navigation items around it; so this particular element will have to be smaller in order to fit on the stage.

The vector aspects of the movie (the text and the scrolling buttons) will scale without issue. However, the bitmap will bloat the reduced-scale Flash movie with unnecessary information (extra pixels that will never be seen). Scale the movie stage to 400 × 300px in the Movie Properties dialog, (CTRL-M), and adjust the text and buttons if you feel the need. I didn't address the former step in this project.

Next, go into Photoshop and export each image again. This time go to the Image Size tab in the Save for Web dialog (as shown in the next image), and type **185** for the height. Since the Constrain Proportions option is on by default, the image will scale to the correct height. Click Apply, then OK.

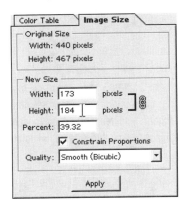

Once you have exported the image at the new scale to the same location (overwriting the old version), you may update it in the Flash movie by simply right-clicking on the item in the library and selecting Update. You may update multiple items by SHIFT- selecting and selecting Update from the context menu.

Update is an indispensable tool, and you should be comfortable using it. This feature will save you a lot of work if you end up making changes to the bitmaps in your Flash movie. Flash knows to update every instance of the bitmap in the movie, using all the same effects, transforms, or any other parameters you have applied. As Deb's photo illustrates, Flash uses the same registration point (your choice of center or upper left) as the original, pre-update photo. For scaling, Flash uses a percentage of the original rather than absolute dimensions. This is nice. It means that you don't have to worry about distorting the aspect of an image if you crop one dimension more than the other.

You should be able to reposition the bitmap layer and publish your movie at its new dimensions. Play with the JPEG Quality setting in the Export Settings dialog (CTRL-SHIFT-F12) to see how much compression you can apply without distorting the image. Personally, I consistently choose the 40 to 60 range. Note that the JPEG settings apply to all raster images in a given movie unless you adjust them individually in the Symbol Properties dialog.

The benefits of scaling bitmaps outside of Flash and using the compression setting in the export dialog should now be obvious. The original movie was about 27KB. After we scaled the movie down, the exported SWF had a file size of 10KB. The final version, with JPEG compression set to 55, is 8KB. That 19KB (the difference between updating the resized bitmap or just scaling it inside Flash) could be the difference between a user waiting for your page to load or clicking the browser's back button. If you are interested in the nuts and bolts of raster images, Photoshop's help feature contains additional useful information.

NOTE

Whenever possible, you should use the technique shown in Chapter 1 for creating an irregular shaped bitmap, which has approximately the same effect as using a transparency. When included, the alpha channel in a PNG image significantly increases the file size of both the PNG and the resultant SWF. However, there are some times when you need powerful raster selection tools to make a cutout realistically around hair, for instance, when a transparency is optimal.

Flash Native Elements

The success of a bitmap image in a Flash movie hinges on manipulations outside of the Flash authoring environment. The following sections consider steps to take within Flash to help fight against file bloat.

Using Symbols

Flowers.swf

Imagine you are walking across the Sahara Desert. You have a pack with all of your outdoor gear, the weight of which could mean the difference between life and death. You figured that it would take you 25 days to make your journey. Based on that number—and your desire to eat three square meals per day—you pack 75 camp stoves into your pack, weighing you down to 1.4 tons, not considering food and water. Since that's not going to work, you'd better rethink this approach.

This may seem ridiculous, but unless you have given serious consideration to optimization already, you are probably doing something similar in your Flash movies. Have you ever drawn approximately same-sized rectangles or circles to serve as the hit area in two different buttons in the same movie? You are essentially using two camp stoves.

TIP

If you are going to reuse any element of a Flash movie—even once—you must create a symbol to optimize the resulting SWF.

The Flash authoring tool converts elements to symbols for you when you import media. For instance, when you import a sound file, it goes into the library automatically—same thing with any bitmap image. When you use a symbol in a Flash movie, the Player can simply refer to something it already rendered and put it in the designated location. This cuts down on file size, which in turn makes your Flash application more usable.

If you catch yourself copying and pasting an element that isn't already a symbol—even simple geometric shapes—stop and convert the original to a symbol. There is no need for your SWF to store the same information twice. We will see this concept pop up again in the ActionScript section of the book. If you find yourself writing the same thing you just wrote, put it in a function (the programming equivalent of a symbol).

Really efficient Flash development takes this a step further by composing elements so that they can be reused. Consider the *Flowers.swf* example on the CD (Chapter05\Examples). The file uses a symbol for an individual petal (they are all the same). The same symbol is used for the leaves on the stem, applying a color effect to make them green. Finally, the flower is a symbol, which in turn is manipulated with color effects to produce the different colored flowers. There are really only two elements in the whole image: the petal and the stem.

Using Layers

The majority of Flash designers have a nasty tendency to cram every piece of a movie onto a few layers, regardless of the movie's hierarchy. This could be because a lot of people are still using a single monitor for development. (See Chapter 20 for tips on monitor real estate.) Whatever the case, this practice is just plain wrong. If you have any identical elements in consecutive keyframes, you are saving useless information in your SWF. Separate persistent elements onto separate layers. Use a keyframe only to change all elements on a layer.

For example, if you have an image that will serve as a static background for a movie, it should be on its own layer, since it will not require any additional attention from the Flash Player once it is rendered the first time. If for some reason you included changing elements on the background layer, using keyframes to mark the entrance and exit of these elements, you would force the player to redraw the entire background at each keyframe. This is a terrible waste of both file size and processor resources.

Using Tweening Instead of Drawing Frame by Frame

Drawing an animation frame by frame is going to generate a much larger file than using tweening. The drawback here is that simple tweening for an object like a hominid isn't going to convey any kind of realistic animation. An easy work-around for this is to draw the character/object you will want to animate and cut it up into its moving parts. In the following image, the head of the minimalist character is being transformed into a symbol so that it can be reused. As the character is animated—it looks like he will be running—the animator will use tweening between the keyframes to move each part of the body. For an excellent implementation of this style of animation, check any of the series at http://icebox.com.

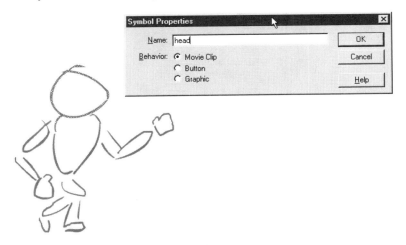

Dynamic Text—Using Only the Font Outlines You Need

When you incorporate input text, such as in a fill-in form, or dynamic text in your Flash movie, you have options for embedding portions of the shape information contained in the font.

▶   **Use a system font (don't embed anything)**   This option can save you a few kilobytes if you are really skimping, but you are giving up control over the appearance of the movie. These fonts are the ones that begin with an underscore, such as "_sans." When a user plays a Flash movie that uses the _sans font, the movie is rendered with the default sans serif font on the user's machine (for example, Arial).

▶   **Embed every character in the font**   This option saves the shape of every character in the font when Flash exports the SWF. For an ornate font with every imaginable character defined, including stuff like ∂, ɜ, ℵ, ®, ™, and §, those shapes add up to make a huge file. This option is probably best reserved for discussion boards on sites dedicated to encoding schemes and symbols or for lazy developers who don't care how long it takes the user to download the movie. To use this option, select the button shown in the following image—the one on the far left under Embed Fonts.

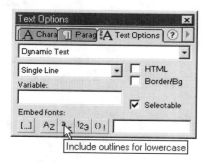

► **Selectively include characters for dynamic text fields**   This is the only sensible approach. If you select the four buttons, as shown in the preceding image, you will allow the text field to draw selected characters from the embedded font. This will cover 99 percent of English-language scenarios. The type-in field to the right of these buttons is for additional characters you want to include. You should start keeping a folder (in the style of code snippets) of characters to paste into here. I use Note Tab Pro (http://notetab.com) to manage clipboard snippets.

Optimizing All Vectors

Whether you draw vector images by hand or import them from another source, chances are your images contain redundant elements. These may include points on a line, fills, or shape corners. Use Flash's optimize tool to simultaneously check shapes for redundancy and remove unnecessary shapes. Using the optimize tool is an entirely intuitive process, but you may rely on one hard rule: for every vector shape, apply the most smoothing that you can without damaging the appearance. If you have a lot of hand-drawn elements in your movie—especially if they are imported from Illustrator or Freehand—you may easily cut 10 percent off the SWF's file size using this rule. See the next image for a sample of the Optimize Curves dialog.

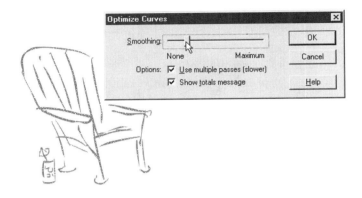

Using Video Tracing

There are a number of visual effects in the Flash repertoire, some powered by ActionScript and some purely visual. In Flash, the gamut of possibilities is as broad as the human imagination. The goal is to capitalize on Flash's strengths, while avoiding the trappings of the author environment (for example, circular buttons, twirling objects, and animated text). In this chapter, we will walk through the process of tracing video, an effect that I find to be not only powerful, but also within Flash's range of execution (and so infrequently used that it is a wonder).

Objectives

Flash is not a standard video editing environment. We are not trying to stream continuous video feeds, like RealPlayer, and we are not trying to incorporate all of the elements associated with normal video (including color). This is not importing a video format directly into Flash, though it is possible to do when adding Flash elements to a QuickTime movie in its native format. The final product looks kind of like a negative of an empty soundstage with actors performing on it.

This process takes shapes from nature that would be impossible to draw by hand. This is a quick visual effect—not the basis of an entire site. This process is good for providing your target audience with the all-time No. 1 best-selling icon in art: the human form.

Disadvantages

The Flash movie will be a large file for the time it will play, as compared to a Flash movie with static text or primitive shapes only. In addition, movies translated from video can require a lot of processing power if the shapes are too intricate. Keep these things in mind when you use this effect.

Choosing Footage

Look at the sites at these two URLs: http://www.mandalay.com and http://www.egomedia.com/. These two sites use the video tracing process. These sites are clean, attractive, and engaging. This incredibly cinematically effective and practically efficient method is just starting to slowly gain popularity. I imagine the reason it hasn't caught on more is that production of this technique can become astronomically expensive in terms of time. However, with added support for more media types and a better user interface in Flash 5, combined with the right video and graphics tools, the process can be significantly streamlined.

Looking at the examples, you should have noticed that you do not see many colors (exactly two: the background and the shapes). You will also notice that you do not see everything you would in a normal video; it is as if you are seeing only the shadows. It is entirely possible to achieve this result by editing any old source video with complex selection techniques and a million hours of hard work, but a little preparation can streamline this process.

In every instance where this effect is well executed, the source video consists mainly of two shades present in two elements: the subject and the background. In the movies at the two URLs I mentioned, the video was intentionally shot with the final product in mind, using a subject and background that would produce the desired quality of contrast.

The video I used for this project is *almost* perfect for the task. It is "Early Nineteenth-Century Quadrille: Step Combinations for figures balancé and Tour de Mains" from the Library of Congress at http://memory.loc.gov/ammem/dihtml/divideos.html, (clip #20 on that page). First, it features two very light-skinned people dressed in black against a very light-colored background. A completely white background and actors with no skin pigmentation would have been optimal. While skin pigmentation can't be helped, you can easily control the background if you are producing your own video.

Next—and more importantly—the content is free. If you want to save an hour's worth of tedious labor, I recommend either shooting your own video with a white backdrop or simply purchasing such a video from a stock footage agency. If you decide to use the video from the LOC, review this video clip in its raw form and try to imagine the final product with just the dancers' clothes and hair.

Getting Started
Flashdance.mov

First, we will cut the video in QuickTime 4 Pro and export it to a series of bitmaps. I used to use a very expensive digital video editor for this task, but now I rely on QuickTime Pro because it is extremely fast, easy to use, and exports directly to the best format for our job: PSD. In addition, it is accessible to anyone ($30), and it does not require you to learn any video editing skills or jargon. Finally, QuickTime is fast and powerful for many of the features Flashers use most, like extracting an audio track from a QuickTime movie for use in Flash. Open your movie in QuickTime and select the range of video you want to export. For the particular clip I chose, we want to end up with a piece of video that starts right when the dancers start dancing and ends as soon as they are done. I chose the frames from 4:18 to 14:20, as shown in the following image. Click the timeline where you want to mark in and SHIFT-click where you want to mark out. With this range selected, copy the video into a new file (Edit | Copy). Save the new file as *Flashdance.mov*. Your new movie should be about 10 seconds long, as seen here:

Close the original QuickTime movie and export *Flashdance.mov* to a series of Photoshop images (File | Export, or CTRL-E). Use the Options button in each subdialog to adjust the settings to those seen here. The great thing about this workflow is that we now have a series of Photoshop images in 256 color-depth grayscale, which is nearly good enough as is for direct import into Flash.

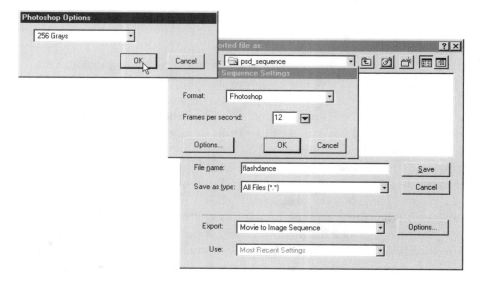

Editing Each Frame in Photoshop

Now that we have a sequence of PSD files instead of a QuickTime movie, we are ready to manipulate each image individually in Photoshop. Fortunately, QuickTime Pro did a lot of dirty work for us by exporting directly to the Photoshop PSD format and saving each image in grayscale. If you are working through this example with a video editing tool that does not offer these options, you can catch up in moments using Photoshop's nifty actions palette and batch-processing capability. Here is an example of how your action for this series of images might look:

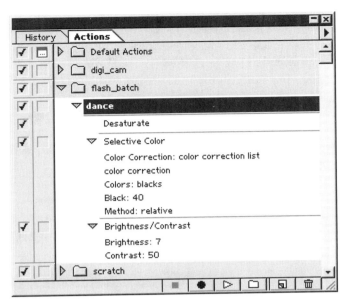

Unfortunately, this is just the beginning for us. Now we have to go back and weed out everything that is not black clothes or hair. You should be able to get this done in less than an hour with the wand tool and quickmasking. I got good results with the wand options set to Tolerance: 30, Anti-aliased, and the Select | Feather option set to 0.2, the lowest allowed. (You want to have the crispest lines possible to translate to vectors.) In addition, the sequence you import into Flash needs to be made up of just two colors, in this case, black and white. You can use any of a half dozen easy techniques to accomplish this. The easiest is probably just to batch an action that increases the contrast (Image | Adjust | Brightness/Contrast).

This process is a terrible chore, so I have included my finished PSD sequence on the CD. Let's pretend you went through those and did all the work; and now we are ready to import the bitmaps into Flash.

Importing the Whole Thing into Flash

First, create a new movie and set your dimensions to match the sequence of bitmaps we are going to import. I also like to change the background color to something other than the background color of the PSD sequence. That way, it is easy to tell which is which.

Next, let's create a new Movie clip to contain the sequence. To keep things modular, you could just as easily import the sequence to the main timeline. Press CTRL-R (or select File | Import) to import and select the first of the series of bitmaps. Flash will prompt you to import the whole sequence.

You now have about 120 frames of bitmaps ready to convert to vectors. This is one of the slickest, most powerful features in Flash (Freehand has it, too): the Trace Bitmap function. Go frame by frame, using Modify | Trace Bitmap. (The dialog is shown below.) You may wish to assign a shortcut key in Edit | Keyboard Shortcuts to convert each bitmap to vectors.

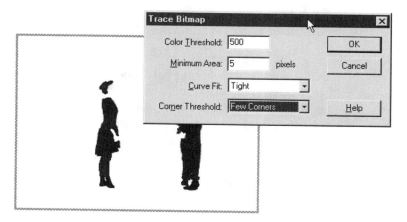

Trace settings are both the least scientific and the most important part of executing this effect. If you choose wisely, you will end up with a good-looking finished product and a reasonable file size. For this particular project, see the settings in the preceding image. Table 3-1 explains what the settings in the Trace Bitmap dialog mean.

Now you should have about 120 frames of vector images and no bitmaps; but you still have 120 bitmaps in the library. Get rid of them. Now all that is left to do is cleanup.

My movie came out to 66KB without any optimizing. It still will not kill you to go through each frame and eliminate redundant vectors. You can do this by going to a frame, pressing CTRL-A (or selecting Edit | Select All), and optimizing

Attribute	Explanation	Value Range (Choices)
Color Threshold	The literal numeric minimum difference in RGB value to be considered as a differentiating factor between two colors. (If two colors do not have sufficiently different RGB value, as determined by this attribute, they are considered one color.) For our example, we only want two colors—black and white—so we go with the maximum value.	0–500
Minimum Area	Number of pixels adjacent to each pixel to consider when assigning a color to that pixel. The definition reveals how this tool works. This should help to understand the relationship between the settings you choose here and the resultant file size and shape accuracy.	1–1000
Curve Fit	How smooth do you want the curves? The closer you are to the pixels end of the choices of attributes here, the more accurate (and bulky) the final image.	Pixels, Very Tight, Tight, Normal, Smooth, Very Smooth
Corner Threshold	How sharp do you want the edges to be? I usually use the Few Corners option for this attribute. More corners mean more vectors, which means a bigger file size. The Many Corners option is good for a static image that you want to look almost as sharp as the original. (Why you would do this, I couldn't guess.)	Many Corners, Normal, Few Corners

Table 3.1   *Setting Options in the Trace Bitmap Dialog*

(CTRL-ALT-SHIFT-C or Modify | Optimize). In addition, there are a few spots that will need some manual touch-up. The woman's hair gets out of place a couple of times as she dances. It is safest to do the manual touch-up first, then go through and optimize each frame. My rule of thumb for optimizing is to use the highest level of optimizing that does not negatively impact the appearance of the image. In this example, it is a very low level.

After I went through my movie, touched up the dancers' hair by hand and optimized each frame individually, I was still at 66KB. Your results may vary, but optimally, you should have less than 1KB per second of animation. That way, you still have room for sound or another layer in your movie without interrupting any user streaming. At this point, you could add a little music loop to the animation (possibly the original—QuickTime will export it for you) or a logo.

Audio

If color is the most subjective medium in all of art, then audio is a close second. Not considering the vast store of conversational fodder the topic of *music* supplies, audio elements like button clicks and voice are enough to keep you awake at night. From microphone type and placement, to mixdown engineering, to compression within the SWF file, there is no other aspect common to all Flash production that has such a complicated, treacherous workflow.

I/O—What Makes a Good Source Sound?

In general, the better your audio source, the better your final Flash movie will sound. Consider a sampling rate of 22kHz with a depth of 16 bits to be the minimum quality for a sound you want to import (44kHz is better). A rate of 22kHz is half the sampling rate of CD-quality sound, and usually sounds crisp and true for any type of uncompressed sound. Anything lower will yield noticeable losses and coloring of the sound.

NOTE

It is entirely possible to get away with lower sampling rates for some sounds like button clicks and short sound effects. I prefer to make the decision on which audio format to use from within the Flash authoring environment to smooth out my workflow. Developers with severely limited storage/system resources may want to import short sounds at lower sampling rates to save disk space and RAM while working with the FLA.

MP3 Is a Compressed Sound Format

Before you get all excited about Flash's new ability to import MP3s, remember that Flash has the ability to compress sound files using a number of codecs covering the spectrum from ultra-squished-long-voice-segment to unnoticeably compressed-home-audio-quality-music. If you bring in a sound that is compressed already and then recompress it upon the compilation of your SWF file, you are going to lose something. Bring sounds in raw if you have the source file.

File Size

Flash is the world heavyweight champion multimedia delivery vehicle specifically because the Player and the content are extremely lightweight (meaning small file size). Audio can easily destroy this feature and must be used with extreme care.

Don't be too proud to sit down with a pencil and paper and draw out a table of priorities for a project before you even begin the storyboard. Looking at a list with "Instant Streaming" at the top and "Audio Quality/Variation" at the bottom can help you make the right decisions before you spend time creating audio you won't use in the end.

Reusing Audio

If you must use audio for every single user event (button mouse-overs, clicks, entering new Movie clips), consider reusing a single audio clip. The value of using sounds for user events is to convey that something has been accomplished, which is really a design crutch. Consider the single most successful use of audio icons as a navigational tool: AOL. The most meaningful and memorable audio icons in AOL are "Welcome!" "You've got mail!" and "Goodbye." These correspond with the most meaningful events for AOL users: connecting to a server, getting email, and terminating the dial-up connection.

The Beat Goes On

Without getting too philosophical, it's safe to say that the modern music world is a looping world. From Philip Glass to Dr. Dre, your users' ears are accustomed to hearing the same music they heard one and a half seconds ago. Use this to your advantage when you compose/employ background music for your Flash project. For instance, instead of bloating a SWF with the full 12 minutes of Miles Davis's "All Blues," just loop the first half of a measure with the vamp.

Compression

Compression is the only difference between very small or very large files in Flash movies that contain any kind of audio. Therefore use as much compression as you can stand when you export. We have already seen this concept when we looked at optimizing curves in vector images; it is the core concept of optimization.

TIP

Optimize elements in your Flash movie as much as possible while retaining the spirit of the original.

More Compression

If you are the one responsible for creating the audio that goes into your Flash movies, spend some time learning how to mix and edit audio. When you do, one of the most useful effects in your repertoire will be compression. This is not file compression like MP3. This is good-old-fashioned-loud-rock-on-cheap-speakers compression. It is an effect that is applied to the audio waveform to push the affected part of the wave into a narrow range of amplitude. The reason this is so important in Flash is that both the Flash Player and the typical system your movies will play on are extremely susceptible to ill effects from extreme lows and highs. Make sure you are remixing, normalizing, or otherwise ending up with a mix that is at an overall high level. The goal is to sound loud and strong without peaks.

Major, Persistent Audio Bugs

Clients with older Win95/Win98 systems often complain about "clicking" in Flash movies with sound. This is a glitch for which there is no sure-fire cure and no certain diagnosis. See Macromedia Technote 14226 at http://macromedia.com/ support/ flash/contents.html. It seems to happen with specific sound cards. Macromedia's approach is that it is not the Flash player, it is the sound cards (yes, these same sound cards that work with every other application under the sun). This is simply one of the drawbacks of using the Flash medium, and it affects only a minority of the audience for Flash content—a minority who have probably grown accustomed to the pervasive clicking in Flash movies. For now, know that in order to effectively troubleshoot this bug in the Flash Player, you must keep one of these machines on hand. The only solution that works with any regularity is to use extremely low sampling rates and bit rates.

Contract Mono

Stereo sound takes exactly twice as much storage space and bandwidth as mono. Stereo music has absolutely no place in Web-deployed Flash multimedia. It won't kill you to mix your audio to stereo, especially when this is the default, for all decent audio apps, but don't rely on Flash to reproduce witty stereo effects you stayed up all night to mix. The default export setting for all sounds is to convert stereo sounds to mono.

Don't confuse stereo ability with panning. While you want to export one track of audio for each sound, you can still efficiently control its panning without doubling the file size.

Audio and Audio Don't Mix

It seems obvious, but it seems to come up over and over in the Flash community: mixing audio inside Flash is generally not a good idea. For example, if you want to have a steady ostinato of crickets with a croaking sound triggered by a user event, fine—split up the audio into a cricket loop and a short event croak. But if you want to have steady croaking along with the crickets, mix the sounds into a *single* loop *before* you import into Flash.

Deconstructing an Example

debsdancedojo.fla

Open *debsdancedojo.fla* from the CD in the Chapter05\Examples folder. Notice that the SWF exported from this FLA in its current state is only 137KB. (This is for instant streaming, animation, audio, and a short video clip, not to mention all the navigation elements for a small business card site.) Click on each button in the SWF to see the final effect of the imported sounds.

Sound Properties Dialog

Look at the library. There are two sounds: "frilly_01," and "taps." Open the properties dialog for "frilly_01." Select it in the library and click on the little letter *i* at the bottom of the library palette or right-click and choose Properties. First note the information on the properties tab, as seen in the following image:

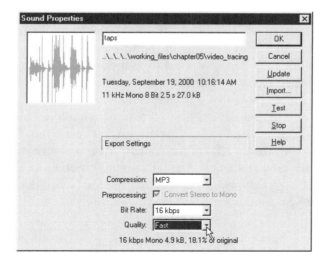

Notice how at the top of the dialog there is information about the original file: 11kHz mono 8-bit (the sampling rate and bit rate at which the music was recorded), 2.5 seconds (the length of the loop), and 27KB (the size of the original file). The most useful information in the dialog, however, is at the very bottom: 16kbps mono (the bit rate and number of channels), 4.9KB (the size of the compressed audio sample), 18.1% of original (the ratio of the compressed file to the original). Watch these two lines of information as you change and test different compression settings for your sounds.

Next in the line of most useful Flash audio features is the Test button, which allows you to preview the sound exactly as it will play in the exported SWF. Use this to play the "Guess a Number" game—just like on long car rides on family vacations. Pick a bit rate between what you know is acceptable and what you know is not. (For example, if you are using MP3 compression, you might start with 128kbps as an upper limit and 8kbps as a lower limit.) If the bit rate you choose yields good audio, try a lower one. The goal is to optimize sound in your Flash movie as much as possible while retaining the spirit of the original. (Is it starting to rub off yet?)

Using "taps" in the Deb's Dance Dojo example as a guinea pig, try using different settings for Bit Rate and Quality, and test the movie (CTRL-ENTER). Just tweaking this sound can make the difference between 115KB and 300KB. For movies in which the audio is imported at a higher sample rate, this difference will be much more dramatic. These audio clips were converted to low sample rates in Cool Edit in order to sidestep the Windows sound card/Flash Player bug.

Bandwidth Profiler

Once you are in Flash's preview mode (CTRL-ENTER or Control | Test Movie), you have a lot of useful tools for testing the performance of your movie (or how well you did at optimizing). Many of these tools are grouped into a console called the Bandwidth Profiler. Open it by selecting View | Bandwidth Profiler (CTRL-B).

You have two choices for the type of graph that will be used to display how the frames of the movie will download: View | Streaming Graph (CTRL-G), or View | Frame-by-Frame Graph (CTRL-F). The frame-by-frame graph merely shows uninterpreted data: the size (in KB) of the contents of each frame in the movie. I can imagine a team development scenario in which this could be useful, but in general, you had better know which parts of your movie contribute the most to the file size before you get this far.

Therefore, the Streaming Graph display option is the more useful of the two. It is a clever, intuitive representation of how the Flash movie streams in a user's player across an Internet connection. The red horizontal line shows the likely maximum amount of data (in KB per second) that a user can receive through his or her Internet connection at the speed designated in the Debug menu. The default is 28.8kbps; there are precious few good reasons to ever change this setting. As you can see in the following image, the streaming graph accentuates those portions of the movie that could potentially cause streaming problems.

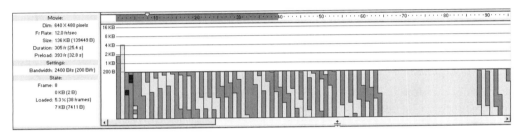

Reading the Streaming Graph

The graph moves from bottom to top, left to right. The meaning may not be clear at first glance. The horizontal axis of the streaming graph represents time (in frames) during streaming playback, while each color change represents a new frame or group of empty frames. The preceding image shows the first frame as a charcoal bar that extends well above the red safety line. This means that the first frame will not stream properly at 28.8kbps, which is not a problem. The user will see the stage and curtain graphics as the first sound downloads. Notice that this sound doesn't slow down the other frames that employ it (three buttons and the pseudovideo demo); once it is loaded, it can be used over and over—*optimization*!

In frame 3 of the streaming graph is a narrow band of black, representing the few empty frames between frames 3 and 15. The next charcoal bar (reading bottom to top) is frame 15. (You can see which frame a bar represents by clicking on it.) The bar runs over onto the next frame of playback (fourth vertical column). This is where the ballet slippers first appear. The playback frames do not line up with the frames downloaded because the Flash player downloads the movie as fast as possible to ensure the best streaming. To get a firmer grasp on this, change the connection speed in the Debug menu to dramatically high and dramatically low speeds (Debug | Customize).

Finally, the streaming graph seems to indicate that the movie will hang up at frame 120 when Deb's photo appears. This would be true if the movie were designed to play straight through without stops. But it isn't, so how do you discern whether this delay is acceptable or not?

Show Streaming

The Show Streaming function models a scenario in which you download your Flash movie from a Web server at the speed designated in the Debug menu. This feature is so valuable it can hardly be overstated. If you test your movies using this feature, you have the assurance that your movies will stream predictably, with a level of certainty to satisfy the most humorless actuary. Here's how it works.

Go to View | Show Streaming (CTRL-ENTER) to start the movie in show streaming mode. Notice the green bar (as in the preceding image) tracking the download process in the timeline. This gives you a real-time update of which frames are ready to play as you download the movie (from the model server into your model browser). Notice that the content of the movie streams into your player in real time, too, so you may sample a typical user experience firsthand.

Use this feature to make an intuitive judgment as to whether the download time is acceptable. In the Deb's Dance Dojo example, the stage graphics and then the ballet slippers come up very quickly while the sound downloads. The pseudovideo in frame 170 takes about 30 seconds to get ready; but with any luck, the user will read some of the text content before proceeding, giving the Player time to download everything. In addition, there is a "loading" MC that comes up very quickly, informing the anxious user of what is happening. This is an acceptable scenario.

Notes on the Optimized Example

The shoe buttons are multiple instances of a single Movie clip. There are a couple of significant points here. One is the assignment of text to the button using ActionScript. As shown in the following image, a very selective group of characters is included in the dynamic text field that serves as a button label. Specifically, I used "aboutscrednialpgm," which exhausts the possible character combinations in the words "about us," "credentials," "rates," "programs," "courses," and "demo." This is especially important because fonts like the one used here (it has a lot of unique shapes and filigree) can really register a hit to the final file size.

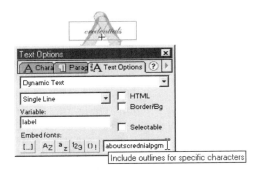

Layers are used to separate elements that remain constant throughout the movie from elements that change—a lot of layers. Since depth is not a huge issue in this movie, it would have been just as easy to put everything on one or two layers. Besides the value of organizing the movie structure, putting things like the buttons and the pervasive title on a separate layer avoids recording superfluous information. If you were to put a keyframe on every frame in the title layer, the final SWF would inform the player of the symbol's presence about 30 times (instead of just once).

Elements are grouped when and where possible—the menu buttons, for example. You may have noticed that some music loop examples in the book are imported at studio-slick, ultra-high-file-size sampling rate and bit depth, while the sounds in this example are puny, dusty little MP3s. This is because of the Windows sound card glitch discussed earlier. These particular clips precipitated the infamous clicking sound at higher sampling rates, so they had to be brought in under a compressed format with a lower sampling rate. Notice also that it is recompressed within Flash. The final selection of a recording-to-compression-to-import-to-recompression scenario is the result of a lot of guessing and frustration (although my frustration threshold has increased as a result of this unresolved Flash Player bug).

Setting	Notes
Default	This uses the settings defined in the Publish Properties dialog (SHIFT-F12). It really isn't very useful if you are interested in optimizing your movies, since you don't know which settings are best until you test sounds individually in the Object Properties dialog, at which point you might as well leave the settings alone.

Table 3.2   *Practical Tips for Audio Encoding in Flash*

Setting	Notes
ADPCM	This compression method also has limited value. It yields file sizes no smaller than MP3, and the perceived quality of sound is diminished. The only redeeming feature of ADPCM encoding is that it allows sounds to be played in the Flash 3 player (F3 can't read MP3).
11kHz sampling rate	You can get away with this setting for things like simple synth waves or short button clicks—waves that are easily or mathematically described. This setting actually causes distortion on previously compressed sounds.
22–44kHz	If you use ADPCM, use the smaller of these two values that sounds OK to you when you use the test feature of the Sound Properties dialog.
4 or 5 bit rate	Use 4 or 5 (whichever is smaller and sounds OK).
MP3	The only well-rounded encoding available in Flash.
16kHz sampling rate	This is the bread-and-butter setting for MP3 encoding. Most audio sounds decent at 16kHz. Remember that the users who have speakers at all have the cheap $2.99 speakers that came with the computer. (These are what you should be using to do the final test for audio optimization.)
24 and 32kHz	This is about as fancy as you need to get for music distributed through Flash. If your audio does not sound crisp (enough for Web users) at this sampling rate, look at your recording/preproduction techniques.
Above 32kHz and below 16kHz	The difference between 16 and 8 is the most significant jump on the scale. You go from pretty good to worthless in a single bound. Don't use 8.
	If you feel you need to use the higher sampling rates, you are probably targeting audiophiles. Audiophiles have a lot of special software and hardware to sate their obsession (including a high-speed connection). You might consider reaching this crowd through a different medium and sparing the typical Web user from the cross fire.
Raw	Don't ever use this. At this point in history, you need to show a little effort to optimize file size when you build something you intend to move to other computers. The only argument that could possibly be made for using a raw sound is that if you deploy a CD targeting users with slower processors, the raw sound will be easier for the older machines to digest.

Table 3.2   *Practical Tips for Audio Encoding in Flash* (continued)

Notice that at the low test rate of 28.8K/sec, the movie hangs up in frame 15 as it waits for the streaming sounds to download. This is by design. The typical solution would be to clobber the user over the head with a "loading" dialog, effectively telling the user, "You are now waiting" (and weighing down the critical first seconds of the movie with another clip). Instead, we rely on the Flash Player's built-in streaming precedence. The animation is controlled by the time in the sound; and the sound won't start until it is ready to stream the whole thing.

There exists a voluminous canon of information on sound in Flash and most of the community sites have discussion areas devoted to this topic. The online help that accompanies Flash is a good general reference to remind you about the different types of encoding. If you already own some decent sound editing tools, the best, most easily accessible source of detailed information on audio is going to be the online help in those programs. Table 3-2 illustrates some general thoughts on encoding and observations from my Flash experience.

Streaming Tricks and Techniques

There is a site (http://www.skipintro.com) that makes fun of the loading/intro movement among Flash designers. This satire brings (or brought—the site has been there for years now) a problem into clear focus: a sequence that says "loading"—no matter how clever—does not excuse the designer from delivering content as soon as the page is loaded. A loading sequence in a Flash movie can be compared to the following:

▶ Being put on hold for customer service: "Your call is important to us" (but not important enough to make us want to pick up the phone just yet)

▶ Missing the last 10 minutes of breakfast at McDonald's while you stand in line

▶ Those advertisements at the beginning of the DVD or VHS you just bought

▶ A prom dress with 30 tiny buttons instead of a zipper

▶ Spending your whole afternoon at DMV (DOT in some states)

Loading sequences and introduction animations are irritating. Don't use them, when possible. However, there will be occasions when you will need to load a huge movie into the user's browser—one that cannot start streaming immediately (like our video tracing example). Instead of the obligatory "loading" slap in the face, consider some of the following ideas as alternatives.

Introductory Text

I refer the reader again to the Mr. Wong series at http://icebox.com. Instead of a simple, mind-numbing, looping animation to indicate that something worth looking at is loading, the user first encounters a warning regarding the content of the movie (the warning is humorous—part of the entertainment itself). Next is a funny (and usually crude) recipe for the user to read through. The recipe requires the user to flip through pages, which enhances the illusion of filling time meaningfully.

A good alternative to flipping through pages is to build an interesting scrolling gizmo. In general, people like things that react to what they do. That is why people like other people, dogs, sports, and Flash. Something as simple as putting your site's favicon on a scroll track instead of the obligatory gradient-shaded ball can bring a smile to someone's face. We will get into the ActionScript behind scrolling later in the book.

The most popular model at the time of writing is introducing a site with fancy, spinning bathos. This may not be the best model, either for streaming or for comprehension. Almost any site will permit, if not require, introductory text. Anyone who remembers Leonard Bernstein's preconcert lectures will testify that art is more enjoyable with a little background knowledge.

This point is worth a little explanation. Think of three other examples of steaming piles of huckster multimedia: motion picture previews, 30-second television ads during the sporting events, and the foreword to a book. What the film preview and the sports ad have in common is context. Viewers know they are seeing a movie preview and not, say, a television news broadcast, because they are in a movie theater and that is what they see before the feature in movie theaters. Similarly, sports fans know they are seeing an ad for an overpriced automobile, overpriced high-tech products and services, and overpriced financial services. There will be no surprises.

The book foreword is a little different. When you pick up a book from an indexed catalog—whether a library, an etailer, or your favorite local bookstore—you have *some idea* of what will be inside, but you really need the foreword or introduction to tell you what the focus of the book is—what ideas the book is selling.

Web-based multimedia is a combination of the two. It is like the movie preview or TV ad in that it has movable bits, and this is what designers fixate on, but the more important issue for users who want to understand what they are looking at is indexing. The Web is an indexed directory just like a library or a Barnes and Noble store. And the sites you build are like books in that they are autonomous packages of knowledge, art, or whatever people think is worth sharing. Most importantly, *users don't know what they are looking at until you break it down into specifics as to what the site is about.*

For these reasons, introductory text—even a one-paragraph blurb—is superior to shocking users immediately with fancy dancing visual metaphors. They won't understand what ideas you are linking to with your spinning 3D objects if you don't at least tell them what kind of ideas you deal with.

Interactivity During the Loading Sequence

Another icebox.com series called Zombie College (again in questionable taste) makes exceptionally good use of the assets in each SWF by using an interactive game as the time filler. The characters in the game are symbols used later in the featured animation. Another example of this technique is the "SouthPark" series on shockwave.com.

This type of padding is ideal when you have already established the premise of the loading animation and the focus is on entertainment. You wouldn't want to offer users an irreverent game with whimsical sound effects while they wait for their medical test results to load.

Interactivity can be as complex as arcade games or as simple as an interesting widget. I especially like trivia quizzes because they are easy to build and require almost no elements that aren't already included in the featured animation.

Simple Beginning Animations

cd_intro.swf

Another viable solution is to incorporate elements into the beginning of the animation that don't tax resources, thus giving the rest of the movie a chance to load. For an example of this approach to streaming large animations, look at *cd_intro.swf* on the CD in the Chapter05\Examples folder.

There are a couple of tricks that fall into this category. The easiest to implement is beginning with the background only. This is such a common cinematic device, I'm surprised this isn't the default Flasher approach.

If you have a background that is composed, optimized, and grouped into a symbol with streaming in mind, it should load instantly if you put it in the first frame of your movie by itself. If you can manage to use just one or two symbols on top of the background in the first few seconds of the movie, you may manage to start without any preload.

Hiding Bitmaps at the Beginning of the Movie

Introducing a bitmap in the middle of a movie can be hard to manage from a streaming standpoint. If you have a continuous animation that includes a bitmap somewhere other than at the beginning, it can be hard to predict how the movie will perform. Consider hiding the bitmap offstage or inside an MC with the visibility set to 0 at a convenient stopping point in the movie. This prevents the infamous skips and stutters that arise from throwing a bitmap into an animation without warning.

If you choose the visibility method, use a separate layer in the timeline for each bitmap. That way, you can hide them individually as you work with the movie. You could just as easily put them all on one layer; but I get confused when I'm trying to figure out which is which on one layer.

In general, I think of bitmaps and animation as an oil-and-water combination. Even more than streaming problems, trying to actually move bitmaps in your Flash movie is going to cause rendering problems on slower processors. In other words, older machines can't keep up with the Flash Player—even in movies that have a small file size—when you try to do too much. Using tweening for effects like zooming in and out on bitmaps generally doesn't work.

You absolutely must test for skips and other symptoms of bad design on a machine with a slow processor before you deploy your Flash movie. Although I am generally unsympathetic to users who have very old browsers, slower processors are a fact of life. It doesn't make sense for most people in big companies to upgrade to a modern, slickified multimedia supercomputer when all they need to use for work is a command-line email client and Word 97. The reality is that a large fraction of any Web audience is using machines as slow as Pentium I with 32MB RAM.

What to Take Away from This Chapter

Optimization is the focal point of one of Flash's most humiliating failures to date—the loading/intro craze. Optimization is the only difference between click-through and click-out. The very first thing some clients do when they review a project is sit at a dial-up-connected computer with a stopwatch (or an actual timer browser plug-in) to measure how long it takes your twirling 3D logo to load. You should plan accordingly.

The crux of optimization is keeping the user's browser pumped full of content from the moment a page is loaded. Although the techniques vary based on the medium, all optimization in Flash boils down to our streaming mantra, "Optimize elements in your Flash movie as much as possible while retaining the spirit of the original."

Audio for Flash

IN THIS CHAPTER:

ome multimedia developers never have to deal with audio engineering. They either receive source audio from clients, are part of a design firm with someone else handling audio or simply outsource audio recording because they understand the scale of the challenge and do not want to deal with it. If you are one of these developers, skip this chapter. Otherwise, this chapter is for you.

The purpose of this chapter is to give you some important background on digital audio as you record and prepare it for Flash. My fundamental approach for Flash audio is to record and edit the best-sounding audio possible outside of Flash and then let Flash do all the resampling and compression.

One common misconception I am particularly interested in dispelling is the idea that the sampling rate, bit depth, and number of channels of the sound file you import into Flash have *anything at all* to do with the size or performance of the exported SWF. The only detrimental thing that a large sound file will do to your Flash movie is bog down your system's performance when you import and export. It is important to understand that the heart of this issue is your budget for hardware or, in special cases, the amount of time it takes to encode unusually long sounds in the SWF.

My way of thinking is that it is easiest and least error prone to maintain a single, relentlessly perfectionist workflow for audio outside of Flash and then use the Flash authoring tool to determine which output format to use for each individual sound. In this chapter I am assuming that people building Flash applications on machines with severely limited resources are not professional developers, for whom this book is designed.

The chapter will cover some nuts and bolts about the process of digitizing sound and sound file formats, since there are some measurable characteristics that we can positively link to perceived qualities. It will also cover some specific tricks and tools to make Flash audio sound as sharp as possible. If you make it all the way to the end of the chapter, you'll find some specific problems and their solutions within the Flash authoring environment.

NOTE

This chapter does not contain a lot of specific information about Flash. Audio within the Flash environment is covered thoroughly in Chapter 3. This chapter merely gets you started with the big concepts and issues in digital recording, should you be at that stage in learning multimedia development. If you are not interested in audio engineering, skip this chapter.

Background

Small-scale audio recording and engineering have been aided immeasurably by the rise of cheap, powerful PCs and cheap, powerful recording software. Although it is easy to dive into the world of audio without much money, it is impossible to start without a little vocabulary. Some of these terms should have been covered in your junior high science class, so this will be mostly review. A few terms are specific to audio recording and PC file formats.

- ▶ **Amplitude**   The volume of a sound wave as measured by the distance between the highest and lowest points in one cycle of the wave. In the context of music recording/engineering, amplitude is *not* the perceived volume of the wave traveling through the air to your ears—which is called *volume*.

- ▶ **Codec**   *Compression* and *dec*ompression scheme, in the form of a file that a player reads, like a set of instructions for encoding and decoding. For instance, WinAmp uses the MP3 codec to decompress the song "Beer Barrel Polka.mp3." Some other application used the same codec to compress the file into MP3 format. Note that any of a number of codecs may be applied to a single file format. For instance, you can have a WAV file encoded with the MP3 format.

- ▶ **Compression (audio)**   An audio effect applied to a waveform to alter its sound. Compression, along with limiting and normalization, is applied to a sound to limit the dynamic range (or amplitude) of the waveform. The perceived effect is that everything is loud. As we will discover later in the chapter, this is a very important effect to use on Flash audio.

- ▶ **Compression (file)**   The type of compression you already know and love. MP3 is a compression scheme. The idea of file compression is that redundant information is discarded. Precisely which information is considered redundant or disposable is the art of good encoding schemes. MP3, along with open-source empire slayer Ogg-Vorbis, are brilliant schemes for compressing audio because they both throw away a lot of information (reducing file size); but they still sound as crisp as the original to most ears.

- ▶ **Frequency**   Ratio measured by the number of times a wave cycles over a period of time. We will deal with sounds whose frequency is measured in Hz.

- ▶ **Gain**   The level of a signal from an audio input device, such as a microphone, line in (from a CD player or synthesizer), or another component of your computer.

► **Hertz (Hz)**   Unit of measure for frequency. Equivalent to one cycle per second. Most of our measurements in audio recording/engineering will be in kHz (kilohertz, or 1000 cycles per second).

► **Loop**   A piece of music that is edited such that it can play over and over successively in tempo. A loop is almost always an integer of musical measures or beats.

► **Multitrack**   Audio with multiple independent channels. The purpose of multitrack recording/engineering is to treat channels (*tracks*—usually abstracted one per sound source) individually and mix them together.

► **Pitch**   The perceived frequency of a sound. This is subtly different from frequency. As discussed shortly, most sounds are not made up of a single frequency, but a mixture of frequencies. The mix and ratios of the different frequencies make up the quality, or *timbre*, of the sound, but if one stands out perceptibly, it is said to be the *pitch* of the sound. When a note is played on a musical instrument, for instance, you hear a pitch. When a door slams, there is not usually a dominant pitch.

► **Reverb(eration)**   The perceived effect of sound waves bouncing off surfaces in an acoustic space in rapid succession (called *reflections*). You hear this in concert halls, bathrooms, the Grand Canyon, and so on, as echo. In professional recording, some type of reverb is typically applied in varying levels to each channel, whether it is from digital effects, the natural ambient resonance of the room, or with special echo chambers.

► **Timbre**   Pronounced *TAM - brr.* (Note: it is all but ridiculous to try to explain the idea of timbre in a few sentences; the idea is elusive enough to keep a coffeehouse full of philosophy grad students on topic for two hours straight.) Timbre is the perceived "quality" of sound. It is the subjective perception of the unique compositions of individual waveforms. It is the way people recognize voices. It is the distinctive sonority of a Guarneri violin or a Fender Rhodes electric piano. Timbre is loosely synonymous with *tone*.

► **Wavelength**   The distance the sound travels in one cycle.

Timbre

Have you ever noticed that it is harder to recognize your friends' and family's voices on the phone than it is in person, not accounting for the advantage of vision? This phenomenon is a perfect microcosm of the challenge of digital audio; namely, to encode physical sound electronically and reproduce it in a different space.

Physical Sound

Let's start with the sound at your friend's end of the phone in our example. In the room from which he calls you, his voice is clear, strong, and unmistakably his. It possesses characteristics that we can describe using subjective commentary the way an author does (for example, "...a deep, sonorous baritone"). This kind of language points to the underlying physical characteristics of the subject's voice. If we had perfect knowledge, we could also describe our friend's voice in terms of the quantifiable parameters of the waveforms that emanate from his mouth, which is what digital recording attempts to do.

The voice is made up of a vastly complex series of waves vibrating simultaneously. These waves are stacked on top of each other, so to speak, according to an order present in all sound called the *overtone series* or *harmonic series*. The gist of the overtone series concept is that an instrument tuned to a pitch—in our case a voice—produces other frequencies that change the color of the sound. These other frequencies are the overtones or harmonics. It happens to be that overtones occur according to a constant set of ratios to the fundamental pitch of a sound (the note that you *hear*). It is the mixture of frequencies in the overtone series that gives the different musical instruments their unique timbre, or aural personality.

Among the musical instruments, some possess more complex timbres than others—that is, they have a more varied or fuller set of overtones complementing the fundamental pitch. Among the instruments that produce simpler waveforms are the flute and the oboe; and to give you a big hint as to where all of this is going, the flute and the oboe were among the first instruments to be convincingly simulated with synthesizers way back in the 1960s. The ("classical") guitar and the human voice are among the more complex waveforms you hear every day.

These factors all come into play when you record music and try to corral it into a usable form in your multimedia projects. Most importantly, you need to know which types of sounds are complex and which are simple in order to make intelligent decisions about factors like microphone type and file compression options.

Table 4-1 shows some examples of sounds and where they fall in the continuum of simple to complex. The simpler a waveform is, the easier it is to record and reproduce with smaller files.

The Computer and Sound

The first challenge in digital audio is converting sound waves of varying complexity in the air to digital information that can be stored in a file. This starts with the microphone, where a little membrane like the one in your ear vibrates sympathetically with the sound waves bombarding it. The microphone converts the waves into minute pulses of electricity.

Simplest
Pure, synthesized waveforms (sine wave, sawtooth, Roland "Synth-lead" type)
Electronic phone ringing
Bird calls
Typical button-click sounds (percussive metal on glass, metal on metal)
Woodwind instruments

Plucked string instruments
Bowed string instruments
Voice
Percussion like cymbals, triangle
Most complex

Table 4.1 *Samples of Waveform Complexity*

At this point the signal is electronic but not digital. It is not quantified in any way; rather it is a reflection of the sound wave—a conversion into electricity of the kinetic energy in the sound wave that hits the microphone diaphragm. Because the signal in this form cannot be recorded in language that humans or machines can understand, it is said to be *analog*. (Yes, analog tape and other such media can store and reproduce audio of this kind, but they can't act on it.)

At this point the signal disappears into a rabbit hole, the complexity of which need not concern the audio engineer. The name and function of that hole is the Analog to Digital Converter (ADC). The process of converting the analog signal from the microphone to a digital file in the computer is where the rubber hits the road for everything discussed in this chapter. This process is called *sampling*.

When the sound card begins sampling, it takes periodic snapshots of the incoming wave of electrical pulses. These snapshots are a measurement of the wave's parameters that describe the sound, which can of course be stored in binary data. Before it will start the sampling process, the sound card's ADC requires an important set of instructions: how frequently to take the snapshots (the *sampling rate*) and how many bits of data to use describing the wave in each snapshot (the *bit depth*).

This scheme is analogous to digitizing photo images, with higher resolution yielding bigger files and a perception of truer quality. The sampling rate is like the image resolution (DPI). The bit depth in audio sampling is analogous to bit depth in images, where you have 8-bit images, 24-bit images, and so on.

Some time before you and I became interested in recording or multimedia, smart people figured out a scheme to determine the minimum sampling rate (or *sampling frequency*, measured in kHz) required to digitize a waveform. The scheme is called the Nyquist Sampling Theorem. The equation for the theorem is

$$F_s \geq 2F_a$$

This simply means that the sampling frequency must be greater than or equal to twice the highest frequency in the original analog signal. For example, if the highest frequency in the sound you want to sample is 15kHz, you would need to sample the sound at a frequency of 30kHz, or 30,000 snapshots every second. If you are interested, you can see a clever proof of the theorem (not for the mathematically fainthearted) at http://ptolemy.eecs.berkeley.edu/~eal/eecs20/week13/nyquistShannon.html.

It turns out that you are reading this book at a marvelous time in the history of desktop digital recording. You see, the generally accepted range of frequencies audible to humans is 20Hz to 20kHz; and the cheapest PCs you can buy on your lunch break at your local office supply store come equipped with sound cards capable of recording at a sampling rate of 44.1kHz. In other words, if you own an even modestly potent PC, you can record high-quality audio.

Making Decisions Based on Timbre

Here are some general guidelines to simplify the decision-making process. You needn't get excited and flustered by the prospect of applying scary physics equations to your multimedia projects.

Record, mix, and edit at the highest sampling rate and bit depth available. If you have a good, high resolution for recording the input, you will retain more of the original's characteristics (just like scanning a document). If you are concerned about RAM or storage and want to use a lower-than-maximum resolution, use a sampling frequency of 44.1kHz and a bit depth of 16 bits as your minimum.

Another thing that will help you save storage space and system resources is to record in mono—always. Don't feel that you're somehow losing sound quality by combining the input channels on the stereo microphone that came with your computer. Real-world, big-time recording—with thousand dollar microphones and hundred thousand-dollar mixing boards—happens one channel at a time with mono microphones.

Once you have captured decent-sounding audio at a high resolution, you can easily *resample* the digitized waveform to a lower sampling rate and/or bit depth. Following the image analogy further, this is like exporting a 300dpi image to 72dpi for Web use. Resampling converts the digital waveform into a smaller amount of data, which means that the resultant file is both smaller in size and of a "lower" quality (sounds less like the original).

Resampling can be executed either in audio editing software or directly from Flash when you export. In addition, compression/decompression-encoding schemes can be applied either in audio editing software or in the Flash export application. This is what makes Flash audio tricky.

In a perfect world, it would make the most sense to import the purest digital sound possible into the Flash-authoring environment. Then you would use the export utility to determine which sounds are OK at low resolution and which sounds require less compression or higher sampling frequency at the cost of bigger file size. In my experience, this scheme works between 60 percent to 80 percent of the time, depending on the waveforms.

The problem is that the Flash Player causes a few specific sound cards on Windows machines to pop and click when playing back some sounds. Unfortunately, these few specific cards are widely distributed, so an appreciable portion of your Flash audience will suffer from this bug. Start with the *perfect world* assumption (import sounds into Flash at high resolution) for all of your audio clips, and work individually with the clips that are affected by the bug. There is more on this in Chapter 3.

Sound File Formats

If you have read everything in this chapter up to this point, you are probably itching to get some specific, practical information. Understanding audio file formats as they relate to audio engineering, and Flash is about as practical as it gets.

A WAV Is Not a WAV
Chapter04 \ Examples\WAV

It is important to understand the difference between the many flavors of WAV. Although WAV is a single file format, Windows provides a wide array of built-in resolution and compression management tools.

▶ **PCM (Pulse Code Modulation)**   This is the scheme that saves the waveform as pure, uncompressed data. This option allows you to choose a sampling frequency and bit depth. You will want to work with PCM WAV files, since this is the purest form of digital audio in the Windows environment. Flash can export PCM audio. This option is labeled "Raw" in the Object Properties dialog for sounds.

▶ **ADPCM (Adaptive Differential PCM)**   This scheme applies a 4:1 file compression to digitized waves when you save them to this format. More specifically, this scheme assumes that your original (and reproduced) waveforms will have 16 bits per channel and tries to expand the compressed file from

4 bits per channel back out to 16 bits at playback. If you use this encoding scheme for some reason, make sure you save to 16 bits to avoid wasting waveform resolution. Flash can export audio to ADPCM format. If you choose this scheme, Flash will choose the optimal (16-bit) settings. This was a good encoding scheme back in its day; but now it is really just lingering for backward compatibility with the Flash 3 player.

▶ **ACM (Microsoft Audio Compression Manager)**   This is not a specific format. It is Windows' (98+) built-in tool for accessing every installed audio codec. Any audio application worth its salt will have an interface with the Microsoft ACM conspicuous in its Save As dialog. It may be a pop-up menu labeled something like ACM/WAV or just a drop-down menu in the dialog labeled Format. You should be able to access every audio format installed on your PC from your audio editor's Save As dialog, as seen here in Sonic Foundry's formidable Sound Forge. Note that this is a good way to get an MP3 encoder on your machine. Some audio editing tools offer you the option of buying an MP3 encoder for an additional cost. By using the Microsoft ACM, you can save this expense by using an encoder you already have installed on your machine.

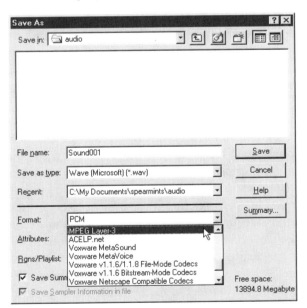

▶ **a-Law/mu-Law**   These formats are very clever, very specialized schemes used in telephony applications to get the maximum signal-to-noise ratio and efficient file compression. Don't bother with these formats for multimedia audio.

►   **Everything else**   You will see a lot of different audio codecs installed on your computer. A lot of applications—speech recognition, for example—have their own specially designed audio formats. These generally do not present any utility to the Flash developer.

There is one important thing to take away from our quick survey of the Windows WAV file format. Just because a sound is a WAV file does not mean that it is uncompressed, has a good sampling frequency or bit depth, or is in any other way optimal for crisp-sounding audio. For a vivid illustration of this concept, listen to all the WAVs in the WAV directory of the Chapter04\Examples folder on the CD. These waves range from pure PCM audio to ultracompressed MP3, yet they are each WAV files.

File Size Equation

You may have noticed the amazing file size difference between the different WAV files in the Examples folder. This is the goal of different compression/encoding schemes, and the current king of this mountain is MP3. Web multimedia is very much concerned with delivering quality audio at the lowest possible file size, as evidenced by Flash's own comprehensive set of audio encoding tools.

While you will generally want to let Flash worry about the details of converting audio elements and make decisions using your auditory perception, you still need to know the factors that go into the size of a resampled sound. Regardless of your Stream scenario, you should always shoot for the smallest SWF file possible with a constant perceived quality of audio. Knowing what contributes most to heavy sound files gets you off to a good start toward having streamlined, clear audio.

The single most important factor in the size of a sound file is the number of audio channels it has. For our purposes we will assume that this number is either one (for mono sound) or two (for stereo sound). Simplifying a sound to mono when you publish your Flash movie decreases the file size by exactly half, *ceteris paribus*.

Next is the sampling frequency. It stands to reason that since samples occur at regular intervals, the sampling frequency is in linear proportion to file size. In other words, changing the sampling rate by a certain percentage changes the file size by the same percentage.

Bit depth does not impact the size of the file in linear fashion, so it is best to sacrifice this setting last when you are resampling to save file size. The equation for a Windows PCM file size demonstrates this:

File Size (in bytes) = Time (in seconds) * ((bit depth)/8) * Channels

Keep the file size equation in mind as you work in the Flash authoring environment, trying to optimize your audio elements. You will be able to bring the majority of audio into Flash as high-resolution PCM WAVs. From there you will use Flash's native tools to resample and compress audio into the best compromise of file size and aural fidelity. I have tried to summarize the process here:

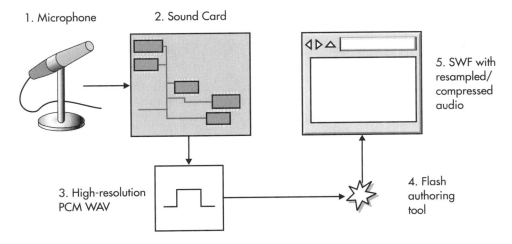

To recap what we have covered so far:

►   Sound is made up of complex mixtures of waves.

►   A microphone captures sound and converts it to analog pulses.

►   A sound card samples the stream of pulses.

►   Use the highest sampling frequency possible.

►   Import the high-resolution sound into Flash.

►   Flash resamples/compresses the audio when it publishes the SWF.

►   More complex sounds require higher resampling frequencies/less compression.

Composing Audio

If you are going to be composing audio yourself—that is, capturing sound from the air with a microphone, or from a musical instrument through a *line in*—you will want to choose tools that can handle high-resolution digital audio. Fortunately, this is no longer expensive or hard to set up.

Requisite Hardware

Some time around the release of the Pentium II processor, the cutting edge of desktop PCs moved well beyond the minimum requirements to produce crisp multitrack digital audio. Whole worlds of enthusiastic amateur music sprang up overnight on the fertile ground of affordable, powerful hardware and software and latent enthusiasm for music.

At the time of writing, consumer PCs come so spectacularly arrayed in high-quality hardware that it is hardly worth mentioning the minimum requirements; but the bar continues to rise with the technology. We will quickly cover the minimum requirements and a few tips on hardware before moving on to the fun stuff.

PC

Assuming you are already a Flash developer, you probably already run some powerful software and have a machine to handle it. That's good, because digital audio can use every bit of what you've got. You probably can't record high-res, multitrack audio with less than 128MB RAM. Processor speed is less a factor, but you will want at least a PII 266.

Sound Card

The sound card's primary task is to convert analog signals to digital, and vice versa. If you don't have a sound card or you need to upgrade, here are just a few things to consider:

▶ The card must be capable of sampling at a frequency of at least 44.1kHz, preferably 48kHz.

▶ Most decent consumer sound cards support 32-bit sampling, but you'll never hear the difference in your multimedia output. Consider 16-bit to be an acceptable performance standard, but probably the mark of a poor-quality card. There are some specialty cards made specifically for digital recording that have a maximum bit depth of 16.

▶ Recording multitrack digital audio requires that you hear the existing tracks while you record other tracks. Both of these jobs are the sound card's responsibility. To do both jobs at once (a necessity for multitrack recording), the card must have a feature called *full duplex*. Almost all cards on the market today have this feature.

▶ If you are planning on going off the deep end into digital recording, you will end up wanting specialized input and output hardware on your sound card to interface with mixing boards, near field monitors, and the like. As is most often the case with music recording, there are few hard standards concerning hardware and software, so don't buy the first thing you find at your local computer warehouse store. Decide exactly what you want to do first, and read up on how to do it.

Microphone

The microphones that come with computers are good enough for recording button click sounds, auditorium-quality speech (though not good enough for important voice-overs that carry a multimedia presentation), and curiously enough, electric guitar amps. Let's assume that this will cover our needs.

If you really want to do it right, you should use what is called a *condenser* microphone to record acoustic sound sources in acoustic space. If you use a condenser microphone, you will also need an analog mixer to send its required "phantom power" and attenuate the signal from the microphone. I know it sounds crazy, but you really do need 1950s technology to get the best input for your digital audio.

At the time of writing there are excellent condenser microphones on the market in the $200 range and mixers for about twice that. If you want to go the Spartan route with your input hardware, you could actually skip the mixer and get an inline preamp to drive the mic. If you will be recording only voice-overs with your mic, this will do the trick just fine.

Recommendations on Software

This is the fun part. This is the part that tells you we have arrived in the Buck Rogers future with flying cars and cures for every disease. The software you can download today as shareware or even freeware is the culmination of close to a hundred years of trying to reproduce audio faithfully. Digital effects presets and macros enable anyone who can read tooltips to perform audio wonders that used to require millions of dollars' worth of equipment, specialized architectural structures, and professional recording engineers.

Sonic Foundry's Acid

I think Acid software is one of the most interesting software products available today, in any category. The central ideas behind the product are

▶ Anyone with a creative spirit can put together interesting music if provided with discreet units of universally compatible music and a tool to join the units.

▶ Put together a hundred thousand of those anyones, and you will get some wonderful music.

Acid uses WAV files that are composed as loops that can be played over and over in tempo with other instruments. With an entry-level version of the software available at $0 (*free*), the new world is definitely accessible to everyone. You can find information and downloads at http://www.sonicfoundry.com/. The software is designed to allow users to compose their loops and save them with all the necessary metadata, so that users can share loops. And if all that isn't enough to prove that Sonic Foundry understands the importance of community involvement in a product, they actually built a site where users can interact, trade loops, and download free, professionally composed music. Lots of independent, noncommercial loop-sharing sites have sprung up as well.

Acid is a particularly good fit for Flashers because it is the premiere prosumer product for loop-oriented music. Loops play an important part in the Flash audio game because background music usually takes the form of loops in order to conserve file size.

Take a look at the example provided in the Chapter04\Examples\Acid folder if you have Acid installed, or glance at Figure 4-1 to see how it works. Note that Acid saves projects with absolute paths to the individual waves, so it will prompt you to find files it doesn't see. They are all in the same folder.

The bass and drum loops are free loops I found at the Yahoo Acid Webring, http://nav.webring.yahoo.com/hub?ring=acidlp&list, which has a wealth of funk and techno fodder on dozens of sites—freely available for anyone who wants it. The guitar track is from my home studio. The high-resolution, studio-slick output was remarkably easy to produce. The entire job, from start to finish, took less than a half-hour, including setup time and tuning an instrument. Here are some of the advantages of Acid for Flash developers that are evident in this example:

▶ The software takes care of marking measures for you. The top half of the screen, which looks similar to the Flash timeline, is measured in beats, and measures the same way that Flash is measured in frames.

► It took me about eight times through a four-bar phrase to play a really good chicken-pickin' riff. The vestige of my blundering is all the excess space before the waveform in the guitar layer becomes active. In the old days, you would have to mix all the tracks first and then trim away the excess manually, finding the best loop in-and-out point by ear. With Acid, you can export only the loop you want by using the marker at the top of the screen in Figure 4-1 that looks like the Flash onion skin marker.

► When I did export, Acid mixed all three tracks based on the position of the sliders in the left pane of the application window.

► The exported WAV is perfectly cropped to a length that will loop inside Flash without adjusting it in the Edit Envelope dialog.

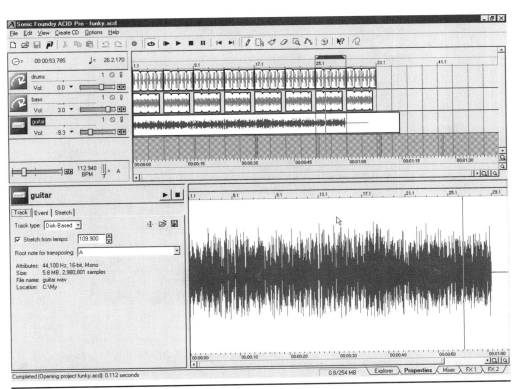

Figure 4.1   *The Acid working environment*

Acid is a terrific tool for Flash developers because it lets you make loops quickly and easily. At $59 for a full-blown professional version, you can't go wrong.

Sound Forge Xp

Sound Forge is another old favorite in digital recording. A low-cost complement to Acid, Sound Forge covers virtually all audio engineering tasks, from manually editing wave forms to applying studio-quality effects.

Another invaluable task Sound Forge performs is saving data within a wave file to mark the beats in an Acid loop. This allows you to use the tempo of the clip you record to synchronize the clip with other loops, or synchronize other loops to the clip.

One of the features I like best about Sound Forge is the ability to view the levels on your input signal in real time, as shown next. This *feels* like analog recording, which is one of the highest forms of praise for a digital recording application. It lets you know immediately if you are going to have trouble with the wave, even before you finish recording.

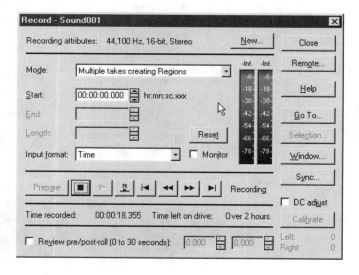

Cool Edit

Cool Edit has been a shareware favorite since before the Internet was a big deal. The central concept of the application is to put a traditional recording studio on your desktop. In fact, if you have *any* professional recording experience, you probably won't even have to read the documentation.

Cool Edit's entry-level version offers you studio-quality tools for an unbeatable price. In addition, you can add features as needed, including effects and a multitrack ability. Multitracking looks like this:

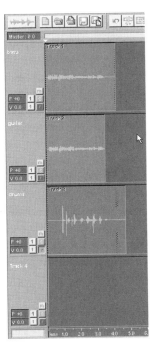

Recording

At the risk of beating a dead horse, let me reiterate the need to record at the highest resolution available through your software and hardware. There are also some other factors that determine whether or not your recording session is successful.

One of the easiest to fix is microphone placement. Placement is easy enough to understand—you just move the microphone to where it sounds good. There are some rules for microphone placement, like angles for specific instruments and distances to achieve specific effects. The easiest approach is this: closer for more details like pops, clicks, and surface noise, and farther away for more ambient aspects of the waveform. For instance, if you want gritty, percussive sounds for button clicks, you can put your microphone right up to a glass as you tap it with a ballpoint pen. The keys to success with microphone placement are experimentation and learning by example. Just remember that placing a microphone in front of something doesn't mean you are capturing the essence of its waveform.

Gain is a deceptively simple concept. If you are still not certain what gain is, think of it as the microphone *in* level. On the surface, it would seem that gain is a simple setting that has a correct and an incorrect value for a given situation. The fact of the matter is that the amount of gain has a lot to do with the perceived quality of the sound you are recording. Sounds recorded at high gain sound hotter or more energetic, while sounds recorded at lower gain sound cooler. Some examples of high gain input in popular recordings are hot Nashville guitar pickin' and Alanis Morrisette's vocals on "You Oughta Know"—it actually clips in spots. An example of beautiful low gain recording is Kevin Eubanks' "Live at Bradleys"—the entire CD.

The reason that gain is so important is that the sound card—or any other audio input device for that matter—has a finite range of input that it can record. If the electrical pulses coming from the microphone are too weak, the sound card can't pick them up. On the other hand, if the pulses going into the sound card are too strong, distortion results. Curious thing about distortion: It is one of the most common icons in modern popular music in that it is used to connote excitement in everything from trash metal to smooth jazz, and it is not even the product of any musical instrument. It is an artifact of the amplification process.

A few more simple precautions should guard against noisy or ugly recording. If you hear a low-level hum, check for fluorescent lights or other electrical appliances in close proximity to your microphone. Watch out for creaky chairs, shuffling feet, sniffles, and sounds from next door or outside. Remain absolutely still and silent for a full two seconds after you finish recording, and record the silence. Listen carefully to your first take to make sure you are not picking up anything you don't want to.

Mixdown/Effects

The traditional role of mixing and applying effects is to polish studio-quality music for production in audio media like CDs and motion pictures. Although we will be using similar tools and processes, our medium and goals are different.

There are two main differences between traditional audio production and producing audio for Flash. In Flash, you know that your audio output is usually going to be compressed and resampled at a lower rate. That means that some of the information contained in the original waveform will be lost by the time your target audience hears it. Careful treatment of the wave in its high-resolution form will ensure that you don't lose nuances that you worked hard to create.

Another key difference between a Web site with audio-intensive Flash and an audio CD is that the hardware for a Web audience is more diverse. You don't know whether users have a high-end sound card designed for 3D gaming audio, a cheap, ten-year-old card, or no card at all. In order to deliver your audio to the less than optimal systems, you have to take special care in the mixing stage.

Compression

Compression, simply put, is limiting the range of the amplitude for a waveform. This has a few perceptible effects. Compression filters out softer sounds in the wave, but also adds an unpleasant hum during silences. If used heavily, compression colors the sound unfavorably, making it sound tinny. The up side of compression, and the reason we use it, is that it makes the overall wave sound louder or hotter. This guards your wave from losing some of its characteristics when you compress or resample the file in Flash. The biggest plus is that compression carries your sound over the hurdles that cheap hardware presents: speakers with bad response, sound cards with a limited range, and low output levels. Of course, crunching your entire wave into a small dynamic range can ruin subtleties in your composition; but the trade-off is generally good.

Normalization

Normalization is the process of scaling the amplitude of an entire waveform such that the highest point is at any user-defined level. This allows you to make sure you are fully utilizing the widest possible dynamic range. While compression generally flattens out the wave, normalization expands the wave to fill the space available to you. Again, this is in the interest of making sure you have a good strong feed to the user's sound card. The stronger every aspect of the original audio is, the better chance it has of surviving file compression and resampling.

You can actually see a striking difference in a waveform as you add compression and normalization. Look at Figure 4-2 to see a waveform before and after normalization and compression.

Before you go wild creating superloud Janet Jackson remixes, consider a couple more factors. First of all, different systems have varying levels of tolerance for waveforms that are very close to the edge of their dynamic range. If you get too close to this edge, your sound can cause distortion. In addition, Flash seems to be especially sensitive to high output waves. The default horizontal guide in Sound Forge of minus six decibels is a good compromise between strong output and caution. In Cool Edit, you have a similar guide, except that the level is measured in percentages. I have good luck normalizing compressed sounds to about 90%.

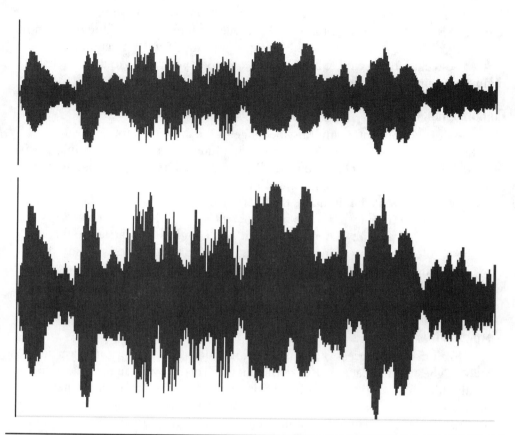

Figure 4.2   *The top window shows a waveform before compression and normalization; the bottom shows the same waveform after compression and normalization.*

Audio in Flash

Once you are satisfied with your audio in a PCM WAV or another platform-specific pure wave format like AIFF, it is relatively easy to deal with it inside Flash. Unless you count the Windows sound card glitch, choosing a compression and resampling is as easy as trying a few settings and listening to the results. This is covered in detail in Chapter 3.

Importing/Updating

Bringing your crystal-clear, studio-quality audio into Flash is a huge drain on your system resources, no two ways about it. This is why you need a powerful, stable platform to run your multimedia applications. Some Flashers will tell you that you should resample your audio to a lower rate before you import it; but there is no reason you can't do it with an adequate PC. Flash assumes that you are importing the best-quality audio you have.

If you are short on RAM, there are a few things you can do to make your life easier when you bring audio into Flash. For instance, you can convert your audio to mono before you import it. You'll end up converting all of your audio to mono inside Flash anyway. Very rarely will you preserve a stereo sound clip. Another thing you can do if you have audio recorded at unusual sampling frequencies is to resample the sound to the next lowest multiple of 11kHz. Flash resamples these sounds anyway right away when you import them.

Event/Stream

You should already know the difference between the Sync options in the sound palette, as shown next. However, a lot of confusion over the Stream option persists.

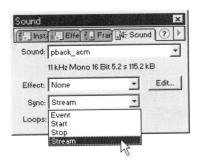

Think of the Stream option as "Synchronize" or "Lock to the Timeline" instead of "Stream." All the other sound Sync options are concerned with either starting or stopping a sound at a point in time. In other words, the playback of the timeline controls when a sound either starts or stops, but other than that, the audio and the timeline are not linked in any way.

The Stream option, on the other hand, causes the timeline to be controlled by the audio playback. The Flash movie becomes like the old VHS videotapes that have channels for video and audio—the tape flies by a single head that reads everything, playing the audio in perfect sync with the video.

By selecting the Stream option, you tell the Flash Player to give precedence to the audio track over the visual elements in your movie. The audio track becomes a crude time code for synchronizing every other element in the movie. The classic application of Stream audio is for animation lip sync, where an animator starts with an audio clip of a character speaking and draws the mouth movements frame by frame. In traditional animation media, animators did this by *scrubbing* a magnetic audiotape of the character's dialogue. Scrubbing consists of moving the tape back and forth by hand or with shuttle controls and watching a readout of the audio's time code in frames. You will notice that Flash allows you to scrub the playhead across a Stream audio clip (more signs of Flash's primal animation roots). You can see this in the next image. Try grabbing the playhead in a scene with Stream audio and dragging it across the section containing the sound. This is what the Stream option is meant for.

Export

Here are some quick tips to keep in mind when you publish a Flash movie with audio. There is more discussion of specific export setting in Chapter 3.

► Audio can weigh down a Web-distributed Flash application to the point of being useless. For things like full-length songs that are self-contained elements of your site, set up a scheme for them to load in the background and show as an available option only when they are ready to play.

▶ MP3 is a compressed format. If you want to take advantage of the amazing strengths of MP3 audio, use the Flash export application to encode your sounds. Import your audio in uncompressed, high-resolution form.

▶ If you use the Stream Sync option for sounds, they must be resampled upon export. You do not have the option to use the format of the sound in which you brought it into Flash. This is one of the reasons you generally don't want to import MP3s.

▶ Determine the best encoding scheme for each sound individually. Specific techniques are discussed at length in Chapter 3.

Troubleshooting

There is a reason for a whole phylum of vocations centered around audio recording and engineering. It's a slippery slope. Reproducing audio that either sounds true to life or just sounds good is hard. If you doubt that it is, try to recall an instance when you were fooled into thinking a recording of a voice or an incidental noise was the real thing. Unless you are a recording artist with a big budget or someone who sweeps the floors in a million-dollar studio, you probably never have.

In the Flash production cycle, faults in audio are usually close to the source (again, not counting the Windows sound card bug). If you have a crisp, clean, strong wave coming into Flash, you will have no problem finding optimal settings for export. Following are some hints on how to find the problem when audio goes bad:

▶ Keep one of the bug-catching sound cards on hand for testing. This can be as simple as adding the card to your setup if you already run Windows 95/98. I use my Web server to test all things crappy and old (including version 3 and 4 browsers). Here is a short list of cards affected by the bug and where you find them, taken from the Macromedia tech note on the subject:

Crystal Audio System	IBM Intellistation E Pro
ESS ES 1869	Packard Bell desktops
ESS Maestro-2E	Dell Inspiron laptops
Sound Blaster Audio PCI 64D	Ubiquitous
Sound Blaster Audio PCI 128D	Ubiquitous
Sound Blaster Live Value with non-2000 drivers	Ubiquitous

► Use your EQ. A little EQ (*equalization*—adjusting levels for frequency ranges) goes a long way to shape a sound. If the encoding scheme you need colors the sound in an unacceptable way, an effective kludge is to apply EQ to the original to offset the change. Note that boosting high frequencies won't bring back parts of the waveform that aren't possible at low sampling frequencies.

► Use a condenser microphone. Unless you only record screaming electric guitars and drum sets, you will get better results from an active, powered microphone. (Come to think of it, you still need good condensers for recording drums to get the overhead wash from the cymbals.)

► Apply EQ, effects, and amplitude manipulations to tracks individually in a multitrack project, such as in Acid. Using a blanket approach on your final mix will make it sound canned.

► Don't use Flash as an audio mixer. Don't play two sounds simultaneously that could be mixed into one wave. Flash won't combine two simultaneous sounds. You'll end up with double the file size for those audio clips.

► Don't loop Stream sounds.

► Edit the Edit Envelope dialog to trim out any silent space at the end and beginning of a sound, like in the next illustration. Remember that the equation for the size of an audio file is a function of time and resolution, not where there is anything interesting in the waveform.

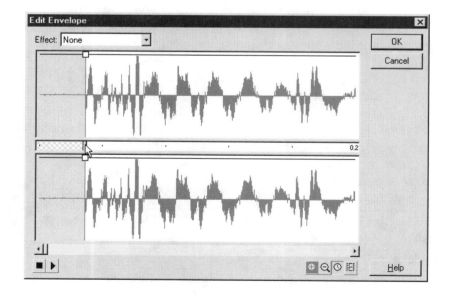

What to Take Away from This Chapter

This has been an introduction to the basic concepts of digital audio. You have by no means completed your Jedi training in this matter. I hope you have gained some insights into how sound flows from the air to your PC and back to the air. You should understand the factors that go into creating and translating high-quality audio. The rest is a matter of experimentation and research into the particular areas that interest you most. Recording is a fascinating endeavor and a little-known but rewarding hobby. Once you start dabbling, you will probably become addicted and start accumulating a formidable home studio.

Printing for the Web

Y ou would think that by now paper would have gone out of style as a medium for everyday communication. With email in every office from the CEO down to the part-time, 16-year-old clerk, the means are certainly there for most to communicate electronically.

It goes beyond the office, too. Half of all urban professionals use handheld PDAs to organize information and move it along electronic channels. (The other half started leaving them in a drawer after the early-adopter chic wore off.) With phones, cars, and every other electronic device talking to each other, trend watchers are increasingly speaking of a paper-free time—not too far in the future—when clothes, dog toys, and beer cans will be linked to a universal network.

Yet people still prefer paper. Managers prefer paper. Harry Potter fans prefer paper. Customers who want a reliable record of a transaction prefer paper. Even I prefer paper, and I worked obsessively to all but discontinue paper usage at my property when I was a hotel manager.

Without contemplating the causes or meaning of this human trait, we accept it as part of the landscape we work in. Flash provides a very clever way to deliver what people want (information on paper) easily. Whatever your method of distribution, you can allow users to print maximum-resolution graphics without any additional plug-ins or document formats.

Overview

Flash's printing feature presents a perfect solution to both developers and users. For users, Flash offers maximum-quality printing at the click of a mouse, without starting another application. From the user's perspective, the printed page magically appears as needed during the course of browsing a site. This is an extension of the already favorable user perception of a seamless site, owed to the Flash Player's handling of loading and unloading content.

This is in sharp contrast with the more familiar model of following a link to a printable page. Before the advent of Flash printing, the user was stuck with either a stripped-down HTML page that printed with any old layout that happened to be rendered by the browser, or a document that required a big, klunky plug-in and redundant user input to start printing. Developers will appreciate the fact that printing is very easy to implement in Flash. It doesn't require any authoring extensions or special tools—just a little know-how.

Printing from Player Versus Print Action

Big_page_printer.swf, big_page_printer.html

The first thing to understand is that we are not talking about printing from the Flash Player's context menu.

Look at *Big_page_printer.swf* from the Chapter06\Examples folder on the CD to see Flash's custom printing capability in action. When you click on the tiny print button, a full-sized 8 ½ x 11-inch page prints out.

This is a good illustration of the biggest difference between a designed Flash printing application and a user printing from Flash's context menu or even the Web browser. The difference is control. If you were to print the movie from the context menu, you would get a single word in a huge font size in the middle of the page. The scale is completely wrong and has little to do with the desired output.

If you open the SWF in your Web browser (*big_page_printer.html*) and use the browser's print function, you could get anything, depending on the browser. I should say anything except the desired effect, because you most likely get a tiny "print" in the upper-left corner and some unwanted headers and footers displaying superfluous information.

Using the Web browser to print Flash content can yield near-satisfactory results if you are careful, but at the expense of the sense of using a custom application, which I feel is one of Flash's top three greatest features. Using the Web browser, or even the context menu, to print puts you back in the same situation you were in when you tried to use HTML as a print medium: second-guessing browser incompatibilities, relying on user proficiency to accomplish critical functions, and generally losing control over the layout of your print material.

Advantages

Printing from Flash has a number of advantages over the old-fashioned method of trying to kludge HTML into an attractive layout. There are even advantages over powerful document formats like PDF.

▶ **Seamless user experience**   The biggest advantage in using Flash for printing high-resolution graphics from the Web is *usability*. There are no extra plug-ins or "readers" to download, and nothing to start running when you want to load a for-print document. The obvious advantages here are a slick navigational scheme for your Flash project, along with the optimized system resource demands (no extra software to start). I think one of the greatest values, however, is enhancing the perception of using a custom application. Users are familiar with dealing with print dialogs on a per-application basis, and having a native print button from your Web site or multimedia project enhances the façade of a specialized standalone application.

▶ **Custom layout** There are really no restrictions on the layout you choose for print documents in Flash. Since it is not necessary for the user to see the print document, you can choose any orientation and dimensions without considering how it would show in a browser window. There are none of the trappings of HTML layout—browser differences, version differences, unwanted output, alignment, or user interference. You just design your print document *exactly* as you want it to appear.

▶ **High resolution** You can set Flash to use the highest resolution available on the user's printer, or you can rely on Flash's vector output to deliver razor-sharp print output. We'll get into the different factors later in the chapter. Either way, a carefully designed print document will come out clean and beautiful, unscathed by the rigors of electronic distribution.

▶ **Compatibility** Printing from Flash works for practically all-modern PC graphics-capable printers. This will be the least of your concerns in the compatibility department.

▶ **Ease of implementation** Printing from Flash requires no additional authoring software and no additional plug-in.

▶ **One version** Developers are not required to compose separate versions for print and Web in order to strip out ads. The ActionScript print action determines which content prints.

Requirements

Windows users must have Flash Player 4.0.25 or above; Mac users need the 4.0.20 version. The user's Player version is easy to determine, and this is the topic of a subsequent section of the book. I recommend requiring users to have the current Player at the front door of your site.

Aside from the appropriate Flash Player, users need only a working printer and printer driver to print your high-quality designs from Flash.

At the run-time level, there are two obvious caveats worth mentioning. Printable material must be loaded before it can be printed. If you try to start printing before your designated printable content is loaded, the print action just dies and the Flash Player continues in its logical playback flow. You get what David Letterman used to call "...the sound of people changing channels." When this happens, users will probably assume that your entire application is broken.

Finally, elements must be pulled out of the library—either onto the stage or in the work area offstage—before printing. This is really an extension of a movie being loaded. If you don't reference an object in the library anywhere in the movie, that object won't be published with the SWF. You have to load the print material into the Flash Player, visible or not. You can make material invisible either by putting it offstage, or by setting its _visibility property to 0 or False.

Setup

Setting up a movie for printing is easier than you might suspect. As always, starting with the end in mind and planning on paper make development time short and sweet.

Specifying Frames with Labels

By default, the Flash Player prints all the frames in a movie or Movie clip in order from first to last. Depending on your preferences for movie structure and hierarchy, variability of print output based on user input, where you put your ActionScript, and even security, you will usually want to limit the range of the Flash movie that is printed.

You control the range with frame labels. There are three basic frame labels to inform the Player about which frames to print—#p, #b, and !#p. When the Flash Player receives a print command, either at the user's behest via the context menu or via ActionScript, it evaluates the action's parameters in the context of these labels. I consider this to be the lowest level of control in Flash printing.

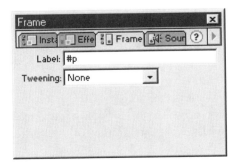

Label a frame with #p as shown above to mark it for printing. When the Flash Player begins printing a movie with one or more frames marked with #p, it prints only these frames.

Imagine a Flash application with animation, introductory text, and superfluous graphical elements on the main timeline. You want to allow the user to print only the last frame of the main timeline in the movie, which is a terse advertisement with a slogan, a tiny bit of product information, and contact info. You could just label this frame with "#p" to target this frame for printing:

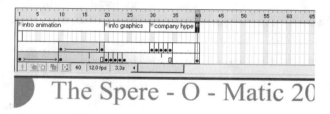

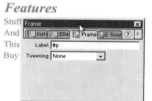

When you assign the #p label to multiple frames in a Flash movie, you will see an error message when you export or test the movie. Don't worry about this. This is just a heads-up to let you know you may get unexpected results if you rely on having unique labels for navigation or logic.

In this example, the movie will print only the frame containing the product and contact info, whether the print command comes from the Flash Player's context menu or ActionScript. At this point, creating a seamless user interface for printing this custom content would be as simple as attaching the print action with the default parameters to a button. Now that's about as easy as something this powerful can be!

Now imagine that you want the same 640 × 480px movie, only with a full 8 ½ by 11-inch page for the print output. Defining a frame with #b and drawing an appropriately sized box will do just this. In the following illustration you see a frame labeled "#b," which contains (on any layer) a box that determines the size of the print area. The #b label acts as a complement to the #p label to provide the simplest method for specifying which frames and what part of them print from the main timeline. This is by no means the only method. We will investigate others shortly.

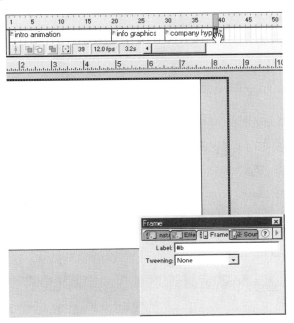

The !#p label, placed anywhere in the main timeline, tells the Flash Player to disable printing for this movie. In addition to negating print actions targeting the main timeline, this label causes the Print option in the Flash Player's context menu to dim, which means that this option is not available.

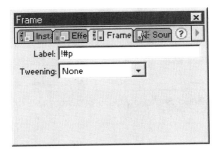

Be aware that users can still print output from movies by using the print capability of the Web browser. There is no reliable way to disable the browser's ability to print Flash content.

Specifying Area

As mentioned above, using the #b label is an easy way to specify the print area of a Flash movie. It yields predictable results. It is the method I personally prefer, but there are more options.

These options are called *arguments* or *parameters* to the print function in ActionScript (more on arguments later in the book). To see the dialog shown in Figure 5-1, just assign the print action to a button or frame in the actions palette while in normal mode.

Movie Stage

The stage defines the default print area for Flash printable content. Far from being a bit of trivia or an obstacle to try to kludge around, this property can be your biggest advantage in quickly developing print applications.

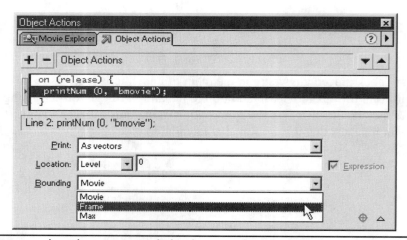

Figure 5.1   *Use the Object Actions dialog box to adjust the print function in ActionScript.*

I like to compose each printable document as a separate FLA on a stage that is 8 ½ × 11 inches. You can count on just about everyone who would print materials from Flash to print to a letter-size page, so using a stage that is scaled to this size ensures that you are designing direct to the page. That way, there are no scaling issues. You are seeing what the user will see at a 1:1 scale.

Using this method has other advantages, too. For instance, bringing in existing print documents (such as PDF documents) becomes as simple as importing them via Freehand and placing them at coordinates (0,0) on the stage. Another advantage is avoiding pixelation that results from scaling bitmap images. This ill effect is a fact of life with some of the other methods of determining the print area.

Loading printable documents from autonomous SWFs also keeps the project architecture sensible. Instead of figuring your (optional) print content into the mix of file size, loading time, and navigation, the print document mirrors in architecture what it is from the user's perspective: an external appendage to the application. The printable document can be treated as a separate entity during development, which frees up RAM between your ears. Similarly, the printable content is available separately, on demand, to the users who want it, without forcing the rest to download it. This effect is magnified by the fact that printable material is generally heavier than Web content.

Max

The Max option makes a composite of all the frames in the printable area of the movie and figures out the minimum area required to print everything. This area is used as the bounding box for the print document, which in turn is scaled to the maximum size possible on the user's printer.

In other words, the Flash Player figures out how big it can make the whole printable document without distorting the scale relationships between printable elements. The next illustration shows an imaginary box (the dotted line) around the bounding box that the Flash Player might compose based on the size and position of the first frame of printable material (the darker graphic) and the size and position of the second frame (the lighter graphic). The dotted line represents the area that the Flash Player will blow up to the biggest dimension possible based on the user's settings in the print driver. If the user has the Paper option set to Landscape, the print output will be larger than if it is set to Portrait.

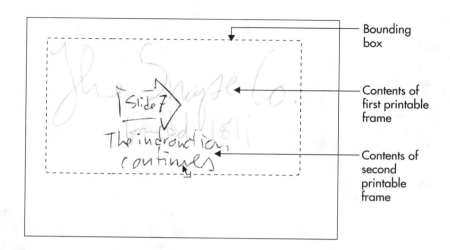

Frame

The Frame option is a similar approach to Max. The core concept is the same—blow up everything to the largest possible size upon output—but the Frame argument takes this goal to the extreme by abandoning concern for the relative scaling between printable elements. The Frame option looks at the printable content in the Flash movie frame-by-frame and scales each frame to the largest print area possible on the user's system.

Look at the next illustration for an example. With the Frame argument to the print action selected instead of Max, the imaginary bounding box that the Flash Player generates in each frame is smaller than the composite box illustrated previously. This translates into bigger output for each element.

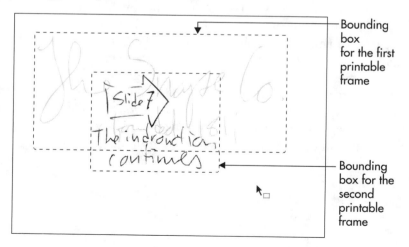

For general-purpose, everyday printing of preformatted business and marketing documents, the Max and Frame parameters are irrelevant. The whole idea of printing from Flash is to create a high-resolution, designed, custom layout that can be printed effortlessly from a custom UI. The key word in the previous sentence is "custom," and using the Max and Frame parameters destroy it by putting the control back in the user's hands. I imagine that these options are indispensable for specialized tasks, such as printing technical drawings at the best size and resolution possible over the Web, but avoid using them for everyday printing tasks.

Printing Options

So far we have designated which frames to print, the limits of the print area, and how printable elements scale within that area. The only argument remaining is Print. This is what determines whether the Flash Player interprets the print output as scalable vectors or as bitmap information.

Vectors

The Flash Player prints output as vectors by default. The obvious advantage is that the vector output will scale to look sharp at any size. This guards against the possibility of output looking pixelated from scaling.

Using the default vectors argument to the print action yields the highest resolution output. If you tried the first example in this chapter and printed the sample page, you can see the difference between vector and bitmap output. The bitmap element (the rulers that make up the left and bottom border) looks good. It is printed at the proper scale at a perceived resolution of 72dpi (the resolution of the screen from which the image was captured).

The vector output, on the other hand, looks excellent. It is so crisp and clean that it looks like it was printed from professional image editing software. This is the type of output that makes vector file formats like Flash and PDF so attractive.

Bitmap
bitmap-option.swf

The bitmap printing option offers the ability to print alpha and color effects. This is its main strength. Although the bitmap option defaults to the highest resolution available on the user's printer, it will scale vector elements in your movie as bitmaps. In other words, you sacrifice the razor-sharp high resolution of the vector output for the ability to print color and alpha effects.

You can see in the following illustration how color and alpha effects are applied to the Movie clip on the stage. Open *bitmap_option.swf* from the Chapter06\Examples folder and click the print button to see the output. Notice that the colors are blended on the overlapping text with alpha effects.

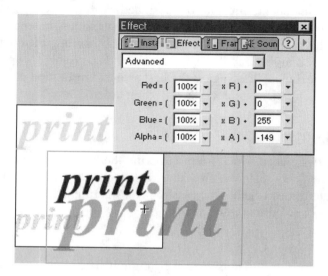

In most cases, the graphic elements in your print content will be static—that is, not the result of user input. Unless you want the user to be able to specify alpha or color levels, take the extra time to compose the elements without relying on these effects. Freehand has a whole category of tools for combining paths. You can use these tools to create flat vector images that simulate the alpha effects.

The quality standards for printed graphics are much higher than Web and multimedia standards. You should always shoot for the highest possible resolution. ("Possible" here takes into account file size and streaming considerations.) Flash provides a powerful solution with vector print output. You get stunningly crisp resolution from a very compact format. Vector output is the bread and butter of Flash printing.

Loading / Visibility

As mentioned at the beginning of the chapter, printable elements must be loaded and present on the stage or work area in order to execute the print action successfully. This turns out to be the critical factor in successfully implementing printing from Flash. The problem presents itself: printable material is generally heavier than material designed for electronic output, and printing is generally an optional function. So how do you keep the heavy print elements from slowing down the users who don't want it?

One solution is to load the print material on demand. In other words, don't load the printable elements into the Flash Player unless the user chooses to print. This is easy to implement by loading an external SWF into a placeholder target, and we will look at this in depth shortly. The only problem is that the users who do want to print are forced to wait longer than would have been necessary.

The best solution is always to load (or start to load) printable material in the background, so that it is available immediately when the user is ready to print. For internal Movie clips, this is easy—you just put the printable elements or the Movie clip containing printable elements last on the timeline. Since the Flash Player loads frames in the order they appear on the timeline, no matter how you alter playback with ActionScript, printable elements that appear at the end of the timeline will load last.

If you want to load an external Movie clip for print content, which is my preference, you need a little bit of ActionScript to ensure that the print material loads last. Here is a sample of what that ActionScript might look like. This ActionScript would be attached to an empty Movie clip that is persistent through the entire main timeline of the movie. All it does is repeatedly check to see if all the frames in the main timeline are loaded. When they finally are all loaded, *printable_material.swf* loads into the Movie clip instance labeled "placeholder."

```
onClipEvent (enterFrame) {
  if (_root._framesloaded >= _root._totalframes) {
    loadMovie ("printable_material.swf", "_root.placeholder");
  }
}
```

Don't worry if you don't recognize anything in this sample code. We'll cover ActionScript from *A* to *Z* in the next section of the book. There is a section of Chapter 10 devoted to the specific task of building a preloader, so you will have plenty of opportunity to catch up.

Internal Versus External Movie Clips

One of the eternal verities of the human mind is that the less material you cram into your brain at once, the more you can clearly focus on that material. This has always been useful information for people who write books on meditation and, more recently, for professional athletes. Even more recently still, developers of all the electronic media have taken this fundamental truth to the bank in the object-oriented programming movement, which I will talk about in the ActionScript section.

The unifying idea behind the author, the athlete, and the programmer is cutting up tasks into the smallest part. When you abstract every little piece of, say, an Olympic high jump, it becomes simple to perfect and maintain each little piece. When you look at a hunk of code, it is easier to break up blocks of code by what they do, abstracting each little function the same way the Olympic high-jumper does.

The same principle applies to designing Flash applications, especially ones with printable content. You will probably use a different set of tools to develop your print content. You may even have separate personnel to develop printable content for a Flash project. Deciding whether to integrate your print material into an internal Movie clip or a separate Flash movie is an important step in building your application.

Internal Movie Clip

Using an internal Movie clip is nice for a number of reasons. Although this method is not optimal for abstracting the parts of a Flash application, it has many real advantages. This seems to be the most popular way to put together Flash movies.

▶ You have your entire movie in front of you at a glance while you are building it. This sounds contrary to the object-oriented approach, but it's really not that different. Either way, you will have to put everything together at some point on a main timeline. When you do, it is nice to have everything in front of you as it will appear in the final Flash movie, instead of using temporary bounding boxes and empty placeholder Movie clips.

▶ If you don't load any additional SWF files from the main timeline, you only make one trip to the server. Loading additional SWFs is no more taxing than loading JPEGs or GIFs of similar file size, but this could be a factor for some sites.

▶ The loading scheme is a no-brainer. You just put the printable material at the end of the main timeline. That means less code to debug and fewer things that can go wrong at run time.

External Flash Movie

Loading printable material from an external SWF file is more closely aligned with the object-oriented frame of mind. This is the method I prefer. The advantages of using this method are as follows:

▶ Translating print documents to Flash applications becomes as easy as exporting a file to SWF from Freehand. You don't waste your time importing, placing, and reformatting a document inside Flash.

► Print documents are abstracted from the Flash application. If your Flash application prints material that changes—for instance, a fax order form for a restaurant that lists a daily special—you will want to change the printable portion often and leave the main application the same. By abstracting the printable content in a separate Movie clip, you allow yourself to focus on the matter at hand and not worry about accidentally changing other elements in the movie.

► The manner in which you load the printable content becomes more flexible. You can use the method shown previously, loading the external SWF after the main timeline has loaded; or you can load on demand. The latter could be a better choice for a timeline with a lot of content—animation, for example.

Picking Apart an Example

index.html, brandchain-brochure.fla, brandchain-site.fla, brandchain-brochure.swp

The CD includes an example of a printing Flash application. It uses both an internal Movie clip and an external SWF to house printable material. We'll use this example to pick apart some solutions for loading and printing Flash elements. Open *index.html* in the Chapter06\Examples folder to see the example Flash application in action.

First open *brandchain_brochure.fla* from the Chapter06\Examples folder and look around in it. There's not much there in the way of interactivity—just two frames of printable content, with a "stop();" action in the first frame. Even this action is not necessary.

The thing to notice here is that this is basically a print document in Flash format. Because this brochure is abstracted into a separate SWF file, it could easily have been converted from a FHx, AI, or PDF document. The brochure designer—whether it is you or a print design specialist—will appreciate not having to deal with any Flash interactivity or scripting at this level of the overall design. Notice that the SWF weighs in at about 75KB.

Next open *brandchain_site.fla* and have a look around. This is where all the pieces come together, so naturally there is a lot more going on. Go to frame 13 of the "printed materials" layer. This is the printable internal Movie clip, which is named "rewards_form." The visible content in this Movie clip instance (labeled "form") never shows, but you can see its registration point, as in the following image. It is the little white dot between the Brandchain logo and the keys at the bottom of the stage. Notice that the Movie clip is almost at the very end of the movie, so it will be one of the last things to load.

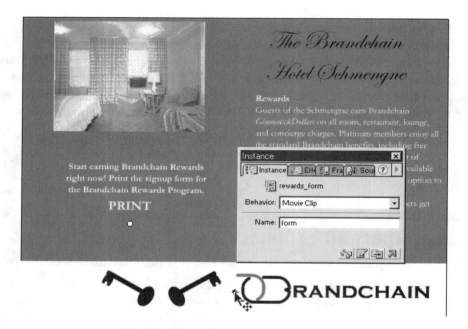

Open the "rewards_form" Movie clip (right-click the MC on the stage and select Edit in Place), and look at the labels. You have a #b label on the frame that holds a bounding box:

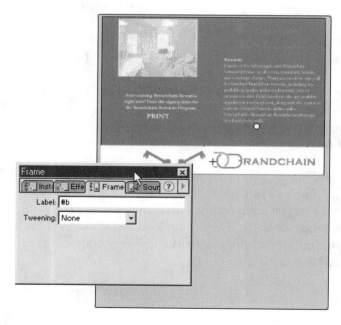

The frame labeled #p holds all the content that will be printed. This is supposed to be a mail-in form for guests of the Brandchain Hotel to fill out and send in for membership in a rewards program. This is a very lightweight form as printables go, so it is a good choice for an internal Movie clip.

Notice the white solid fill in the printable frame in this Movie clip. This is an easy way to change the background color of a printable Movie clip. The default background color is whatever you set in Movie Properties (CTRL-M). Most printers see white as transparent or null.

Finally, look at frame 14 of the "placeholder" layer. There is an empty Movie clip called "placeholder" just offstage in the upper-right corner. This is where *brandchain_brochure.swf* loads. Since this Movie clip is offstage, the movie will not show when it is loaded.

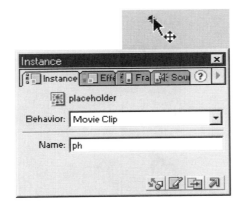

Interested parties can pick apart the loading logic and print actions, which reside in the print buttons. We will cover all of this in the ActionScript section of the book.

What to Take Away from This Chapter

The ability to print high-resolution graphics from the Web has bewitched developers since the early days. Flash's solution seems to summarize all the good ideas that have preceded, including the best interface—your own.

Flash and the Web Browser

OBJECTIVES

- ► Learn the Basics of JavaScript

- ► Review a Simplified Introduction to Object-Oriented Programming

- ► Survey the Basic Built-in JavaScript Objects

- ► Discover the Rudiments of Window Manipulation

- ► Add Data Storage Using JavaScript Cookies

- ► Examine the Communication Between JavaScript/ActionScript Using FSCommands

Introduction to JavaScript

I f you're new to programming, this chapter is for you. We are going to delve into some background material on JavaScript, including the most basic tasks in scripting. Don't waste energy trying to construct a mental map of JavaScript; this chapter is meant to get you started by example with a few rules that will have you writing code in a jiffy. The significance of the different kinds of code, how they all come together, and how it all relates to Flash will become clear in Chapter 7.

Background

Flash 4 was a mixed blessing for multimedia developers. On one hand, we finally had the ability to deliver logic-capable, lightweight, vector-based content over the Web using a plug-in that almost everyone had. On the other hand, ActionScript in version 4 was a monumental challenge to even the most dedicated kludge makers.

ActionScript was originally designed to perform simple tasks, such as checking to see if the frames in the movie were loaded and performing rudimentary manipulations of native objects on the stage. What's worse, the interface for Flash ActionScript didn't allow the developer access to the underlying logic.

Macromedia quickly learned, however, that developers were going to get around the interface one way or another and write advanced scripts using the full power of the language. Developers built everything from interactive games with homemade collision detection to shopping cart front ends. So in version 5, Macromedia decided to let developers tinker under the hood and get at the core scripting language. It turns out that the core scripting language is ECMAScript, the same core as JavaScript. This is why we are going to spend some time on JavaScript, lingering on some details that aren't necessarily critically important to create a pop-up ad banner.

The history of JavaScript, like almost all Web standards, it seems, reads like a Russian novel. Once upon a time, when the great Mozilla roamed the earth, there was a great deal of excitement about creating entirely new Web technologies all the time—that is, new categories. One of these revelations was JavaScript, something analogous to the first pair of air-breathing lungs in terms of continuous development of Web-based multimedia. It started at Netscape, and this was the first time I can remember people talking about the browser wars being over.

ECMAScript came about like this: Netscape submitted its new scripting language to the European Computer Manufacturers Association for consideration as a standard. It was accepted, and Netscape has pretty much carried the ball since then. That was 1995.

When JavaScript first hit the streets of Geocities, it was a magnificent revolution. Suddenly anyone with a little interest and time to tinker could do Web programming. The early days of JavaScript defined what it meant for a Web site to be interactive: image swaps, pop-up windows, form handling.

Today JavaScript is implemented almost as widely as HTML. Its modern uses range from embedded script that HTML coders don't even realize is JavaScript to server-side workhorses and desktop macrosss.

Defining JavaScript

The first point in any discussion of what JavaScript is, is what it isn't, which is Java. That is, JavaScript has no relation to Java. At the time JavaScript was released to the public, the fully featured, cross-platform *programming* language Java was in the limelight. It was the dawn of Net civilization; and at that time, it seemed that Netscape was building an empire that would last for a thousand years. In the spirit of a dominant suite of developers' tools, Netscape named their new scripting language after Java, which they were also responsible for distributing to client computers. Confusion has continued steadily since then. (There's always that critical gray area where you try to decide whether it's necessary for contract purposes to explain to your client that you are building a JavaScript application, not Java.)

Client Side

The next big concept we should try get a grip on is the idea of server side and client side. While the core ECMAScript has been extended to include most of the entire scripting spectrum, with custom objects for everything from Web server database interfaces to desktop application macros, the bread and butter of ECMAScript as implemented in JavaScript is on the client side. In other words, the JavaScript that we will be interested in is executed inside a Web browser. This type of JavaScript is the most useful for everyday HTML hacking necessities, and this type of JavaScript is most closely aligned to core ECMAScript and, therefore, ActionScript.

Look at Figure 6-1 to get a better idea of what is going on. When you load a Web page containing JavaScript into your Web browser, the server just spits out the page as if there were a static page. It is up to the Web browser, also known as the *client*, to interpret and process the instructions given by JavaScript.

JavaScript is an interpreted language, which means that it consists of instructions that are read by an interpreter at run time. This is different from compiled languages like C+ +, which are compiled to an executable and require no interpreter. The

Client   Server

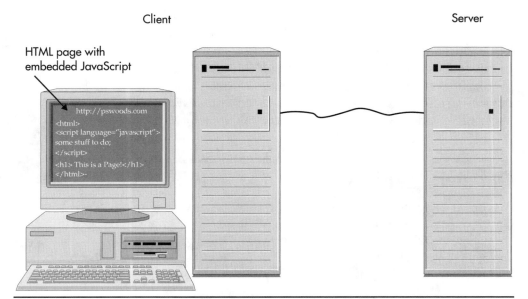

HTML page with
embedded JavaScript

Figure 6.1   *Client-side JavaScript is loaded like a normal HTML page and executed
inside the browser.*

interpreter that we will be interested in is contained within the Web browser. When
JavaScript is loaded into a browser, the built-in interpreter reads the instructions
contained within the script and executes them.

Human Readable

You'll be glad to know that JavaScript is easy on the eyes. First of all, its built-in
functions and objects have names that say what they do. In fact, someone with no
programming experience can look at a simple script and guess what it does by
simply reading it.

JavaScript uses Unicode, a set of characters similar to ASCII, except that it has
a lot more international characters in the same set. Unicode, like most character sets
you will run across in your travels, can be thought of as an extension of ASCII.
The set begins with the same characters as ASCII and then includes other characters
specific to the needs of that set. For most of us, this aspect simply boils down to
the fact that we can use a regular text editor to write JavaScript.

JavaScript is case sensitive, but you shouldn't rely on this feature for naming
conventions, since ActionScript is not case sensitive. One of the time-honored
traditions of JavaScript hackers is to name objects with an initial lowercase letter,

with an uppercase letter for each new word, omitting spaces. For example, "theJavaScriptFunctionName" would be a perfectly acceptable name, in keeping with the JavaScript tradition. This is the naming scheme I prefer, and it works well in ActionScript, too. You may have already noticed that the custom objects in Flash (like gotoAndStop) follow this pattern.

Robust Language

JavaScript is the perfect language for a lot of tasks, including learning programming. While it is relatively easy to learn the basics, the concepts you learn in JavaScript apply to virtually every other language. This is especially true in ActionScript, since the two languages share a common core. If you take the time to learn the JavaScript basics, you will probably use JavaScript every day—the concepts at least, if not the actual language, for window manipulation, DHTML, or CGI.

JavaScript is also a perfect introduction to Object-Oriented Programming (OOP), which we will cover in the next chapter. The idea of OOP will come up over and over, and it should serve as your guide when programming in Flash.

If you become very interested in JavaScript, the sky's the limit for what you can do with it. Look at the JavaScript section at your local bookstore and browse the contents of the books directed toward professional developers. You'll find that in general, at least half of the material out there deals with things outside the Web browser.

HTML Tags and Alerts

include_JS_from_external_file.html, in_line.html

In this section, we will begin with examples of JavaScript in an HTML page. For the remainder of the chapter, we will go over examples, learning a few basics. We will then put the big picture together in the next chapter.

Look at the following example code. This is the simplest possible scheme for including JavaScript in your HTML page. It simply loads a script from an external file.

```
<!DOCTYPE HTML PUBLIC "-//W3C//DTD HTML 4.0 Transitional//EN">
<html>
<head>
    <title>My Little Page of JavaScript</title>
<script language="JavaScript" src="alert_01.js"></script>
</head>
<body>
```

```
<h1>This is JavaScript.</h1>
</body>
</html>
```

You can see this example in action in the Chapter06\Examples folder: *include_JS_from_external_file.html.* You should see a little dialog like the one shown next, after which a page should load that says "This is JavaScript."

There should be no mystery as to how HTML works. You have the most Spartan hierarchy of tags, complemented by the script tag. If you don't already understand everything except the script tag, you need to brush up on HTML before you can continue. Go to Webmonkey or WDVL.com and take a good hour or two to learn HTML.

For the rest of us, let's look at the script tag. The language attribute is not strictly necessary, since the default language in all browsers of which I am aware is JavaScript. It's good practice to use it, though; and this is definitely a tag that you should have in your snippet library, so it's not like you're going to have to type it over and over. You can also include the JavaScript language version, such as "JavaScript 1.0." We are not going to get deep enough into the language that the version will make a difference; so just let the browser make whatever assumptions it likes.

The src attribute is only necessary when you load an external file. Most of the JavaScript we will use in this and the next chapter will be written in line in the HTML page. When this is the case, the script will appear as follows:

```
<!DOCTYPE HTML PUBLIC "-//W3C//DTD HTML 4.0 Transitional//EN">
<html>
<head>
      <title>My Little Page of JavaScript</title>
<script language="JavaScript">
<!—hide

//pop up an alert window
alert("JavaScript is, like, totally fun!");

//show-->
```

```
</script>
</head>
<body>
<h1>This is JavaScript.</h1>
</body>
</html>
```

In this example (*in_line.html* on the CD), we have the same JavaScript as before, only this time it is included in the same page as the HTML. First notice the comment about the line that begins with "alert." The double slashes (*//*) indicate that the following text is a single-line comment.

The next thing you should notice is that the JavaScript itself—a single line that pops up an alert—is nested within an HTML comment, the tag for which is "<!-- -->". The comment in turn is nested within the script tag. This is done so that browsers that can't read JavaScript will not display the contents of the script in the user's window. Notice that the last line of the HTML comment begins with a double slash. This makes this line become a comment within the JavaScript, so that the browser doesn't show an error when it tries to process "show-->" as JavaScript. If this seems tricky or confusing at all, just ignore the reasons why and memorize this (in the form of a snippet) as your standard JavaScript tag:

```
<script language="JavaScript">
<!--hide
(insert brilliant programming here)
//show-->
</script>
```

Finally, look at our single line of JavaScript. I think you can figure out the syntax from the example, but just in case, you can look at the following. The *argument* in the following code simply means *the stuff we want to pass to the alert function.* Argument is synonymous with *parameter.*

```
alert(argument);
```

Variables

name_variable.html, name_variable_concatenated.html

You have undoubtedly heard of variables in some context. You may even be familiar with variables from your previous experience with Flash. Nonetheless, we will construct our own definition for this easily recognized but hard to pin down idea.

Simply put, a *variable* is a container for information. In most senses, a variable is like a physical container, such as a bucket. You can put something into it, store it, retrieve it later, and dump it into something else. Unlike a physical container, however, a variable can duplicate its contents and pass it to another container. Let's look at an example. The following code is from *name_variable.html* on the CD.

```
<script language="JavaScript">
<!--hide

var wifesName = "Hilde Weinmargestrasse";
alert("The name of the farmer's wife is...");
alert(wifesName);

//show-->
</script>
```

The string literal "Hilde Weinmargestrasse" is assigned to the variable wifesName. This means that the container called wifesName now holds the value "Hilde Weinmargestrasse." For the remainder of the script, every time we want to know the name of the farmer's wife, we can simply refer to this variable. Notice that the variable name is not in quotes, while the string literal is in quotes. The quotes are what make it literal.

Notice the difference between the first alert and the second alert. The first one is a string literal—it is in quotes. The second time we use the alert function, the argument is not in quotes. That's because it is a variable. If you were to put the name of the variable in quotes (for example, "wifesName"), the second alert would say "wifesName" instead of "Hilde Weinmargestrasse". To summarize in programming parlance, the argument to the alert function can be either a string literal or a variable.

NOTE

Using var is not strictly necessary, but it is good practice, as it defines the scope of the variable. We'll talk more about this later. For now, just understand that this is an instruction to the interpreter (the Web browser) to create a new variable in memory instead of assigning a new value to an old variable of the same name.

```
<script language="JavaScript">
<!--hide

var wifesName = "Hilde Weinmargestrasse";
```

```
alert("The name of the farmer's wife is " + wifesName + ".");

//show-->
</script>
```

This example pops up a single alert, as seen in the following image. You can open the HTML file, *name_variable_concatenated.html* on the CD. In this example, we use both string literals and variables in the same command. Notice that the variable name is separated from the string literals by a plus sign. This is called *concatenation*. When you use the plus sign like this, you tell the JavaScript interpreter to take each item and combine it with the others into one.

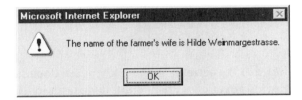

Data Types

Variables can hold different types of data. In some languages, you have to define what type of data a variable will hold and then stick with it. Not so with JavaScript. You use the same declaration for any type of variable. Not only that, you can change the type of data that a variable holds simply by assigning a different type to the variable. We will be talking about the three most commonly used data types: Boolean, number, and string.

Boolean
boolean.html

Boolean data takes the form of either true or false.

```
<html>
<head>
      <title>My Little Page of JavaScript</title>
</head>
<body>
<p>"5=4" is
<script language="JavaScript">
<!--hide
```

```
var isItTrue = (5==4);
document.write(isItTrue);
//show-->
</script>
</p>
<h1>This is JavaScript with Variables.</h1>
</body>
</html>
```

The preceding example (*boolean.html* on the CD) assigns the Boolean value false to the variable isItTrue. The JavaScript interpreter compares the numbers four and five to see if they are equal. Of course they are not, so it returns a value of false. We could have just as easily written it like this:

```
isItTrue = false;
```

You will also notice that the script is in the body of the document instead of the head, as in the previous example. Placing the JavaScript in the body has the advantage of making it possible to write visible text in the user's window. This is what document.write() does.

String

preformatted_ text.html

We have already talked about strings in the context of string literals. A string as a data type is simply zero or more characters in succession. It can be a single letter or data block of text containing a chapter of a book.

Let's look at some special characters, called escape sequences, that can be contained in strings. *Escape sequences* are special string characters that stand for something else. The following table illustrates the most commonly used escape sesquences:

Escape Sequence	JavaScript Interprets As
\n	Newline
\t	Tab
\r	Carriage return
\"	Literal quote
\'	Literal single quote
\\	Literal backslash

Let's look at an example using the escape sequences. The following code can be found in the file *preformatted_ text.html* on the CD. Notice that there are two sections of JavaScript with an HTML document. This is perfectly acceptable. Beginning with the declaration of the bigFatString variable, you see a lot of slashes. Let's look at each instance and what it means.

```
<html><head>
<title>My Little Page of JavaScript</title>
<script language="JavaScript">
<!--hide
bigFatString="//A Poem\\\\ \n\nPuppy in my lap
    \rHe just came into the house\rIt was raining hard"
//show-->
</script>
</head><body><pre>
<script language="JavaScript">
<!--hide
document.write(bigFatString);
//show-->
</script>
</pre></body></html>
```

The two forward slashes have no special significance. The four backslashes after the text "A Poem" are interpreted as two escaped backslashes. The output appears as "//A Poem\\." Next we have two newline escape sequences. This is probably the most commonly used escape sequence in Flash. Finally, there are carriage return escape sequences between the lines of the poem. The output appears as follows:

```
//A Poem\\

Puppy in my lap
He just came into the house
It was raining hard
```

Number

Although it may seem like an obvious data type, there are actually a few fine points about numbers that need to be discussed. Operations that use numbers in JavaScript are not quite as precise or intuitive as you might imagine.

The number data type supports an optional decimal and an optional exponent. For example, if you have an exceptionally large number, like 6,000,000, you can express it exponentially like this:

```
bigNum=6e6;        //exponential
smallNum=0.0023;   //decimal
redColorNum=0xfFF;//hexadecimal
```

You don't have to give any special designation to variables containing different kinds of expressions of numbers. JavaScript knows from the context how to evaluate the number.

As alluded to previously, there some slight imperfections in the way JavaScript handles numbers. When you're handling very large numbers—that is, numbers with a lot of digits—it is possible for some of the digits to get dropped. This happens when the 64-bit container for the number runs out of room. In all likelihood, this will never have a noticeable impact on anything you ever read in JavaScript, unless you are figuring space shuttle trajectories or something.

Something you will see when dealing with a number data type is *NaN*, or Not A Number. You will occasionally see this value where you expect a number to be returned. Ninety-nine percent of the time this is due to an error in your code, as it results from mathematical operations like dividing by zero or figuring the square root of a negative number. NaN is actually considered a core property in JavaScript, and not part of the number data type.

Control Structures

So far we have stored a little bit of information in a variable. This is interesting and useful for about the same amount of time it takes the computer to process these scripts. The real power of scripting in any context is making decisions based on dynamic circumstances. *Control structures*, also known as control blocks, give JavaScript the ability to make decisions.

If, Else If, Else

simple_if.html, more_ifs.html, nested.html

The following sample, *simple_if.html* on the CD, employs the simplest and most common control structure, "if." It demonstrates the correct syntax for the if control structure: if (something is true) { do this stuff; }.

```
<html>
<head>
<title>My Little Page of JavaScript</title>
<script language="JavaScript">
<!--hide
if (5 == 5){
    alert("Eureka!");
}
//show-->
</script>
</head>
<h1>I find that to be highly logical, Captain.</h1>
</body>
</html>
```

The script starts by testing to see whether the condition in parentheses is true. If it is, it executes everything between the brackets. You probably noticed, but there are two equal signs in the condition that the if control structure tests. This is called a comparison operator, which we will talk about shortly. When you want to assign a value to a variable, use one equal sign. When you want to check to see if two values are equal, use two.

NOTE

Start developing a literal, written checklist for debugging your JavaScript. High on the list should be checking your comparison operators. It is very common to use the assignment operator "=" accidentally instead of the comparison or relational operator "==," possibly because it is more intuitive to do so.

The following example, *more_ifs.html* on the CD, shows two possible extensions of the if control structure. The indentation used in this block of code is the traditional way of keeping your code clean and easy to read. Any text editor worth its salt will offer you the option of maintaining an indentation scheme automatically.

```
<script language="JavaScript">
<!--hide
if (5 == 4){
    alert("Eureka!");
}else{
    alert("Let me try that again.");
}
```

```
if(7 == 6){
      alert("Now I've got it!");
}else if (7 > 6){
      alert("Is this right?");
}else{
      alert("Oh, I give up.");
}
//show-->
</script>
```

There are two if control blocks—the first extended with "else," the second extended with "else if" and else. The JavaScript interpreter goes through the code looking for the first condition that is true in each control block. In the first block, it looks to see whether five is equal to four. It is not, so it executes the instructions labeled with else.

The next control structure first tests the hypothesis that seven is equal to six. Obviously, it is not, so it tests the next hypothesis. This one is true. Seven is greater than six, so it pops up the alert "Is this right?" Since it found a condition that was true, you will not read the statement inside the else label. As soon as the JavaScript interpreter finds a condition that is true within the if control structure, it executes the commands and then exits the control structure.

It's possible to have nested control structures—a control structure within another control structure. Look at the following example (*nested.html* on the CD). Here we are checking to see if a user can guess someone's age. The user gets two tries, after which he is forwarded to a different page if he can guess the correct age.

```
myAge = 29;
usrGuess = prompt("Guess my myAge.","type guess here");
if (usrGuess == myAge){
   window.location="secret.html";
}else{
   usrGuess = prompt("Guess my age?","type guesshere");
   if (usrGuess == myAge){
   window.location="secret.html";
   }else{
   window.location="forgot.html";
   }
```

Now obviously this is not the optimal security scenario, (the secret information is contained within the HTML page); this is just illustrating nested control structures.

There are several new things in this example: "window.location" is used to redirect the user's browser to a new URL, and "prompt" pops up a window as seen here. The user's response in the pop-up is the value of the variable usrGuess.

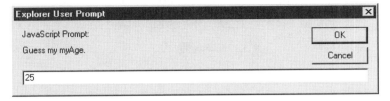

If you follow the flow of the script, you see that the user has two chances to guess the age—once in the outer control structure and once in the nested control structure. The script is technically not incorrect, but it is definitely not in good style. The fact that we have copied several lines verbatim is a sure sign that there are better solutions available.

While

while.html

"While" is a better solution to the challenge posed in the previous example. Consider the following, which is from *while.html* on the CD:

```
myAge = 29;
usrGuess = 0;
while (usrGuess != myAge){
    if(usrGuess > myAge){
        usrGuess = prompt("My age is lower than your guess.",
    "type guess here");
    }else{
        usrGuess = prompt("My age is higher than your guess.",
    "type guess here");
    }
}
```

This solution functions just a little bit differently than the previous example. Instead of defaulting after two erroneous guesses, this code continually prompts a user until he gives the correct age. The most striking difference, however, is the length of the script. There are far fewer lines using the while control structure than there were using nested if control structures.

The JavaScript interpreter processes the while control structure as you would guess. While the condition in the parentheses is true, it will execute commands inside the curly braces over and over. When the condition is no longer true, the interpreter exits the loop. In our example, the condition is that the value of the variable usrGuess does not equal the value of the variable myAge.

Do While

do_while.html

The following code (*do_while.html* on the CD) presents a little bit better solution. The "do while" control structure executes the contents of the brackets before it evaluates the condition in parentheses.

```
myAge = 29;
usrGuess = 0;
var i=0;
do {
    usrGuess = prompt("Guess my age.","type guess here");
        if (usrGuess == myAge){
            window.location="secret.html";
            break;
        }
    i++;
}while (i < 2);

if (usrGuess != myAge){
    window.location="forgot.html";
}
```

There's another new thing in this script. The condition that the do while control structure tests is whether the variable *i* is less than two. We increment the variable *i* by one each time we loop through the control structure by writing "i++". This is called a *unary* operator, which we will talk about in a moment.

Break is also new. This built-in JavaScript function does exactly what it sounds like, which is to break out of the control structure. This is included for the case in which the user guesses the correct age the first time. If we didn't include break at this point, the do-while loop would continue to execute until the condition was met.

Our script is getting better. We didn't have to declare the variable *usrGuess* at the beginning of the script (although fussbudgets would insist that it is proper to do so). We reincorporated the feature that allows the user only two guesses, and our script is still cleaner and smaller than the original.

For

for.html

The following example (*for.html* on the CD) uses a "for" control structure to streamline our little example further. You should be beginning to form the impression that better code is smaller code. While this is not an applicable axiom in all cases, it definitely is a trend you will see in all the code you write.

```
myAge = 29;
usrGuess = 0;

for (i=0; i<2; i++){
    usrGuess = prompt("Guess my age.","type guess here");
        if (usrGuess == myAge){
            window.location="secret.html";
            break;
        }
}

if (usrGuess != myAge){
    window.location="forgot.html";
}
```

A for loop is a kind of shorthand for automatically incrementing a counter variable like we use than the previous example. The syntax can be summarized this way:

```
for (initial value; test; increment){ execute this stuff ;}
```

Switch

switch.html

The "switch" control structure isn't used much, but it's handy when you need it. Switch is a good choice when you have more than two possible outcomes for testing a condition, each of which requires different JavaScript to execute when it is true. Consider the following example (*switch.html* from the CD):

```
var usrPassword = prompt("What is the password?",
    "type pword here");
```

```
switch (usrPassword){
case 'TNPRock':
      window.location="Carls_Home_Page.html";
      break;
case '123doggy':
      window.location="Steves_Home_Page.html";
      break;
default:
      window.location="forgot.html";
      break;
}
```

The script assumes that there are two users: Carl and Steve. If Carl types his password, TNPRock, his browser is redirected to Carls_Home_Page.html. If Steve types his password, he goes to his home page. If any other password is typed, the user goes to forgot.html. This method has a convenient shorthand that saves you from typing a lot of extra brackets and code. I like it because it is easy on the eyes—it is easier to comprehend what is going on at a glance for scripts with a complex flow.

Operators

We've already seen several types of operators in action in the examples. Now we will look at the most important categories of operators, with descriptions of what each one does.

Assignment

There are two basic flavors of assignment operator. The first is the kind we have already seen. The value of the thing on the right side of the equal sign is assigned to whatever is on the left. By extending this simple definition, you might guess that the following is true (it is):

```
theAge = theIq = theShoeSize = 48;
```

In this example, each of the three variables receives a value of 48. Just remember that assignment works from right to left. In other words, the following would not work (it would return "undefined"):

```
48 = theAge = theIq = theShoeSize;
```

The other type of assignment operator performs an arithmetic function. For example, you might want to double the value of the variable each time you go through a control structure. For example:

```
TheNumber = TheNumber * 2;    //the long way
TheNumber *= 2;               //the right way
```

Arithmetic

Arithmetic operators act on numbers just as you expect them to, as we have already seen. The only thing that could possibly trip you up here is confusing the addition and subtraction operators with the other functions performed by the plus and minus signs. The following table shows the arithmetic operators.

Arithmetic Operator	Functrion
+	Addition; concatenating strings
−	Subtraction; negation
*	Multiplication
/	Division
%	Modulus (known abroad as *remainder*)

The arithmetic operators follow the same precedence you learned in fifth grade algebra, but you can override them with parentheses. Look at the following example:

```
x=12;
y=3;
z=1;
newNum = y + z / x; //newNum will be 3.08
newNum = ( y + z ) / x; //newNum will be 0.33
```

In the first statement with arithmetic operators, z is divided by x first because division takes precedence over addition. (Remember *My Dear Aunt Sally*?) In the next statement, the sum of y and z is divided by x because they are grouped in parentheses. If you get results you don't expect from arithmetic operators, check to see if it might be the operator precedence. Parentheses are a sure cure for these problems every time.

Relational

We've already seen how relational operators are used to construct a condition tested by a control structure. The following table lists the most common relational operators.

Relational Operator	Translation
==	Is equal to
!=	Is not equal to
< (or >)	Is less than (or greater than)
<= (or >=)	Is less than or equal to (or greater than or equal to)

Logical
logical.html

Logical operators allow you to construct more complex conditions for your control structures. The following example shows how you can use logical operators in our password example to allow more than one possible password. This code is taken from *logical.html* on the CD.

```
var pWord = "jellyfish";
var curTemp = 72;
for (i=0; i<2; i++){
    usrPassword = prompt("What is the password?",
  "type pword here");
    usrTemp = prompt("What is the current Temperature?",
  "type temp here");
        if ((usrPassword == pWord) && (usrTemp == curTemp)){
            window.location="secret.html";
            break;
            }
}

if ((usrPassword != pWord)||(usrTemp != curTemp)){
    window.location="forgot.html";
}
```

This example requires the user to give a password and the current temperature (a number). The if control structure nested within the for loop has a condition expanded with the && logical operator. If you were to translate this into plain English, it might read, "If the user guesses the correct password, *and* the user guesses the correct number for the temperature, go to the secret page."

In the last bit of code, we use the "or" logical operator ("||"), aka "pipes." This reads, "If the user guessed the wrong password, *or* if the user guessed the wrong temperature, kick him out to the nonsecret area.

Unary

Unary operators are used to automatically increment and decrement variables, as in the for loop. One handy unary operator we didn't see in the examples is negation (–). This is just the minus sign. For instance, if you wanted to find the absolute value of a number, you might write

```
If (theNumber < 0){
theNumber =  -theNumber;
}
```

You will sometimes see the unary operators ++ and – – on the left side of a variable instead of the right. This doesn't make any difference in JavaScript unless the variable being incremented is also having its value assigned to another variable. For instance:

```
TheNum=7;
elNumero = TheNum++ +2 //elNumero will be 9 and TheNum will be 8

X = 2;
Y = --X + 7; //Y will be 8 and X will be 1
```

If the increment comes before the variable, the increment operation takes precedence over the rest of the arithmetic operators—it is figured into the output. Otherwise, the increment is figured afterward. The same is true for decrement. In other words, a unary operator takes precedence over arithmetic operators only if it is on the left side of its operand.

Arrays

Arrays are special types of containers for holding data. Instead of the bucket, an array is more like a fisherman's tackle box or toolbox with compartments. Some arrays have labels on the compartments, while others simply provide an ordered set of generic containers.

Literal

literal_array.html

A literal array is defined by simply typing in the values. Look at the sample code (*literal_array.html* on the CD):

```
<script language="JavaScript">
<!--hide
var usrList = new Array ( "Steve", "Joe", "Mike","Ron");
document.write("The users are " + usrList[0] + ", "
   + usrList[1] + ", " + usrList[2] + ", " + usrList[3] + ".");
//show-->
</script>
```

The array is defined by creating a new array object and assigning values to it. In the next line of code, we access the elements in the array by using index numbers. The elements are indexed with sequential integers, starting with zero. You can also assign values to individual array elements using this property.

```
usrList[1] = "Jose";        //changes "Joe" to "Jose"
```

This type of array is handy for breaking down large chunks of data, especially if they are defined by discrete lines. For instance, as you'll see when we read about cookies in the next chapter, this type of array is a nice choice because it breaks down a large piece of data, the cookie, into individual elements. The weakness of this type of array is that you do not have anything like random access to the individual elements. If you want to find something in an array, you either have to know the exact order of elements or go through each element individually and check to see if it is the one you want.

Associative

associative_array.html

Associate arrays allow you to give each element in an array a unique name by which to refer to it. Instead of using arbitrary numbers, in the following code (*associative_array.html* on the CD), we construct an associative array that holds a unique password for each user.

```
<script language="JavaScript">
<!--hide
var usrList = new Array ();
usrList["Steve"]="8usrStv98";
usrList["Joe"]="joeIsKewl";
usrList["Mike"]="domin8r";
usrList["Ron"]="1dummy";
document.write("Steve's password is " + usrList["Steve"] + ".");
//show-->
</script>
```

Now we have a list of passwords associated with the users they belong to. This is a handy way to store information temporarily within your script, especially when you want to store information about specific objects and be able to refer back to them.

Arrays Within Arrays

quasi-multiple_array.html

Suppose you wanted to represent tabular data like a spreadsheet with a new JavaScript application. It turns out that arrays are perfect for this task. As we will discover in the next chapter, JavaScript's native containers for information are very flexible regarding what they can hold. Arrays are no exception. Among the different types of data an array can hold is another array. Look at the following example (*quasi-multiple_array.html* on the CD):

```
var usrList = new Array ();
usrList["Steve"]=new Array();
usrList["Joe"]=new Array();
usrList["Mike"]=new Array();
usrList["Ron"]=new Array();
usrList["Steve"] ["Telephone"]="818 555 1212";
usrList["Steve"] ["Address"]="513274 Avocado St Apt D";
document.write("Steve lives at " + usrList["Steve"] ["Address"] + ".");
```

An associative array is created for each user in usrList. Two elements are defined for Steve's list, and values are given to them. As you probably already guessed, this can go as deep as you want, building arrays inside arrays inside arrays. . .

Functions

As I mentioned before, if you're writing something more than once in your JavaScript, there is probably a better way to do it. Frequently that better way will be a function. The *function* is a piece of code that you can call when you need it. You can use it over and over without having to retype it.

```
if (newPersonTemperament == "friendly"){
    sayHello();
}

function sayHello(){
    alert("hello");
}
```

This simple code shows a function called sayHello(). It only executes when it is called from inside the if control structure, which of course only happens if a new person is friendly. The obvious advantage of using this function is that it applies to all new people, not a just special case. The syntax for declaring a function is as follows:

```
function nameOfTheFunction(optional arguments){
    Stuff to do;
}
```

The optional arguments are anything you want to pass to the function to do something with. It could be a number, a string, or any data type. In the following example, we pass numbers to a function that spits out the product of the number.

```
var firstNum = prompt("What is the first number to multiply?",
    "- number here");
var secondNum = prompt("What is the second number to multiply?",
    "- number here");
theAnswer = productFiggerer(firstNum , secondNum);
alert("the product is " + theAnswer);

function productFiggerer(x,y){
    var elProducto = x * y;
    return elProducto;
}
```

There are several things to notice here. First, look at how the main script calls the function:

```
theAnswer = productFiggerer(firstNum , secondNum);
```

Two arguments—the values from the user input—are fed into the function, but the function calls them something else. This is perfectly acceptable. When you get up and running with JavaScript, you will be calling functions from different parts of your script; so the best thing to do is to name the variables that are local to the function in a way that makes sense *within* the function. The parentheses in the first line of the function declaration act as a sort of terminal between the function and the rest of the script. The names don't need to match, and usually don't.

Next look at how the function gives its output back to the script that called it:

```
return elProducto;
```

"Return" is the function's way of breaking out of itself and going back to the script that called it with the current value. In this case, it is the product of the two numbers.

Abstract Scripts by Utility

The best broad, sweeping rule for writing JavaScript functions is to abstract blocks of code by what you want them to do. For instance, in our last variation on the password theme, there are two main tasks we kept performing over and over: adding a new user to the list and filling out the information for the user. Let's construct one script with two functions—one to add a user and another to fill out the user's information.

```
var usrList = new Array ();
addUser("Steve");
addUser("Joe");
addUser("Mike");
addUser("Ron");
addStats("Steve", "Telephone","818 555 1212");
addStats("Steve", "Address","513274 Avocado St Apt D");
document.write("Steve lives at " +
   usrList["Steve"] ["Address"] + ".");

//add a user to the array
```

```
function addUser(newGuy){
usrList[newGuy]=new Array();
}


//flesh out the array for a user based on the arguments
function addStats(userName, infoCat, theVal){
usrList[userName] [infoCat]=theVal;
}
```

This is basically the same as before, except that we have put the interfaces to the arrays into functions. If you wanted to be really tricky, you could use a characteristic of all functions in JavaScript, like this:

```
<!—hide
var usrList = new Array ();
addUser("Steve","Joe","Mike","Ron");
addStats("Steve", "Telephone","818 555 1212");
addStats("Steve", "Address","513274 Avocado St Apt D");
document.write("Steve lives at "
    + usrList["Steve"] ["Address"] + ".");

function addUser(){
      for (i=arguments.length-1; i>=0; i--){
            usrList[arguments[i]]=new Array();
}
}


function addStats(userName, infoCat, theVal){
   usrList[userName] [infoCat]=theVal;
}
```

The only thing that has changed is the addUser function. This function now makes use of the default value between the parentheses and any function declaration: an array called "arguments." A good exercise at this point would be to figure out how to write such a function for the addStats feature.

NOTE

The functions in the preceding example are extremely susceptible to errors. For instance, if this were built into a form as a front end for a database, a user could cause problems by trying to add information to an array that doesn't exist. If you wanted to correct this, you would have to add a check to the addStats function. I omitted this in the interest of keeping the scripts simple.

JavaScript Built-in Functions

Lots of functions are built into JavaScript to help you cut down on your development time. We're going to take a very quick look at three of the most useful: eval, escape, and unescape.

Eval does what it sounds like it does: it evaluates whatever is fed into it, kind of like a little JavaScript interpreter within the interpreter. This is especially important to Flash developers because of the nature of the interface between Flash and the Web browser. Often you will need to pass an argument to a function in a form that isn't yet fully digested. Here is a contrived example:

```
var myString="2 + 5";
var mySum=adder(myString);

document.write(myString + " = " + mySum + ".");

function adder(args){
elSum=eval(args);
return elSum;
}
```

The functions performed are slightly absurd, but you can see how eval works. It takes the string "2 + 5" and evaluates it as an independent block of JavaScript. The result is of course seven; so the output from this entire script reads "2 + 5 = 7." This works with absolutely any block of JavaScript that you dump into the eval function. Keep this in mind later when we are trying to use JavaScript in conjunction with ActionScript.

The escape and unescape functions work together to code and decode strings into a form that can be passed via http. This will be important when we deal with cookies in the next chapter. It is also very important for any Web application using CGI scripts that are called in the following form:

```
http://pswoods.com/examplor.php?studentID=Joe%20Schmoe%20from%20Buffalo
```

The following code shows by example how the escape and unescape functions change a string so that you can use it with dynamic Web applications, cookies, or however you like.

```
var myString="I am Iron Man - na na na na na na nuh na na na!";
var webFriendlyString=escape(myString);
var peopleFriendlyString=unescape(webFriendlyString);
```

```
document.write(webFriendlyString + "<p><p>");
document.write(peopleFriendlyString);
```

The output looks like this:

> I%20am%20Iron%20Man%20-%20na%20na%20na%20na%20na%20
> na%20nuh%20na%20na%20na%21

I am Iron Man—na na na na na na nuh na na na!

All those funny characters in between these powerful moving words serve to encode the spaces between the text, as well as special characters like the ampersand that might throw off Web applications. If these functions weren't built into JavaScript, you would have to write your own parsing engine using regular expressions every single time you wanted to send a string like this over the Web. When you get down under the hood of this amazing scripting language, you'll discover that a lot of hard work has already been done for you.

JavaScript Tools

"You get what you pay for" is one of the eternal verities of human interaction, which is unfortunate for Web developers. JavaScript, along with server-side scripting languages like Perl and PHP, has always been free. That's great, except that with this blessing comes the curse of free IDEs (Integrated Development Environments), which have traditionally been built by well-meaning but inexperienced college students and other assorted young enthusiasts. This situation is in sharp contrast with programming languages like Java, which enjoy attention from large, well-funded software companies.

The few good products that make it out of basement apartments and into the world aren't always easy to find. So I've included a blatant, unpaid, unsolicited endorsement for three of my favorite tools for developing JavaScript.

Note Tab Pro and Edit Plus

Note Tab Pro (http://notetab.com) was the first in a long line of text editing applications to use a special interface for code snippets. This is by far its best feature. The interface allows you to choose a set of snippets from as many sets as you like. (The program is fully extensible.) I divide my snippet libraries by programming languages—one for JavaScript, one for ActionScript, and so on. After you've worked on several projects with any particular language, you find the same problems coming up over and over. If you have a slick snippet library that you can drag and drop into your documents, solving a new problem becomes as easy as remembering what you called it the last time. The following image shows part of the HTML library included with Note Tab Pro.

Note Tab Pro is open for any interested party to develop not only snippet libraries, which are as easy as cutting and pasting, but also entire language schemes to check and highlight syntax. Other features include ftp, autocomplete, and scripting to automate anything the application does. Note Tab Pro is shareware, and the price tag is a very lightweight $20. Free light versions are available.

Edit Plus (http://editplus.com) is very similar to Note Tab Pro. It has the same kind of snippet interface, and it is in the same price range at $30. At the time of writing, I am migrating to Edit Plus simply because some generous soul has composed an exhaustive syntax scheme for ActionScript that you can plug into Edit Plus to turn it into a powerful text editor made just for Flash.

1st Page 2000

The immediate advantage of 1st Page is that it is free. There are no advertisements, no nag screens, and no prescribed course of action for the user other than to enjoy the software. In my opinion, this software is an unbelievable windfall for people who want to learn scripting by way of JavaScript.

The 1st Page software does have a good system for storing code snippets. It's no Note Tab Pro, but it gets the job done. The number one advantage is being able to view your work as you go, without leaving the development environment. In other words, you don't have to launch your giant, feature-bloated Web browser just to see whether the last line of code you wrote caused a glitch. Figure 6-2 shows a full-screen view of 1st Page. There are tabs along the bottom of the screen that let you toggle between open documents, just like in other high-end text editors. What's different here is that you have tabs across the top of the screen to toggle between the source code, a rather good set of documentation, and a preview of the document featuring a JavaScript debugger.

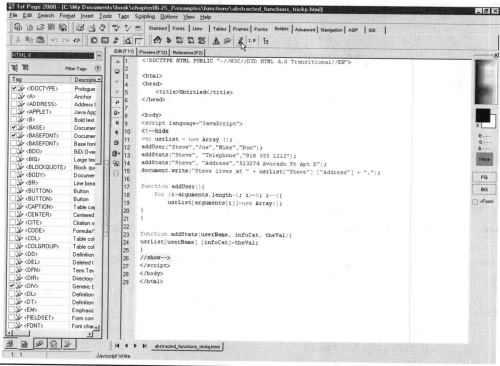

Figure 6.2   *The 1st Page IDE*

The 1st Page software also includes copious amounts of extras, for example, prewritten scripts in a number of languages, wizards, and a very intelligent scheme for bookmarking the directories on your drive that you use most often so that you can get to them quickly from the application. I prefer the look and feel of 1st Page for developing JavaScript over any other application. I use this as my external editor from Dreamweaver, so that I can open any documents that I want to hand code in a familiar environment.

Dreamweaver

Macromedia certainly doesn't need any help from me to market this popular application. But just in case there's anyone out there who hasn't tried Dreamweaver, read this carefully.

Dreamweaver takes the idea of saving code snippets as custom objects to the extreme. First of all, you have the option to use JavaScript functions built by either Macromedia or third-party developers. These take the form of a custom interface built by the developer that allows you to enter all the necessary parameters. You do all of this without getting your fingers dirty in the code. The following illustration shows an interface for a function that will be attached to a hypertext link. This function pops up a new browser window.

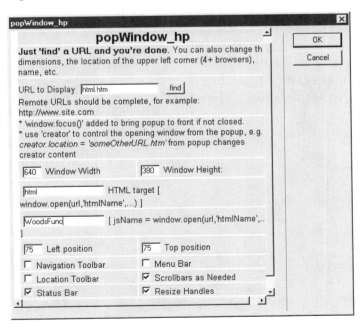

Building a JavaScript object and an interface like this is not as hard as you think. If you spent a solid week with some decent JavaScript books, you could pull it off. The biggest advantage to using this type of interface is the consistency you get when you use the same tool, either between multiple developers working on the same project or for yourself between projects. It is a lot easier to look at a drop-down menu and a clearly written description than it is to look at a big, messy block of code you forgot to comment.

Dreamweaver also has a dazzling array of visual tools, DHTML and CSS. The new UltraDev version incorporates visual tools for back-end development. However, it has yet to address the extremely popular scripting languages PHP and Perl.

What to Take Away from This Chapter

JavaScript is here to stay. Just about any serious Web developer engaged in scripting uses JavaScript every day. It is an easy-to-learn, fun scripting language that serves as a good introduction to the world of programming. It shares a core canon of objects with ActionScript, so it is an optimal starting point for us. After working through the examples in this chapter, you should have a very good feel for the general flow of JavaScript.

Whether or not you get stuck in this and the following two chapters, you should find a good JavaScript reference for your bookshelf. While JavaScript is easy pick up quickly, there are numerous subtleties you can easily miss. In addition, you should also find an online resource with which you can use as a quick, searchable index. At the time of writing, my favorite is at http://www.devguru.com/Technologies/ecmascript/quickref/javascript_intro.html.

JavaScript Part II

IN THIS CHAPTER:

I n this chapter, we are going to talk about objects within the context of JavaScript and how to use them. We will start by constructing our own objects from scratch while we talk about the definition of objects in general. Next we pick through a few of the built-in objects in JavaScript while we investigate how they all fit together.

Introduction to OOP

Introductions to modern programming languages usually begin with the obligatory, big, confusing treatise on Object-Oriented Programming, or OOP. I'll try to avoid the big and confusing part.

On the most general level, OOP simply aims to reduce some of the unpleasant things about programming by packaging reusable code into neat little bundles. The most obvious advantage is that you save a lot of typing. In addition, by using objects, you have a comprehensive solution at your disposal that was composed by someone who is a master programmer. Another thing about not typing a solution to a problem that has been solved before is that it cuts down on typos. Abstracting code into objects also makes it easier for a developer to look at a piece of code and understand it immediately. All of these factors add up to an easier process—from coding through troubleshooting.

Objects

dog _ object.html

Objects take on many forms. An object may be as simple as a single line of code within your JavaScript, or as sophisticated as a GUI module in an expensive IDE. An object can be abstracted into a separate file, such as the first example in the previous chapter.

To keep the concept general and simple at this point, let's define objects as self-contained units that can be used over and over, like a Flash Movie clip. Before I start droning on and on about metaphors for objects and the nuances of OOP, let's look at an example.

```
<html>
<head>
    <title>My Doggy</title>
<script language="JavaScript">
<!--hide
```

```
var dog=new Object();
dog.name="Huckleberry";
dog.color="mostly white with rusty ears";

function lifeStory(){
       alert("This is " + dog.name  + ". " +
       "As you can see,  " + dog.name + " is " + dog.color + ". ");
}
//show-->
</script>
</head>

<body>
<a href="#" onClick="lifeStory();">Just an Introduction</a>
<p>
</body>
</html>
```

This example (*dog _ object.html* on the CD) builds an object called "dog." It starts by creating an empty object, then begins to flesh out the object by assigning values to the properties "name" and "color." Very simple. The only other thing you may not have seen is the onClick event for an HTML hyperlink. When a user clicks on a link with an onClick event, the JavaScript interpreter fires up and executes everything within the quotes.

Properties and Methods
dog _ method.html
The previous example showed how to assign properties to an object. This particular example is actually about as deep as the concept of properties goes. You have a thing, and you know something about it—that's the whole idea of object properties.

Let's take a look at how to define a method using the following example. You can find the file containing this code on the CD: *dog _ method.html*.

```
<html>
<head>
       <title>My Doggy</title>
<script language="JavaScript">
<!--hide
```

```
var dog=new Object();
dog.name="Huckleberry";
dog.color="mostly White with rusty ears";
dog.intro=shortIntroduction;

function shortIntroduction(){
     alert("This is " + this.name + ". As you can see,  "
   + this.name + " is " + this.color + ". ");
}

//show-->
</script>
</head>

<body>
<a href="#" onClick="dog.intro();">Just an Introduction</a>

</body>
</html>
```

This example shows the method dog.intro being constructed. You may have noticed that the properties called in the shortIntroduction() function has changed from dog.name and dog.color to this.name and this.color. The word "this" has a special significance in JavaScript. It is a sort of placeholder for the name of the current object. In our script, the object that calls the function is "dog," so that is what the function uses in place of "this."

That should be enough to form our definition of an object method, again keeping it general and basic. In the previous example, we saw that dog.intro() not only looks like a function in its syntax, it also called an actual function from the object. For now, let's assume that an *object method* is something that an object can do, or a function of the object.

Constructors

dog_constructor.html, experimental_dog_prototype.html

In the following sample we are going to build a dog. In the previous example, we simply added properties manually to an object. This accomplishes no more than just storing data in arrays. In order to start taking advantage of the power of objects, we're going to use a constructor to flesh out some of the properties and methods for an object automatically. This code is taken from *dog_constructor.html* on the CD.

```
<script language="JavaScript">
<!--hide

function shortIntroduction(){
     alert("This is " + this.name + ". As you can see,    "
  + this.name + " is " + this.color + ". He is "
  + this.age + " old.");
     if ((this.tail == true) && (this.numLegs == 4)){
          alert("He has four legs and a tail.");
     }
}

function dog(name, color, age){
this.name=name;
this.color=color;
this.age=age;
this.numLegs=4;
this.tail=true;
this.intro=shortIntroduction;
}

var huck = new dog("Huckleberry", "mostly white with rusty ears", "5
months");
var mopey = new dog("Mr. Mopey", "mousy brown with grey streaks", "17
years");
mopey.numLegs=3;

//show-->
</script>
</head>

<body>
<a href="#" onClick="huck.intro();">Huckleberry</a><p>
<a href="#" onClick="mopey.intro();">Mr. Mopey</a>
```

The thing we are calling a constructor is the function named "dog." It is a special kind of function that creates a new dog when it is called. The only information it requires (the arguments) are name, color, and age. The constructor makes assumptions about dogs in general to flesh out the remaining properties and methods. The constructor assumes that all dogs have four legs and a tail. Since almost all dogs do have four legs and a tail, it is easier to use this information in the constructor and change these properties manually for dogs that do not have four legs and a tail. In fact, this is what we do for the dog named Mr. Mopey who has only three legs.

Notice how we call the intro method in the body of the HTML document. Huckleberry has his own intro method, which checks to make sure that he has four legs and a tail before announcing to the world that he does. When Mr. Mopey's intro method is called, the if control structure finds that he does not have four legs, so it takes the easy way out by skirting the subject.

It makes your code cleaner to abstract constructors further by separating parts that are the same for every single object it builds. To do this, you use a prototype. The following code is from *experimental_dog_ prototype.html* on the CD. This JavaScript sample functions exactly as the previous one, except for the constructor function. The parts that are the same for every dog—the number of legs, the existence of a tail, and the method "intro"—are separated from the function as prototypes. The word "prototype" is the reserved JavaScript word to tell the interpreter to ascribe all things on the right to the object class listed on the left.

```
function dog(name, color, age){
this.name=name;
this.color=color;
this.age=age;
}

dog.prototype.numLegs=4;
dog.prototype.tail=true;
dog.prototype.intro=shortIntroduction;
```

For those of you who sat in the first three rows in college with your hands up, this *will* be on the test. Defining custom objects, however simple, is essential to writing clean, efficient code. This carries over into Flash as well.

NOTE

The word "constructor" is loosely synonymous with "class," which you will hear used in many discussions on OOP. More specifically, a constructor is said to create a class, which is a model for the objects it builds.

Using with
with.html

Suppose we had a whole bunch of things to do with a particular object—Mr. Mopey, for instance. We would find ourselves typing "mopey.something" over and over; when you are typing something over and over, rest assured there is a better way to do it.

The best way to do this in JavaScript is using "with." The following example (*with.html* on the CD) shows how to use it.

```javascript
function shortIntroduction(){
      alert("This is " + this.name + ". As you can see,   "
   + this.name + " is " + this.color
   + ". He is " + this.age + " old.");
      if ((this.tail == true) && (this.numLegs == 4)){
           alert("He has four legs and a tail.");
      }
}

function dog(name, color, age){
this.name=name;
this.color=color;
this.age=age;
}

dog.prototype.numLegs=4;
dog.prototype.tail=true;
dog.prototype.intro=shortIntroduction;

var huck = new dog("Huckleberry",
   "mostly white with rusty ears", "5 months");
var mopey = new dog("Mr. Mopey",
   "mousy brown with grey streaks", "17 years");
mopey.numLegs=3;

with (mopey){
      temperament="nasty";
      fleas=true;
      confirmedKills=5;
      houseTrained=false;
}
```

As you can see, this is an updated version of our dog constructor. The author of the script thought it was necessary to include a lot of extra information about the dog Mr. Mopey, for safety's sake.

The syntax is easy to understand. You just state which object you want to use and go to work. How it works is an interesting subject. "with" defines the *scope* of the statements contained within the curly braces. Scope just means the area of the script in which you're currently operating. If you are at the highest level in the script, such as the first code that executes (var huck = new dog... in this example), the objects you use affect the entire script. This scope is called *global* in most programming languages (though some hard-core hackers scowl if you use this weighty nomenclature on a lighthearted language like JavaScript). The scope of objects that only exist nested within other objects (like functions) are said to be *local* to the object that contains them.

Closet Objects

neat.html, substring-n-indexOf.html

By now you have noticed similarities between the custom objects we have built from scratch and the built-in parts in JavaScript. For instance, when we want something to appear in the browser window, we use the method document.write(), which looks a lot like huck.intro(). The similarity is owed to the fact that document is an object with its own built-in methods. In fact, just about everything in JavaScript is an object. Strings are objects, numbers are objects, arrays are objects, browser windows are objects. It goes on and on.

As built-in JavaScript objects, simple data types have built-in functions. The string data type has an unusually large number of functions, which is great for developers. So many of the problems we encounter building Web applications center around exchanging data back and forth as long, slapped-together strings (like when you call a CGI script: '../flip.cgi?stuff=yeah&burger=big%20burger&fries=no%20thanks'. JavaScript provides you with a whole slew of tools to manipulate strings and discover useful information about them without working too hard. The escape and unescape functions we looked at in the last chapter are examples of this.

The following example shows a few of the neat things you can do with built-in string functions. This is just a demonstration to give you an idea of how extensive the complement of string functions in JavaScript is. This script is from *neat.html* on the CD.

```
<script language="JavaScript">
<!--hide

/*a string as it might appear from another source, such as a cookie
this script looks in  two strings to see if they contain
the word "elvis" */
var banjoString="rock=hard|sore=rojo|water=deep|
    morpheus=happy|elvis=swingin";
var otherString="this is a big long string
    with nothing at all about the King of Rock 'n' Roll";

function parseString(line){
      //define a regular expression to match against-this is cool
      var regExp=/Elvis/i;
      var isItThere=line.search(regExp);
      //if the word 'elvis' (ignoring case) is not in the string
      if (isItThere == -1){
            document.write("There is nothing in this string.")
      }else{
      //otherwise, parse the name/value pairs in a known format
            better=line.split("|");
            pairs=new Array();
            var indexer = "";
            for (i=0; i<better.length -1; i++){
                  indexer=better[i].split("=");
                  pairs[indexer[0]]=indexer[1];
                  document.write("<a href='#' onclick='alert(\""
    + indexer[1] + "\");'>" + indexer[0] + "</a><p>" );
      }
  }
}
parseString(banjoString); //creates links that pop up matching alerts
parseString(otherString); //returns "There is nothing about Elvis…"
//show-->
</script>
```

Let's take a quick look at two pairs of string functions that you will be using a lot, both in JavaScript and in ActionScript. The first pair of important string functions is "split" and "join." As you may have guessed from the example above, split divides a string into an array using a designated delimiter. For example:

```
var theString="thisQisQaQstring";
myListOfWords=theString.split("Q");
```

myListOfWords is now an array containing the values "this," "is," "a," and "string." This kind of scenario comes up over and over in Web development because it is often necessary to pass data back and forth on a single line. (Luckily, this kind of data transfer is slowly becoming outmoded.) Usually you will want to choose a standard delimiter, like the pipe (|), a semicolon (;), or any character that is extremely unlikely to be used in a variable name or value.

"Join" is the exact opposite of split. It zips up an array into a single string using the delimiter of your choice, using the syntax:

```
var delimitedString=myArray.join(delimiter); //for example…
var myList = new Array("milk", "eggs", "buns", "hot dogs");
var portableList = myList.join("|");
```

In this example, the variable portableList will be a long string containing all the values of myList, separated by a pipe: "milk|eggs|buns|hot dogs".

The second most handy pair of string functions is "substring" and "indexOf." They tell you what characters are in a string at the location you designate, and provide a numeric index of a character or group of characters, respectively. These two functions are used a lot to do a primitive, clumsy kind of pattern matching. The basic idea of pattern matching is that you have a string, and you want to determine whether certain combinations of characters are present in the string.

Let's look at substring first. Substring uses the following syntax (which is totally screwy, so don't feel bad if you have a hard time getting a feel for it):

```
var myNewVar = myString.substring( index of 1st character,
   index of last character + 1);
```

In other words, if you want to get "weise" out of "Budweiser," you would use "substring (3,7)." The letter *w* has an index of 3 (the index starts at 0, just like with arrays). The index of *s* is 6, but you have to add 1 to it. It helps me to remember that the second argument to the substring function is the sum of the first argument and the number of letters you want. So in the case of "Budweiser," I know that 3 is the first argument—and I want four letters total—so the second argument must be 7 (3 + 4 = 7).

The indexOf method works a little more intuitively. It returns the index of the first character of a matching substring in the string you are testing. For example:

```
var myString="JavaScript";
var w = myString.indexOf("v"); // w will be 2
var x = myString.indexOf("S"); // x will be 4
var y = myString.indexOf("Script"); // y will also be 4
var z = myString.indexOf("donkey"); // z will be -1
```

If you try to feed indexOf a substring that doesn't exist, it returns a value of −1. This little quirk in the function makes indexOf so valuable you could hardly live without it. One very common line of code in JavaScript is this:

```
if (someString.indexOf("desired result") != -1) { ...
```

This code translates, "if someString doesn't not contain 'desired result'…" or "if someString contains 'desired result'…" This is a handy way to quickly and easily check to see if a substring you are looking for is present. The following example (*substring-n-indexOf.html* on the CD) uses this technique, along with the substring and split functions.

```
/*this script looks to see if the substrings 'cool' and 'http://'
exist in a string. if they do, it creates a link to the URL */

//declare string variables
var myString="I saw the coolest thing today at
http://suck.com/ It like totally rocks.";
var anotherString = "Dude - you have got to check out
http://www.shockwave.com They have SouthPark cartoons. Hella cool.";
var yetAnother = "I say, old man - how are you faring these days?";

function parseString(line){
//check to see if the string has the requisite substrings
if ((line.indexOf("cool") != -1)&& (line.indexOf("http://") != -1)){
var startIndex = line.indexOf("http://");
var endIndex = line.length -1;
//grab the string from the beginning of the URL to the end of the
string
var biteSizeChunk = line.substring(startIndex, endIndex + 1);
//grab the URL only (assuming a space follows immediately)
```

```
var chunkEndIndex = biteSizeChunk.indexOf(" ");
var theURL = biteSizeChunk.substring(0, chunkEndIndex +1);
//weed out the special characters, etc to show the site domain only
for display
var bitsOfChunk = theURL.split("/");
var outputLabel = bitsOfChunk[2];
document.write("Check out the cool stuff at <a href =\"" + theURL +
"\">" + outputLabel + "</a><br> ")
        }else{
                document.write("Nothing cool to report here.")
   }
}

parseString(myString);
parseString(anotherString);
parseString(yetAnother);
```

A Smattering of Built-in Objects

In general, the deeper your understanding of built-in objects in any language, the cleaner, faster, and more reliable your code will be. JavaScript has a lot of useful objects incorporated into the core language, and it has many of these objects in common with Flash. Let's take a look at some of the most basic and useful objects.

Object

object_object.html

The "object" object is the model for all other objects in JavaScript. This is a very useful bit of information when you consider that the core properties and methods of the object object are available to every other object in JavaScript. The following code (*object_object.html* on the CD) is an enhancement of our first script that built a dog object. This version uses the toSource() function to show all of the source code that went into the dog object.

```
<html>
<head>
     <title>My Doggy</title>
<script language="JavaScript">
<!--hide
var dog=new Object();
```

```
dog.name="Huckleberry";
dog.color="mostly White with rusty ears";
dog.intro=shortIntroduction;

function shortIntroduction(){
      alert("This is " + this.name + ". As you can see,  "
   + this.name + " is " + this.color + ". ");
}


//show-->
</script>
</head>
<body>
<script language="JavaScript">
<!--hide
function showSource(){
      whichObj = eval(window.document.elFormo.text1.value);
      document.write(whichObj.toSource()+"<BR>");
}
//show-->
</script>
<a href="#" onClick="dog.intro();">Just an Introduction</a>
<p>
For which object do you want to see the source?
<form name="elFormo" onSubmit="showSource(); return False;">
      <input name="text1" type="text" onFocus='this.value="";'
  value="type 'dog' and enter">
</form>
</body>
</html>
```

Open this file to see how it works. You must use Netscape or another
ECMAScript-compliant browser for this example, as the toSource method is
not currently supported in Microsoft Internet Explorer.

This is an incredibly clever and useful function. With the baby-simple syntax
whichObj.toSource(), you can refer to the source code for an entire object. At this
point you could print it out as it is here, or you could use it to create other objects.

Although the toSource() method—or even the prototype property—may not be
the bread and butter of everyday JavaScript, the lesson is clear. Learn JavaScript
from the top down. Get to know the built-in objects, including object, first. This
will illuminate features of the language that are inherited from the basic objects.

Math

distance_calculator.html

"Math" is a bread-and-butter object that you will use constantly. Whether you are building a game or a simple script to deal with currency, you will be glad that JavaScript has an extensive object for handling just about any situation you can throw at it. Let's look at the following example (*distance_calculator.html* on the CD), a very simple distance calculator:

```html
<html>
<head>
      <title>Distance Calculator</title>
<script language="JavaScript">
<!--hide
function calculator(){
x=window.document.elFormo.lati.value;
y=window.document.elFormo.longi.value;
z=Math.sqrt(x*x + y*y);
window.document.elFormo.distance.value=Math.round(z);


}
//show-->
</script>
</head>
<body>
<h1>Distance Calculator</h1>
<form name="elFormo"onSubmit='calculator();return false;'>
      <input name="longi" type="text" value="diff. in
longitude"onClick='this.value="";'>
      <br>
      <input name="lati" type="text"
   value="diff in latitude" onClick='this.value="";'>
      <input type="submit" value="calculate">
      <p>
      <input name="distance" type="text" value="distance">
</form>
</body>
</html>
```

In the calculator function, we first use the math object to figure the square root of the sum of the squares of the two input numbers. We also use the math object to round off the answer to an integer. We could do both of these things with simple arithmetic, but it gets really ugly really fast. In addition, using the math object instead of hacking out our own methods is more efficient in terms of memory demands at runtime.

In this example we used the .round() method of the math object to round off the distance to the nearest integer, just like we learned in elementary arithmetic back when dinosaurs roamed the earth. There are other ways you can round off a number in JavaScript. You could use .ceil(), which rounds up to the next highest integer, or .floor(), which chops off any decimal remainder (rounds down). This is generally how things work in ECMAScript—within any built-in object, you have one way of doing things that works for 99 percent of all situations; but you also have built-in methods for special cases. The moral of the story is that you should learn *all* of the built-in methods.

By now you have noticed that forms are objects, too. Each element within the form object is a nested object, like a Movie clip within a Movie clip. The syntax we use to refer to form elements helps paint a picture of how an HTML document containing JavaScript fits together.

```
x=window.document.elFormo.lati.value;
```

"window" refers to the Web browser window, which is of course an object. "document" is the document that is currently loaded—in other words, itself. Next is the name of the form, followed by the name of the form element, followed by the property of the form element object that we are looking for, "value."

Another interesting point about HTML forms is that they are accessible even if you don't name them. This is because client-side JavaScript objects in general are also arrays. So the following two statements are equivalent in the context of our current example:

```
x=window.document.elFormo.lati.value;
// x gets value of "lati" text field
x=window.document.forms[0].elements[1].value; // same thing
```

The math object has more methods than you will ever need. If you are trying to do something mathematically with a number but don't know how, open the object hierarchy tool in First Page 2000. A partial screen is shown here. You can probably figure out which one to use by its descriptive name.

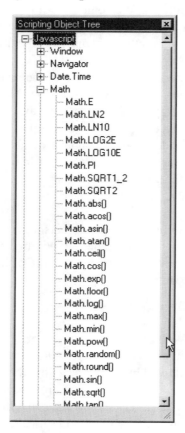

Date

clock.html

There was a time not long ago when the fashionable useless Flash gadget was a clock. These clocks were made using an interface between Flash and the Web browser, which will be covered in the next chapter. Building this kind of bridge was common practice among advanced developers because it afforded them the opportunity to use a more sophisticated scripting language—JavaScript. Today it is easy to build a clock using native ActionScript; so of course this gadget has gone out of fashion.

The following example (*clock.html* on the CD) reads the system clock and displays the time remaining until midnight in one text box and the number of years remaining until 2005 in the other text box.

```
<html>
<head>
   <title>El Clock</title>
<script>
<!--hide

startCrystal=new Date(2005, 00, 01, 00, 00, 00);

function getTime() {
   var today = new Date();
   var youthRemaining = startCrystal.getFullYear()
   - today.getFullYear();
   window.document.elFormo.Logan.value = youthRemaining;
   var hours = 23 - today.getHours();
   var minutes = fixer(60 - today.getMinutes());
   var seconds = fixer(60 - today.getSeconds());
   var rightNow = hours + ":" + minutes + ":" + seconds;
   window.document.elFormo.elClocko.value = rightNow;
   timeOut= setTimeout('getTime();',1000);
}

function fixer(elNumero){
   if (elNumero < 10){
       elNumero = "0" + elNumero;

   }
   return elNumero;
}
//show-->
</script>
</head>
<body onLoad="getTime();">
<form name = "elFormo">
<input name="elClocko" type="text" value="">
CountDown to Midnite
<br>
<input name="Logan" type="text" value="">
Years of Youth Remaining
</form>
</body>
</html>
```

Since date is derived from the object object, the syntax for creating a new instance looks exactly the same. getHours(), getMinutes(), and getSeconds are all methods of the date object. Their respective meanings should be obvious.

The last line in the function getTime() is interesting. The built-in function setTimeout() calls the function within which it is nested. In other words, the getTime function calls itself every 1000 milliseconds (every second). This type of function is called *recursive*. Recursive functions are especially handy when you want to parse through a structured blob of data when you don't know the exact structure. You'll be surprised how often this comes up.

JavaScript DOM

Understanding the JavaScript Document Object Model, or DOM, is critical to being comfortable with the language. The flavor of JavaScript used inside the Web browser uses the DOM as a blueprint. We have already seen numerous examples of elements being defined in the context of the DOM; now we're going to dig into the details.

Structure

Figure 7-1 shows the browser object hierarchy. I illustrated it in similar fashion to the standard Explorer interface to reinforce the concept of hierarchy. As you may have already guessed from the examples, navigating the DOM is just like navigating a physical file structure. You have things inside things inside things.

There are a lot more objects available to JavaScript programmers in the browser-specific DOMs for both Microsoft Internet Explorer and Netscape Navigator. Figure 7-1 represents the most basic core object categories you are likely to use in everyday, fully compatible scripting.

Dot Syntax

When we wanted to name elements in the form, we used the following syntax:

```
window.document.form[0].elements[1].value
```

Notice how this way of naming objects traces a line down the tree of the DOM. This works the same for any object. For instance, if we wanted to check to see if any version of the Flash Player was installed on a user's machine, we might use this:

```
if (navigator.plugins["Shockwave Flash"]) {...
```

In this line of code, we don't include "window" because we're assuming that "window" is the scope we are already operating in. That's a pretty safe bet. If you

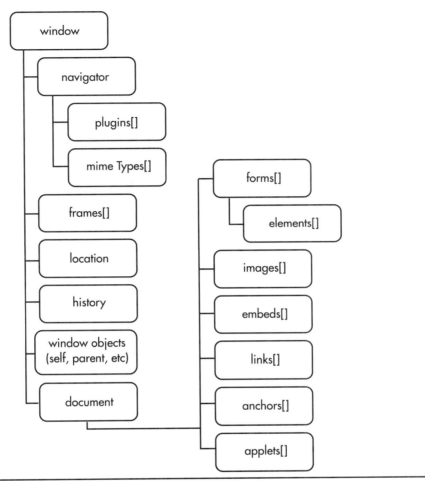

Figure 7.1   *The JavaScript Document Object Model*

are writing JavaScript in a single window and not referencing anything outside that window, the top-level scope will always be "window."

The navigator object has a child object called "plugins," as shown in Figure 7-1. If a user has the Flash Player installed, the array "plugins" will have an element called "Shockwave Flash."

It looks as though there is no condition being tested within the parentheses in this example, but this is actually a shorthand method. Any time you look to see if an object is present, it returns one of two Boolean values. If it is present, it returns true.

Window Manipulation

If you develop any kind of content whatsoever for the Web, then you deal with windows. The only question is whether you choose to do something interesting with them.

The window is the centerpiece of the JavaScript Document Object Model, from far-out DHTML to button-down, everyday corporate hacking. Opening, closing, and communicating between windows is essential to Web development. In this part of the chapter, we look at some basic techniques for window manipulation.

Open a Window

simple_popup.html

The following example (*simple_popup.html* on the CD) shows a very simple way to open a new window using JavaScript.

```
<html>
<head>
      <title>Window Maker</title>
<script language="JavaScript">
<!--hide
function theBigPopper(){
window.open("http://suck.com","theNewWindow");
}
//show-->
</script>
</head>
<body>
<a href="#" onClick="theBigPopper();">Suck dot com</a><p>
</body>
</html>
```

If you actually opened this example and tried it, you probably noticed that you could have done the same thing in HTML, and it would have been easier. In addition, if you use the HTML link attribute "target='_blank'," the new window retains the preferences set in the original window. In the JavaScript version, you get the default Web browser layout, with toolbars, menu bars, and everything else. We'll look at how to customize pop-up windows shortly.

The window is opened within the function theBigPopper(). "open" is a built-in method of the window object. Its syntax is as follows:

```
window.open(URL,name of the new window, options);
```

Window Options

options_popup.html

Considering the current level of intolerance for pop-up windows, it is very important to give these windows the best possible presentation. If your window is sloppy, has unnecessary toolbars, or is positioned in the upper-left corner of the screen, chances are, users will simply close it. The popular identifier for dealing with pop-ups is "whack-a-mole."

Open the following example (*options_popup.html* on the CD) to see a little bit better approach to popping up the window. In this case, it makes sense to use JavaScript instead of the standard "target" attribute of the HTML link tag. We have a custom-sized window that has been stripped of most of its tools and options.

```html
<html>
<head>
      <title>Window Maker</title>
<script language="JavaScript">
<!--hide
function theBigPopper(){
window.open("http://suck.com","theNewWindow",
   "width=400,height=300,location=no,menubar=no,resizable=yes,
   screenX=175,screenY=175,status=no,toolbar=no");
}
//show-->
</script>
</head>
<body>
<a href="#" onClick="theBigPopper();">Suck dot com</a><p>
</body>
</html>
```

Notice that all the options are listed within a single set of quotes. If you're used to HTML attributes, you may have a tendency to put the values in the name-value pairs in quotes. Just remember, you are not writing HTML; you are writing one long string of data as a JavaScript argument.

Similarly, although JavaScript is generally tolerant of white space (spaces, tabs, newlines), this particular argument would be the Deep South on a map of tolerance in JavaScript. If you include spaces between the comma-separated values, the options won't register with most browsers. IE with translate if you screw up and includes spaces; but don't count on this function to clean up your code.

Window Option	Description
width=400	Sets width of the new window to the specified number of pixels (400 in this case).
height=300	Sets height of new window.
location=no	Sets whether the address bar will show in the new window. Possible values are "yes" and "no."
menubar=no	Sets whether the menu will show.
toolbar=no	Determines whether the toolbar ("back," "home," "reload," etc.) will show in the new window.
status=no	Determines whether the new window will have a status bar. Warning: it freaks out some users if they don't have a status bar on a window.
scrollbars=no	Determines whether the new window is allowed to have scroll bars. You can just leave this option alone unless you deliberately want to hide content out of sight.
resizable=yes	Determines whether the user will be able to grab the lower-right corner of the new window to resize it.
screenX=175	The horizontal distance from the left edge of the opening window to the left edge of the new window, in pixels (here, it is 175).
screenY=175	The vertical distance from the top edge of the opening window to the top edge of the new window.

Table 7.1   *Window Options*

Table 7-1 shows some of the more common window options. These should all work on any JavaScript-enabled browser.

A New Window Can Be an Object

simple_popup_with_wireless_remote.html

Opening a new window is all well and good, but what if you want to do something with it after it has opened? It turns out that you can treat the window that you opened as an object from within the same script.

The following example (*simple_popup_with_wireless_remote.html* on the CD) shows a window with a lot of options being opened and subsequently manipulated by channeling its properties into the object newWin.

```
<html>
<head>
    <title>Window Maker</title>
<script language="JavaScript">
<!--hide
function theBigPopper(){
    newWin=window.open("http://suck.com","theNewWindow",
    "width=400,height=300,location=no,menubar=no,
    resizable=yes,screenX=175,screenY=175,status=no,toolbar=no");
}
function channelChanger(){
    newWin.location="http://yahoo.com";
    window.self.blur();
}
function turnItOff(){
    newWin.close();
}
//show-->
</script>
</head>
<body>
<a href="#" onClick="theBigPopper();">Suck dot com</a><p>
<a href="#" onClick="channelChanger();">Change the channel.</a><p>
<a href="#" onClick="turnItOff();">Turn it off.</a><p>
</body>
</html>
```

We use the same method of the window object to open a new window in this example, but with an important difference: it is preceded by "newWin=." This makes it easy to refer to the new window by simply calling the newWin object.

Recall that before, when we wanted to point the user's browser to a new address, we used the syntax "window.location='http://newurl.com/'." We do the same thing in the function called channelChanger, only with the newWin object.

The other little item in the channelChanger function causes the window in which the script resides to go behind all other open windows. This is done to cure an age-old scourge of JavaScript development: the challenge of navigating the contents of one window from another window. There have been numerous clever and effective solutions to this problem over the years. There is one I especially like that the author packaged as a Dreamweaver behavior. You can find it at http://www.pawluk.com/public/.

Notice which object the blur method affects. This is one of the objects directly under the window in Figure 7-1. These objects are most useful to the poor souls who still use frames (Godspeed to you, brave ones). You will also find a lot of uses for window.self. You can use the window.self object to close a window, make a window full screen, or to employ many DHTML tricks.

Another handy object at this level is a window.opener. This object refers to the window that spawned the current window. You can use this object to complete the circle of communication between windows.

Using pop-up windows just because you know how isn't going to win any friends. But driven by a compelling idea, applications that exist in multiple, simultaneous, custom windows can be breathtaking. When you use JavaScript to manipulate windows, just remember that there should be a good reason for opening a new window.

Cookies

Cookies were a headline item in the early days of the Web, and we have the media to thank for widespread misconceptions and panic over cookies. To this day there are large numbers of users who consider cookies to be too great a security risk to be useful. While this isn't a seminar on security, I do want to get the point across that it is OK to use cookies. In fact, the once ubiquitous practice of warning users before installing a cookie seems to be evaporating steadily.

There are two stages of cookie use: writing and reading. Although the cookie object itself is easy to manipulate, care must be taken to save your information in a way that you will be able to find it again.

Cookie Object—Save and Retrieve

messy_cookies.html, messy_cookie_reader.html, better_ cookies.html

Every Web scripting language has a tool kit for cookies. JavaScript is an appealing solution for Flashers because it operates in the same client-side environment—the Web browser. The combination of Flash in JavaScript using cookies allows Flashers to add long-term memory to their multimedia applications without server-side scripting.

I believe that this obvious combination has been largely overlooked so far in the history of Flash development. You don't see a lot of Flash applications using cookies, and it's a shame. I think this is probably because the first big prospectors' rush was to the gleaming valley of server-side scripting, where Flashers built applications using combinations like PHP and MySQL, which are designed to store data on the server; but when you want to store user-specific information with absolutely no storage cost, almost no programming, and no extra processes running on your server, cookies are a fast, easy way to get the job done. Server-side scripting languages are equipped with cookie functions, too, but we are going to look at using cookies with JavaScript in this section.

The following example shows the simplest possible scenario for writing a cookie. Notice the escape function zipping up the cookie contents before the cookie is set. This is a necessary step. This code is from *messy_cookies.html* on the CD. Make sure to copy this and the next example onto a local drive on your PC.

```
<html>
<head>
        <title>Window Maker</title>
<script language="JavaScript">
<!--hide
var theString=prompt("Give me a string to write to the cookie.","");
document.cookie=escape(theString);
document.write("<h1>Cookies</h1><p>Now go to <a
href='messy_cookie_reader.html'>another page</a>
    and retrieve the cookie.")
//show-->
</script>
</head>
<body>
</body>
</html>
```

The cookie object is easy to get at. You simply assign any string to document.cookie. This example redirects you to another page to demonstrate that the string is being saved on your hard drive, not simply in a variable within the script. If you are still skeptical, you can exit your browser, shut down your machine, unplug it from the wall, and move your PC to a different room. The cookie will still be there when you come back to the same directory.

The following code demonstrates the simplest possible application of reading a cookie. The sample is *messy_cookie_reader.html* on the CD. Don't forget to copy it to the same directory as the previous example.

```
<html>
<head>
        <title>This is not a good cookie scheme.</title>
<script language="javascript">
        alert(unescape(document.cookie));
```

```
</script>
</head>
<body>
</body>
</html>
```

Employing cookies is really that easy. There are, however, a few additional conventions that will make your cookies much more useful. First of all, you will want to use the standard naming convention to separate your cookie from any others that might exist for the same directory. Unless you specify otherwise, cookies apply only to the directory where the document that created them resides. To set the name of a cookie, use the following syntax:

```
document.cookie="cookieName=the|real|content";
```

This is confusing. The equal sign in the string that you assign to the cookie is not evaluated by the JavaScript interpreter at this time because it is in quotes. It is just another character (part of a string literal). This allows you to have multiple cookies for the same top-level directory (up to about 14, I think). When you call document.cookie, it might look like this:

```
"PSWFirstCookie=stuff|and|too;PSWOtherCookie=
    more|useless|stuff;yetAnotherCookie=more..."
```

JavaScript knows that the stuff between "cookieName=" and the semicolon is one cookie. Each time you assign a value to document.cookie, some logic executes somewhere deep in the bowels of the JavaScript interpreter. It looks to see if the cookie name already exists for the current directory. If it does, it overwrites that cookie with the new value. If the cookie name does not exist there already, the JavaScript interpreter creates a new cookie with that name and tacks it onto the end of the existing document.cookie.

In other words, document.cookie can be made up of several individual cookies. Let's look at an example to get a handle on this idea. The following code is from *better_ cookies.html* on the CD.

```
<html>
<head>
    <title>Window Maker</title>
<script language="JavaScript">
<!--hide
cookieName = "PSWoodsCookie";
var expiry = new Date("December 31, 2002");
expiry=expiry.toGMTString();
```

```
function cookieSetter(){
     var someWords=new Array();
     for(i=1;i<=3;i++){
        someWords[i]=prompt("Type in short phrase "+ i, "");
     }
     var usefulInfo = someWords.join("|");
     document.cookie=cookieName + "=" + escape(usefulInfo)
   + ";expires=" + expiry;
    window.location.reload();
}
function cookieReader(){
   var theCookie = document.cookie;
   var splitAlongEqual=theCookie.split("=");
   var afterTheEqual = unescape(splitAlongEqual[1]);
   var splitAlongPipe = afterTheEqual.split("|");
        for (i=1;i<=3;i++){
        document.write("Phrase number " + i + " was \""
   + splitAlongPipe[i] + "\"<br>");
   }
}
//show-->
</script>
</head>
<body>
<script language="JavaScript">
<!--hide
if (document.cookie.indexOf(cookieName) != -1){
     cookieReader();
}else{
     document.write('<a href="#" onClick="cookieSetter();">
   You do not have a cookie. Set one now.</a><p>')
}
//show-->
</script>
<p>
You can reset your cookie if you like. Click
   <a href="#" onClick="cookieSetter('PSWoodsCookie');">here</a>.
<p>
Now look at the contents of document.cookie. Click
   <a href="#" onClick="alert(document.cookie);">here</a>.

</body>
</html>
```

The only really new part of the script is the line that writes the cookie. First, we have added the name of the cookie and an equal sign to the beginning of the cookie string. Next, we added an expiration date to the cookie. This is necessary if you want the cookie to survive between browser sessions. By default, the cookie expires when the user closes the browser. (I cheated and sneaked an expiration date into the first example.)

To see exactly how we got this date, look at the first two lines of the script. The expiration date of the cookie has to be in an arcane format called GMT. This is not a problem, though, because you can convert a date in any other format to this version by simply using a handy method of the date object toGMTString().

The rest of the script is really just string handling drudgery. You should be able to follow what is going on with all the pipe business. The pipe is an arbitrarily chosen delimiter that makes it relatively easy to break apart the string once we retrieve it from the cookie. You could use any format you want to save your cookie data.

Take some time to dig into this script. This method of storing and retrieving data—whether in the form of name-value pairs or just multiple strings—is relatively easy; but the elaborate string methods required are a pain. By the time you get to XML, you will be ready to send voluminous packets of data back and forth without jumping through a lot of hoops.

Other Cookie Considerations

There is one more attribute of cookies that you can cram onto that crowded little line: the scope of the cookie. As mentioned previously, the cookie refers to the directory of the originating document by default. If you want to change this, which you will almost certainly want to do, you have two options.

The first and most common option is to set the path (on the server). This is as simple as naming a folder in the directory path of the originating document that syou want to use. This has a simple syntax. You just tack it onto the end of your cookie, like so:

```
document.cookie=cookieName + "=" + escape(blahBlah)
    + ";expires=" + expiry + ";path=/myfolder";
```

Remember, you have to choose a folder that is above the originating document in the directory path. For instance, the above line of code would work for a document at the URL "http://stuff.com/myfolder/docs/archive/cookie_writer.html." The scope of the cookie would be everything in myfolder.

Another way to do it is to use "directory" instead of "path." The syntax is the same, except for the slash.

```
document.cookie=cookieName + "=" + escape(blahBlah)
   + ";expires=" + expiry + "; directory=pswoods.com";
```

The directory method is handy if you want to use the same cookie across multiple subdomains; for instance, if you wanted to use a global cookie for a username and password at sales.stuff.com, bs.stuff.com, and corporate.image.stuff.com.

What to Take Away from This Chapter

If you didn't pick up on the central message of this chapter, it is *everything in JavaScript is an object*. If you keep this in mind as you write your scripts, you will do well. Understanding how JavaScript is built from the top down will help you not only within this language, but also in every other language that you undertake to learn.

Flash, HTML, and the Browser

IN THIS CHAPTER:

Veteran Flashers remember a time when any kind of advanced client-side Web scripting had to be completed with JavaScript, passing variable values to Flash only after the interesting problem solving was done within the browser. Although Flash does have a better set of scripting tools now, it is still dwarfed by the magnificent power of JavaScript. For instance, JavaScript allows you to use regular expressions using the same syntax and vocabulary as Perl—a powerful toolset when you want to match strings against complex patterns (as with form validation, for instance). We will take an in-depth look at the regular expressions toolset in PHP for server-side pattern matching in Chapter 16. In addition, browser-specific client-side objects like "cookie" and "window" can only be accessed through JavaScript.

This chapter shows you how to connect Flash with the Web browser. We will cover the two different ways this happens, depending on platform, and how to control parameters in the <OBJECT> tag and <EMBED> tag. Each concept will be illustrated in an example.

Keep in mind, however, that this material is meant to be a theoretical background for you. There is a continually increasing number of ready-made solutions floating around the Web that allow you to complete most of these tasks with well-crafted scripts or graphical interfaces for your HTML editor. What we're trying to do here is provide enough background so that you can customize JavaScript generated from these interfaces. Without a few tidbits of knowledge about the inner mysteries of the Web browser, you would have a hard time knowing what is going on in these scripts.

Bridged Applications

As you may have guessed from the not so subtle foreboding in the previous chapter, the Flash Player becomes an object accessible via JavaScript when it is included in an HTML page. In a perfect world, that would be all you need to know to go to work, but client-side scripting is one of the least perfect worlds imaginable.

In addition to the eternally frustrating arbitrary differences between Netscape and Internet Explorer, you are dealing with entirely different technologies—completely divergent methods of embedding the Flash Player in the Web page. Not only that; there's a particular platform issue that makes applications using bridged Flash and JavaScript inaccessible to an appreciable portion of your potential Web audience.

Make no mistake—building this kind of application is currently a hard row to hoe. We can only hope that this style of scripting will become more compatible and more feasible in the future. The emergence of solutions for JavaScript/Flash bridged applications from Macromedia for the Dreamweaver products is an indication that this is a realistic dream.

Plug-in Versus ActiveX

The biggest difference between embedding methods on different browsers and platforms is between *plug-ins* and *ActiveX controls*. You probably already have a good idea of what a plug-in is—just a little application that runs inside the browser. Plug-ins typically have a few methods that can be executed via JavaScript, but not much else in the way of interacting with the resources on the client computer (the computer on which the Web browser is running).

ActiveX, on the other hand, is a nebulous adjective in the taxonomy of Microsoft products. In the context of Flash and other Web technologies, we are interested in ActiveX controls. ActiveX controls interact directly with other elements in the Microsoft *Component Object Model*, which is used for everything from 32-bit desktop applications to Windows itself.

The extent to which ActiveX can access the resources on the client computer is simultaneously a hope for the future of Web-based applications and a cause for concern. If you remember the early days of the Web, you will recall a big stir over this issue. People were in an uproar because of the lack of security offered to users of ActiveX components. The only security measure in place was a dialog when users installed a new ActiveX control—a dialog that included, " trust". This scheme persists as the basic security precaution; but the ruckus has died down. In general, users will install a new ActiveX control from a recognized company, especially if there is a promise of an entertaining payoff.

The cool thing about ActiveX for the Flash developer is that the Flash Player ActiveX control downloads automatically when required. The user doesn't have to *do* anything to keep up-to-date with the latest Flash Player (except to acquiesce to the agreement to accept updates). There are some parameters to control this behavior in the <OBJECT> tag, which we will get to later.

ActiveX runs on Wintel computers in Microsoft Internet Explorer. That's it. The rest of the mainstream browsers and platforms will be running the Flash Player as a plug-in. The immediate significance of this is that we will need a snippet of VBScript (the ActiveX lingua franca) to direct the flow of scripts on Windows/IE browsers to equivalent instructions.

ActiveX is a fascinating technology, despite its numerous serious drawbacks. If you are interested in learning more, check out this insightful and entertaining resource: http://www.njnet.edu.cn/info/ebook/activex/contents.htm. ActiveX offers the possibility to run complex applications inside a Web browser that use elements and resources from both the client and server machines, like server-based productivity applications. There have been numerous experiments with these types of applications, including one of my favorite places to see a good presentation of collected news sources, http://octopus.com.

The type of technology that plays back Flash content is one issue; the path to the Player is another. When we are ready to use the Flash Player's methods, we have to use the correct path to the Player's object, just like with any other object:

```
window.document.write("this is getting tricky");
```

In the previous line of code, we name the path to the document object, then name the method "write." Nothing tricky here. The document object is in the same path in any JavaScript-capable browser, but IE and Netscape have different paths for an embedded Flash Player. In Netscape, the path is "document.movieName," while in IE the path is "window.movieName." The easiest way to get over this hurdle is with a simple control structure:

```
function rewind(){
    if (navigator.appName.indexOf ("Microsoft") !=-1){
        window.flashMovie.gotoAndStop(1);
    }else{
        document.flashMovie.gotoAndStop(1);
    }
}
```

Unfortunately, such logic is necessary every time you want to call methods of the embedded Flash Player object. You have several choices for accomplishing this. You could simply use the same type of control structure every time you want to invoke a method; but that's not very good coding style. You could break this control structure out into its own function, where the function returns the path to the Flash Player object. If that method appeals to you, check out John Croteau's article at http:// www.flashbible.com/Members/FSCommand/FlashMethods.htm, where there are a half dozen different approaches to doing this.

I have come to the conclusion that the best approach to cross-platform, cross-browser compatibility is to simply detect the user agent type on the server side using a script and serve different documents for each application and platform. The commercial application BrowserHawk, which we will discuss at the end of this chapter, makes short work of this method, and it is much easier to keep your code clean. Assuming this scenario, the remainder of the examples in the chapter will use only the IE Flash Player object path. If you want to adapt these scripts to cover both types, you can easily add the logic to do so.

Embedded Multimedia Object Requirements

At this point you'll be glad to know that there are some common elements to all platforms and browsers when it comes to controlling an embedded Flash object with JavaScript. Following are the requirements that must be fulfilled before JavaScript can act on the Flash Player object.

▶ The multimedia object appears within the <OBJECT> tag (for ActiveX) or the <EMBED> tag (for plug-ins).

▶ The browser must recognize the SWF MIME type.

▶ The user must have a plug-in that can play the Flash file.

▶ The SWF file must be loaded. This doesn't necessarily mean that the entire file must be loaded, just everything in the scope of the Flash Player method you want to use.

Some of these concerns are obviously addressed in your browser detection scheme, but you should still keep all of these in mind if you want to build an application that executes a Flash Player method via JavaScript as soon as the page loads. In this kind of scenario, the easiest way to set your script in motion at the right time is to initiate it from the Flash movie.

Connecting Flash and the Browser

bridge.html

Let's pick apart an example to get an idea of how to build an application using JavaScript and Flash. We will be looking at the code from the example called *bridge.html* in the Bridge folder on the CD. Please take a moment to look at it in your browser, so that you will know what the desired result of each of these functions is.

We'll start with the parts of the script that will be common to all of the examples in this chapter. The following code is the last JavaScript function in the head of the document, plus one tiny snippet of VBScript.

```
//the function 'movieName_DoFSCommand(command, args)'
// is the default terminal for outgoing FS commands.
function bridge_DoFSCommand(command, args) {
    if (command == "alert"){
        alert(args);
```

```
    }else if (command == "popup"){
        popup(args);
    }else if (command == "changeBG"){
        changeBG();
    }else{
        alert("No FSCommand params rec'd.");
    }
}
// done hiding -->
</script>

<script LANGUAGE="VBScript">
<!--
//this little snippet just points the flash ActiveX control to
//                       'movieName_DoFSCommand()'.
Sub bridge_FSCommand(ByVal command, ByVal args)
    call bridge_DoFSCommand(command, args)
    end sub
//show-->
</script>
```

First off, look at all the comments in the script. Our scripts are getting a little more complicated now, and at this size, comments are mandatory in any scripting language.

The function bridge_DoFSCommand() is a standard feature in any page in which you want to receive JavaScript commands from Flash via FS commands. "Bridge" is the name of the embedded Flash object for this particular example. This part will need to change to match the name of the Flash Player object as you have named it in your individual movies. It takes as its arguments the "command" and "args" parameters from the Flash FS command action, as seen next.

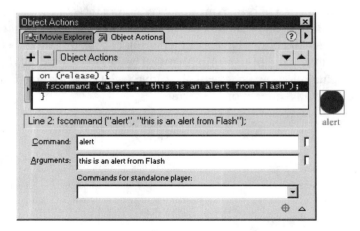

I typically use an if control structure to route the FS commands from Flash to different functions, as we did for the function changeBG();. As you can see, you can also just write their JavaScript in line.

TIP

Use this rule of thumb for determining whether to break out a piece of code into a separate function: if it is something you will reuse, or something that will take more than two or three lines to complete a single idea, it belongs in a separate function. In addition to preventing redundant code, this practice keeps your code clean and easy to read.

The little snippet of VBScript is the ActiveX equivalent of the bridge_DoFSCommand(). You could rewrite everything you do with JavaScript within this VBScript function, but that's not how we do things. Instead, we use it as a hub to reroute FS commands from the Flash Player ActiveX control to the JavaScript bridge_DoFSCommand() function. This is the best scenario because IE can easily execute core JavaScript without any problem, but you can't count on other browsers to deal with VBScript.

FS Commands and Flash Player Methods

Next we look at the functions initiated from the HTML links in the body of the page. These functions use methods of the Flash Player embedded object.

```
//these functions use methods of the flash player
// object to manipulate the flash movie with JavaScript.
function tellFlash(){
     var userInput = prompt("What do you want Flash to say?","");
     window.bridge.SetVariable("userInput", userInput);
}

function bigBoy(){
     var girth = windowbridge.TGetProperty("mc", 2);
     window.bridge.TSetProperty("mc",2, girth*2)
}

function spin(){
     window.bridge.TCallLabel("_root.circleMC","end");
}
```

The first function, tellFlash(), assigns the value from the user prompt to the variable userInput. It then feeds the variable's value into the global level of the Flash movie using the method SetVariable(). The first argument to this method is the name of the variable inside the Flash movie, while the second argument is the value. For a complete reference on Flash Player methods and properties, see http://www.macromedia.com/support/flash/publishexport/scriptingwithflash/scriptingwithflash_03.html.

The spin() function is nothing shocking. It calls a frame label within the named target. The target identifier "_root." is actually not necessary in this example; I just included it to demonstrate that you can reach any object within the movie, no matter how deep. If you don't understand this, don't worry. We will get into target paths in the next chapter.

The function in bigBoy(), on the other hand, is very interesting. In two short lines you have data flowing in both directions across our JavaScript/Flash bridge. TGetProperty() is only one of a number of Flash Player object methods that query the Flash movie for information and return it to the JavaScript function. In this case, we get the property XScale from the Movie clip instance named "mc."

Communicating Between Windows

slide_show.html, pic.html, flash.html, flash.swf

The previous example was hard on the eyes, so we'll do something pretty for the next exercise. Open the file *slide_show.html* on the CD. The application consists of the main page, *slide_show.html*, and two other pages opened from the main page in separate windows. The pop-up window with the Flash movie controls the other pop-up window to create a slide show. Let's look at the code in *slide_show.html* first.

```
<script language="JavaScript">
<!--hide
function popper(){
    if (navigator.appName.indexOf("Microsoft")!= -1) {
        pos1="left=25,top=25";
        pos2="left=300,top=175";
    }else {
        pos1="screenX=25,screenY=25";
        pos2="screenX=300,screenY=175";
    }
    theRealBigPopper(pos1,pos2);
}

function theRealBigPopper(pos1,pos2){
```

```
        flashWin=window.open("flash.html","flashWin","width=220,
height=170,location=no,menubar=no,resizable=yes," + (pos1)
+ ",status=no,toolbar=no");
        picWin = window.open("pics.html","picWin",
"width=420,height=325, location=no,menubar=no,resizable=yes,"
+ (pos2) + ",status=no,toolbar=no");
}

function next(){
        picWin.next();
}

function prev(){
picWin.prev();
}

function closer(){
        flashWin.close();
        picWin.close();
}
//show-->
</script>
```

Nothing new here. This page runs the popper() function as soon as it loads using the onLoad() attribute of the <BODY> tag. The JavaScript inside the quotes executes as soon as the entire HTML page is loaded, not counting images or embedded objects. In this page it looks like this:

```
<body onLoad="popper();">
```

Notice also that in this page the longest function is popper(), which deals with the differences in syntax between the two major browsers. This is just how it is with JavaScript. Now aren't you glad you chose Flash instead of DHTML?

The function closer() does exactly what you would expect—it closes the windows flashWin and picWin when it is called. The method for closing a window from Flash is one of the top 20 all-time most frequently asked questions on Flash bulletin boards and discussion groups. This is the method you use. You can also put it into the body tag of an HTML document and just load that document with a GetURL action from Flash. The body tag for such a document would look like the following line of code. Now you can be the smarty-pants-wise-guy who chimes in first the next time someone asks about this in your favorite Flash community!

```
<body onLoad="window.self.close();">
```

This popper function opens two new pages, picWin and flashWin. Notice how these objects come up again in the curious syntax in the "next" and "prev" functions.

```
picWin.prev();
```

This calls a custom object—in this case a function—inside the object picWin. Let's take a look at what is inside this object, which we will find in the document *pic.html* on the CD.

```
<script language="JavaScript">
<!--hide
var slideNumber=1;

function loadCarousel() {
    for(loop = 1; loop <= 12; loop++)
    {
        var loader = new Image();
        loader.src = "slide_show" + [loop] + ".jpg";
    }
}

function next(){
    slideNumber++;
        if (slideNumber == 13){
        slideNumber = 1;
    }
    document.images[0].src="slide_show" + slideNumber + ".jpg";
}

function prev(){
    slideNumber--;
    if (slideNumber == 0){
        slideNumber = 12;
    }
    document.images[0].src="slide_show" + slideNumber + ".jpg";
}

//show-->
</script>
</head>
```

```
<body onLoad="loadCarousel();">
<div align="center"><img src="slide_show1.jpg" name="theSlide">
</div>
```

Let's follow the script through the order in which it runs. We have another function being called from the onLoad attribute—the body tag loadCarousel(). The only purpose of this function is to load all the images into the memory of the client computer. This makes the image swap appear instantaneously.

The two remaining functions only execute when called, and you can see that there is nothing within this page that calls them. These are the functions being called from *slide_show.html*.

Notice how these functions name the image of which they change the source. Since the image was given a literal string for a name, it can also be called another way:

```
document.images[0].src="slide_show"
    + slideNumber + ".jpg";  //swap image
document.images.theSlide.src="slide_show"
    + slideNumber + ".jpg";//          same thing
```

Any images placed in an HTML page using the <IMG> tag are accessible via the "document.images" object, which takes the form of an array. Including the descriptive name attribute in the <IMG> tag merely makes it easier to come back and edit the script later.

The last page in this application that we need to look at is *flash.html* on the CD. This page contains an embedded Flash Player object—specifically, the movie *flash.swf*. Internally, this movie has two simple actions, as shown here:

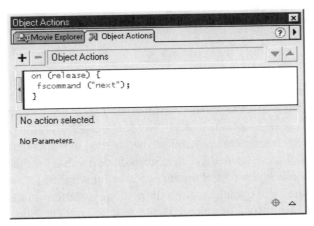

The script for this Flash/JavaScript bridge is more streamlined than what we've looked at so far. This is because data is only traveling one way across the bridge.

```
<script LANGUAGE="JavaScript">
<!--
//hand-coded functions
function prev(){
     window.opener.prev();
}

function next(){
     window.opener.next();
}

function flash_DoFSCommand(command, args) {
     if (command == "prev"){
          prev();
     }else if (command == "next"){
          next();
     }else{
          alert("No FSCommand params rec'd.");
     }
}
// done hiding -->
</script>
<script LANGUAGE="VBScript">
<!--
Sub flash_FSCommand(ByVal command, ByVal args)
     call flash_DoFSCommand(command, args)
     end sub
//show-->
</script>
```

Everything should be familiar except the "next" and "prev" functions. These functions call functions in another page, just like the first example of this section. Notice the object in which these functions reside: "window.opener." This is part of the core of the JavaScript DOM. It refers to the window that opened this one. Obviously, only pop-up windows that were opened via JavaScript have a value for this object.

To summarize, *slide_show.html* opens two pop-up windows. One of them loads a series of 12 images and cycles through them using a standard image swap. The other contains a Flash movie that controls the unit swaps. The Flash movie sends FS commands through a path from the flash_FSCommands function to the window that opened it to the other pop-up window to the "next" and "prev" functions.

Using Cookies to Add Client-Side Memory to a Flash Application

I really like this next application. In fact, I originally built it for myself to keep track of what I do with my time. (You know how sometimes days can just run away from you?) I happen to think that cookies are one of the most useful Web technologies. If it weren't for the difficulties of implementing a fully compatible cookie in Flash/JavaScript applications, I would use this type of application a lot more.

There is nothing new in this example, except the way we put everything together, and the code is thoroughly commented. I will just point out a few things that bear explanation.

The script starts with the flashReadCookie function, where we check to see if the cookie named captainsLog7 already exists on the client computer. The style of this function suggests the pessimistic view of the application. You generally want to put the most likely condition first in a control structure, so that the JavaScript interpreter can just look at the first possibility, match it, and exit the loop. In this function, our first condition is that the user's computer does not already have our cookie.

```
var check=document.cookie;
if (check.indexOf(cookieName) == -1)
{
```

At this point the next function that is likely to run is flashCookie, after the user types some input and presses ENTER. The next illustration shows this command in the Flash movie. Don't worry if you don't understand it. We will cover ActionScript thoroughly in Chapters 9 through 14.

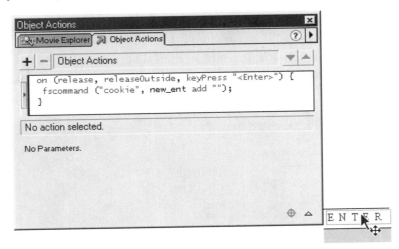

The function flashCookie begins with a standard date manipulation. All of this code is needed just to get that little time stamp.

```
function flashCookie(flashInput)
{
var days =new Array("Sun","Mon","Tues","Wed","Thu","Fri","Sat");
var myDate = new Date();
var myDayNumber = myDate.getDay();
var myDay = days[myDayNumber];
var myHour = myDate.getHours();
var myMinutes = myDate.getMinutes();
if (myMinutes < 10){myMinutes = "0" + myMinutes;}
var myTime = myDay + " [" + myHour + ":" + myMinutes + "] ";
```

You will have this type of scenario to get a date in a certain format over and over. You might as well develop a function and put it in your snippet library so you don't get sick of typing it. There are a few noteworthy things here. First, the method getDay() for a date object returns an integer between zero and seven, inclusive, with Sunday being the first day. We exploit this aspect of the method to return the correct text value for the current date from the array called days.

The single-line if loop corrects the value of the minutes variable if it doesn't contain a zero. This is so you don't return time that looks like "4:9" instead of "4:09." This line actually exposes a very interesting aspect of JavaScript:

```
myMinutes = "0" + myMinutes;
```

The variable myMinutes was a number up to this point. By simply adding a zero in quotes, it magically becomes a string without any special instructions. The same thing happens to myHour in the next line of the script.

Next the script executes a whole bunch of menial hacking to cut up the entire contents of the document.cookie into just a string that we want. We covered this in the previous chapter. The difference here is that we're not interested in name-value pairs; we just want one big string. Once we get the string, we return to the flashCookie function with the variable "the_values."

```
var muchoVal=the_values.length;
//if the cookie is more than a thousand chars,
   chop some chars off the end.
if (muchoVal > 1000){
   the_values=the_values.substring(0,1000)
}
```

Here "the_values" gets truncated if it is more than 1000 characters. After 1000 characters, the text will be off the visible page. In addition, a cookie has a maximum possible size of about 4KB, so you don't want to push your luck by overcrowding it with information. The if control structure translates "If the string is more than 1000 characters, cut it back down to 1000 characters."

At this point there's nothing left to do except roll everything into one string and write the cookie. We add the newline character manually so that there is a break between each line of user input.

```
cookieValue = myTime + flashInput+ "\n" + the_values;
setCookie(cookieName, cookieValue, retiresAt);
```

There's absolutely nothing tricky about the script. It's just long. In addition, the function names might be confusing because they are the culmination of a lot of snippet squirreling. This is typical of scripts that run on for more than 30 or 40 lines. Just make sure when you work on a long script that all the variable names are something that will make sense to you when you or someone else comes back to it. Another way to keep bits of script more manageable is to break them into separate JavaScript files, like the first example in Chapter 6. In this case, we could abstract the cookie reader and writer functions into their own JavaScript files.

Compatibility
flash.swf

At the time of this writing, the Mac version of IE can't run JavaScript/Flash bridged applications using FS commands. The calls you make to the Flash Player methods and the FS commands from the Player to the browser just evaporate. This is about as big as compatibility issues get. If you are developing for any kind of broad Web audience, you will have to carefully consider what to do with Mac/IE users when you employ bridged applications.

You might want to consider using the GetURL function in ActionScript instead of FS commands. Version 5 of IE for the Mac supports this kind of outgoing data. Instead of using an actual URL, type **javascript:**, followed by the exact script you want to execute. For instance, we might make this substitution in *flash.swf* in the slide show application:

```
fscommand ("prev");   //one way of doing it
getURL ("javascript:prev();");//same thing, only more compatible
```

It was actually necessary to use getURL in the slide show example to get it to work on both IE5 and Netscape Navigator on all platforms. For reasons hidden in the unfathomable depths of the application, Netscape doesn't like executing image swaps initiated from an FS command. This is a good illustration of how getURL is generally more compatible than FS commands.

Flash HTML

The HTML we use to embed the Flash Player in a Web page is easy to use and understand, and it works without a hitch across different browsers and platforms. Learning the different options available is just a matter of course for the Flash developer—part of your apprenticeship. This part of the chapter covers everything you need to know regarding HTML for everyday Flash applications.

Attribute Choices for <OBJECT> and <EMBED>

The <OBJECT> tag and the <EMBED> tag are alternate choices for embedding the Flash Player in an HTML page as an object. The <OBJECT> tag targets browsers that support embedded ActiveX controls (Microsoft Internet Explorer running on the Windows platform). The <EMBED> tag is used for the Netscape-style embedded plug-in object, which is used on every other Web browser/platform combination.

We will use the following example for the remainder of the discussion on Flash HTML tags. This set of tags is typical of a Flash application using FS commands.

```
<OBJECT
    classid="clsid:D27CDB6E-AE6D-11cf-96B8-444553540000"
  codebase="http://download.macromedia.com/pub
   /shockwave/cabs/flash/swflash.cab#version=5,0,0,0"
    ID=flashMovieName WIDTH=640 HEIGHT=480>
    <PARAM NAME=movie VALUE="flashMovieName.swf">
    <PARAM NAME=quality VALUE=high>
    <PARAM NAME=bgcolor VALUE=#FFFFFF>
    <EMBED
    src="flashMovieName.swf"
        quality=high bgcolor=#FFFFFF
        WIDTH=640 HEIGHT=480
        swLiveConnect=true
        NAME=flashMovieName
        TYPE="application/x-shockwave-flash"
        PLUGINSPAGE="http://www.macromedia.com/shockwave/
```

```
download/index.cgi?P1_Prod_Version=ShockwaveFlash">
    </EMBED>
</OBJECT>
```

First notice that the <EMBED> tag is nested within the <OBJECT> tag. Don't let this confuse you. They do the same thing. For IE running on Windows, the <OBJECT> tag is processed and the <EMBED> tag is ignored. For every other combination, the <OBJECT> tag is ignored and the <EMBED> tag is processed.

The first few attributes of the <OBJECT> tag *should* be mysterious to you unless you are an ActiveX programmer. The "classid" attribute is a static, specific identifier that applies only to the Flash ActiveX control. Never change this. The "codebase" attribute is a different story. The browser compares the version number in this attribute with the installed ActiveX control on the user's machine. If the codebase attribute designates a higher version number than what is already installed, the new Player downloads automatically.

There is an analogous attribute within the <EMBED> tag: "PLUGINSPAGE." This isn't quite as slick as the ActiveX approach. If the browser reads the <EMBED> tag and ignores the <OBJECT> tag, it uses this attribute to check whether or not any version of the plug-in is installed. If it is completely absent, it offers the user the option to go to the plug-in download page.

The "ID" attribute of the <OBJECT> tag gives the embedded ActiveX control a name by which to refer to it. This is what makes window.flashMovieName point to this ActiveX control. The analogous attribute in the <EMBED> tag is "name."

The meaning of the rest of the tags is obvious, but we will belabor the subject in the interest of being thorough. First look at the "quality" attribute. The possible values are best, high, autohigh, autolow, and low. The best choice for any widely distributed animated Flash application (*just about everything you build*) is either autohigh or autolow.

Autohigh begins with anti-aliasing turned on, with smoothing applied to bitmaps. If playback begins to fall behind because the processor can't keep up, these appearance features are dropped in favor of faster playback, which is generally a good trade-off. Using this feature ensures that users on slower machines will not suffer huge skips while your movie bogs down the Flash Player.

Autolow is the frowning, sensible identical cousin to autohigh. It starts with the assumption that the client processor is going to need all the help it can get, turning off anti-aliasing at first. Only when it is sure that the processor can handle the animation will it reinstate the high-quality appearance features.

The swLiveConnect attribute in the <EMBED> tag is an unfortunate necessity for running a Flash/JavaScript bridged application. Setting this attribute to true tells the browser to start the Java virtual machine, which is a considerable load on any system, given the user's expectation for lightweight Web applications. Enable this attribute only when you need to have Flash and JavaScript communicate.

There are lots of additional parameters available, but the usefulness declines sharply at this point. You have "play" and "loop," each of which can be either true or false. As we will learn in the next chapter, these parameters should really be controlled within the Flash movie.

The "scale" attribute is an interesting one. The possible values are showall, noborder, and exact fit. Exact fit stretches the movie to fit the specified dimensions without trying to maintain the height/width ratio. The other two values maintain this ratio. Showall places emphasis on fitting the entire stage into the designated area, while noborder focuses on filling the entire space.

The "base" attribute can be used to resolve relative URLs. For instance, if you have a directory of Flash movies that interact with PHP pages in another directory, you might save a lot of typing and troubleshooting by using this attribute.

Templates

FS _ template.html

You will undoubtedly develop your own preferences for what goes into your Flash HTML, specific to different kinds of applications. Flash provides a brilliant tool to help you streamline the process of customizing HTML for different applications. This tool takes the form of templates. Templates are the HTML documents that reside in the Html folder in your Flash installation directory. They are fully customizable.

The Flash implementation of HTML templates is like a miniature Web publishing system using simple placeholders that are populated by variables from the Flash authoring environment. You can use these placeholders to reduce or even eliminate the need for manual markup or coding in the pages you publish from Flash, including complex applications with JavaScript.

I have included a sample template that incorporates some of the JavaScript functions we have been using in this chapter. Let's take a look at this template, *FS _ template.html* on the CD.

```
$TTPSW_FSCommand
$DSPSWoods' Custom FSCommand Template$DF
<HTML>
<HEAD>
<TITLE>$TI</TITLE>
<script LANGUAGE="JavaScript">
<!--
function $TI_DoFSCommand(command, args) {
    if (command == "alert"){
        alert(args)
    }else{
```

```
                alert("No FSCommand params rec'd.");
        }
}
// done hiding -->
</script>

<script LANGUAGE="VBScript">
<!--
Sub $TI_FSCommand(ByVal command, ByVal args)
     call $TI_DoFSCommand(command, args)
     end sub
//show-->

</script>
</HEAD>
<BODY bgcolor="$BG">
<OBJECT classid="clsid:D27CDB6E-AE6D-11cf-96B8-444553540000"
codebase="http://download.macromedia.com/pub/shockwave/
    cabs/flash/swflash.cab#version=5,0,0,0"
 ID="$TI" WIDTH=$WI HEIGHT=$HE>
 $PO
<EMBED $PE WIDTH=$WI HEIGHT=$HEsw      LiveConnect=true NAME="$TI"
 TYPE="application/x-shockwave-flash"
 PLUGINSPAGE="http://www.macromedia.com/shockwave
    /download/index.cgi?P1_Prod_Version=ShockwaveFlash"></EMBED>
</OBJECT></BODY></HTML>
```

Everything in this example with a dollar sign in front of it is a placeholder that will be filled in when you publish your Flash movie, as seen in the following image. Notice that the $TT and $DS variables (template title and description start) show up in the export dialog.

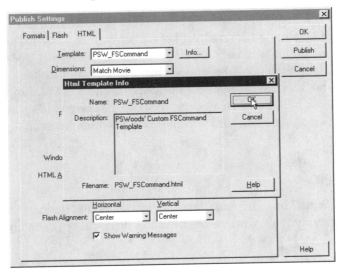

The title ($TI) placeholder pops up eight times in this template. We use the title of the SWF as the name of the embedded Flash Player object for the sake of simplicity. If you do this, make sure you don't use the underscore character (_) in the name of your Flash movie because it will screw up the pointers to the *_FSCommand() function. Notice that all of our JavaScript functions will be named automatically. That's worth a lot of typing and debugging right there. I strongly recommend building your own templates for each general application you develop (one for Flash/JavaScript bridged applications, one for a SWF in an invisible frameset for full-screen effect, etc.). For a complete list of template variables, see Appendix C.

Dreamweaver Integration

Macromedia offers a small array of free fabricated JavaScript functions to control a Flash movie that you can drop into an HTML page using the slick Dreamweaver behaviors interface. These are available at http://Macromedia.com/exchange. The scripts cover the basics, focusing mostly on playback, but there is also a routine for retrieving cookies.

Once you become comfortable with the Macromedia Extension Manager, you will probably want to start crafting your own behaviors to use with Dreamweaver based on your needs. This isn't much harder than creating your own HTML templates for the Flash authoring tool.

Browser/Plug-in Detection

I don't usually give away the ending to a story, but in this case I feel it is my duty. We're going to talk about the basics of browser and plug-in detection, but we're not going to build a comprehensive "net" or detection scheme. Although the basic concepts involved are much easier to swallow than most of what we've already done in this chapter, building a good detection scheme is a giant, thankless task. It is best left to people who hack JavaScript and VBScript for this kind of thing all day every day. It's not so much that it takes a genius to write the scripts; it's just that it takes a huge amount of time, patience, and testing (none of which I personally am well suited for).

The Basic Idea

The basic idea behind browser and plug-in detection is that the performance of Flash and JavaScript and how they interact is radically different between browsers and platforms—even between different versions of the same browser, thanks to the marketing geniuses who built the browsers that everyone uses.

So developers must make decisions—*big* decisions. You must decide first how low you are willing to limbo to make your content backward compatible. You have to decide whether to force users to install the Flash plug-in or a modern browser. Then you have to decide whether to offer some watered-down design for these mysterious mountain people who don't have this free technology. And then you have to decide whether to deliver the non-Flash content via redirection or by dynamically generating it in the same page. But you can't execute any of your decisions at runtime until you know which browser and plug-in the user has.

This happens in two basic stages: using client-side scripting to look for the Flash Player plug-in or ActiveX component, and reading the "$version" variable within the Flash movie. Let's look at how the first one works in the context of JavaScript.

Outside the world of IE and Windows, we may safely assume the browser treats the Flash Player object as a plug-in accessible via JavaScript. While the embedded object is available through the "embeds[ ]" array, the entry that records the Player itself is found in an array called "plugins," which is under "navigator" in the DOM. We can write a simple query in a single line to check for the installation of the Flash Player, like this:

```
if(navigator.plugins["Shockwave Flash"]){ do some stuff...
```

It's that simple. If everyone in the entire world used Netscape, version 3 and up, our entire detection scheme wouldn't be much more complex than that.

Using a Commercial Solution

News flash: Not everyone uses the same browser! IE makes things complicated. First of all, IE on the Windows platform treats the Flash Player as an ActiveX control. For this reason, you need to have some VBScript sprinkled into your detection scheme. The other quirky thing about IE before version 5.0 is that you can't detect the Flash Player at all on the Mac platform.

These little tidbits are more than an interesting slice of life in the day of the JavaScript hacker. These factors, along with a dozen others, are the reasons that a comprehensive detection script is a big application combining separate files, languages, and techniques, instead of a couple lines in the head of your HTML document.

Luckily, some tenacious, detail-conscious hackers have blazed a trail before us. There are about half a dozen widely distributed, well-known detection applications that require nothing more of you than to plug in values for a few variables. We'll look at three different detection schemes that you might want to use instead of undertaking to reinvent the wheel yourself.

First, Macromedia offers its Flash Deployment Kit free of charge at http://macromedia.com/exchange. If for some reason you don't have Dreamweaver, you can use the deployment kit simply as a template for your Flash applications, manually updating variable values to fit your needs specific to the application. Otherwise, get the Flash 5 Dreamweaver integration kit, which includes a graphical interface for the detection application and lots of other features. The dialog shown next constructs the detection application based on your input.

Now we've gone from a simple if control block to an impossibly complex application to something that's at least as easy as our simple script. This is my personal favorite among the detection solutions available at the time of writing.

Old-school Flash guru Colin Moock has been dealing with Flash Player and browser detection since Flash was a pup, and he makes his own effective approach commercially available at his Web site, http://moock.org. His original script is a similar approach to the more recently emerged Macromedia equivalent. He uses a combination of JavaScript and VBScript abstracted by function into separate files. If you don't have Dreamweaver and you want a script that is very easy to customize by changing the values of a couple of variables, this is for you.

The last detection solution I want to mention is called BrowserHawk (http://browserhawk.com), a Java server component (there is an ActiveX/COM version for IIS nuts) that does everything the client-side solutions do, plus some other stuff.

The biggest difference between BrowserHawk and the type of JavaScript detection schemes we've already talked about is that you send more precisely targeted content to a specific browser. In other words, instead of sending 15 control structures in the head of an HTML page to address all the differences between Netscape and IE, you send either the code for Netscape or the code for IE.

Another advantage of this particular product is that it automatically queries the manufacturer's database for updates. This takes the pressure off you to maintain your detection application.

BrowserHawk also has a lot of other little knickknacks that seem like they would be really useful for high-traffic sites. For instance, it gives you the option of returning <META> tags only to search engines spiders, in case you are worried about other people in your industry stealing your secret method for getting high search rankings. This is not the first application of its kind, but it's the first I've seen or heard of that is cheap, easy to use, and effective. BrowserHawk is a good choice for high-traffic sites that want to serve Flash content. Figure 8-1 shows the interface for the editor component of the BrowserHawk software. This is where you can visually set up rules and associations for different browsers.

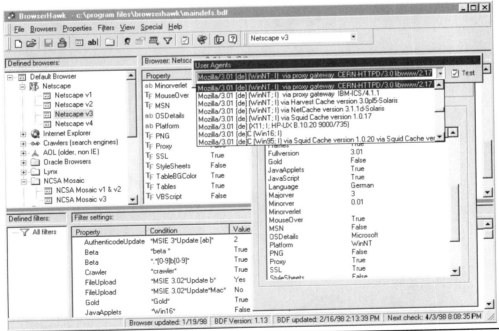

Figure 8.1   *Use BrowserHawk's editing component to set up rules and associations for a range of browsers.*

What to Take Away from This Chapter

Putting Flash content into a Web page is not a simple matter. Understanding the bridge between the Flash Player and the browser is the bridge between the Flash developer and rest of the Web development world. Of paramount importance is understanding all of the caveats, cross-platform differences, cross-browser annoyances, and generally how the Flash Player behaves in every environment. Once you have figured all of that out, your next big job is to assemble some object-oriented solutions—whether your own or a set of third-party plug-ins.

PART III

ActionScript

OBJECTIVES

- ► ActionScript Overview

- ► Learn All About Movie Clips

- ► Build Projects Using Smart Clips

- ► Deconstruct Examples of Programmatic Movement

- ► Acquire Preparatory Skills for Working with Dynamic Data Sources

- ► Understand URL Encoding and HTTP Methods Get and Post

Introduction to ActionScript

IN THIS CHAPTER:

JavaScript Differences

ActionScript Object Models

Where ActionScript Can Fit into a Flash Movie

Deprecated Actions

ActionScript Panel Options

ActionScript Flow Control

This chapter is an introduction to Flash ActionScript. I'm assuming that you now understand JavaScript, whether from the previous three chapters or from your own experience. As we go through this chapter, I won't stop to explain things that were covered in the JavaScript section.

We will start with a comparison between JavaScript and ActionScript, moving on to a demonstration of all the places within a Flash movie where ActionScript can reside. Finally, we will cover the ins and outs of the ActionScript panel in the Flash authoring environment, using the most common basic playback actions as examples.

JavaScript Differences

If you have spent any amount of time developing in Flash 5, you have already heard some discussion on the similarities and differences between Flash 5 ActionScript and JavaScript. I will try to give the subject a comprehensive treatment without succumbing to the developer's most alluring temptation: ranting over minutiae.

Access to Objects

You may have wondered why we spent all that time in the previous chapter on developing a bridge to manipulate windows and cookies. If JavaScript is so similar to ActionScript, wouldn't it make more sense to access these objects directly from Flash? The problem is that you can't access any of the window-specific objects from Flash.

This makes sense if you think about it. The Flash Player itself is an embedded object within the window in the JavaScript DOM. Therefore, the broadest scope of any ActionScript function or method is the Flash Player. There are plenty of actions that have effects outside the Player, but these are accomplished by exchanging data at the border between the Player and some external medium (usually the Web browser), as we saw in the previous chapter.

Flash-Specific Objects

Although Flash and JavaScript share a core complement of objects, Flash contains objects not found in JavaScript, and vice versa. For instance, objects like "window.history" or "document.cookie" would make no sense within a Flash movie, so there are no such objects within ActionScript. In addition, objects that exist in both Flash and JavaScript, such as "date," are not accessible between a Flash movie and JavaScript without building a bridged application as we did in the previous chapter. In other words, you can't define a variable called "theDay" using the Date object in JavaScript and expect to be able to use that variable automatically in Flash.

The up side of all this is that Flash has a ton of custom objects to make your life easier. For instance, "color" is an object in Flash that you can use to dynamically control the RGB color values of a Movie clip. The coolest object built into Flash 5 ActionScript is "XML," and we will be spending a great deal of time exploring the subject and all its methods in Chapter 18. This object allows you to exchange data to and from Flash in structured packets.

There are also objects for sounds, Movie clips, and mouse events, each with a dazzling array of methods to make your work easier. Macromedia did a very good job of dividing the elements of a Flash movie and assigning them to objects. Each object has an impressive complement of useful and intuitively named methods and handlers.

Limited Scope of "function" and "eval"

In the previous three chapters of the book, we saw "eval" used as a directive to process everything within a string literal as raw JavaScript. We called this a JavaScript interpreter within an interpreter. The way eval works in ActionScript is a little more watered down. In ActionScript, eval really means "evaluate variable references." eval in ActionScript cannot be used to evaluate statements. The following code shows two expressions using eval in ActionScript.

```
a=2;
b=4;
c=eval("a")+b;   //kosher -- c gets value of 6
c=eval("a+b");   //doesn't work -- c is undefined
```

The way you build functions in ActionScript is also limited relative to JavaScript, but this is no cause for alarm. The following code shows an alternative method for building a function in JavaScript using a built-in constructor.

```
var circleArea = new Function("r", "return Math.Pi*(r * r)");
document.write(circleArea(7)) ;
```

We didn't cover this built-in JavaScript constructor in any of the previous chapters because it is generally less efficient than the standard way of building a function. Using the function constructor requires the function to be evaluated every time it is called, which works out to poorer performance. On the off chance that you are an experienced JavaScript coder and you use this constructor, just be aware that you can't use it in Flash.

The last critical difference between JavaScript and Flash that you need to be aware of is the character sets used by each. We already know that JavaScript uses Unicode, but Flash uses something slightly different—ISO-8859-1 and Shift-JIS. You can think of all of these character sets as extensions of the ASCII character set, which encompasses 99.9 percent of the work you're likely to do in Flash. If you don't already know an application where the character sets will make a difference, I wouldn't worry about it.

What Is an Object in Flash?

Programmatic_slug_path.swf, slug.swf

If you got sick of hearing about objects in the previous section, you should take a swig of Pepto-Bismol before you read the next paragraph. Flash's approach to objects is similar to that of JavaScript (on the simple side), but there are added dimensions in Flash.

For instance, Movie clips are treated as objects within Flash. Regardless of the ActionScript code you have attached to a Movie clip, the clip itself is an object with built-in methods and properties galore. Look at the example *Programmatic_slug_path.swf* on the CD. The following code is repeated over and over to make the slug move diagonally from upper left to lower right.

```
if(slug._x<525){
slug._x+=5;
slug._y+=5;
}
```

This code utilizes two of the many built-in properties that are present at all times in all Movie clip instances on the stage. These are "_x," the horizontal position in pixels from the upper-left corner of the stage, and "_y," the vertical position from the same point.

Flash also has the ability to treat external files as objects. This aspect of Flash is greatly expanded in Flash 5. This is one of the clear signals that our favorite multimedia technology is ready to play with the grown-ups in the Web world.

You probably already know that Flash can load external SWFs into any level of a movie, including any Movie clip. This is worth dwelling on for a moment. One of the most interesting things about importing an external SWF into a Movie clip or movie "_level" is that the imported movie takes on all the properties of its container.

In other words, if you import *slug.swf* into a Movie clip instance named "Bob," the slug movie will be positioned where Bob was, have the same scaling, rotation, and color effects applied—you name it.

This little nugget can be very handy. Suppose, for instance, you want to apply humorous deformations to people's faces, with the selection of the images being based on user input. Instead of either hacking a mile of code or storing huge Movie clips in the movie—the same deformation for each image—you use the container Movie clip as a constructor of sorts. The cool thing is that you build the constructor visually using the native tools in the Flash authoring environment. Remember this when you want to apply the same properties to multiple Movie clips or to a dynamically selected Movie clip—importing a SWF is usually the best way to do it.

The most important type of external object in Flash—at least for buzzword compliance and getting you into the inner sanctum of your favorite discussion forum—is XML. We will be spending a great amount of time covering XML in Chapter 18, but it is worth mentioning here. The basic idea behind loading an XML document into a Flash movie is that you are creating an object with a custom hierarchy. The hierarchy is defined within the XML document, where data is arranged and described. You could think of an XML object loaded from an external file as the ultimate array. You could also think of it as the result of a database query.

In a more banal sense, everything you can see on the stage and in the work area of a Flash movie is an object. Everything that is rendered as vectors gets stored as an object within the FLA. This may seem a little less practical in terms of how to code a cool game, but this is fundamental to understanding how Flash thinks.

Finally, everything we talked about in JavaScript is an object in Flash. Native objects, custom objects, functions, arrays, and so on, all act as objects, just like they do in JavaScript.

ActionScript Object Models

We covered the basics of ECMAScript in the section on JavaScript. The good news is that almost everything we learned is going to apply in ActionScript. The other good news is that the things that don't apply, such as window manipulation and cookies, will probably be useful to you in your everyday Web development. Finally, the best news: all the new stuff you have to learn for ActionScript deals with Flash-specific objects that are designed to make your life easier. There's no bad news.

Table 9-1 shows which objects we covered in the JavaScript section first as objects that are unique to Flash. All of the built-in objects in Flash are listed in this table.

Similar to JavaScript	Unique to Flash
Array	Color
Boolean	Key
Date	Mouse
Math	Selection
Number	Sound
Object	XML
String	XMLSocket
Movie clip	

Table 9.1   *Flash's Built-in Objects*

The Movie clip object is by far the most useful and interesting object in the Flash environment. I have listed it across both columns of the table, even though it is unique to Flash. A closer look at some of the uses for this object will reveal why I have done this.

Paths to Objects

customDOM

In Flash, every object besides Movie clip is accessible the way math and date are available in JavaScript. For example, you can call the hide and show methods of the Mouse object from anywhere in a Flash movie; you don't have to define a path like window.document.mouse.

In JavaScript, we call this the Document Object Model. This static structure provides us with a clear, easy-to-understand way to call all the different parts of a document containing JavaScript.

On the surface, it appears that there is no such structure in Flash. You can call any built-in object from anywhere in the movie. However, as we begin to dig into ActionScript, you will notice that paths to objects take on a familiar form, and if you think about it, you will realize that the way you place nested Movie clips within a Flash movie is a lot like building your own Document Object Model. Let's look at an example. This is from *customDOM* on the CD.

```
var boxes=new Array("enter name","enter rank","serial number");
document.form.name=boxes[0];
document.form.rank=boxes[1];
```

```
document.form.serial=boxes[2];

if (boxes.length>1){
    _root.document.title="Some Questions";
}else{
    _root.document.title="A Question";
}
```

Now this example is a little bit ridiculous from a functional standpoint: we have a logical control structure to query the length of an array that we just wrote out by hand. The point is the structure of the Movie clips. I have named them to mimic the structure of an HTML document containing JavaScript. The name "_root" is a reserved word in ActionScript that refers to the main timeline of the movie. It is analogous to "_level0" in Flash 4.

The rest of the elements are accessible according to their place in the overall hierarchy, just as in JavaScript. In our example, "title" is the name of a dynamic text field inside the Movie clip instance named "document."

These are the names given to the Movie clip *instances* on the stage, not the names of the Movie clips in the library. The following illustration shows the name "form" being assigned to the Movie clip of the same name. The name could just as easily have been "ArchieBunker," which rounds out my point about the nature of Movie clips. By choosing a structure and naming convention for your Movie clips, you are really creating a custom Document Object Model.

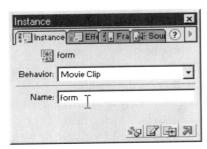

As your Flash applications grow in complexity, you may find it helpful to use a Flash movie with a standard Movie clip structure as a template. For instance, you may be in the habit of loading a separate HTML page for a Flash movie with a fill-out form. In this case, the fastest, easiest way to build this application without errors is to do it the same way every time.

This accomplishes roughly the same thing as a SmartClip or a Movie clip in the permanent library, but the shades of meaning are a little different. With the Movie clip that you drop into your movie, you are required to make decisions about what to name the clip and where to place it in the movie hierarchy, whereas an FLA used as a template allows you to plug in a few variables and be on your merry way.

Mileage will vary greatly among practitioners of this method. If you have followed the train of thought this far, you should be starting to develop a sense of the most important fundamental verity of Flash ActionScripting.

It is commonly thought and advertised among commercial proponents of Flash (as well as many high-profile Flash designers) that the most useful feature of a Movie clip is an independent timeline. This may be true for designers using Flash primarily for hard-coded animation, but looking around, you have to wonder if that's what developers (and audiences) are really interested in. My humble hypothesis is that Movie clips are most useful to mature developers as a means of structuring the logic of the Flash application.

Consider the following hypothetical example. Suppose we wanted to add another slug to the first example in this chapter. In addition to the slug that moves from top left to bottom right, now we want one that moves from right to left horizontally, much slower than the first slug. Would it make more sense to have two Movie clips, each with tweened animation, or would it make more sense to simply name another instance of the same Movie clip? In terms of file size, the latter makes more sense by a factor of about 10.

To be fair to timelines, I should mention that timelines are the very thing that allowed developers to create complex applications in Flash 4. Things like two frame loops to continuously check or update elements, frame labels on the main timeline to mark sections of the application, and alpha tweens were all clever hacks, and useful in their time. That time has now passed, and Flash 5 offers much better tools to manage the elements of your application. If you really dig into the uses of methods like attachMovie and handlers like onClipEvent(enterFrame), you will start to write cleaner applications that rely less on the timeline.

Timelines in Movie clips are not likely to go away anytime soon. However, timelines in Movie clips are also not likely to be a major factor in professional Flash development that isn't focused on hard-coded animation for entertainment. Keep this in mind as we talk about ActionScript. We will cover Movie clips in depth in the next chapter.

Access to Built-in Objects, Properties, and Methods

dogConstructor.fla

You have probably already figured out that since the dot syntax for accessing objects works the same as in JavaScript, you can easily *port* (attached to a new programming environment) JavaScript applications to Flash that use objects common to both. The following code is from *dogConstructor.fla* on the CD. It uses the "object" object. This code is unchanged from when we first saw it in Chapter 7, except that we've replaced "alert" with "trace."

```
function dog(name, color, age){
this.name=name;
this.color=color;
this.age=age;
this.numLegs=4;
this.tail=true;
this.intro=shortIntroduction;
}

var huck = new dog("Huckleberry", "mostly white with rusty ears",
"5 months");
var mopey = new dog("Mr. Mopey", "mousy brown with grey streaks",
"17 years");

mopey.numLegs=3;

function shortIntroduction(){
    trace("This is " + this.name + ". As you can see,  " + this.name
+ " is " + this.color + ". He is " + this.age + " old.");
    if ((this.tail == true) && (this.numLegs == 4)){
        trace("He has four legs and a tail.");|
    }
}

huck.intro();
mopey.intro();
```

Here we see the constructor function "dog" using the built-in characteristics of the object object, just as we did in the JavaScript section. At this point, it should come as no surprise that methods of the objects, such as string and math, work exactly as they do in JavaScript. Following is a smattering of examples:

```
var myString="This is like, totally Quwell.";
var whereIsQ=myString.indexOf("Q");
var myNum=Math.sqrt(5);
var myWholeNum=Math.round(myNum); //etc...
```

So core ECMAScript works inside Flash. What's even better, all of the built-in objects unique to Flash have their own methods and properties. We saw two of the most common ones in a slug example: _x and _y.

The underscore is a vestige of Flash 4. It indicates that these are built-in properties. Following is an illustration showing properties inherited by all Movie clips.

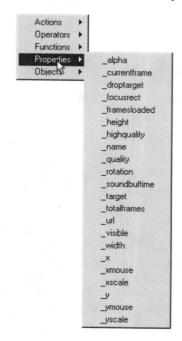

Where ActionScript Can Fit into a Flash Movie
slide_show.fla

In this part of the chapter, we will use *slide_show.fla* on the CD as an example. This application shows some of the different places that ActionScript can reside within a Flash application. We will discover that with each different location for ActionScript, there is a unique nuance to how the script executes, how it is called, and how wide its default scope is. There are strengths and weaknesses in each of the different choices for where to put ActionScript in your Flash application.

Main Timeline

slide_show.fla

To veteran Flashers, timelines are the most familiar place to put ActionScript. Although there are more options nowadays, timeline-based ActionScript remains a good method for building scripts that are sensitive to the context of the Flash movie playback.

The first example we will look at in this chapter uses functions at the root-level timeline, also known as the main timeline. This code is from *slide_show.fla* on the CD.

```
var counter=1;
var numSlides=12;
var oldSwapNum=1;

function loadPic(counter){
     attachMovie( "ph", ["ph"+counter], counter );
     loadMovie(["ss"+counter+".swf"],["ph"+counter]);
     _root["ph" + counter]._x=650;
     _root["ph" + counter]._y=490;
}

function terminal(){
     nav.duplicator(counter);
     counter++;
     if (counter<=numSlides){
          loadPic(counter);
     }
}

function picSwapper(swapNum){
     _root["ph" + oldSwapNum]._x=650;
     _root["ph" + oldSwapNum]._y=490;
     _root["ph" + swapNum]._x=210;
     _root["ph" + swapNum]._y=100;
     oldSwapNum=swapNum;
}

loadPic(counter);
```

This example uses the main timeline as the central terminal for all the actions in the application. There is one particular action that requires a little bit of extra attention before we continue: attachMovie is used to pull a Movie clip out of the library, give it an instance name, and assign it to a z-index depth. The syntax looks like this:

```
attachMovie(name of the Movie clip, instance name, z-index depth);
```

You assign the name of the Movie clip in the Linkage dialog, just as we did for a shared library item in Chapter 2. The following image shows the Linkage dialog for the "placeholder" Movie clip in this example.

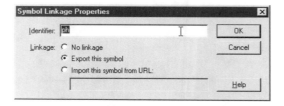

NOTE

The first argument of the attachMovie action is the name you give the Movie clip in the Linkage dialog, not the name of the Movie clip as it appears in the library.

The other thing to notice about this piece of code is how we refer to the new Movie clip instances that we create. When we name them in the attachMovie action, we call them by the arbitrary name "ph" (short for placeholder), plus a suffix generated by the counter variable. Using this method, Movie clip instances will have the names "ph1," "ph2," and so on. We do this so we can keep track of the different Movie clip instances. This is a very common coding practice.

After we load the SWF into the placeholder, we set the x and y coordinates. This presents a problem because we can't use a combination of string literals and variables and the dot-delimited path syntax.

It turns out that the brackets we use for naming individual array elements work just as well as dots for naming a path to an object. This makes sense when you think about it (or if you even vaguely remember any of my incessant droning about the object nature of all elements in JavaScript and Flash). When we use the following code, we are referring to a built-in array of Movie clip instances that is always available from the _root object:

```
_root["ph" + counter]._x=650;
```

To get the big picture, let's look at how the entire application fits together. The main idea is that we are pulling Movie clips out of the library to making navigation buttons for each external SWF we load. In other words, when a SWF is loaded, its button appears, but not before. This is an alternative solution to the problem of what to show while heavy files are loading. We only give the user the option to view those things that *can* be viewed. The slick part is that we give that option immediately and update it in real time.

Looking at the code above, it is easy to see how we load the first external SWF, but it is not clear anywhere within the FLA how or even *whether* an additional movie will be loaded. The loadMovie action only occurs within the loadPic function, and it is only called once within this FLA. The answer is in *slides.fla.*

External File

slides.fla, slideShow.swf

The second frame of the main timeline in *slides.fla* contains the following action. This Flash file is used to publish every one of the slide SWFs.

```
_root.terminal();
stop();
```

When loaded into *slideShow.swf*, this ActionScript acts just as it would if it were on the timeline of a nested Movie clip. It calls the function "terminal" on the main timeline, which increments a control variable called counter and starts the next loadPic function. This action will not be executed until the image has fully loaded. This is because the SWF will not reach the actions in the second frame until the image in the first frame has loaded.

Using this ActionScript in this location is especially handy in this application. It allows us to control which images a user can try to view without using a clunky timeline structure or a complicated loading script.

Nested Movie Clips

Let's look at the code that duplicates the buttons. This is found on the timeline in the Movie clip "navigation." The instance of this Movie clip on the stage is called "nav."

```
MCx=0;
MCy=0;

function duplicator(num){
if((num-1) % 3 == 0){
   MCx=0;
   MCy+=50;
}
_root.nav.attachMovie( "thumbnail", "thumbnail"+num, num )
_root.nav["thumbnail"+num]._x=MCx;
_root.nav["thumbnail"+num]._y=MCy;
_root.nav["thumbnail"+num].picNum=num;
MCx+=50;
}
```

This code is very similar to what we saw on the main timeline of the movie. The main difference is that we are now on the timeline of the Movie clip. Notice that we are still not concerned with the playback of the timeline; this is just a convenient way of placing these Movie clips with some simple code.

The primary difference between this code and the functions in the main timeline of the movie is how we place the Movie clips on the stage. If you look at the last line of the duplicator function, you see that we place each Movie clip 50 pixels to the right of the previous one. The first line of code in this function uses the modulo (%) to start a new line *after* every third Movie clip. The subtitle for this code is something like this: "Subtract one from 'num.' If the remainder of this number divided by three is zero, then a row of three has been filled up. Start a new line." This is why you see rows of three when you play the movie. The following line of code assigns the number to the text field labeled picNum in each Movie clip.

```
_root.nav["thumbnail"+num].picNum=num;
```

Notice that we use _root.nav throughout this block of code to refer to Movie clip itself. We could just as easily have used "this." In other words, it can also look like this:

```
MCx=0;
MCy=0;

function duplicator(num){
if((num-1) % 3==0){
   MCx=0;
   MCy+=50;
}
this.attachMovie( "thumbnail", "thumbnail"+num, num );
this["thumbnail"+num]._x=MCx;
```

```
this["thumbnail"+num]._y=MCy;
this["thumbnail"+num].picNum=num;
MCx+=50;
}
```

In this contrived example, there are not a whole lot of good reasons to embed this code in a Movie clip timeline. In this case, the most attractive benefit of doing it this way is that we can simply drag the Movie clip on the main stage to control the layout. Otherwise, we would either have to set the x and y coordinates of the first Movie clip we attach manually or use a dummy Movie clip and get its x and y coordinates with additional ActionScript.

Button

If you dealt with Flash 4 at all, you probably know just about everything there is to know about buttons. We will still touch on them briefly. (I will try to make it interesting.) Here is the code from the only button in our movie. You won't find it on the stage anywhere, because it resides in a Movie clip that gets pulled onto the stage when the movie runs. You can find it by double-clicking on the Movie clip "thumbnail" in the library.

```
on (release) {
    _root.picSwapper(this.picNum);
}
```

This is interesting because this code will be reused for each Movie clip. In the case of a button, "this" refers to the Movie clip that contains the button. The variable picNum will be assigned in the "navigation" Movie clip. So for the Movie clip instance "thumbnail1," the value of picNum will be 1. This number gets passed to the function picSwapper on the main timeline.

You should already know that you have a wide array of choices for the state of the button that triggers your ActionScript. You should also know that you can declare multiple states to trigger one block of ActionScript, and that you can define different consequences for different states of the same button. Following is an example of such a button's actions. This button was on a site that used a custom cursor and tooltips.

```
on (rollOver) {
    tip._visible = 1;
    tip.gotoAndStop(5);
    cursor.gotoAndStop(2);
}
```

```
on (rollOut) {
   tip._visible = 0;
   cursor.gotoAndStop(1);
}
on (release, releaseOutside) {
   getURL ("popper.html", "upper");
}
```

Attached to a Movie Clip Instance

In version 5, Flash introduced the ability to attach ActionScript directly to Movie clip. This new feature creates a lot of new possibilities, not the least of which is repeated checking that used to be done with two frame loops on a timeline. Following is the code attached to the titleFader Movie clip instance on the main timeline.

```
onClipEvent(load){
      var timeout=3000;
}

onClipEvent(enterFrame){
   if (getTimer()>timeout){
      if (this._alpha > 0){
         this._alpha -= 5;
      }
   }
}
```

This ActionScript replaces two very common tasks that used to be performed by the timeline back in Flash 3 days, and to a lesser extent in Flash 4. This script simply waits for three seconds and then gradually fades out the Movie clip. By this time you should recognize everything except getTimer() and onClipEvent().

getTimer() is just a built-in function that returns the number of milliseconds elapsed since the Movie clip started playing. This is compared to the arbitrary variable "timeout," which we set to 3000, or three seconds.

The interesting thing is the onClipEvent() action. It takes one argument: the type of clip event that you would like to use to trigger the ActionScript contained within the curly braces. This works just like the different button actions, except that the events are different. The following image shows the different clip events available for this action.

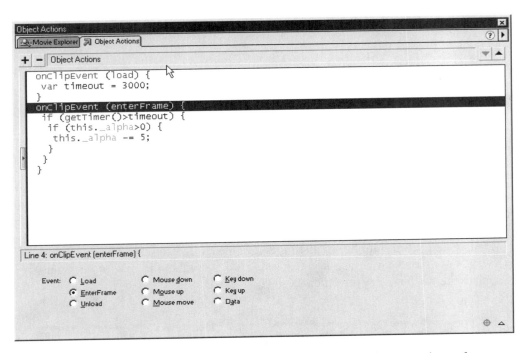

When you use onClipEvent(enterFrame) for a Movie clip that contains only one frame, the ActionScript in the curly braces executes continuously. This is a much more handy and elegant way to handle checking and smooth transitions. Say good-bye to two frame loops and unnecessary tweening.

SmartClips

SmartClips are a special kind of Movie clip. We will talk about them in great detail in the next chapter. The most important difference between the Movie clips we have talked about so far and SmartClips is that the latter are designed to be used with a graphical interface to enter variable values. This is a programming professor's dream illustration of an object.

The ActionScript in a SmartClip still resides entirely within the Movie clip, but there are significant differences. First, the variable names in a SmartClip are typically locked. The programmer who designs the SmartClip decides which variables can have their values changed. These variables show up as a text field or a drop-down list in the GUI for the clip.

There is an additional place where actions can reside in the general SmartClip structure: in the GUI itself. You can design your own front end for the clip. (We will do this in the next chapter.) You may incorporate anything from form validation to a video game in your custom GUI.

Deprecated Actions

Before we dive into the deep end of ActionScript, you should be aware that you have options in Flash 5 that aren't necessarily good ones. I am talking about *deprecated actions*. Calling a particular action deprecated is just a nice way of saying, "Don't count on being able to use this in the future; it's on its way out."

In every instance in Flash 5 where an action is deprecated, a new equivalent is available, often with improved features or flexibility. The equivalent action is always referred to in the ActionScript Dictionary included with the Flash 5 installation.

Deprecated actions are highlighted green in the snippets gutter. Using these actions is not strictly wrong, but you should stop using them in new projects and translate them wherever convenient.

ActionScript Panel Options

When Flash 5 was in beta, you could sense a cumulative sigh of relief among serious Flash developers as an undertone to the general excitement. It appeared that Flash 5 would be one of those rare cases when a software manufacturer picked up on everything developers wanted to do with its product. There were many signs that the new version was built to accommodate any developer—from graphic artists wanting to do a little animation to hard-core scripting junkies.

One of the clearest signals was the new ActionScript panel. Not only was the underlying logic of the application exposed, but developers were also given a much more comfortable environment in which to tinker. For those of you who don't remember, the following image shows the ActionScript panel in Flash 4. It was a suffocating little box that you couldn't resize, could not type directly into, and couldn't use to import or export. It was a real drag for anyone who tried to do anything interesting with ActionScript.

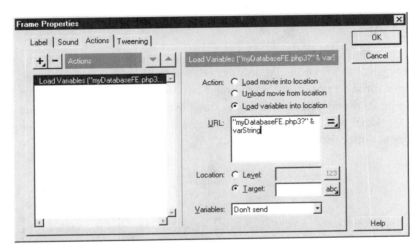

Things are much better now. We are going to take a short look at the different options available for getting ActionScript into the actions panel, just in case you missed any of the cool new features.

Normal Mode

When you first install Flash, the actions panel operates in normal mode by default. When you are in normal mode, you lose the ability to type ActionScript directly into the panel. There are several cool features in normal mode that are geared toward less experienced coders.

One nice thing about normal mode is that it automatically adds handlers for you when they are needed. (A *handler* is the type of ActionScript you use on buttons and Movie clips. It begins with some form of "on," followed by the state that triggers the action, followed by the action executing curly braces.) For instance, if you add a getURL action to a button in normal mode, it will add the handler "on(release){ }" in the proper place automatically.

Another nice thing about normal mode is that it spells out the syntax of every action for you and gives you a list of choices where applicable. When I can't remember the proper syntax for an action, instead of looking it up, I find that simply switching to normal mode is faster and less vulnerable to error.

Expert Mode

If you haven't figured it out already, you can set the actions panel to start in expert mode every time you open it. To do this, go to Edit | Preferences | General.

You have three choices for composing ActionScript within this panel in expert mode: typing it in manually, selecting actions from the hierarchical pop-up menu that appears when you click the plus sign (see the following image), or using the little snippets gutter on the left.

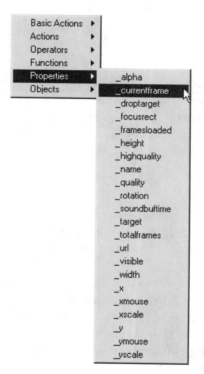

My personal preference is for a combination of manual typing and double-clicking in the snippets gutter. I find that if I leave the actions panel sized so that it covers the entire screen, I can see all the available methods I might have to use in tedious applications like date manipulation. In cases like these, it is easier for me to use the expanded ActionScript panel than any of the other options: type all of the actions by hand, scroll through a long list in the snippets gutter, or go stumbling through a pop-up menu. When you have the ActionScript panel expanded like this, you can toggle the visibility of an expanded ActionScript panel using CTRL-ALT-A.

Import from File

In an ongoing effort to promote better living through snippets for developers worldwide, Macromedia has incorporated two useful tools for bringing your saved code into the ActionScript panel. The result of the options is the same, but each appeals to a different subculture of hard-core hackers.

My favorite method is importing ActionScript from an external file. You can select this option from the pop-up menu in the upper-right corner of the ActionScript panel, as seen in the following image. I like this method because it doesn't require me to remember the path to the file—you use a standard Windows open file dialog. In addition, this meshes well with my practice of saving snippets as text files.

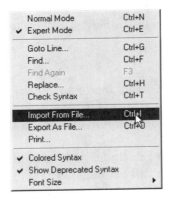

Include File

For those with the command line penchant, you can type the path to the text file you want to include as ActionScript, as seen in the following bit of code. The effect is the same as when you use the "src" attribute in the script tag in HTML: it is as if the contents of the external file are present where you put the placeholder.

```
#include "myScript.as"
```

This is a little different from JavaScript in that the include action is really an instruction to the Flash compiler. In other words, Flash grabs the code from the external file and publishes it in the SWF. After that, the published SWF does not refer to the external file; it is not needed at run time.

This brings up an interesting point about the nature of Flash as it is published for the Web and how it affects ActionScript. A Flash movie is compiled into binary byte code (the SWF) when you publish it. This is something similar to a machine-readable executable; it needs very little additional interpretation. This is a great scenario for the Web, because it means that the Player is small and the Flash application starts quickly. The one drawback to this scenario is that because the SWF is a hunk of binary code geared toward machines instead of people, you can't make up variable identifiers on the fly like you can with purely interpreted languages.

ActionScript Flow Control

The following sections present a smattering of the most important commonly used actions associated with navigation, flow control, and playback. Hopefully you are already familiar with all of the basic playback actions. I include these to remind you of a few nuances that are often overlooked. I will try to keep things interesting.

GetURL

As we are discovering the seemingly increasing unreliability of FS commands, getURL is becoming more practical and more popular. At the time of writing, this action is your best bet when you're trying to send JavaScript commands from a Flash movie to the browser.

getURL is also important for its traditional function of using the browser to call a Web address. The syntax for this action is

```
getURL (address, window, method);
```

"address" is of course the URL. "method" is an optional argument that allows you to designate either the POST or GET http command. "window" has some interesting applications that I think tend to be overlooked often by Flashers. Table 9-2 shows a few of the possible values for the window argument and what they mean.

With frames falling out of fashion in recent years, you may not even be aware of some of the cool tricks you can do with them. One of the most useful ones is hiding a page in a frame with a width or height of zero. This trick came about in the early days of Flash when opening a site as a full-screen display was seen as a great technical achievement. Luckily, the full-screen craze has ended, but this trick remains useful. To use this trick, you set up a frame like this:

```
<frameset rows = "0, *">
<frame frameborder=0 marginheight=0 noresize name="hidden" src="functions.html"    >
<frame frameborder=0 marginheight=0 noresize src="myMovie.swf" name="FlashApp">
</frameset>
```

Value	Meaning
_self	Opens the URL in the same window that holds the Flash movie issuing the call
_blank	A new, separate window
_parent	The window above the current window in a frameset hierarchy
_top	The outermost window in a frameset hierarchy
hidden	A window arbitrarily named "hidden"
killerJoe	A window arbitrarily named "hidden"

Table 9.2   *Possible Window Arguments for the getURL Action*

In addition to providing a fully customized display (no unpredictable space like you get in an HTML document), you have the ability to add a head and title. But the best part—and the point of all this—is that you have a hidden page that can contain anything. This is a good place to put JavaScript. By using the getURL action to call JavaScript in the hidden frame, you reduce compatibility issues that arise from using Flash and JavaScript together to practically nothing. If you wanted to call a function in a page named "functions.html" in the frameset shown above, you could use the following action:

```
getURL("javascript:alertFunc('" + alertMsg + "')","hidden");
```

In this example we call a JavaScript function named alertFunc and pass it the argument alertMsg, which is a variable in our imaginary Flash movie. There are a lot of different things you can do between windows from Flash by simply using and calling window names in this way.

LoadMovie

The gist of the loadMovie action is that you are loading an external SWF into a placeholder. You are probably fairly familiar with this action, but we will still go over a few nuances in case you missed them.

The most common application of this action is to load a movie into a dummy Movie clip. The power of this action comes from being able to determine which Movie clips to use at run time based on logic in the main movie without having to weigh down the application by including all possible choices. Take the following code, for example:

```
if (currWeatherIndex>=0 &&currWeatherIndex < 4){
    weatherMC="frownyCloud.swf";
```

```
}else if(currWeatherIndex>=4 && currWeatherIndex < 8){
   weatherMC="sunAndCloud.swf";
}else if(currWeatherIndex>=8 && currWeatherIndex <= 10){
   weatherMC="smileySun.swf";
}else{
   _root.errorRoutine();
}
loadMovie (weatherMC, "placeholder");
```

This code evaluates the value of the variable currWeatherIndex and groups it into one of three categories (corresponding to the current weather). After the control structure executes and assigns the appropriate value to the variable weatherMC, it loads the appropriate Movie clip into the instance named "placeholder." This is a very common application of the loadMovie action.

There are just a few other things you should know about this action. Every transformation (scaling, color effects, etc.) and translation (movement of the x and y coordinates) applied to the placeholder—both before and after the loadMovie action executes—are applied to the loaded movie. This can be important if you're using ActionScript to apply a precise position to the loaded movie.

The problem occurs when you have a difference in registration points. In other words, the center of your placeholder Movie clip as it registers in Flash must be the same as the center of the loaded SWF. It turns out that the registration point of all loaded movies is the upper-left corner. So the easiest way to match them is to go into your placeholder Movie clip and move it so that the upper-left corner of what you see on the stage is on the registration point. The following image shows how you would do this if you were using a square as a placeholder for an image of the same size.

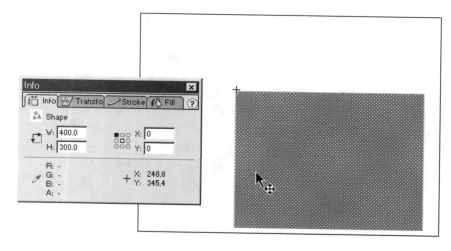

Another interesting thing about the loadMovie action is the ability to load a movie into a particular level. If you started on Flash in version 5, you may not even be aware of levels, since they are much less important now than they once were. The levels in the movie are sort of a blend of the movie hierarchy and the z-index stack. The main timeline of the movie always occupies "_level0." You can specify a level instead of a target Movie clip instance when you load an external SWF, but not both.

There is one good use for this feature: loading a new movie into the main timeline. You might want to do this if you were maintaining a site manually and wanted to keep movies separated into files, in keeping with the old HTML paradigm. In other words, when the user clicks to navigate to a new page, you load a new movie into the main timeline instead of loading a separate HTML page.

IfFrameLoaded Versus _framesloaded

IfFrameLoaded is a sort of shorthand to create a control structure based on whether a particular frame is loaded. This particular action is a vestige of the Flash 4 approach to scripting: concealing the real logic in dumbed-down actions. Appropriately, this action is deprecated in Flash 5.

You should be using the _framesloaded property instead. This property exists by default for every Movie clip. In addition to the satisfaction you get from doing *real* coding, this property is also a lot more versatile in what you can do with it. Following are a couple of examples to get your creative juices flowing. If you spend a little time getting intimate with this property, you'll probably find yourself creating more interesting (and less frustrating for the user) loading schemes.

```
/*a cheapo connection speed detection - you might load a movie with a few
bitmaps  - one to a frame - and execute this code after a couple of
seconds*/
if(_framesloaded>=_totalframes){
    getURL("broadband.html","_self");
}else{
    getURL("straightOuttaLocash.html","_self");
}


/*an action on a dummy movie clip - controls a loading bar in the style of
the old JavaScript %loader*/
onClipEvent(enterFrame){


_parent.percentLoadedDisplay.gotoAndStop(Math.round(_root._framesloaded));
}
```

Button Event	Explanation
Press	The user presses the left mouse button.
Roll Over	The mouse cursor touches the hit area of the button. This corresponds with the moment that the mouse cursor changes from an arrow to a hand.
Release	The user releases the left mouse button while still over the hit area of the button.
Roll Out	The user moves the cursor off the button without having clicked.
Release Outside	The user releases the left mouse button while outside the hit area of the button.
Drag Over	The user moves the cursor onto the button while holding down the left mouse button.
Drag Out	The user moves the cursor off the button while holding down the left mouse button.
Key Press	The designated key is pressed. You can capture keystrokes by entering this handler in normal mode.

Table 9.3   *Mouse Events*

onMouseEvent and onClipEvent

Here are a couple of tables explaining the uses of the different event handlers available in Flash 5. Table 9-3 deals with the possible events for buttons, while table 9-4 deals with Movie clips.

Movie Clip Event	Explanation
load	The Movie clip loads for the first time. This only happens once per Movie clip instance.
enterFrame	This event occurs every time the Movie clip plays a new frame. The ActionScript within this handler executes after the ActionScript in each respective frame of the Movie clip timeline. If there is only one frame in the Movie clip, this handler executes in rapid succession.
mouseMove	The user moves the mouse. This is handy for situations in which you are tracking the mouse position and want to conserve system resources. The ActionScript in this handler will only execute each time the user moves the mouse.

Table 9.4   *Movie Events*

Movie Clip Event	Explanation
keyDown, keyUp	Similar to the button event handler Key Press, except that you can capture both states of the key press.
mouseDown	The user presses the left mouse button.
mouseUp	The user releases the left mouse button.
unload	The Movie clip instance is unloaded from the stage/work area.
data	This handler is used primarily with the loadVariables action. It marks the point in time when the last variable is loaded from the source, whether it be a text file or a CGI application.

Table 9.4   *Movie Events* (continued)

What to Take Away from This Chapter

Flash 5 is a curious beast indeed. It has some things in common with DHTML in that it uses a similar scripting language to control both visual and text elements. It has similarities with video editing, where you deal with timelines. Some elements are mutual to Flash 5 and XML: creating a custom structure for your data and being able to separate that data from the presentation, for instance. If there's anything I would like to get across an this chapter, it is that Flash 5 ActionScript is much deeper and protean than text effects and preloaders. You will do well if you can keep the many faces of ActionScript in your mind as you approach new projects.

All About Movie Clips

In the previous chapter, we saw how you can use Movie clips to structure the ActionScript in your movie. In this chapter, we are going to look at some common ActionScript-related uses for Movie clips. Some of the exercises in this chapter are specific tricks with limited application, like creating a custom mouse cursor. Other skills we will look at in this chapter, such as building SmartClips, have a broader scope.

When Do You Use a Movie Clip?

lion.fla, slideShow.fla

The most common use for Movie clips is creating a hierarchy for graphical elements. In Figure 10-1, you can see how the cartoon lion's leg is nested within the Movie clip for the whole lion, which in turn is nested within another Movie clip.

Figure 10.1   *The hierarchy of graphical elements is shown in this cartoon*

This use is undoubtedly familiar to you already. Notice that the static graphic itself, the leg, is a graphic symbol and not a Movie clip. This is to save on both file size and the amount of information that the client computer has to process at run time. Remember that Movie clips contain a number of properties and methods that other symbol types do not contain.

Another good reason to use a Movie clip is the power of independent timelines. (If this seems to contrast with what I said in Chapter 9, just hold your horses—we are only talking about the animation here.) In Figure 10-2, you can see a very simple Movie clip timeline from the example *lion.fla* on the CD.

This is the bread and butter of passive, entertainment-oriented animation. However, this is not what we are going to talk about in this chapter. I just included this to reinforce the primary purpose of timelines, which is hard-coded animation.

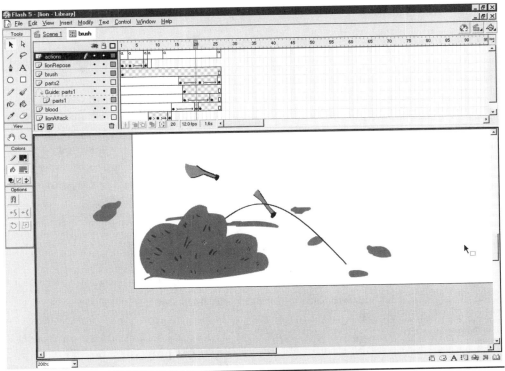

Figure 10.2 *A simple Movie clip timeline using,* lion.fla, *an example on the CD*

This example would have been cumbersome to build with ActionScript alone, but was very easy to do with timeline-based tweening.

Where we used to loop between two frames on the timeline, we can now (in Flash 5) continuously check and update elements in the movie using the onClipEvent handler. As we saw in the previous chapter, this handler—or rather group of handlers—can execute code on just about any event or interval you can imagine.

```
onClipEvent (load) {
    var timeout = 3000;
}

onClipEvent (enterFrame) {
    if (getTimer()>timeout) {
        if (this._alpha>0) {
            this._alpha -= 5;
        }
    }
}
```

When you use a Movie clip like this—continuously checking for or updating an element in the movie—make sure you provide a way to remove the clip once you're done with it. For example, the previous block of code makes no provision within itself to stop checking the _alpha property of the clip. This wastes system resources and should be avoided. One solution is to nest a clip like this within another empty Movie clip and attach it dynamically at run time. This way you have the option to remove the Movie clip when it is no longer needed. The alternative is to move the playhead to a point on the timeline where the clip is no longer on the stage or work area.

A Movie clip can also serve as a placeholder for external SWFs. We saw this in the *slideShow.fla* example in the previous chapter. This is actually a popular method for organizing an entire site. Many Flash developers construct their movies with nothing more than multiple instances of a blank Movie clip acting as placeholders for the content, which resides in an external Flash movie. I had a short-lived affair with the style of Flash movie architecture myself, but I think the tools in Flash 5 solve all the problems that this scheme originally addressed.

The Movie clip can be a container for data in more ways than one. In one sense, each Movie clip holds the information that makes up its properties: position, color, frames loaded, and so on. In another sense, you can use a Movie clip to collect and send data, such as in the case of the fill-out form that exists within a separate Movie clip. This is handy for the sake of sending only the variables you need to another application, like a CGI form mail script or a database servlet.

The other way a clip can be a container for data is the simplest use for a Movie clip. You take an empty Movie clip and load it with data. This approach is good for situations where you will want to look for information in the same place in a number of movies or Movie clips. An example of this would be a template used for Flash movies across an entire site (for instance, if we added a title to each of the images in the *slideShow.fla* example in the previous chapter) or a custom UI for SmartClips, which requires a standard Movie clip container for variables to be passed from the UI to the Movie clip instance on the stage. We will cover this later in this chapter.

Movie clips are perhaps most useful as a constructor or prototype for other Movie clips. When you look at it this way, a Movie clip in the library is like an object class, and Movie clip instances on the stage or work area are objects created from this class. This may seem like the most obvious thing in the world, especially since this is one of the first things emphasized in the online tutorials that come with a Flash installation; but this little nugget is even more valuable than simply saving file size by reproducing redundant graphics programmatically.

By creating Movie clips with reusable ActionScript that is sensitive to the context in which it is used, you can code your applications more efficiently and reduce the amount of time it takes to build Flash movies with multiple instances of similar logic-driven elements. This is exactly what SmartClips are for, and we will cover them in depth later in this chapter.

Instances

An *instance* is nothing more than a named copy of a Movie clip on the stage or work area of your Flash movie. You should already be very familiar with this concept. We will quickly review the idea of instances just to be safe.

Movie clip instances in Flash 5 have retained familiar strengths from Flash 4—lowering file size with repeated animations and serving as simple containers for data. In addition, there are new, extremely useful methods that treat Movie clip instances more like the objects they really are.

Attach/Duplicate/Remove

We've already seen several examples of the .attachMovie() method in this book, but we haven't really talked about why it is advantageous to use this. After all, for everything we've done so far, it would be just as easy and effective to duplicate a Movie clip instance that was hovering offstage in the nonvisible work area.

For instance, consider this example from the previous chapter, where we dynamically pulled a Movie clip from the library and placed it on the stage:

```
function loadPic(counter){
    attachMovie( "ph", "ph"+counter, counter );
    loadMovie("ss"+counter+".swf","ph"+counter);
    _root["ph" + counter]._x=650;
    _root["ph" + counter]._y=490;
}
```

If, instead of using the export linkage to name the Movie clip in the library, we had placed the clip on the stage and named the instance "ph," we could accomplish the exact same thing thus:

```
function loadPic(counter){
    duplicateMovieClip ( "ph", "ph"+counter, counter );
    loadMovie("ss"+counter+".swf","ph"+counter);
    _root["ph" + counter]._x=650;
    _root["ph" + counter]._y=490;
}
```

You may be wondering "What's the big deal?"—the perceived result is exactly the same. To get to the answer, imagine the following scenario. Suppose this Movie clip instance called "ph"—the one that we are duplicating a number of times—contains multiple tweened bitmaps and is a container for 600 variables. Each instance would significantly bog down the movie, so it would be in our best interest to eliminate any unnecessary instances.

Even if you don't have 600 variables in a Movie clip, it still takes up space in the client computer's memory. Remember that you start with a couple dozen properties for any Movie clip before you add any graphics or custom variables, as you can easily see from a glance at your debugger, shown here:

Saving memory by deleting objects after they have run out their useful lifetime is one of those things they teach you in a first-year programming course in college. It's just a good habit. The way we retire Movie clips is with the .removeMovie clip() method. Its syntax looks like the following, with instanceName being any Movie clip instance that was created by either attaching or duplicating. You cannot remove a Movie clip that was not created by either attachMovie() or duplicateMovie clip().

```
_root.instanceName.removeMovieClip();
```

Swap Depths

swapDepths.fla

Another handy method that is available in Flash 5 is .swapDepths(). This method changes the z-index of the Movie clip, which is a geeky way of saying "which one is closest to you" or "which one is on top." In other words, the higher the z-index, the closer to the top of the stack. The syntax for this method looks like this:

```
_root.someInstance.swapDepths(target);
```

The Movie clip instance you feed into the swapDepths() function trades its z-index with the clip that used the method ("someInstance" in the preceding line). The argument to the swapDepths function can also be the absolute z-index. For instance, if you knew that you wanted your Movie clip to end up with a z-index of 11, you could write it like this:

```
_root.someInstance.swapDepths(11);
```

On the CD you will find a FLA called *swapDepths*. This movie uses five instances of MC1 on the stage. As you can see from the following code, this trick is not as treacherous as some would have you believe. This is the only logic required to swap depths in the movie.

```
z=6;
function bringToFront(mcName){
    mcName.swapDepths(z);
    z++;
}
```

The meaning of the function bringToFront() should be obvious. The Movie clip instance that calls this function receives a new z-index higher than any other already assigned. The following code is contained within the button that lives inside the Movie clip. This is what calls the function and causes the Movie clips to drag.

```
on(press){
    _root.bringToFront(index);
    this.startDrag();
}
on(release, releaseOutside){
    this.stopDrag();
}
```

Just for fun, I added a maximize and minimize function. The minimize function is as follows. It is attached to the button shaped like a minus sign.

```
on(press){
    this.prevPosX=this._x;
    this.prevPosY=this._y;
    this._x=0;
    this._y=472;
}
```

When the user clicks this button, the clip moves to the lower-left corner of the stage, but not before recording its current position. When it's time to execute the following code, which is attached to the square-shaped maximize button, the MC will remember its previous position.

```
on(press){
    _root.bringToFront(this);
    this._x = this.prevPosX;
    this._y = this.prevPosY;
}
```

The clip will also come to the front. This is a much closer approximation of the type of application window functionality than you typically see at present in Flash Web design. For some reason, probably because it takes two less lines of code, designers seem to be fond of minimizing a window in place—leaving it hovering over the material that the user wants to use. While this does have a precedent—there is exactly one desktop application that I've seen, an MP3 player, which uses this functionality—it's probably better to stick with a scenario that real-life users will easily understand

Our example is a pretty good setup if you have nothing on your stage but translucent faux-windows; but you should be aware that this method is limited. For instance, if you had another element in your movie that you wanted to remain in front of the windows, you have to swap the z-indexes between Movie clips so that they stay within a given range. You would also want to keeping a running total of the number of minimized windows and prevent them from totally overlapping and obscuring each other.

Dragging: Two Approaches

Dragging is an essential element in building engaging visual applications. It has been literally decades since the first widely distributed consumer visual operating system was released, and marketing types still tout products as supporting "drag and drop" as if it were something revolutionary. Users like the feeling of picking something up and moving it—from their first lacquered, drool-resistant wooden puzzle made of geometric shapes all the way up to visual programming IDEs. It's just hardwired in the human machine.

There are two basic approaches to drag and drop within Flash. The most common and most efficient of the two is the built-in *drag* action. This action takes a Movie clip instance as an argument. This action makes that Movie clip follow the mouse cursor. The alternate method is to code your own version by continuously querying the mouse position and updating the position of the Movie clip. One reason you might want to do this is the fact that you can only drag one Movie clip at a time.

Drag

animalSounds.fla

The drag action is very easy to use. Its syntax is as follows:

```
startDrag (targetPath, true, leftLimit, topLimit, rightLimit, bottomLimit);
```

Appropriately, targetPath is the path to the Movie clip instance. The next argument is a Boolean representing whether the Movie clip that is going to be dragged should lock its center to the point of the mouse cursor. If you set this to false, not only will the Movie clip not be centered, it will start dragging from wherever it is on the stage at the time the action is executed—whether or not the mouse is over it. The remaining arguments should be self-explanatory—they are the number of pixels from the upper-left corner of the stage that make a bounding box. If you leave these arguments blank, you can drag the clip anywhere.

The following code is from *animalSounds.fla* on the CD. This code is attached to the button inside each animal sound Movie clip at the bottom of the stage. There is other code attached to these buttons, but it is omitted here for the sake of simplicity.

```
on (press) {
    this.startDrag( false, 0, 0, 640, 480 );
}
on (release, releaseOutside) {
    this.stopDrag();
}
```

The first thing you'll notice is that immediately after telling you the syntax for this action, I turned around and changed it. This syntax is unique to Flash 5, and keeps with the scripting style we have already covered. The only drawback to doing it this way—with the action appended to the target path as a method instead of the target path being an argument to the action—is that it is not compatible with Flash 4; Flash 5 won't convert it for you if you try to export it. The moral of this story is *make sure you decide which version you will publish before you begin work.*

The next thing to note in this example is the handler we used to stop dragging. By adding the releaseOutside handler, you eliminate the possibility of the user releasing the mouse at a time when the cursor is ahead of the Movie clip. This happens when the Flash Player can't keep up with the mouse because it can't redraw the Movie clip fast enough.

DropTarget
animalSounds.swf

If you haven't already done so, look at the compiled output from this example (*animalSounds.swf* on the CD). It's a game to help you learn some of your most important animal sounds. This is a classic application (the functionality, not the animal sounds) of dragging in Flash. The key actions in this example are drag and stopDrag, the actions that we've seen already. The trick of knowing which Movie clip, if any, the user drops the word on its easily achieved using the _droptarget property.

The property _droptarget belongs to the Movie clip that is being dragged. Let's look at the rest of the script attached to each of the buttons we looked at previously to see how we will use drop target in this example.

```
on (press) {
    this.startDrag( false, 0, 0, 640, 480 );
}

on (release, releaseOutside) {
    this.stopDrag();
    if(this._dropTarget == "/pig"){
        _root.correctAnswer("pig","oink");
    }else{
        _root.sendHomer("oink");
    }
}
}
```

correctAnswer() and sendHomer() are the names of functions on the root timeline of the movie. We've seen this in previous examples, so I'll just mention one aspect that we haven't talked about so far. In order for Movie clips to be able to talk to functions on timelines above themselves, the nested Movie clip must be in a frame that contains the function. For instance, suppose you have a function on the main timeline in frame 1, and on the same layer you have a blank keyframe in frame 2. If you try to call the function from a Movie clip while the main timeline is in frame 2, it won't work. However, you can still call the function from frame 2, but you can't pass it any of the variables from the Movie clip unless the Movie clip is on the same or a previous keyframe and exists at the point where the function is created. It works the same way going down the hierarchy, which is a little more intuitive.

The _droptarget property returns the full path to the Movie clip instance on which the user drops the draggable Movie clip. The reason for the slash is that this is the way targets were named in Flash 4. You can easily convert it to the modern syntax by using the eval function, like so:

```
if(eval(this._dropTarget) == "_root.pig"){
```

Another point to consider when you are using the _droptarget property is that it will still return a string if the user drops the dragging Movie clip onto a Movie clip instance that is not named. For instance, if we had a Movie clip that served as a title at the top of our example, but it didn't have a name, you would return the value "instancex," where *x* is its index number in the array of Movie clip instances on the stage.

Custom Cursor
customCursor.fla

One feature very high on the list for "most bang for the buck" in Flash 5 is the ability to hide or show the mouse cursor at any time. Since we already know how to drag a Movie clip, the obvious application is to create a custom mouse cursor.

The following code is the only ActionScript in the example *customCursor.fla* on the CD. The effect we are going for is replacing the typical hand-shaped pointer that appears when you hover over a button or link. Our custom cursor resembles the two-finger gun employed by people who think they're funny when they wink and make the "giddy-up" sound to indicate that they understood what you said.

```
on (release, releaseOutside) {
    getURL ("http://suck.com");
}
on (rollOver, dragOver) {
    Mouse.hide();
    attachMovie("cursor","cursor",3);
    cursor.startDrag(true, 0, 0, 400, 300 );
}
on (rollOut, dragOut) {
    Mouse.show();
    cursor.removeMovieClip();
}
```

As you can see, we've added even more possible events to the event handlers than before. This is because you want to be sure to always have the mouse pointer in correct state. Using a custom cursor is especially susceptible for a number of reasons. You are using the cursor for some kind of navigation, so you have to have handlers in every portion of the application where the user might navigate. In addition, you might be opening up separate windows or affecting other parts of the HTML page in which the movie is embedded, which will lead the focus of the user (and hence the mouse) elsewhere. If you use a custom mouse cursor, set aside some extra time for testing and debugging.

Continuously Update Position

The drag action is so easy to use and performs so well that it is hard to imagine why you would want to use anything else. One possible reason might be the desire to drag something under a custom cursor. Since you can only drag one Movie clip at a time, you might want to drag the cursor and use the handler onClipEvent(enterFrame) in the Movie clip if you want to have the *appearance* of dragging. The problem with this scheme is that it is incredibly taxing on the client processor.

Another application in which you might want to use this scheme is mouse trailers, for example, if you wanted to have a Movie clip or a series of Movie clips follow the mouse in varying levels of delay. Simple dragging won't work for this type of effect.

Hit Test

The *hit test* is an old concept in the study of building video games. The idea is to check whether visual elements are touching on screen. Creating a hit test in Flash 4 was a bear, but some people managed, driven by their vision for a cool game and the desire for recognition in the quickly growing Flash community. What was once part of the canon of the Seven Mighty Tasks of Flash Kludging is now as easy as using a simple method.

Games

lion.fla

Take a look at *lion.fla* on the CD. This movie flows as follows. At the beginning the only Movie clip on the stage is the lion hiding in the bush. A function in the main timeline called recyclor() attaches the antelope Movie clip and chooses its vertical position at random. After that, the only logic contained in the movie is attached to the blank Movie clip in the upper-left corner of the stage. The ActionScript for it is

```
onClipEvent(enterFrame){
    if(_root.caribu._x <= -20){
        _root.recyclor();
    }else{
        _root.caribu._x -= 7;
    }
    if(_root.brush.hitTest(_root.caribu)){
        _root.killor();
    }
}
```

When the "caribu" Movie clip intersects the "brush" Movie clip on the screen, the function killor() is called in the main timeline. The hitTest() method is used on the "brush" Movie clip with the argument _root.caribu.

Tooltips

customMenu.fla

Here is another application of the hitTest() function. This code can be found in *customMenu.fla* on the CD.

```
startDrag (tip, true, 0, 0, 400, 300);
tip._visible=false;

function partGoToer(partNum){
    theCurrentPart.removeMovieClip();
    attachMovie("part" + partNum, "theCurrentPart",3);
    theCurrentPart._x=52;
    theCurrentPart._y=122;
}

//hide and show tooltip
onClipEvent (enterFrame) {
    if (_root.part1.hitTest(_root._xmouse, _root._ymouse, true)) {
        _root.tip.gotoAndStop(1);
        _root.tip._visible = true;
    } else if (_root.part2.hitTest(_root._xmouse, _root._ymouse, true)) {
```

```
      _root.tip.gotoAndStop(2);
      _root.tip._visible = true;
   } else if (_root.part3.hitTest(_root._xmouse, _root._ymouse, true)) {
      _root.tip.gotoAndStop(3);
      _root.tip._visible = true;
   } else if (_root.part4.hitTest(_root._xmouse, _root._ymouse, true)) {
      _root.tip.gotoAndStop(4);
      _root.tip._visible = true;
   } else {
      _root.tip._visible = false;
   }
}

onClipEvent (mouseDown) {
for(i=1;i<=4;i++){
   if (_root["part" + i].hitTest(_root._xmouse, _root._ymouse, true)) {
      _root.partGoToer(i);
   }
  }
}
```

SmartClips

Just in case you missed all the excitement about SmartClips, I will give you a quick rundown. A SmartClip is basically a Movie clip that functions as a wizard or macro within the Flash authoring environment. The idea is that a highly skilled Flash scripting developer builds a little application in a Movie clip and publishes it in a reusable form for anyone to use.

SmartClips also offer the author the ability to create a custom UI. This is especially handy if the instructions for using the clip are difficult to explain with text. For example, you might have a SmartClip that includes the ability to change the color of the graphic elements of the SmartClip. Instead of a fill-in form for RGB values, it would be much easier for the user to have three sliders and a preview of the color.

If that's not enough to get you excited about SmartClips, consider that Macromedia offers its extension manager and an environment on the Web for Flash developers to exchange SmartClips freely. This new scenario goes a step beyond the tradition of exchanging FLAs and code snippets, and makes managing extensions for Flash *and* Dreamweaver easy.

Using SmartClips

mathenator.fla

Let's start from the point at which you have some SmartClips in your library. In case you don't already, we will use an example from this chapter as if we were opening it from a permanent library.

Start with a new Flash movie of any dimension. Ordinarily, you have a SmartClip stored in your permanent libraries folder in the Flash application directory, but we are going to open our library from a FLA on the CD. Choose Open as Library (File | Open as Library, or CTRL-SHIFT-O) and select *mathenator.fla* on the CD. You should have the blank stage and one Movie clip in your library. Notice that the smart Movie clip has a different symbol—it's like a Movie clip except that it has a vertical column of horizontal bars representing the data that is passed to the movie from the SmartClip.

Drag the SmartClip onto the stage and close the library palette so that you don't get confused. Next you have to open the clip parameters panel, which you can do either of two ways: from the context menu on the Movie clip instance, select Panels | Clip Parameters or by selecting Window | Panels | Clip Parameters.

Fill in any values you like for the three variables and test your results. Obviously, this SmartClip is not the zenith of Flash development, but you get the idea. Even if you are stumbling through the process for the first time, it will probably take you less time to use the SmartClip than it would to write the code just to add and display the sum of two numbers.

Building SmartClips

The fundamental reason for SmartClips is to save time when you build a movie that contains problems that have been solved before. The popular conception is that this scenario primarily applies to senior scripting developers who make the Movie clips for less experienced or graphics-oriented developers. Personally, I believe that the best application of SmartClips is putting a friendly interface on your snippets library. If I had all the time I've spent writing the code over and over again for a time delay in ActionScript (although I did eventually save a Movie clip in my permanent library in Flash 4 that still required manual editing), I think I'd write a novel and ride a motorcycle across America.

Another way to look at it is in terms of the object-oriented model. A Movie clip is a class that acts as a template for the objects it creates—the Movie clip instances on the stage. SmartClips provide a clear line of abstraction between variables that change and the ones that stay the same between objects in the same class. This is because the variables that can be changed stand alone in the clip parameters panel.

The least optimistic reason for building SmartClips is that the ability to create custom UI ensures that you can boil down your programming, no matter how complex, to a level that anyone can understand. If you think it is necessary, you can go as far as creating a wizard with alternating form fields and embedded QuickTime movies explaining exactly what each variable means.

What Are SmartClips Good For?

During Flash 5 beta testing, I was certain that the ability to create and exchange SmartClips would revolutionize the Flash community overnight. Since Flashers had been free and sharing code and tricks in the past, it seemed only natural that the new, vastly improved medium of exchange would catch on like wildfire. At the time of writing, however, the exchange of SmartClips is still in early infancy. Flash 5 has been out for four months, but there are currently exactly 4 SmartClips on Flashkit.com (one of which is mine) and less than 40 SmartClips at the newly opened Macromedia Exchange for Flash.

Hopefully things will turn around by the time this book hits the shelf; but just in case, let me suggest a few applications for SmartClips.

Scrolling is one of those things—at least it was in Flash 4—that wasn't exactly brain surgery or rocket science, but there were enough little catches and gotcha's to make it sufficiently inconvenient and time consuming for any Flash developer. In addition, every publicly shared solution I saw in the Flash 4 days required that you change some variables that were buried deep within the movie. These solutions also required that you make specific measurements, like the height and width of the visible area. This kind of solution was not optimal, even for experienced developers, because it required the developer to fully comprehend the big picture of what the Movie clip was doing. Even if you are capable of taking in this much information, it takes time to upload it all into your brain.

What if you had a SmartClip for scrolling that allowed you to drag and drop an area on your movie stage, size it to custom dimensions by whatever method you choose, and have it scroll any Movie clip you point at? After all, every visual IDE for programming languages like Java and C++ has a feature like this—why not Flash? The last example we will look at in this chapter does precisely this.

Example: Addition
mathenator.fla

Let's rebuild from scratch the arithmetic SmartClip that we saw earlier. If you get stuck, refer to *mathenator.fla* on the CD. Start with a blank movie and create a new Movie clip called "mathenator." (This is going to be your SmartClip.)

Inside this Movie clip, create a dynamic text field and assign it to display the variable "answernator," using the Text Options dialog:

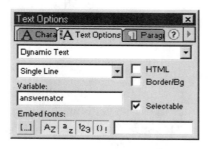

Assume that when we planned the design of this SmartClip, we decided that we would take three variables from user input: "num01," "num02," and "opernator." The input will come in the form of the clip parameters panel, which we are not going to worry about at the moment. Since answernator is the visual output for this application, following is the only ActionScript we will need for this SmartClip. It resides in the timeline of the "mathenator" Movie clip.

```
answernator = opernator + ", "  + num01 + ", " + num02 + " equals ";
if (opernator eq "add") {
   answernator+=  num01+num02;
} else if (opernator eq "subtract") {
   answernator+=  num01-num02;
} else if (opernator eq "multiply") {
   answernator+=  num01*num02;
} else if (opernator eq "divide") {
   answernator+=  num01/num02;
}
```

At this point we've gone as far as possible in terms of creating a reusable object class in the previous version of Flash. Without SmartClips, it would be up to the user to make sure that the three input variables got to where they needed to go.

Right-click on the "mathenator" Movie clip in the library palette and select Define Clip Parameters, as shown in the next image. You could also get there from the options menu in the library palette (provided that the "mathenator" Movie clip was selected).

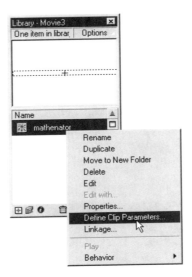

This is where the developer of a SmartClip defines the variable for which the user (another Flash developer) will enter values. We already decided that we wanted to have three variables for user input, "num01," "num02," and "opernator," so enter them here:

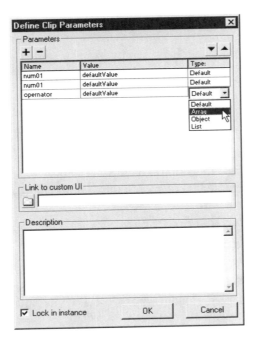

Finally, we have to define the data type for each variable. "Default" is fine for the first two variables (it works for any number or string); but because of our lazy logical scheme for detecting which operator the user selected, we have to limit the choices. This is a perfect example of when to use an array. To assign the possible values to the array, double-click on the Value column in the "opernator" row. Use the plus sign button (shown next) to add values to the array. Notice also that you have space at the bottom of the Define Clip Parameters dialog to add any text you want to pass on to the user. It is always a good idea to include instructions, no matter how tedious and redundant it may seem.

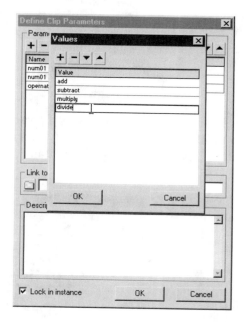

That's it! You now have the same SmartClip we used at the beginning of this section. You can either use this clip (and all SmartClips) within the movie in which it is native (where you created it) or drop it into any movie from an external library.

Building a Custom UI for Your Smart Clip
preloaderSmartClip.fla, preloaderUI.fla, preloaderUI.swf

This example is based on *preloaderSmartClip.fla* and *preloaderUI.fla* on the CD. The benefit of the preloader SmartClip is that it allows the user to choose a Movie clip that will be used as the preloader animation. Try this SmartClip out to see how it works. (You will have to save *preloaderSmartClip.fla* and *preloaderUI.swf* in the same directory if you are working from your hard drive.)

The first thing you should notice that is different about this Movie clip is the custom user interface, which is shown in Figure 10-3.

The entire user interface for this SmartClip consists of a single text field that passes the variable "clipName" to the SmartClip on the stage, and a whole bunch of the explanation—including visual aids—to get the user up to speed with the SmartClip.

The logic of the SmartClip itself is incredibly simple. The following bit of code resides on the timeline in the top level of the SmartClip. The only thing it does is stop the main movie from playing and attach the Movie clips that the user designates.

```
_root.stop();
attachMovie(clipName,"clip",1);
```

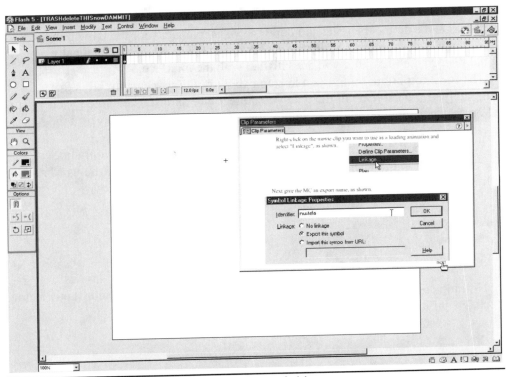

Figure 10.3   *Using a SmartClip with a single text field*

The only other code in the movie is attached to the "blank" Movie clip within the SmartClip, as shown here:

```
onClipEvent(enterFrame){
    if(_root._framesloaded >= _root._totalframes){
        _root.play();
        _parent.clip.removeMovieClip();
    }
}
```

As soon as the movie is loaded, it will begin to play, and the user's Movie clip (which we named "clip" when we instantiated it inside the SmartClip) will be removed. The weakness of this scenario is that it relies on the user to have enough sense to delete the SmartClip from the timeline after the first frame, which may or may not happen. This would be easy enough to fix, but it would result in extra code that is not part of the focus of this exercise.

Finally, open the FLA that creates the custom UI with a SmartClip, *preloaderUI.fla* on the CD. We define the logic and build the visual elements for the UI within this FLA, but it is the compiled SWF that acts as the actual interface. Theoretically, you could discard the FLA after you are satisfied with the interface.

The most important thing to understand about building a custom UI is that ultimately you must feed all the data you collect into an instance named "xch," (short for "exchange"). In our example, this instance is in its own layer in the upper-left corner of the stage, as seen in Figure 10-4.

When you boil down this movie to what it actually *does*, there is only one interesting action in the entire FLA. It is attached to the button over the word next in frame 4. It looks like this:

```
on(release, releaseOutside){
_root.xch.clipName=clipName;
nextFrame ();
}
```

Nothing could be more simple. We simply pass our variable to the instance named "xch," and Flash knows what to do from there.

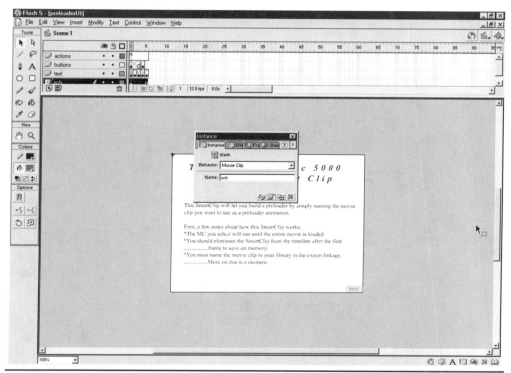

Figure 10.4 *Feeding data in an instance*

There remains one step. We have to link the SWF to the SmartClip in the Define Clip Parameters dialog in *preloaderSmartClip.fla*. Switch back to this file and open the Define Clip Parameters dialog for the Movie clip "preloader" in the library palette. If you did not notice it before, look at the section of the dialog labeled Link to Custom UI. To link to the SWF we just looked at, simply click the folder icon seen in the next image and browse for it. It should go without saying that if you move the SWF, you'll have to change this. If you use Macromedia's extension manager to both install and create SmartClips, this will be taken care of at installation time.

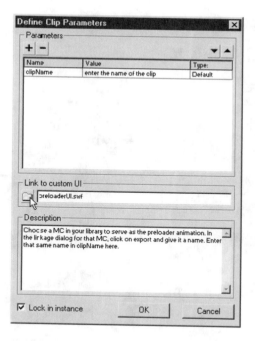

Example: Scrolling Window

We're not going to pick this entire example apart. For one thing, the structure of the movie goes pretty deep. (That's not to say that it is complex from a scripting point of view, just that there is a lot of ActionScript.) The other reason is that the code is not what you would call *clean*, and you would be better off not using this as an example of elegant ActionScript.

I originally built this for my own use. The point of including this example is to show how you can use SmartClips to extend the Flash authoring environment to include any components you can imagine, including UI elements that are standards in "real" programming languages.

The real logic that we want to reuse with the SmartClip is the scrolling, which can be found in 00copyThisToo | second frame, controllerMC layer | scrollLogic. This action is simple.

```
onClipEvent(enterFrame){
    distance=_parent._parent.lowerlimit-_parent._parent.upperlimit;
    proportion=(_parent._y-_parent._parent.upperlimit)/distance;
    _parent._parent._parent.document.document._y
=-proportion*_parent._parent.documentScrollDistance;
}
```

The way this action is set in motion is also simple. (It even uses a model of a two-frame timeline, which is a sure indication that this application was developed in a hurry.) This action is attached to the button in the same Movie clip.

```
on (press) {
    startDrag (this, false, 0, _parent.upperLimit*1.1, 0,
_parent.lowerLimit-_parent.scrollBar._height);
    this.gotoAndStop(2);
}
on (release, releaseOutside) {
    stopDrag ();
    this.gotoAndStop(1);
}
```

If you pick apart this SmartClip all the way down to the level of understanding how the parts interact, you will discover several kludges, poorly chosen variable names, and other residue of building an application without an adequate plan. In my experience, some "adjustment" is necessary whenever you build an application with scrolling content. The lesson to take away from this, and our entire discussion of SmartClips, is that once you slug through a common problem, you should never have to solve the same problem again.

What to Take Away from This Chapter

Movie clips are probably the single most useful and interesting element of any Flash movie. The power of Movie clips is what allowed Flash developers to hack the most innovative applications on the Web in Flash 4. In Flash 5, the subtle but mighty power of Movie clips continues to broaden the horizon for dedicated Flashers. Any time you take to stop and reflect on the different possible meanings and uses of Movie clips is time well spent.

Using Flash Native Objects

lash's built-in objects are like an allegiance of comic book superheroes, each with its own complement of amazing superpowers, easy-to-understand character, and a few idiosyncrasies. In this chapter we are going to deconstruct four examples, each featuring a different superhero.

Date

clock.fla

The date object has a straightforward, if tedious, interface. While it does take 20 lines of code just to get the time in the format you want 99 percent of the time, it's easy coding; so I'm not complaining. At least we don't have to do this in JavaScript and try to pass it to the Flash movie through the browser any more.

The sample we are going to use as a study of the date object is *clock.fla* on the CD. Please familiarize yourself with the output (the published SWF) and the structure of the elements on the stage before you continue.

We have three instances of the same Movie clip called hand. There's one for seconds, one for minutes, and one for hours. Each contains a graphic centered on a spot that makes a natural clock hand axle. Since this is done inside the Movie clip, there is no need to edit the registration point using Modify | Transform | Edit Center.

Once we have the graphic elements in place, we are ready to start using the date object. The following code is from the instance of the Movie clip "blank." It is the only ActionScript in the entire movie.

The first thing we have to do is to create an instance of the date object. This looks exactly the same as it did in JavaScript, except that we have to tell the Movie clip when to execute it.

```
onClipEvent(enterFrame){
myDate=new Date();
```

Now we are ready to start pulling the values we want from the date object. This object contains a lot of information, and it has a bazillion methods built in to output this information in any format you can imagine.

The only information we need from the date object that we created is the current seconds, minutes, and hours. We query the date object *instance* ("myDate," not "Date") like this:

```
mySeconds=myDate.getSeconds();
myMinutes=myDate.getMinutes();
myHours=myDate.getHours();

//you know how the hour hand doesn't jump all at once? - it just
creeps?
hourAdjustment=myMinutes/2;
```

The variable "hourAdjustment" is going to add a little bit of rotation to the hour hand to simulate the way a real clock's hour hand moves gradually between numbers, instead of jumping between them. The proportion is derived by dividing the fraction of the circle that one hour takes up by the fraction of a circle (one hour) that one minute takes up. The end result is smooth movement of the hour hand.

Next we perform the actual rotation. This is straightforward. We just rotate each hand to where it should be based on the current time.

```
//apply the correct rotation to each MC instance
_root.minutos._rotation = myMinutes*6+180;
_root.secondas._rotation = mySeconds*6;
_root.horas._rotation  = myHours*30 + hourAdjustment + 180;
```

The block of code above executes every time the Movie clip enters a frame, or practically continuously. The only problem is that we will keep working with the same date object until we change it. In other words, the date object gets the time from the computer's system clock when it is first created—after that, it does not update itself. That is why we need the following code:

```
delete myDate;
}
```

This simply deletes the old date object and replaces it with a new one, thus keeping the Movie clip updated with the correct time from the system clock. When the whole block of ActionScript starts executing again, it will have a fresh date object to work with.

This method is a little more processor intensive than the JavaScript way—checking every one second, or a larger fraction of a second. In this movie, the frame rate is set to 12; so it will execute this code about 12 times every second, which is definitely overkill for this application. On the other hand, looping through frames takes attention from the processor, too. I like the method we used in this example because it is easy, clear, and probably nearly as efficient as the alternative.

Key

itemAction.fla, lion.fla

This section discusses the example *itemAction.fla* on the CD. This is a skeleton of a game, with only three components, that makes use of the key object in ActionScript. Take a moment to play the game so that you will understand what the actions mean. The objective is to get the player, the little walking figure, to the doughnuts at the top of the screen without being hit with a memo. If the player gets hit with a memo, he must curtail his break time and go back to work. The focus of this example is on the player's motion, which is controlled by the arrow keys. Notice that you can move the player diagonally by holding down two adjacent keys.

The following code is from the main timeline of this application. You should recognize the first portion of this code from the *lion.fla* example in the previous chapter. It is 95 percent postconsumer's recycled code.

```
Mouse.hide();
function recyclor(){
   memo.removeMovieClip();
   attachMovie("memo","memo",1);
   memo._x=650;
   memo._y=Math.round(Math.random()*400);
}

function killor(){
   memo.removeMovieClip();
   attachMovie("msg","msg",3);
   msg.msg="You lose! Back to work.";
}

function winnor(){
   memo.removeMovieClip();
   attachMovie("msg","msg",3);
   msg.msg="You win! Yay, donuts!";
}
```

First the mouse pointer is obscured from view—there's nothing for it to interact with, so there's no point in showing it. The function "recyclor" first deletes the current memo and then adds another one on the right side of the stage. This function only gets called after the memo has drifted off the left side of the stage.

The remaining functions simply call the Movie clip exported as "msg" from the library. This Movie clip contains one element—a text field to display the variable "msg." Each function assigns a string to this variable. The only difference between the two functions is the string.

The remainder of the actions in the main timeline are new. These are the actions that make use of the key object.

```
//feed values to the keyController MC instances for the key they will
respond to, and direction to move the character
    up.diffX=0;
    up.diffY=5;
    up.keyVal=Key.UP;

    down.diffX=0;
    down.diffY= -5;
    down.keyVal=Key.DOWN;

    left.diffX=5;
    left.diffY=0;
    left.keyVal=Key.LEFT;

    right.diffX= -5;
    right.diffY=0;
    right.keyVal=Key.RIGHT;

player.swapDepths(2);
recyclor();
```

First notice that you don't see a constructor (like "someVar=new Key();") anywhere. In other words, you don't need to create an instance of the object to start using it, like we did with date.

The names of the variables "diffX" and "diffY" were chosen arbitrarily. These represent the amount of desired movement per frame that will be applied to the player when each respective key is held down. "Key.UP," "Key.DOWN," and so on, are properties of the key object. These values correspond to the arrow keys.

The following code is attached to the player instance. As a gesture of dark irony, I attached the motion mechanism for the memo to the player. We also see our old friend hitTest.

```
onClipEvent(enterFrame){
    if(_root.memo._x <= -20){
        _root.recyclor();
    }else{
        _root.memo._x -= 15;
    }
    if(this.hitTest(_root.memo)){
        _root.killor();
    }
    if(this.hitTest(_root.donuts)){
        _root.winnor();
    }
}
```

As this code executes on each frame, it first checks to see if a memo slid off the left side of the stage. If it did, a new cycle starts via the function "_root.recyclor." Otherwise the code decrements the memo's x coordinate by 15 pixels. Finally, it checks to see if the player is intersecting either the memo movie clip or the doughnuts.

Because we defined three variables for each instance of the controller Movie clip, the code that executes continuously inside each instance can be more streamlined and efficient. This is especially important to our little game, since there are four of these Movie clips, plus the player Movie clip, which is also continuously checking and updating.

```
onClipEvent(enterFrame){
    if(Key.isDown(_parent.keyVal)){
        _root.player._x -= _parent.diffX;
        _root.player._y -= _parent.diffy;
    }
}
```

The control block in this code translates loosely, "If the key we designated earlier is down, move in the direction we designated earlier." For instance, in the case of the UP ARROW, the value of "_parent.keyVal" (an arbitrarily chosen variable name) is "Key.UP." The other key object, "isDown," returns true if that key is down. When this condition is true, the code inside this block executes and the player appears to move.

Array

pizzaSpreadsheet.fla

In Chapter 6, I briefly mentioned the ability of arrays to exist within another array. The way arrays are implemented in JavaScript and ActionScript is not exactly the same as multidimensional arrays in other programming languages, but it's close enough to be extremely useful. In this example, we fake a multidimensional array. The goal is to represent data in columns and rows, with one array representing one axis, and the other array representing the other. In this example we will build the purest practical application of this concept, a spreadsheet.

This example is *pizzaSpreadsheet.fla* on the CD. The entire application is run from the only frame on the main timeline, with the exception of the handler for pressing the ENTER key and the SmartClip from Macromedia Exchange for handling the tab order. We will not consider the latter two.

The first thing we have to do is initialize all the arrays we will want to use. For the layout of our spreadsheet, it would make sense to deal primarily with arrays for department code in the vertical axis, and weeks in the horizontal axis.

However, this would require a separate entry for each department code for each week, with nothing obvious tying them together. This is just like designing a little spreadsheet. In the end, I decided that I would rather have arrays for each department code, because it would most likely facilitate the easiest access to information that would be needed for management accounting, toward which the spreadsheet is obviously oriented. In other words, if profits for this restaurant were to drop suddenly, the manager would immediately look at trends in revenue and labor expense. Having these items in their own arrays makes it easy to track information this way.

```
var revenue=new Array();
var flour=new Array();
var pepperoni=new Array();
var cheese=new Array();
var tomatoes=new Array();
var labor=new Array();
var totalExpenses=new Array();
var netProfit=new Array();
var deptCode=new
Array(revenue,flour,pepperoni,cheese,tomatoes,labor,totalExpenses,netProfit);

totaller();
```

We now have one über-array called deptCode, which contains as its elements all of the arrays defined before it. There are nine arrays within the array deptCode. We can access elements at the lowest level with the following syntax:

```
deptCode["labor"]["wk1"] = 5475;
```

This assigns the number value 5475 to the element labeled wk1 within the array "labor," which in turn is an element within the array deptCode.

At this point you may be thinking that this is a silly way to figure the bottom line of a mom-and-pop pizza stand. After all, it would take about the same amount of scripting and less ingenuity (thinking) to make each vertical column an instance of the same Movie clip and just do the arithmetic manually. For the application of graphic display, a solution using Movie clips might be equally viable, but this approach would quickly run out of steam as you increased complexity and the need to manipulate the arrays.

You will see the same basic nested for loops repeated over and over in this code. The function of these loops is to go through each element in each array. There are two dimensions to our system of arrays and therefore two levels in the control structure. The structure could easily be broken out into its own function, but the meaning would be much harder to comprehend at first reading. For the sake of keeping this example simple, I have kept them separate.

The following code is the beginning of the "totaller" function, which is everything that executes when the ENTER key is pressed. In other words, this is what recalculates the totals and fills out the spreadsheet.

```
/********here's where it happens*****************/
function totaller(){

//re-initialize the array element values
for (i=0;i<deptCode.length;i++){
    for(j=1;j<=5;j++){
        deptCode[i]["wk" + j]=0;
    }
}
delete i;
delete j;
```

The first order of business is to clear out the previous values in the arrays. This is not strictly necessary for the first iteration of this function, but for each subsequent round, it is.

The outermost for loop goes through each element in the array deptCode. Remember that each element in this array is itself an array. That is why, when the inside for loop calls "deptCode[0]["wk1"]," it is actually accessing the element labeled "wk1" within the array "revenue."

Using this structure, we quickly assign a value of zero to 40 elements. This is one of the primary conveniences of using arrays this way.

Our goal is to calculate a bunch of interrelating totals from the user input. So far, we cleared the arrays of any meaningful numbers. The next step is to get the numbers from the user input.

```
//get cell values from user input
for (i=0;i<deptCode.length-2;i++){
    for(j=1;j<=4;j++){
        deptCode[i]["wk" + j]=_root["cell" + (i+1) + j];
    }
}
delete i;
delete j;
```

To understand what is happening here, look at how the text fields are named on the stage. Each one is named cell, with an affix that describes its coordinates. The first number is its row number, and the second number is its column number. This has nothing to do with programming proper; it is just a convention I chose to make parsing through the information easier. You can also choose letters of the alphabet, names of U.S. presidents, or color names, but anything other than sequential numbers would require additional scripting.

Once you observe this, it's easy to see what is happening. We are going through each array element one by one, just like before, only this time we are assigning a value from the corresponding text field on the stage. This works because our naming scheme fits well with the structure of our arrays. It would be ideal if we could simply name the text fields as array elements, but unfortunately, Flash 5 does not yet have this ability.

We have all the user input safely nestled in our arrays, and we are ready to start computing totals. We will start by going down each column and figuring the total expenses from each week.

```
//find total expenses for each week
    for(j=1;j<=4;j++){
        for (i=1;i<deptCode.length-2;i++){
            totalExpenses["wk"+j]+= number(deptCode[i]["wk" + j]);
        }
        _root["cell" + "7" + j]=number(totalExpenses["wk"+j]);
    }
delete i;
delete j;
```

Since we are figuring the total expenses, we don't want to include revenue or net profit in the computation. We also don't want to include the value of total expenses when we are trying to figure out a new value of total expenses—not that it would hurt since it is zero, but it would be bad style. So we start iterating through the deptCode array on the second element ("i=1") and stop before we evaluate the last two ("i < deptCode.length-2"). After we figure the total expenses for each week, we fill out each text field in the "total expenses" row on the stage. Notice that there is no need to fill out any other text field so far, since the other text fields are just user input—they require no change.

You may have noticed the top-level function "number" in this block of code. This is required because Flash can get confused when you combine strings, variables, and raw numbers, as we do in this script. If we didn't use the function "number" to tell Flash exactly what we want, we would get unpredictable results, with some of the totals being concatenated strings of the individual number values.

Next is figuring the net profit, which is simply the difference between two numbers that reside in known locations within each array. Therefore, it is only necessary to loop through the weeks, so there's only one "for" loop.

```
//find net profit for each week
    for(j=1;j<=4;j++){
        netProfit["wk"+j]=revenue["wk"+j] - totalExpenses["wk"+j];
        _root["cell" + "8" + j]=netProfit["wk"+j] ;
    }
delete j;
```

Finally, we find the sum of each horizontal row. I have no idea how real spreadsheet programs work, but I'm sure it's not like this. In our example, we employ only addition and subtraction, so it really makes no difference which direction we go.

```
//extend the rows across to find the month total
    for (i=0;i<deptCode.length;i++){
        for(j=1;j<=4;j++){
            deptCode[i]["wk5"]+= number(deptCode[i]["wk" + j]);
        }
        _root["cell" + (i+1) + "5"]=number(deptCode[i]["wk" + j]);
    }
delete i;
delete j;
}
```

Nothing new conceptually here. You might have noticed that the way "for" loops are nested is opposite to the way it was before. This is not necessary at all. This is just my way of indicating to myself which direction we're working across the array matrix. If I see "i" on the outside, I know that I'm working *across* horizontally. I conceptualize the user input as moving this way because of the tab order. In the loops where we moved through the entire matrix, I used the same method because it is easy to visualize. When I see "j" on the outside, it is easy to tell at a glance that I'm moving vertically on the matrix of arrays.

The only other code required to make this thing work is something to set the "totaller" function in motion. I chose a button with a keyPress handler for the ENTER key. This is different from the methods we used with the key object—it is a special handler available only to buttons.

```
on (keyPress "<Enter>") {
    _root.totaller();
}
```

Sound

campfireMixer.fla

Our last example is a fun little project. All of the code we will be discussing is in *campfireMixer.fla* on the CD. Please take a moment to familiarize yourself with how this movie works.

The idea is that we're taking aural elements from a scene and mixing them together using recording console–type faders. The reason we are using sounds from nature instead of synchronized music is because we currently lack a 100 percent reliable solution for controlling synchronous music tracks from some kind of time code. I suppose you could use very short samples triggered over and over any timeline loop, but there's still no guarantee that the sounds would start at the same time. Since we are attaching and starting sounds with ActionScript, which executes commands in order and not simultaneously, it is impossible to synchronize these events down to the electron.

The ActionScript behind this application is so simple I'm hesitant to include it in the book, but the application is fun to play with and it has a high "neat" rating. At the time of writing, every Flash community has a tutorial or an open source FLA with a single sound fader, but no one seems to have thought of a mixer. I think this is a terrific interactive widget; it has the potential to engage users for a long amount of time relative to its file size. This is a good measure of usefulness in our business.

The application begins on the main timeline. First we create a unique sound object for each sound.

```
var crickets=new Sound("_root.cricketsFader");
crickets.attachSound("crickets");
crickets.setVolume(0);
crickets.start( 0, 999 );

var fire=new Sound("_root.fireFader");
fire.attachSound("fire");
frie.setVolume(0);
fire.start( 0, 999 );

var stream=new Sound("_root.streamFader");
stream.attachSound("stream");
stream.setVolume(0);
stream.start( 0, 999 );

var guitar=new Sound("_root.guitarFader");
guitar.attachSound("guitar");
guitar.setVolume(0);
guitar.start( 0, 999 );
```

You can easily guess what each method of the sound object does just from reading its descriptive name. I'll elaborate where it is not insulting. Like the date object, the sound object requires a constructor. Each of the sound object instances we create in our example uses an optional argument. This defines the scope of the sound object. If you leave this blank, the sound object will apply to the entire timeline. The other interesting thing about this argument is that sound objects without it cannot be manipulated individually. Try deleting this argument from the sound constructors in this example and see what happens.

The "attachSound" method pulls a sound symbol out of the library. The argument to this method is the name of the symbol in its export linkage.

The scale of the "setVolume" method is 0 to 100. It may seem backward to set the volume of the sound before it ever starts playing, as we do in this example. This is because there is a tiny delay between the execution of each command. If we switched the order, the sound would start playing for a moment at full volume before going back down to the level we want.

Finally, the "start" method takes two arguments: the point and the sound at which you want to start playing in seconds, and the number of times to loop the sound. In other words, if you want to chop off the first three seconds of the sound and loop it twice, you could do something like the this:

```
mySound.start(3,2);
```

There is one obvious improvement we can make to the code for our sound object, and we haven't talked about it yet in this section of the book. Any time you want to use multiple methods of a single object—that is, what Flash considers a proper object—you can use this construct:

```
with(stream){
attachSound("stream");
setVolume(0);
start( 0, 999 );
}
```

This works with custom objects, built-in objects such as date and math, and Movie clips. It does not work with arrays.

For the faders, we use four instances of the same Movie clip. The following code is attached to each. Only the target of the "setVolume" method changes between them.

```
onClipEvent(mouseMove){
    faderVal=100-Math.round(this.button._y/2.685);
    _root.crickets.setVolume(faderVal);
}

onClipEvent(load){
    _root.crickets.setVolume(0);
}
```

The variable "faderVal" is just a simple algebraic expression to determine the position of the button on the fader. You should also notice that the handler for this code is "mouseMove" instead of "enterFrame." Since the volume of each sound object doesn't need to change when the mouse is not moving, there's obviously no reason to waste system resources by continuing to check for movement of the slider button.

What to Take Away from This Chapter

Objects are there to make your life easier. Learn to use all of the built-in objects in Flash 5. Make silly little applications like the ones in this chapter. Even if they don't seem to address particular problems that are in front of you now, they help you get familiar with the techniques they use. You aren't really done learning Flash until you know and understand every built-in object, property, method, and action.

Mouse/Keyboard Interaction

IN THIS CHAPTER:

Mouse Interaction and Usability

The User's Perspective

Rotation

For... In

_Name Property

Combining Conditions with Logical Operators

In this chapter, we are going to look at the big topic of creating interactivity with the user's mouse movements. Everything in this chapter will be a discussion of the example *fakop.fla* on the CD. Please take a moment to open *fakop.html*, the sample HTML frame for the movie, and get a feel for how the menu works. As you can see in the next illustration, you engage the menu by moving your mouse to the upper-right corner of the screen.

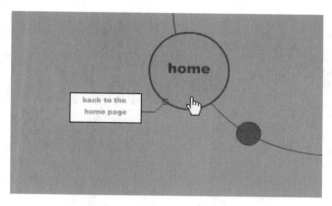

We begin with a terse foray into the even bigger topic of usability, followed by a breakdown of what a typical user might perceive as he uses the example for the first time. After that, we will look at the nuts and bolts of this Flash movie, including a few tricks we haven't seen before, such as the for...in loop.

Mouse Interaction and Usability

In case you didn't notice when you tried it, I should point out that the example is my take on Yugo Nakamura's famous menu concept from his original Mono*Crafts Web site (http://yugop.com). This is especially interesting as we begin our discussion of usability in the context of mouse interaction, considering that Nakamura's site makes no attempt whatsoever to ensure that users will be able to find any useful information quickly by using familiar navigation. I believe that the example discussed in this chapter is extremely usable—even to the point of being a viable navigation system for a commercial Web site. This section of the chapter discusses the impact on usability of mouse interactivity in Flash.

The Idea of Usability

If you have not already been mired in a knock-down-drag-out, circular flame war over usability (or at least a discussion of it), the most basic core principles are as follows. There are plenty of other issues—probably enough to make a career out of—but we are just going to focus on the things that have an immediate impact on using mouse interaction for a menu application in Flash.

▶ **Familiarity** The usability pundits, including Guru-in-Chief Jakob Nielsen, seem to focus on familiarity as the primary feature of a good design. "If the user has seen it before, the user will know how it works," goes the argument.

▶ **Being able to find things quickly and intuitively** This is the second commandment at the very general level. Obviously, this criterion is in a slightly different category. It is more an effect of implementing a good design than a cause.

▶ **Compatibility** This is probably the most familiar usability topic to anyone who uses the Internet, developers and users alike. Compatibility means basically that users have the proper tools to render the design on their machine. In the case of Flash, the big variable in this category is whether the user has a new enough version of a Flash Player installed. For our example, we will not consider compatibility issues like browsers, browser version, or platform. We will assume that if the user has the Flash Player, compatibility is taken care of. For a full treatment of compatibility, including metrics for measuring how well screen space is used, check out Jakob Nielsen's "Designing Web Usability."

▶ **Use of common navigation tools** In case you missed one of the biggest events in the Flash world in 2000, you should be aware that usability talking head Jakob Nielsen caused a foundation-shaking uproar in the Flash community with his short article on Flash usability. You can find the article at http://www.useit.com/ alertbox/ 20001029.html One of the biggest usability issues for Flash developers, according to the article, is whether the design makes use of the most common navigation tools, including the back button, bookmarks, standard hypertext link color schemes, and cookies. The problem with Flash, according to this argument, is that an entire Web site exists within a single file that does not interact with the Web browser's built-in navigation features.

No matter who you ask, the most sensible approach for determining the usability of a particular design is always the following axiom: The ultimate goal of usability is to present users with an interface that allows them to find the information they want quickly and easily. In design, however, there exists a continuum between a primary focus on easily accessible, useful information and a primary focus on attractive, engaging design elements. For any particular design, at what point do the benefits of a tricky interface outweigh the necessary sacrifices made in the area of standard navigation tools? Or, to put it another way, is it worth scaring off newbies, tech-hypochondriacs, and people who otherwise have no tolerance for alternative navigation methods for the sake of attracting people who share your joy for interactive widgets?

How Does the Example Compare?
fakop.html, fakop.fla

Our example, *fakop.html*, is perfect fodder for discussion on this subject. It employs a nonstandard navigation menu and disables the standard navigation tools of the Web browser. In other words, it does everything usability experts say we ought not do. Following is a look at how the example stacks up to the criteria we just discussed, including several advantages not commonly considered in discussions on usability.

First of all, our example fails miserably in the area of familiarity. Unless you correspond with me regularly, you have probably never seen anything quite like this menu before. What's worse, probably 90% of typical Web users wouldn't know where to find the menu without bright flashing lights and animated arrows pointing them to it.

Therein lies the problem. People approach new knowledge and experiences as a problem to be solved in the context of what they already know. To put it another way, people describe things (to themselves, if we are talking about learning a new skill) in terms of things they already know. For instance, when chewing gum was first introduced to the fever pitch postwar consumer market, it was likened to "candy that you don't swallow," for lack of better imagery that all Americans were likely to share. In slightly more recent history, gummy, animal-shaped candy might have been described as "gum that you *do* swallow."

The Web is the same way. When a certain searchable index became the most popular Web site in the world in the early days of the Web, usability conscious developers reasoned that if they built their sites with the same interface, a majority of people would instantly know how to use their site. "It's like a Yahoo that has information about our company," went the pitch, and it didn't take long for this simple idea to become exalted dogma, complete with high priests and millions of devoted followers.

So basically what we are asking as we examine this chapter's example under this criterion is, "Is this navigation menu like Yahoo?" The answer is obviously no, but there is at least one up side.

While Flash applications that make use of complex mouse interaction may not conform to standard *Web* navigation techniques, it is entirely possible to closely mimic standard navigation widgets from familiar places like operating system dialogs and scroll bars. For instance, if you were designing a resource site for users of 3D Studio Max, you might get the most mileage for your screen space with a simulation of that tool's viewport pan and rotation tools. This navigation system would be incomprehensible to the average Web user; but to the target audience it is vastly more efficient than standard HTML, as well as endearing because of its reference to Max, the focus of the community it serves. An excellent real-life example of this kind of menu is The Freehand Source (http://www.freehandsource.com/).

The example's rating in the next category, *ability to find things quickly and easily*, is less a definite answer and more a function expressed as a learning curve. Obviously, first-time users could find the information they are looking for faster with a familiar HTML menu. However, once you learn to use the example menu, there are additional benefits that could never be acquired with simple HTML.

First of all, the menu is always in the same place on the user's screen. This is in contrast to the usual HTML scenario, where the menu is the upper-left corner of the page, where it remains regardless of the user's position on the page. In other words, the farther you go down the screen, the harder it is to get somewhere else on the site.

The other advantage in this category is that once the menu is activated, very little movement of the mouse is required to make any selection. This is in contrast to the sprawling HTML menu, which is typically about 100 pixels wide and anywhere from about 400 to thousands of pixels tall.

Another, similar advantage of Flash over HTML is an unmatched ability to represent hierarchical structure. Our little wheel of menu items represents a simple, flat information structure for the sake of simplicity; but it could just as easily be a little wheel of even smaller wheels, which would contain individual entries in each category.

On the issue of *making use of the browser's native navigation tools*, we could easily obtain a high score by breaking out each section into a separate movie, which in turn would be framed in a separate HTML page. This would allow the user to bookmark specific sections, use the back button, and accept cookies in a fashion to which she is already accustomed. I chose the structure as it appears on the CD for the sake of simplicity.

Conclusion

This example would probably not be the first choice for a huge international site receiving millions of hits from street-level consumers, at least not at this point in history. Such sites are primarily concerned with serving the most people with the least amount of confusion possible. Another thing to consider is that sites that already receive heavy traffic are probably not interested in novelty—certainly not in the navigation menu.

On the other hand, I believe this type of menu is perfect for a more specialized site that seeks to differentiate itself from competitors. There are some types of sites where users are actually seeking an engaging experience in addition to the raw information. Two common examples are entertainment sites and purveyors of high-ticket consumer goods. In this kind of user base, users are more likely to explore the site, taking their time to enjoy the atmosphere, even if that atmosphere initially presents obstacles to finding the information they want.

Complex mouse interaction is as basic to mature multimedia projects as color and typography, and knowing when and how to use it is tricky. It is a simple fact of life that employing slick interactivity will attract some users and repel others. I hope our discussion has shed some light on the subject.

The User's Perspective

There are two main problems with this kind of interactivity as it is currently employed on the Web. First of all, there is too much of it—it pops up in places where it doesn't belong, giving Flash a bad name. And second, it is usually conceived of as a technical achievement rather than a user enhancement.

When I decided to include an entire chapter on mouse interaction, the classic Yugop menu was the first thing to come to mind (and the second and the third). But it bothered me that while the effect was ubiquitous on second-rate sites, you never saw it in the mainstream. After much thought on the subject, I think I figured out why the idea doesn't mesh well with a commercial project.

At first glance, the Yugop menu seems like it would be a perfect GUI widget to increase the usability of a menu: as you move the mouse closer to a menu item, that menu item responds by moving toward the mouse. What could be easier? The problem is that there is never a point where the menu stands still and lets you click with confidence. The result is a kind of nervous energy that radiates from the menu as if it were a living (or at least intelligent) thing. The reason the menu is designed this way goes back to the idea that spawned the entire site: interacting primarily in the dimension of time, rather than the horizontal and vertical axes of the monitor.

Now that's all fine and good for a site that exists as a piece of fine art; but how does that help us build an interactive menu for a commercial site? You can't exactly sit in your client's office and pitch far-out, abstract ideas. And the other, more common approach, starting with a technical idea like "I want to use a cool new technique," doesn't sell well, either.

The middle road that we are taking with this example is *starting with the user interaction in mind*. First I took my favorite interactive elements from the Yugop menu: the behavior of the menu items to move toward the mouse, and little tooltips. Then I added a feature from the Windows operating system: autohide. The second feature, combined with the idea of clicking on labeled buttons to navigate to a different portion of the site, provides enough familiar territory for new users to get their bearings.

Whenever I design a Flash application in which I can't immediately imagine every line of pseudocode, I draw it out by hand first, making notes like "menu rotates counter to vertical mouse movement," or "autohide when mouse moves 10 pixels beyond left or lower perimeter." If you think of it *first* in terms of how you would use it, the code practically writes itself. If, on the other hand, you think of it in terms of how to make it a cool menu with lots of widgets, you typically end up with something less useful.

Rotation

We are finally ready to break down the code line by line. The following code is from the Movie clip instance labeled "menu," which contains all five menu items and is located just offstage to the right.

First look at what happens within the load clip event handler. We will talk about how the for...in loop works shortly. In this case, the control structure loops through each instance of the "circleMC" Movie clip (the circular menu items). First it hides the nested Movie clip instance within each one called "toolTip." Then it accesses an array called "tooltips" in the main timeline to assign the unique text to each tooltip.

```
onClipEvent(load){
    for(name in this){
        this[name].toolTip._visible=0;
        this[name].toolTip.text=_root.tooltips[name];
```

```
        }
    }
```

Next is the most conspicuous feature of the application: the rotation of the menu. The general notion is that the menu rotates in response to the vertical distance between the mouse cursor and the imaginary horizontal line 125 pixels from the top of the stage. (Remember that Flash measures vertical distance from the top, not the bottom.)

We use this distance to figure out how much we want to increment or decrement the menu's _rotation value. The farther we get from the line without going over 125 pixels in distance, the more we rotate the menu. The ratio vertDist/10 was chosen by trial and error. This fraction seems to offer the best compromise between moving quickly between menu items and being stable enough to use easily.

If the variable vertDist is more than 125 pixels (the mouse cursor is more than 125 pixels below our imaginary line), we set the value to 125. This is so that the variable rotIncrement, which is going to be responsible for rotating the menu, has the same possible range of values in each direction.

```
onClipEvent(enterFrame){
vertDist=_root._ymouse-125;
if (vertDist > 125){
    vertDist = 125;
}
rotIncrement=Math.round (vertDist/10);
```

The following chunk of code has several interesting elements. We will talk about the for...in loop in the next section, and complex conditions with multiple logical operators in a subsequent section in this chapter. Right now, we are just going to talk about the flow of events and how the menu gets rotated.

The long condition in the if control structure can basically be read as follows: "If the Movie clip is rotated more than –130 degrees *and* the user's mouse is above our imaginary line, *or* if the Movie clip is rotated more than 60 degrees *and* the user's mouse is below our imaginary line, then do the following stuff..." The only reason we need to bother with all these braces, marks, and squiggles is so that we do not waste the user's time by rotating the blank part of the circle over the stage. We are setting a limit on how far we will rotate the menu in each direction. Combining the conditions that test the position of the mouse cursor with the conditions that check the current value of the rotation is a safeguard against *bouncing*—the effect you might get if you tried to reset the rotation when it went out of bounds. Try removing the conditions that test the value of vertDist and see what happens.

Next we increment the rotation of the Movie clip by the value of rotIncrement. It may not be obvious why it is always incremented, since half of the time we actually want to decrement the rotation, that is, turn the Movie clip counterclockwise. However, if you refer to the previous block of code, you will notice that when the mouse cursor is above our imaginary line, the value of rotIncrement will be negative. Incrementing the rotation by a negative number is the same as decrementing it.

Finally, we have another for…in loop. The function of this code, just as the comment says, is to keep level all of the Movie clips nested within this one. If this movie clip ("menu") is rotated 20 degrees, all the Movie clips inside it will be rotated −20 degrees. This is what keeps the text on each button parallel to the horizontal axis.

```
//if the menu is within the designated range of rotation, make it
respond to user mouse movement
if ((this._rotation > -130 && vertDist < 0) || ( this._rotation
< 60 && vertDist > 0)) {
     this._rotation+=rotIncrement;
}

     //counter-rotate all inner MC's to make them level
       for(name in this){
           this[name]._rotation= -this._rotation;
       }


}
```

For…In

ForElipsisIn.fla

In this section we are going to take a closer look at the for…in loop and how it works. The basic idea of the for…in loop is that you designate an object and then cycle through every nested object contained within, executing the code inside the control structure on the nested objects.

First, let's look at the basic syntax. In the following code, which shows the syntax of the for…in loop, you see something called a *variable iterant*. This is just fancy programming talk, meaning "a special variable that applies to every object in a list." This variable acts as a placeholder for each of the objects contained within the object you designate. If you are familiar with any old-school languages, the for…in loop is just like a for each loop.

```
for(variableIterant in object){
    variableIterant.someMethodOrProperty(); //i.e. do something
}
```

For instance, you may choose an array as an object, using the word "name" as the identifier for your mystical "variable iterant" variable. In the following example, we iterate through the array ages, using the variable "name" as a placeholder for the name of each element. Because this is an associative array, the label on each array element is a name we have assigned. If this were a simple array, these labels would be simple index numbers. In this example, the variable identifier "name" was chosen arbitrarily. It could just as well have been "Saskatoon."

```
ages=new Array();
ages["Jonny"]="47";
ages["Jane"]="19";
ages["Joe"]="14";
ages["Janice"]="99";

for(name in ages){
    trace(name + " is " + ages[name] + " years old.");
}

/*has the output...
Janice is 99 years old.
Joe is 14 years old.
Jane is 19 years old.
Jonny is 47 years old. */
```

Next let's try something a little closer to what we use in the rest of the chapter. The code in this example comes from *ForElipsisIn.fla* on the CD. This movie features five instances of the same Movie clip, named "Circle One," "Circle Two," and so on. Each was manually rotated to an arbitrary position, shown here:

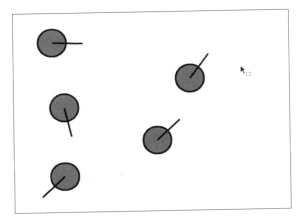

The following code is on the main timeline of the movie. This is the only code in this example.

```
for(MC in _root){
    trace(MC + "'s rotation is " + Math.round(_root[MC]._rotation) + " degrees.");
}

/*yields the output
$version's rotation is 0 degrees.
Circle Five's rotation is -45 degrees.
Circle Four's rotation is 135 degrees.
Circle Three's rotation is 75 degrees.
Circle Two's rotation is -55 degrees.
Circle One's rotation is 0 degrees. */
```

This time we used "MC" as our variable iterant, again chosen arbitrarily. We are iterating through the root level of the movie, so the code in the middle of the loop will act on any object at this level, as you can see. The variable $version is something that was added in Flash 4 to help with automatic user agent detection. It is always there.

Now that you have a better handle on the for…in loop, let's take another look at the code attached to the menu Movie clip. It should be obvious what is going on at this point. We are iterating through the object identified as "this," which you will recall is simple shorthand for "the current Movie clip or object." Therefore, we are iterating through the menu Movie clip, changing the rotation of each object within it. When we write "this[name]._rotation," we are talking about the rotation of each object within the current Movie clip.

```
//counter-rotate all inner MC's to make them level
    for(name in this){
        this[name]._rotation= -this._rotation;
    }

}


onClipEvent(load){
    for(name in this){
        this[name].toolTip._visible=0;
        this[name].toolTip.text=_root.tooltips[name];
    }
}
```

Don't let the last line in the code above confuse you. When we write "_root.tooltips[name]," we are referring to an array in the main timeline that was specifically constructed to exactly match the objects contained within this Movie clip. You should get used to moving data around this way, because this is how you will bring data into a Flash movie when we start working with external data sources in Chapter 14.

```
tooltips=new Array();
tooltips["home"]= "back to the home page";
tooltips["about"]= "about lil ol us";
tooltips["mission"]= "some hokey, canned bs";
tooltips["products"]= "our stuff we sell";
tooltips["contact"]= "a fill out form";
```

_Name Property
fakop.fla

Way back in Chapter 3, I talked about reusing Movie clips as navigation objects in order to save on file size. This trick is used in our *fakop.fla* example, this time with an added twist. If you look at each "circleMC" instance within the menu Movie clip (the circles that comprise the navigation buttons), you will find the following code attached to each. Originally this code was in the for…in loop, but I separated it for the sake of pedagogical clarity.

```
onClipEvent(load){
    label=this._name;
}
```

The crux of this trick is giving each Movie clip instance a name that you want to display at run time. In other words, we are creating Movie clip instances that display their own names. For example, I named the Movie clip shown in the next illustration "mission," so that when the code above executes, the dynamic text field that displays the variable "label" will read "mission."

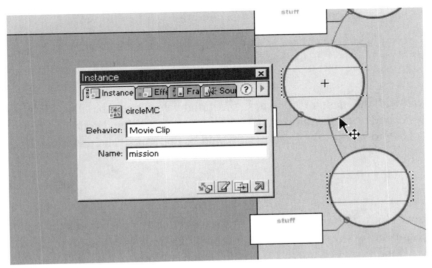

We are simply making use of the _name property that exists for all Movie clips. Since this property exists for every Movie clip already, using this method is more efficient in terms of memory than it would be to assign a value to the variable "label" from an array or some other tedious method.

Combining Conditions with Logical Operators

The code we will examine in this section is attached to the blank movie clip instance called "checker" in the upper-left corner of the stage. We'll also use this code as a review of the logical operators && (logical *and*) and || (logical *or*).

The first order of business in this section of code is to set the variable called "switcher." This is an arbitrary variable name I chose to signify whether the user wants the menu to be on screen. Anytime you have a variable that toggles between two states, it makes the most sense to use the Boolean values true and false. That way, you have more options to construct conditions, for example:

```
if(switcher){...       //true if switcher is set to true
if(!switcher){...       //true if switcher is set to false
or if(switcher != true){...      //same as above
```

We start with the menu off screen, so the initial value should be false. If we had used either the second or third example above in our long, convoluted condition below, we wouldn't have to set the initial value—it would be undefined, and therefore not true.

```
onClipEvent(load){
    switcher = false;
}
```

The next block of code simply determines whether the user wants the menu to pop out or disappear. This code is a little bit on the ugly side because of the complexity of the two conditions considered. Take a moment to look at it while I paraphrase the meaning in plain English.

(First condition): if the mouse cursor is in the upper-right section of the stage, *and* the switcher variable is set to false (meaning that the menu is either hidden or moving to the right toward being hidden), change the switcher variable to the value true (meaning that the menu should start moving back to the left toward its on-screen position).

(Second condition, else if): if the switcher variable is set to true, *and* the user moves the mouse out of the menu area (either to the left *or* down), change the switcher variable to the value false.

```
onClipEvent(enterFrame){
    if((_root._xmouse >= 540 && _root._ymouse <= 100) && switcher == false){
        switcher = true;
    }else if((_root._xmouse <= 360 || _root._ymouse >= 250) && switcher == true){
        switcher = false;
    }
```

Let's look at the same block of code in another way. Recall that the logical operator && makes it so that both statements in the condition must be true in order for the code inside the control structure to execute. Therefore, another way to write the first condition would be with three nested if control structures, as follows:

```
if(_root._xmouse >= 540){
    if(_root._ymouse <= 100){
        if(switcher == false){
            switcher = true;
        }
    }
}else if ...
```

If you find yourself writing deeply nested control structures like this, or multiple else if control structures with duplicate code executed within them, take another look at what you are really testing. The number of control structures should always match the number of possible outcomes for which you are testing. Using the two most common logical operators, && and ||, you can construct complex conditions that reflect what you're testing more accurately than nested if and else if loops.

The last bit of code to look at in this example is a simple control structure that moves the menu left and right on demand. It appears as follows:

```
if(_root.menu._x >590 && switcher==true){
    _root.menu._x -=10;
}else if(_root.menu._x < 870 && switcher==false){
    _root.menu._x +=10;
}
}
```

This one is easy to translate. If the horizontal position of the menu Movie clip instance is more than 590 pixels (it is somewhere to the right of its on-screen position), *and* the variable switcher is set to the value true (the user wants the menu to be on screen), decrement its x position by 10 pixels (move it toward its on-screen position). If, on the other hand, the menu movie clip instance is to the left of its off-screen position *and* the variable switcher is set to the value false, move 10 pixels to the right.

What to Take Away from This Chapter

In the Flash 4 days, complex mouse interaction was a sign that someone had both mastered the scripting language and completely discarded any notion of usability. Today things are different, or at least they *can* be different. On one hand, it is much easier to script complex interactions because of increased power and ease of ActionScript, not even considering the growing number of drag-and-drop interactivity scripts available from Macromedia Exchange and elsewhere in the Flash community. On the other hand, the novelty of Flash for Flash's sake has completely evaporated; and users are tired of useless tricky gizmos, no matter how complex or clever their conception. At this point you should have a new trick or two to employ in your own Flash movies using mouse interaction, as well as a few ideas about usability to encourage you to use your superpowers only for good.

2D Motion in the Flash Universe

I n my humble opinion, one of the most interesting and satisfying things you can do with any programming or scripting language is create motion. Whether it be motion that simulates the physics of the real world or simply motion that is pleasing to the eye, creating autonomously moving objects in an application gives you a profound sense of satisfaction. It is something that touches the human need to create in a deep way.

Thumbnail Physics

It is entirely possible to simulate the physics of the natural world—gravity, friction, wind velocity, the statics of rigid bodies, and so on—with a powerful scripting language. The accuracy of physics emulation is critical when you are building something like a controller to land a lunar module or a flight simulator to train young, green pilots.

In our case, we are not going to bother ourselves with details and equations regarding real-world physics. Rather, we will take the approach of intuitively constructing code to emulate the visual output we want.

Acceleration

acceleration01.fla, acceleration02.fla

The first example we are going to look at is *acceleration01.fla* on the CD. This simple movie shows a small circle beginning from a static position and accelerating as it moves to the right. The following code is what makes the ball go:

```
onClipEvent(load){
    xVelocity=0;
    acceleration=.9;
    this._x=this._width/2;
    this._y=this._width/2;
}

onClipEvent(enterFrame){
    this._x += xVelocity;
    xVelocity += acceleration;
```

We have one variable to define the velocity of the object, xVelocity. This is the amount by which the x position of the Movie clip is incremented each time the code executes. In other words, if this variable is set to 5, the Movie clip will move to the right five pixels each time the code executes. This is what gives the impression of fluid motion.

The "acceleration" variable is the amount by which the velocity is incremented each time that code executes. Because the velocity becomes greater with each iteration, the Movie clip is moved by a slightly larger amount in each successive frame. This is what gives the impression of fluid acceleration.

If we were doing this experiment in a physics lab, we would use a nice long table with runners on the side to give us enough room to perceive the effect of acceleration and to keep our test subject in line. Since we have limited space to work with on our monitors, we will use an old video game trick to create the illusion of continuous motion.

```
//move the ball back to the left side of the screen a la asteroids
if (this._x-this._width/2>=640){
        this._x=0-this._width/2;
    }
}
```

This is what the code means: if the left edge of the Movie clip (assuming it is symmetrical) is flush with or beyond the right edge of the stage, we will place the Movie clip's right edge at the left edge of the movie stage.

Because of the decidedly unscientific method we chose to apply acceleration to the Movie clip, it would be helpful to add a slider to change the value of the acceleration variable. Using a slider, we can adjust the value visually at run time and observe the effects. That way, we can decide which value has the most pleasing outcome with continuous visual feedback. The following code is from *acceleration02.fla* on the CD. This action is attached to the "slider" Movie clip, which you will remember from the audio fader example in Chapter 11.

```
onClipEvent (mouseMove) {
    _root.ball.acceleration=this.percent/50;
}
```

The variable "percent" has a range of 0 to 100, so the value of _root.ball.acceleration will have a range of 0 to 2.

The reset button simply sets all of the variables back to their original values, including x position of the ball. The code shown next is attached to the invisible button over the text that says "reset."

```
on(release){
ball.switcher=false;
ball.velocity=0;
ball._x=0-ball._width/2;
}
```

Bouncing

bounce01.fla

In previous chapters we saw how the Flash 5 method hitTest() makes collision detection easy. In this chapter, we are going to use the old school method of defining imaginary boundaries. In our first example, *bounce01.fla* on the CD, our imaginary boundary will be the lower extent of the movie stage.

```
onClipEvent(load){
    velocity=0;
    acceleration=.9;
}

onClipEvent(enterFrame){
//add switch to facilitate start and reset
if(this.switcher==true){
    this._y += velocity;
    velocity += acceleration;
//bounce off the bottom border of the movie
    if (this._y+this._width/2>=480){
        velocity=-velocity;
        this._y=480-this._width/2;
    }
}
}
```

Only two things have changed between the last example and this one: we have changed the orientation from horizontal to vertical, and the Movie clip now bounces instead of recycling back to the other side of the screen when it encounters its boundary. In other words, it bounces off the floor instead of going from left to right.

Notice that we are still using half the width of the Movie clip instance as an adjustment when we test to see if the Movie clip instance is at the border. This only works because the clip is a circle with a registration point at the center (so the vertical distance is the same as the horizontal distance).

Since the Movie clip continues to accelerate without any obstacles like gravity or friction, you might think that it would just continue to speed off the screen after the first time it bounces. However, if you look at the method we use to increment velocity, you can see why this isn't the case.

Since we *add* the constant acceleration to the dynamically changing velocity, we are continuously increasing the speed toward the bottom of the movie stage. While the Movie clip is moving up, the velocity is decreasing by the amount of the value of "acceleration" each time the code executes.

While the Movie clip is moving down, adding acceleration to the velocity obviously makes the clip move faster. This description sounds a lot like gravity, but there are still several elements missing. The most obvious is that the object continually gains momentum, bouncing higher each time. We will correct this idiosyncrasy in the next example.

Gravity

bounce02.fla, bounce03.fla

While we did change the name of one variable from the previous example, and the beginning value is a little higher, the change is actually very subtle. The only substantial difference between this example and the previous one is the order in which the variable values are incremented. This code is from *bounce02.fla* on the CD:

```
onClipEvent (load) {
    yVelocity=0;
    gravity=1.5;
}


onClipEvent (enterFrame) {
//add switch to facilitate start and reset
if (this.switcher==true) {
    yVelocity+=gravity;
    this._y += yVelocity;
    if (this._y+this._width/2>=480) {
        yVelocity=-yVelocity;
        this._y=480-this._width/2;
    }
}
}
```

Now, instead of applying the acceleration before the Movie clip is moved, it is applied afterward. The end result is that the ball bounces to the same height every time.

The essence of the previous problem is that we were adding energy to the ball's motion when it hit the floor instead of taking energy away. In the real world, kinetic energy is translated into all kinds of different neat stuff when objects collide: heat and sound waves just to name a couple.

In addition to the energy translated to an object upon collision, objects also lose energy as they travel—most importantly to the medium (like air) through which they are traveling—by means of friction. In the next example, we will combine these phenomena into a single variable that we will call lossOfEnergy. The following code is from *bounce03.fla* on the CD.

```
onClipEvent(load){
    yVelocity=0;
    gravity=1.5;
    lossOfEnergy=.95;
}


onClipEvent(enterFrame){
//add switch to facilitate start and reset
if(this.switcher==true){
    yVelocity*=lossOfEnergy;
    yVelocity+=gravity;
    this._y += yVelocity;
    if (this._y+this._width/2>=480){
        yVelocity=-yVelocity;
        this._y=480-this._width/2;
    }
}
}
```

The feeling you get from viewing the compiled output of this example should be familiar territory. It is that dreamy computer world in which the effects of friction and collisions are understated, and everything moves just a little faster than slow-motion instant replay. It's like walking on the moon, and there is something very pleasing about it. Maybe people just like the idea of escaping from gravity once in a while. I don't know—ask Freud.

Here's how the code works. The switch is the same as in the previous example: when a user clicks on Start, the variable "switcher" is set to the Boolean value "true." This sets the ball in motion.

Velocity and gravity interact the same as they did in the previous example. We have added the variable lossOfEnergy, a fraction by which the velocity is multiplied in each iteration. This is our universal simulator for friction, impact, and everything else that slows down a moving object.

Bouncing off the Walls

bounceWithWalls.fla

Our next example adds nothing but complexity to the commonsense principles we have already explored. This movie, *bounceWithWalls.fla* on the CD, adds several features: movement on both axes, four walls against which to bounce, and sliders for the variables gravity and lossOfEnergy.

The code that we will look at in this example is attached to the ball-shaped Movie clip. We start by initializing some of the variables we will use:

```
onClipEvent (load) {
    // define the limits of the box
    leftEdge= _root.box._x;
    rightEdge = _root.box._x+_root.box._width;
    topEdge = _root.box._y;
    bottomEdge = _root.box._y+_root.box._height;
    gravity = 3;
    lossOfEnergy=.94;
}
```

Instead of tediously defining four boundaries by rote, we dynamically get the values for the extents of the ball's motion area. We query the dimensions of the Movie clip instance "box," which doubles as a visual aid in the application output. This way, if we wanted to change the dimensions of our little virtual racquetball court, we could simply resize the "box" Movie clip instance visually to suit our taste (although it would require the addition of the properties _xscale and _yscale to the mix). This is generally an efficient and elegant way of doing things.

The next passage of code should look familiar. Everything is the same as in the previous example, except that there are more circumstances to consider.

```
onClipEvent (enterFrame) {
    xVelocity *= lossOfEnergy;
    yVelocity *= lossOfEnergy;
    yVelocity = yVelocity+gravity;
    this._y += yVelocity;
    this._x += xVelocity;
```

First of all, the ball is simultaneously moving horizontally and vertically. Therefore, we apply lossOfEnergy to the velocity of each direction. On the other hand, we only want gravity to affect the vertical axis, so the variable gravity only turns up once in this block of code.

Now the only thing left to accomplish in moving the ball is to determine whether it is bouncing off a wall. The following big, ugly block of code accomplishes this.

```
if (this._x+this._width/2>rightEdge) {
        this._x = rightEdge-this._width/2;
        xVelocity = -xVelocity;
    } else if (this._x-this._width/2<leftEdge) {
        this._x = leftEdge+this._width/2;
        xVelocity = -xVelocity;
    } else if (this._y+this._width/2>bottomEdge) {
        this._y = bottomEdge-this._width/2;
        yVelocity = -yVelocity;
    } else if (this._y-this._width/2<topEdge) {
        this._y = topEdge+this._width/2;
        yVelocity = -yVelocity;
    }
```

I can think of several other ways to do this, but each of them requires either checking four possible outcomes or constructing an unwieldy algorithm to reverse the velocity based on a hit test (using individual MCs as boundaries on each side instead of numeric constraints). So we'll stick with the easy way.

It's just like before, only there are four walls. Don't get confused because there are three "else if" segments of the control structure and no "else." This is necessary because the control structure needs to test four conditions simultaneously. Consider the possibility of the ball bouncing in a corner. The x velocity needs to change, but so does the y velocity.

Trigonometry

For a lot of people, the word "trigonometry" is just a set of words that together form a fuzzy memory of suffering through least-favorite high school classes. Unfortunately for those people, we are going to have to move (just a weensy bit) beyond that understanding to do our next set of examples. Don't worry, though—

we'll keep it much shorter and much, much sweeter (no homework) than your high school math class.

Short Review

Figure 13-1 illustrates everything we will need to know about trig. The reason that things are so simple in our trig review is that we are only interested in finding the relationship between two points on a two-dimensional coordinate system.

When we are looking for the angle between points (the centers of Movie clip instances), it is easy to think of it in terms of the opposite (difference in _y) and adjacent (difference in _x) sides of an imaginary right triangle. In other words, the best starting point for finding the angle between points is first finding the difference between their x and y positions on the movie stage. If you imagine the x distance as the adjacent side of a right triangle (as in Figure 13-1) and the y distance as the opposite side, you can use trigonometry to find the measure of the angle.

The Old Way

tangentGetter.html, follow01.fla

This example, while it is updated to Flash 5 syntax, uses the basic workflow I used to use in Flash 4 to find the angle between Movie clips. We will not go into minute detail for this example; it is included mainly to show how ridiculously complex the process used to be. Hopefully, this will bring the relative ease of using the Flash 5 ActionScript Math object into sharp relief and inspire you to create cool games and organic applications.

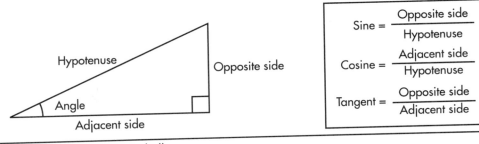

Figure 13.1   *Trig in a nutshell*

My old method started with a simple JavaScript HTML page to generate a list of tangent (opposite over adjacent, or _y over _x) values for each integer from 0 to 90. The following code is from *tangentGetter.html* on the CD.

```
<script language="JavaScript">
<!--hide

for(i=0;i<=90;i++){
    document.write(Math.tan(i*Math.PI/180) + ", ");
}

//show-->
</script>
```

In reality, my old method rounded the numbers off to four decimal places, but I left it alone in this example to bog down performance a little. This is because we used to have to emulate arrays in Flash 4, which was really just a whole bunch of simple string handling, whereas now we have actual arrays.

The following code is from *follow01.fla* on the CD. The output from the HTML page above is pasted directly into the array tangentLookupTable, which actually would have been one giant string in Flash 4.

```
onClipEvent(load){   tangentLookupTable=new Array(0,
0.017455064928217585, 0.03492076949174773, 0.052407779283041196,
0.06992681194351041, 0.08748866352592401, 0.10510423526567646,
0.1227845609029046, 0.14054083470239145, 0.15838444032453627,
0.17632698070846497, 0.19438030913771848, 0.2125565616700221,
0.23086819112556311, 0.24932800284318068, 0.2679491924311227,
0.2867453857588079, 0.3057306814586604, 0.3249196962329063,
0.3443276132896652, 0.36397023426620234, 0.3838640350354158,
0.4040262258351568, 0.4244748162096047, 0.4452286853085361,
0.4663076581549986, 0.48773258856586143, 0.5095254494944288,
0.5317094316614788, 0.554309051452769, 0.5773502691896257,
0.6008606190275604, 0.6248693519093275, 0.6494075931975106,
0.6745085168424267, 0.7002075382097097, 0.7265425280053609,
0.7535540501027942, 0.7812856265067173, 0.809784033195007,
0.8390996311772799, 0.8692867378162264, 0.9004040442978399,
0.9325150861376615, 0.9656887748070739, 0.9999999999999999,
1.0355303137905693, 1.072368710024 6826, 1.1106125148291927,
1.1503684072210094, 1.19175359259421, 1.234897156535051,
1.279941632193 0787, 1.3270448216204098, 1.3763819204711733,
1.4281480067421144, 1.482560968 5127403, 1.5398649638145827,
```

```
1.6003345290410506, 1.6642794823505173, 1.7320508075688767,
1.8040477552714235, 1.8807264653463318, 1.9626105055051503,
2.050303841579296, 2.1445069205095586, 2.2460367739042164,
2.355852365823752, 2.4750868534162964, 2.6050890646938005,
2.7474774194546216, 2.904210877675822, 3.0776835371752526,
3.2708526184841404, 3.4874144438409087, 3.7320508075688776,
4.010780933535842, 4.331475874284157, 4.704630109478451,
5.144554015970307, 5.671281819617707, 6.313751514675041,
7.115369722384195, 8.144346427974593, 9.514364454222587,
11.430052302761348, 14.300666256711895, 19.08113668772816,
28.636253282915515, 57.289961630759876, 16331778728383844);
counter=0;}
```

The next block of code is the actual quasi-trig. We measure the x and y distance from the Movie clip to the mouse and compare it to each individual value in the lookup array until we find one that matches. At any point in the "while" control structure, the value assigned to the variable "counter" is the angle in degrees that corresponds to the tangent in the lookup array. (Is this tedious or *what*!)

```
onClipEvent (enterFrame) {
    xDistance=_root._xmouse-this._x;
    yDistance=_root._ymouse-this._y;
    theTangent=Math.abs(yDistance)/Math.abs(xDistance);
    while (tangentLookupTable[counter]<theTangent) {
        counter++;
    }
    correctRotation=counter+90;
```

Finally, we have to correct the rotation for any instance in which the x distance and y distance are not both positive. The following code corrects each of the three quadrants of the stage that would otherwise make our application malfunction.

```
    if(xDistance < 0 && yDistance >0) {
        correctRotation=0-correctRotation;
        //lowerLeft;
    }else if(xDistance < 0 && yDistance < 0) {
        correctRotation+=180;
        //upperLeft;
    }else if(xDistance > 0 && yDistance < 0) {
        correctRotation=180-correctRotation;
        //upperRight;
```

```
    }
    this._rotation=correctRotation;
    counter=0;
  }
```

If this seems like a lot of work, consider the following factors that I sorta cheated around:

- ▶ Flash 4 had no clip event handlers. Continuous loops were handled with a two-frame Movie clip with a gotoAndPlay(1) action in the second frame.

- ▶ There were no arrays, so I used one long string to hold the lookup table, and as a result...

- ▶ There were about four more lines in the "while" loop, which served to iterate through the comma-separated values in the long string.

- ▶ Some people actually went a step deeper into Kludge World and used the Sine trig function (opposite over hypotenuse), which in turn necessitated the use of an arithmetic-oriented method (Newton's method) of determining the square root of a number. (The length of the hypotenuse is the square root of the sum of the squares of the opposite side and the adjacent side, hence the need for a square root function.)

The New Way
follow02.fla

Now that you have suffered as a smith's apprentice in the hot, sweaty furnace room, you are ready to appreciate the fact that we now do everything with lasers in a climate-controlled laboratory. The difference is that dramatic. Check out the equivalent example, *follow02.fla* on the CD.

```
onClipEvent (enterFrame) {
    xDistance=_root._xmouse-_x;
    yDistance=_root._ymouse-_y;
    correctRotation =
Math.atan2(yDistance,xDistance)*180/(Math.PI)+90;
    this._rotation = correctRotation;
}
```

That's all the code there is. There are a few new concepts in there, though; so we will linger on this example for a moment.

First of all, the method Math.atan2 is something a little different from the primary trig functions we already talked about. It measures the arc tangent of an angle, which is just the inverse of (one divided by) the tangent. The cool thing about this method is that *it takes as its arguments the lengths of the opposite and adjacent sides of our imaginary triangle* (as opposed to just an angle, as the rest of the trig methods in Flash do).

The last pedagogical speed bump to overcome is the idea of radians. The output of the atan2 method is measured in radians. I know that it sounds like a made-up unit from a low-budget science fiction TV show, but it's real. Ask any high school math student if you don't believe me.

One radian is equal to $180/\pi$. The reason this measure was chosen is so that one lap around a circle can be described by an absolute scale, with two easy-to-measure halves. Figure 13-2 should make this a little clearer.

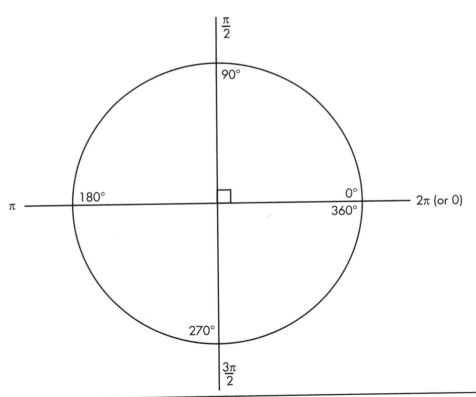

Figure 13.2   *Familiar points on a circle, measured in radians*

As you can see in Figure 13-2, starting from the right side of the circle, a counterclockwise rotation of 90 degrees is equivalent to $\pi/2$ radians. Similarly, at any point on the circle, you can convert degrees to radians by multiplying by π and you can convert from radians to degrees by multiplying by $180/\pi$.

The end result of using this nifty little method is supersmooth performance (at least compared to the first trig example). There is much less code to execute, so it is easy for the Flash Player to keep up.

Pythagoras and His Wicked Gaming Apps
follow03.fla, follow04.fla

In the next two examples, we will expand on our already towering trigonometry knowledge and add some code to calculate the distance between objects. I already casually mentioned the Pythagorean Theorem, but I'll flesh it out a little more clearly right now. Using Figure 13-1 as a reference, the following equations will always be true for the length of the sides:

$$(\text{hypotenuse})^2 = (\text{opposite side})^2 + (\text{adjacent side})^2$$
$$\ldots\text{which simplifies to} \ldots$$
$$\text{hypotenuse} = \sqrt{(\text{opposite side})^2 \quad (\text{adjacent side})^2}$$

If you have a handle on that, this code from *follow03.fla* on the CD should make perfect sense.

```
onClipEvent (enterFrame) {
    xDistance=_root._xmouse-_x;
    yDistance=_root._ymouse-_y;
    correctRotation = Math.atan2(yDistance,xDistance)*180/(Math.PI)+90;
    this._rotation = correctRotation;

_root.distance=Math.round(Math.sqrt((xDistance)*(xDistance)+(yDistance)*(yDistance)));
}
```

We have condensed the previous example into fewer lines and added the variable "distance." This variable uses the Pythagorean Theorem to find the distance from the registration point of the arrow Movie clip instance (this._x and this._y) to the mouse cursor (_root._xmouse and _root._ymouse). The distance is displayed in a dynamic text field on the movie stage.

Our final foray into math is going to be another exercise in thumbnail physics. We return to this subject now because we needed the trig background to build this example. This effect simulates decelerating as an object approaches the mouse cursor, whether the mouse is stationary or moving. The farther the object is from the mouse, the faster the object (our same little arrow) will move toward it.

The following code is from *follow04.fla* on the CD. The only code in this lively little number is attached to the arrow Movie clip instance.

```
onClipEvent (enterFrame) {
    xDistance=_root._xmouse-_x;
    yDistance=_root._ymouse-_y;
    correctRotation =
Math.atan2(yDistance,xDistance)*180/(Math.PI)+90;
    this._rotation = correctRotation;
    this._x+=(xDistance)*.13;
    this._y+=(yDistance)*.13;
}
```

Though the style is the same as in our former examples, the execution is a little different. Each time the code executes, the arrow moves closer in each axis to the mouse cursor by the amount of the distance times 0.13.

Connected Objects

The next set of experiments studies a particular method for connecting objects with lines. My favorite example of this *kind* (it is in Java) of technique on the Web is at http://sodaplay.com/constructor/index.htm. The examples we will cover here should be just enough to get you started and whet your appetite.

Elastic Band

connect01.fla, connect02.fla, bounceWithWalls.fla

Our first example, *connect01.fla* on the CD, simply connects the draggable Movie clip instance to the point of its original position with a line. The following code initializes some variables and moves the line Movie clip instance into position.

```
onClipEvent(load){
    xCenter=this._x;
    yCenter=this._y;
    _root.line._x=xCenter;
    _root.line._y=yCenter;

}
```

The following code acts as a custom button, as we discussed in Chapter 11. When the user clicks on the Movie clip instance, it becomes draggable.

```
onClipEvent (mouseDown) {
    if (hitTest(_root._xmouse, _root._ymouse, true)) {
        this.startDrag ();
    }
}

onClipEvent(mouseUp){
    this.stopDrag();
}
```

And finally, the code that "draws" the line:

```
onClipEvent(enterFrame){
    _root.line._xscale=this._x-xCenter;
    _root.line._yscale=this._y-yCenter;

}
```

It may not be immediately obvious how this works. The success of this effect hinges on the fact that the line, drawn at a 135 degree angle from horizontal, describes a box that is 100 pixels high and 100 pixels wide. Therefore, when the distance in either axis is 100 pixels, the scale of the line in that axis will be 100 percent (also 100 pixels).

It is worth mentioning at this point that this method of drawing a connector line is very clever. (I didn't invent it.) I personally used to use a vertically aligned line segment, combined with the awful, long method we went over in the previous section to rotate the line. Then you still had to use the PT to scale the line to the correct length. Performance was suboptimal, to say the least. If you have any ideas about other ways to create a connector line, forget them. This one is hands-down the most efficient.

The next example, *connect02.fla*, is a combination of the first connector example, *connect01.fla*, and the bouncing off walls example, *bounceWithWalls.fla*. The idea is that there are two balls bouncing around with a line connecting them. Maybe "idea" is too flattering a word for this exercise; this is a very common type of task for Flash gaming—tracing the motion of one object with another. Once you become comfortable writing code like this that can keep up even on slow processors, the Flash gaming world is your oyster.

```
onClipEvent(load){
   // define the limits of the box
   leftEdge= _root.box._x;
   rightEdge = _root.box._x+_root.box._width;
   topEdge = _root.box._y;
   bottomEdge = _root.box._y+_root.box._height;
   gravity = 3;
   lossOfEnergy=.94;
}

onClipEvent (enterFrame) {
      xVelocity *= lossOfEnergy;
      yVelocity *= lossOfEnergy;
      yVelocity = yVelocity+gravity;
      this._y += yVelocity;
      this._x += xVelocity;
      if (this._x+this._width/2>rightEdge) {
         this._x = rightEdge-this._width/2;
         xVelocity = -xVelocity;
      } else if (this._x-this._width/2<leftEdge) {
         this._x = leftEdge+this._width/2;
         xVelocity = -xVelocity;
      } else if (this._y+this._width/2>bottomEdge) {
         this._y = bottomEdge-this._width/2;
         yVelocity = -yVelocity;
      } else if (this._y-this._width/2<topEdge) {
         this._y = topEdge+this._width/2;
         yVelocity = -yVelocity;
      }

   xCenter=_root.ball2._x;
   yCenter=_root.ball2._y;
   _root.line._x=xCenter;
   _root.line._y=yCenter;
   _root.line._xscale=this._x-xCenter;
   _root.line._yscale=this._y-yCenter;
}
```

You will notice that the code from both the onClipEvent(load) and the
onClipEvent(enterFrame) handlers in *connect01.fla* have been combined and

included in the enterFrame handler in this example. This is because the anchor point of the line is no longer stationary; it is attached to the other MC, ball2.

The other ball MC has the same code attached, except for the code that pertains to the line segment. When you have a scenario like this, with one programmatically moved MC tracking the movement of another, you often have to experiment to find the best place to attach code so that the Flash Player can keep up and redraw connectors and such smoothly. While the serious Flash geeks (people who run benchmarking tests for fun on their days off) are at present engaged in a conversation over which is more efficient/fast—multiple handlers or one big block of code in a single handler—I have found a few general guidelines in my experience that seem to hold true most of the time:

▶ When you are tracking the movement of an MC that is moved by ActionScript, do the tracking and the movement in the same block of code. This seems to be the only way for the two to occur simultaneously.

▶ Let each object control its own movement. I seem to get jerky results when I try to use one MC as a controller for the movement of multiple MCs. There doesn't seem to be any limit within the domain of everyday use on the number of clips that even slow processors can process simultaneously.

▶ Delete variables and MCs that are no longer required. The less memory the Flash Player has to dedicate to dead weight, the more resources it will have available for the desired tasks.

Making the Final Break from Timelines

connect01.fla

The software engineers who worked on Flash 5 did an extraordinary job, bringing the application ahead three version numbers' worth between Flash 4 and Flash 5. For my money, one of the most insightful additions to the programmatic motion toolset is the updateAfterEvent(); action.

This action typically comes at the end of a block of code within an onClipEvent() handler. It updates the stage with the new information obtained in the code preceding it. Consider the following modified version of *connect01.fla*:

```
onClipEvent(mouseMove){
    _root.line._xscale=this._x-xCenter;
    _root.line._yscale=this._y-yCenter;
    updateAfterEvent();
}
```

This version is subtly different from the original. Because the handler onClipEvent(mouseMove) executes at the exact moment when the user moves the mouse, the block of code begins at times that might not necessarily coincide with the Flash Player's playhead entering a frame. The updateAfterEvent() action makes sure that the code above it will take effect immediately, without having to wait for the next movie frame. In general, this marks a movement away from the Flash 4 scripting style that relies on various aspects of the animation metaphor to provide a structure for scripting. This is a good sign.

What to Take Away from This Chapter

The college professors' long-time favorite bumper sticker is true: "Physics is Phun." You don't have to wear a lab coat, a pocket protector, or even army-issue glasses to emulate the physics of the real world in a way that is visually pleasing. The examples in the chapter serve as a foundation for you to get started with the basic principles of moving objects in Flash. Even if you go on to use the *real* physics equations and heavy math, don't consider yourself above using a few tricks. After all, computers will never match the joy of physics that comes from a paper airplane or a high-bounce ball from a grocery store vending machine.

Web Data and Site Architecture

I n this chapter we will cover the most important issues in this part of the book. It seems to me that the prospect of Flash's success in the future rests squarely on its ability to become an integral part of Web sites that a lot of people might like to use and visit repeatedly; and that ability depends on Flash developers' ability to become good architects, handling data from dynamic sources and using it in a way that is as easy to understand for the user as it is easy to maintain for the developer. Like it or not, database-backed Web development is forevermore a fact of the modern world; and in order to become relevant in this world, Flashers need to learn how to deal with Web data and how to structure data-driven apps.

Notice that I keep saying "become." To my knowledge, the most highly trafficked site in recent memory using Flash extensively as a front end was one of the all-time great e-commerce flops, providing fodder for critics in every area from navigation to download speed.

To put it bluntly, Flash has yet to become an integral part of a single successful high-traffic commercial Web site. If you have never thought about this before, take a moment to let it burn in. Open directory portals don't use Flash anywhere. Giant book merchants don't know it exists. News Web sites shun Flash, even when it seems like the obvious choice to illustrate info-graphics. Doesn't this seem strange to you? Didn't you ever wonder why the entire Web development world except for entertainment sites—almost without exception—eschews Flash.

The reason can only be because Flash developers have so far failed to grasp the niche of Flash within the framework of a data-driven Web site, including the issues of compatibility, data handling, and Flash application architecture.

Web Data

With this epoch of Flash history in mind, we will consider the following questions in this chapter:

- ▶ Where do you put data from a dynamic source in your Flash movie?
- ▶ Do you need a timeline?
- ▶ How much data can you get at once?
- ▶ Is it better to get as much data as possible, or just get data on demand as the user surfs?
- ▶ What is the best way to build a menu, in terms of efficiency? In terms of usability?

▶ What are the trade-offs between disabling the browser's navigation features and having virtually limitless functionality in Flash?

▶ How do you structure your Web tree with SWFs in the mix?

▶ How is the structure of your data-driven Flash app affected by who updates the site?

As you can see, these are not simple, tutorial-driven questions. You will have to wrestle with these on your own. This chapter aims to help you start thinking about important decisions you will have to make in order to build a Flash front end for a data-driven Web site.

NOTE

The examples in this chapter make use of a shared library, as well as relative addressing of text files within the structure of the Chapter14 folder. I recommend copying the entire folder to a writable drive ("c:\My Documents\," for example) so that you don't become frustrated with warnings telling you "Unable to open..." In other words, if you change the relative directory structure of the examples, they won't work.

Use a Text File to Simulate Dynamic Data

simpleReadTextFile.fla, classifieds.txt

Obviously, the first-stage function of a Flash front end for a data-driven Web site is to bring in data. Our first example shows a very simple method for loading variables from a text file.

Although this is a simple, introductory exercise, you should not discount the value of using text files as a data source. When you work with a live, dynamic data source (PHP and MySQL, for example), it is always best to begin with a text file as a placeholder for your actual source of data. In other words, the text file is a prototype for an actual dynamic data source. Using this static, reliable data source (a text file) allows you to forget temporarily about the possible complications caused by glitches in the middleware and focus on crafting your Flash application.

The following code is from *simpleReadTextFile.fla* on the CD. This code is attached to the blank MC "hub" in the upper-left corner of the stage.

```
onClipEvent (load) {
    loadVariables ("../classifieds.txt", this);
}
```

Here we are using the loadVariables action to load everything found within the file *classifieds.txt*. If you're not already acquainted with the operating system shorthand "../," it simply means to go up one directory. In other words, the loadVariables action will look for a file called *classifieds.txt* in the parent directory of the folder that holds the SWF.

The second argument in this action tells Flash where to load the data. This will be a topic of much discussion in this chapter, but for right now, just note that we are loading everything into an empty Movie clip. Our visual output takes this into account. You will notice that the names of the text fields follow this pattern: _root.hub.headline04. In other words, we reach to the location of the data from the root level of the stage, rather than assigning values within the data-loaded MC. This will change later in the chapter.

URL Encoding

ReadURL-EncodedFile.fla, Bat-URLEncoder.html

The next example is *ReadURL-EncodedFile.fla* on the CD. As you can see from the following code example, this Flash movie uses the same ActionScript as before.

```
onClipEvent (load) {
    loadVariables ("classifieds.txt", this);
}
```

The difference is in the text file. Open it and take a look at it. The whole thing is marked up with funny characters like this:

```
headline01=Clean%20Fill%20Wanted%0D%0A&story01=No%20Gravel...
```

Compare this with the easier to read format in the previous example:

```
headline01=Clean Fill Wanted&story01=No Gravel...
```

If you look at these two snippets carefully, you will notice that each space has been replaced with the cryptic sign "%20." This is called *URL encoding*. The idea is that you take a long string, usually made up of name-value pairs, and replace any characters that may not flow well over the Internet—like spaces—with a special markup. You've probably seen this in the address bar of your browser. For instance:

```
http://altavista.com/cgi-bin/query?q=%22britney+spears%22&kl=XX&pg=q&Translate=on
```

You can tell at a glance what might be on this page. The domain is AltaVista, so you know that it's a Web search. It looks like I did a search for Britney Spears. At the end of the line, something called "Translate" is turned on, and there are some cryptic variables with the values "XX" and "pg."

While we don't know exactly what all of these variables mean, we can see the data is being passed from the Web browser (where I typed "Britney Spears" in a search box) to some kind of Web application located at altavista.com/cgi-bin. The reason that the data has to be marked up this way, with all the funny signs and glyphs, goes back to the language that the Web browser uses to talk to this application, namely, the HyperText Transfer Protocol (HTTP). We'll talk about that a little more in just a moment, but for now just realize that we transfer data this way when we want it to appear as a single URL.

As you may have already guessed, URL encoding is nothing more than replacing spaces and other special characters in the query strings with their hexadecimal equivalents. For this reason, URL encoding is also sometimes called *hexadecimal encoding*.

When we're talking about using Flash as a front end for a data-driven Web site, we are typically talking about retrieving data from somewhere on a Web server, and that is what we cover in this chapter. That means that the process of URL encoding data takes place on the server, and is therefore outside the scope of this chapter. On the other hand, it is very likely that it will be you designing a mechanism to send data *to* a server application. The same rules apply in either case; so we will dwell on the details for a moment.

There are two basic approaches to marking up data as URL encoded: using pattern matching to replace specific characters, and using the escape function. The following code is from the HTML document *Bat-URLEncoder.html* on the CD.

```html
<html>
<head>
        <title>Bat-URL Encoder</title>
</head>

<body>

<form name="elformo">
        <textarea name="inputText" rows=10 cols=50 value="paste your text here"
></textarea>
        <input type="submit" onClick="URLEncoder(document.forms[0].inputText.value);">
</form>

<script language="JavaScript">
<!--hide
function URLEncoder(elStringo){
    pieces=new Array();
```

```
littlePieces=new Array();
bigString=elStringo;
//now the form input - prob. a lot of text - is all in 'bigString'
pieces=bigString.split("\&");
//at this point you have pairs like this: name=value...
bigString="";
for (i=0; i<pieces.length; i++){
    littlePieces=pieces[i].split("\=");
    //now you've split the name=value pairs into an array with 2 elements
    bigString+=escape(littlePieces[0]) + "\=" + escape(littlePieces[1])+ "\&";
}
document.write(bigString);
}


//show-->
</script>
</body>
</html>
```

This simple HTML/JavaScript form is what I used to create URL encoded text files. Its function is simply to take the input from the form (the contents of the old text file pasted into the form) and spit it out in a form that looks like a URL.

Everything in this code should be reviewed except the escape function. The escape function (a method of the String object, therefore also available in ActionScript) takes a string and converts every special character to its hexadecimal equivalent. This method by itself would be enough, except that we need to retain the characters & and = in their original form. That is why the function URLEncoder is 15 lines long instead of 1. When you send data *from* Flash, the Flash Player typically handles this function automatically, so it is possible you may never have to do this kind of string handling inside Flash.

What to Do with Data

I'm starting to feel like an old man—I find myself constantly bragging about how hard things were in the old days of Flash 4. The next bit of ActionScript we're going to discuss makes my heart swell with nostalgia as much as anything. You see, back in my day, we had to use a two-frame loop on a timeline to check continually to see whether data was loaded. Not only that, we either had to know the exact identifier of the last variable we would receive from the server application *or* add a variable to signify the end of the list. In the context of history, the onClipEvent(data) click event handler seems like flying cars, two-way wristwatch video phones, and silver jumpsuits with funny disks circumscribing the shoulders—all at once.

onClipEvent(data)
onClipEvent-data-.fla

The idea of onClipEvent(data) is to give you a clip event handler that will execute code after it has received a chunk of data. It does not execute until all of the data has been received.

The following example, *onClipEvent-data-.fla* on the CD, loads Chapters 20, 21, and 22 from Jane Austen's *Pride and Prejudice* into the variable "text." The first bit of code we will look at is attached to the arrow button in the middle of the stage.

```
on(release, releaseOutside){
    loadVariables ("variable.txt", "_root.hub");
}
```

Here we see the familiar loadVariables action, except this time it is loading data into a Movie clip other than itself. This is done to demonstrate that the data clip at a handler is really working.

The only action attached to the MC "hub" in the upper-left corner of the stage is as follows. As you can see from the following image, this code does not execute until you click on the button, thereby loading data into this Movie clip.

```
onClipEvent (data) {
    trace("Data received, captain!");
}
```

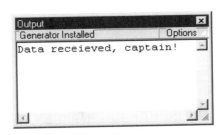

Designate a Hub
dataHub.fla, instructions.txt

You may have wondered why we are using a blank Movie clip as a container for the variables we received from the text files. It almost seems like it would make more sense to save them in the main timeline (_root) so that the variables would be more easily accessible from anywhere in the movie.

The big problems with that line of thinking don't really crop up until you start *sending* data to Web applications. For example, one of the most common CGI applications used by small businesses is a Perl or PHP form mailer. If you're not familiar with these, they're just small scripts that take the results of any form—no matter what the content—and email the results to an address designated within the script. The scripts are also one of the first things for which Flash developers try to build a front end. You begin to run into problems when you write something like the following:

```
loadVariablesNum ("../cgi-bin/mailer.cgi", 0, "POST");
```

The problem is that you may have a lot of variables you don't want to mail in the main timeline—variables that increment as you move through a control structure, for instance. You may not mind if the form is for personal use or if you are an old-school Perl programmer who has nothing better to do than to write unwieldy regular expressions into your script to customize it for your Flash application. I mind.

However, the most compelling reason to use a hub for incoming *and* outgoing data is purely human. When I am building a Flash application, it is much easier for me to see the big picture when objects—visual and otherwise—are grouped according to function. Using a blank Movie clip as a hub for data works nicely in this respect. You always know where your data is and that there is nothing there *but* your data.

Our example to demonstrate a data hub is a little silly. This movie, *dataHub.fla* on the CD, uses data from a text file called *instructions.txt* to scale and place the visual elements in our little newspaper page. The following code is in the MC "hub" in the upper-left corner of the stage.

```
onClipEvent (load) {
    loadVariables ("instructions.txt", this);
}

onClipEvent (data) {
    _root.followInstructions(logoScale,logoX,logoY,numberArrows);
}
```

As with the previous examples, the code that executes on this Movie clip is very simple. The clip is meant as a container for transfer, so it may not be bogged down with irrelevant code.

When we look at the main timeline, we see code that pertains to placing objects at the root level of the movie, which holds true to our pledge to group code by function. The following snippet is the only code in the only frame on the main timeline.

```
function followInstructions(logoScale, logoX,logoY,numberArrows){
    //scale and place the logo according to the vars from the text file
    with(logo){
        _xscale=logoScale;
        _yscale=logoScale;
        _x=logoX;
        _y=logoY;
    }

    //place the number of arrows designated in the text file
    for(i=1;i<=numberArrows;i++){
        attachMovie("arrow","arrow" + i,i);
        with(_root["arrow" +i]){
        _x=Math.random()*600 +10;
        _y=Math.random()*760 +10;
        _rotation=Math.random()*360;
        scaleFactor=Math.random()*50;
        _xscale=scaleFactor+50;
        _yscale=scaleFactor+50;
        }
    }
    logo.swapDepths(_root["arrow" + numberArrows] );
}
```

You can see a result in the following image. The logo is scaled and placed according to the dimensions given a text file. The number of arrows designated in the text file appears scattered all over the stage.

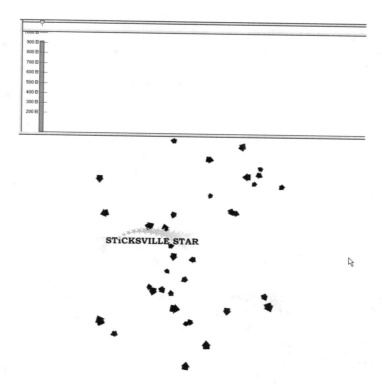

There's one thing in this code we haven't talked about before in this book: "with." "with" is a useful shorthand trick that will save you from writing a long, carpal-tunnel-inducing object path over and over. It translates simply, "using the object path within the parentheses, execute all the code within the curly braces." In our example, the control block described by "with" is shorthand for the following:

```
_root["arrow" +i]._x=Math.random()*600 +10;
_root["arrow" +i]._y=Math.random()*760 +10;
_root["arrow" +i]._rotation=Math.random()*360;
_root["arrow" +i].scaleFactor=Math.random()*50;
_root["arrow" +i]._xscale=scaleFactor+50;
_root["arrow" +i]._yscale=scaleFactor+50;
```

A More Flexible Way to Handle Incoming Data
associativeArray.fla, simpleReadTextFile.fla

There's still another, better way to handle data within our little hub. The methods we've used so far were *pretty* good, so long as the following applied.

► We know exactly which variables will be loaded from the data source.

► The number of variables is static, or

► We have control over the data source, so that we can name the variables in a sequential pattern, like "story1=," "story2=," "story3=," and so on.

I guess that's not over-the-moon unrealistic, but chances are that sometime in your career as a Flash developer you will work on a project where you don't have total control over every aspect. Databases and middleware that handles database data are two cases in which you are most likely not to have total control. Besides, hard-coding *anything*—even something as basic as the number of variables you are loading—just isn't programming *chic*.

We have twice covered one particular type of object in this book that is particularly adept at storing name-value pairs in a more or less open structure with more or less random access. (*Hint*: we built a spreadsheet with it.)

I'm talking about associative arrays. The following code demonstrates how we might use such an array to store name-value pairs that we received from a data source. We are now covering *associativeArray.fla* on the CD. This code is attached to the MC "hub" in the upper-left corner of the stage.

```
onClipEvent (load) {
    loadVariables ("../classifieds.txt", this);
    nameValPairs=new Array();
}


onClipEvent (data) {
    //dump the newly acquired data into the array "nameValPairs"
    for(name in this){
        nameValPairs[name]=this[name];
    }

    for(pair in nameValPairs){
        _root[pair]   = nameValPairs[pair];
    }

}
```

You will immediately notice that the visual output is exactly like our first example, *simpleReadTextFile.fla*. We're just going about it a different way. There are two big conceptual differences between the first example in this one. First, we have all of our data in an associative array. This is especially handy if we plan to manipulate the data and send it back to the application on the server. Arrays have a bazillion handy methods for manipulating their contents, so it is much easier to work with our set of data than if we simply had a bunch of variables. The other big difference goes back to the idea of grouping entities by function. In the first example, we used the label on the individual text fields to point to the hub's object path. In this example, we transfer the data to where we want it—the _root level. Now we can simply label the text fields according to what we want them to hold.

Recall from Chapter 12 that the for…in loop cycles through the designated object, like "for each" in other languages, acting on every element within that object. In this case, we first cycle through the hub itself immediately after we have received all of our data, adding each single variable identifier (name) and value to the associative array called nameValPairs. Next we cycle through the array we just created to call the variable identifiers and values back out and move them to the main timeline.

A potential weakness of this method is effectively duplicating information in memory. After this code executes, you have a copy of the variable identifiers and values on the main timeline and the same data (in a more useful form) in the associative array in the hub. That much isn't bad. The bad part is that you still have all the variable identifier value pairs in the hub just sitting there taking up space.

This problem is easy enough to fix. For instance, you could build your associative array in a second hub and just removeMovieClip("hub") when you are done, or you could add something like the following to your data clip event. Test this example using the debugger to see which variables are persistent in _level0.hub.

```
for(name in this){
    if (this[name].indexOf(nameValPairs) == -1){
        delete(this[name]);
    }
}
```

The code above cycles through the elements in the "hub" object (the MC instance on which the code executes). If the element is not part of the associative array named "nameValPairs," it is mercilessly wiped out. It is considered good form in the programming world to clean up objects that are no longer needed in order to save memory.

Handling Data in Other, Suboptimal Formats

pipeDelimited.fla

Our next adventure in Dataland is a typical source of data: the character-delimited flat file. Databases, like everything else, have widely varied interfaces and file formats between manufacturers. A common solution to the need to exchange data between different types of databases is to export the contents of a table in a standard format, in which the values for each cell are separated by a standard character. The most common characters used to delimit (separate) the cell values are the comma, the tab, and the pipe (|).

Suppose you had a client with a very modest database that he wanted to publish on the cutting-edge Flash-enabled Web site, only he didn't want to pay to have someone develop a script to pull query results out of a mirror of his database on the server. One solution would be to hard-code all of the data into your Flash application by copying and pasting.

Let's look at a better solution. What if we could export the tables to a pipe-delimited format and load those files directly into Flash? Our next example, *pipeDelimited.fla* on the CD, does just that.

First, let's take a look at the contents of the file. Luckily, there's not much data there.

```
Last|First|Age|Fave|____|____|__|____|Woods|Paul|29|Beer|Doggy|Huck|1
|Dog Food|Woods|Irene|33|Ice Cream
```

Now open the example FLA and look at the MC "hub" in upper-left corner of the stage. You'll find the following code attached. The following image—the output from the script—should shed some light on what is going on in the last four lines of the script.

```
onClipEvent (load) {
    loadVariables ("pipeDelimited.txt", this);
}

onClipEvent (data) {
    for (line in this) {
        bigHunkaText=line;
    }

    values=new Array();
    values=bigHunkaText.split("|");
    for(i=0; i<values.length; i++){
        lineString+=values[i] + "\t\t";
        if((i +1) % 4 == 0){
            trace(lineString + "\n");
            lineString="";
        }
    }
}
```

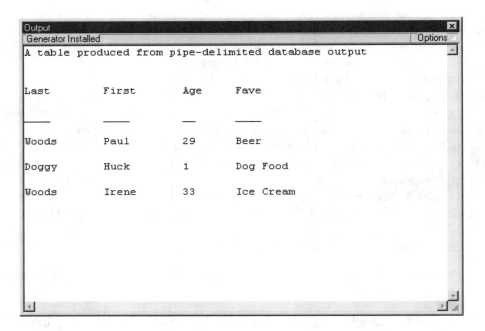

Nothing should be new in this script. Because the file looks like one long line of characters to Flash, it loads the data, but does not recognize a variable assignment statement. Therefore, it is necessary to assign the blob of text to a variable within the Movie clip and then break it up with Flash along the pipe character. This character is used as the separator to display the long string called "bigHunkaText" into the array called "values."

This scenario is not as far-fetched as you might think. Suppose you designed a site for a client who wanted to publish content from a desktop database like Microsoft Works or ClarisWorks, but didn't want to go to the expense and trouble of hosting and learning to maintain a live database. She could simply run the same queries after she updated her content and save the output as a tab-delimited text file.

A Few Words About HTTP GET and POST

index.htm

Flash communicates with outside data sources on a Web server through the browser by using the same dialect as the browser—HTTP. There are two methods available for this task: GET and POST. Up to now, we have not been concerned with the subtleties of communication with a Web server because we have not been communicating with a Web server—we are just reading text files from a local drive. But when you want to go live with your Flash application, hooking it up to your dynamic data sources, you will have to choose one method or the other. This section will give a little background to help you make your decision wisely.

First of all, let's look at how something more familiar, a Web browser, communicates via HTTP. When you click on a link or type in a URL and click "go," you start an HTTP *transaction*. The transaction consists of a *request* from the browser, and a *response* from the server, if there is one at the location you pointed at.

Although you can't see what the browser and the server are saying to each other, they send a *header* back and forth with each request. To demonstrate this, you can use your telnet instead of your browser to send an HTTP request. The following image shows what I saw when I sent the request "GET /pswoods/index.htm /http/1.1" to my own site in my telnet client.

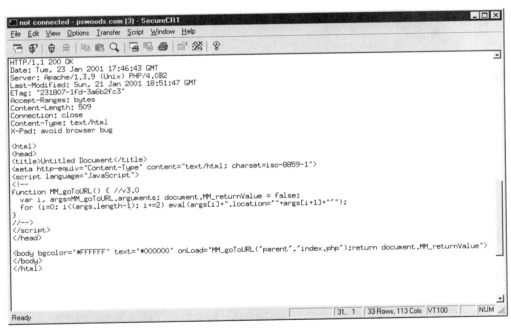

The message that I sent was an HTTP request using the GET method; and the result you see in the image above is the HTTP response, the output from the HTML page called *index.htm*. The extra stuff before the recognizable HTML code is the HTTP header from the server.

NOTE

Don't worry about the syntax of HTTP headers; you will never have to type them manually In Flash.

The unique thing about the GET request that I sent to the server is that it is only a header. This is the main difference between GET and POST. When you send a GET request, you are sending a single URL encoded string of limited size. Along with the method (GET) and the URL, a GET HTTP request can also send additional data in the form of an HTTP_QUERY_STRING. This could be anything from "?name=woods" to the contents of an entire HTML form.

The things to remember about GET are

▶ GET is ideally suited for small query strings, like the one you send with a search engine form or when you want a plain HTML page (when you want to _get_ something _from_ the server). This is how a Web browser does most of its HTTP requests (static pages, images, etc.).

▶ Different browsers and even different Web servers cache GET requests differently. Most of the time, if you send two identical GET requests from the same machine, only the first one will make it to your Web application on the server.

The main thing that differentiates POST is that it sends a body along with the header in separate strings. This is how most HTML forms are submitted. The things to remember about POST are

▶ POST is ideally suited for sending large amounts of data, like the results of a form with lots of fields (when you want to _post_ something _to_ the server application, like a bulletin board post).

▶ POST is necessary when you want to send data to the server repeatedly, such as in chat applications.

▶ POST is (theoretically) not limited in the amount of data it can send via HTTP.

Keep these factors in mind as you start hooking up your Flash applications with the actual live data sources. If your "classified" page of your data-enabled newspaper won't update after you change some entries in your MySQL database, check to see if you are sending a GET request. (You should use POST for requests for frequently updated data.)

Building Menus Dynamically

dynamicMenu.fla

This is the point at which we begin to approach the complexity of real-life Flash applications using dynamic data sources, so it is doubly important that we keep things simple, efficient, and logically organized. This example is *dynamicMenu.fla* on the CD. The first code example should be familiar. It is found in the MC "hub" at the upper-left corner of the stage.

```
onClipEvent (load) {
    loadVariables ("../classifieds.txt", this);
    nameValPairs=new Array();
}

onClipEvent(data){
    //dump the newly acquired data into the array "nameValPairs"
    for(name in this){
        nameValPairs[name]=this[name];
    }
    _root.menuMaker();
}
```

Everything here is just as simple as before, except that we call a function in the main timeline as soon as our hub is loaded with its associative array. This function has three jobs: pull a Movie clip from the library, assign some variable values to that Movie clip, and finally, place the Movie clip on the stage. The following code executes the first two of these three jobs.

```
function menuMaker(){
    counter=1;
    menuY=220;
    for(element in hub.nameValPairs){
        //we only want to make a menu item for the headlines
        if(element.indexOf("headline") != -1){
            attachMovie("menuItem","menuItem_" + element, counter);
            _root["menuItem_" + element].label=hub.nameValPairs[element];
            //get the number of the headline (corresponds to the number of the story)
            _root["menuItem_" + element].articleID=element.substring( 8, 10 );
```

The counter variable is nearly insignificant; it merely keeps track of how many Movie clips we placed on the stage. This will become meaningful in the next section of this function when we start placing the Movie clips in rows of two. "menuY" establishes the initial value of _y for the first Movie clip we attach.

Next is the for…in loop that iterates through the associative array nameValPairs. We only want to attach a menuItem Movie clip for headlines, since we will only display the individual articles after the user clicks on the button that overlays each menu item. If the name of the element in the array contains the string "headline," we attach the Movie clip.

Finally we assigned the variables called "label" and "articleID" to our new Movie clip instance. "Label" is the name of a dynamic text field contained within each menuItem Movie clip instance (the text that displays). Later, articleID will be used on the invisible button that overlays each menu item.

```
//place the menu items in two columns
if(counter % 2 ==0){
    _root["menuItem_" + element]._x=300;
    _root["menuItem_" + element]._y=menuY;
}else{
    menuY += 30;
    _root["menuItem_" + element]._x=55;
    _root["menuItem_" + element]._y=menuY;
}
counter++;
    }
  }
}
```

The remainder of this function is just as tedious as the first half, and less exciting. The first line checks to see if counter is an even number. If it is, the new Movie clip is moved to the right column (_x=300). Otherwise, menuY is incremented by 30—the height of each row in our grid of menu items—and the Movie clip is placed in the left column (_x=55).

Now that the menu is drawn, the user has the opportunity to click on the different headlines in order to read an article. The following code appears on the invisible button in the Movie clip exported as menuItem in the library.

```
on(release,releaseOutside){
    _root.showArticle(this.articleID,this.label);
}
```

When the user clicks on this button, the function showArticle() in the main timeline is called with the arguments articleID and label. The value of each of these variables will be different in every Movie clip instance because we assigned them as we were going through the nameValPairs array in the menuMaker() function.

```
function showArticle(ID,headline){
    for(MC in _root){
        if(MC.indexOf("menuItem") != -1){
            _root[MC].removeMovieClip();
        }
    }

    article.story=hub.nameValPairs["story" + ID];
    article.label=headline;
    article._x=55;
}
```

The first order of business in this function is to delete all of the menu items we just worked so hard to create. Don't worry, it will be very easy to bring them back. Next the text for the story is pulled out of our array in the hub Movie clip instance and assigned to the large text field in the article Movie clip instance. Finally, the headline of the story is moved over to an article Movie clip instance, and it is brought onto the stage.

When the user has read the article, she may elect to use the homegrown back button just to the left of the section heading.

```
on(release,releaseOutside){
    _root.back();
}
```

This button calls the function back() in the main timeline; and finally, we have something beautifully simple on the main timeline:

```
function back(){
    article._x=-560;
    menuMaker();
}
```

Because we got rid of all the clutter on the stage before we brought out the article Movie clip instance, all we have to do now is move the article Movie clip instance back offstage and redraw the menu. An equally viable solution would have been to draw the menu inside a blank Movie clip used as a placeholder. Then, instead of destroying our entire menu every time we display an article, we can just move the container Movie clip offstage. I chose this solution with the following section in mind.

Site Architecture

The best way to get the full impact of the differences between the following examples is simply to look at them. Literally look at them—visually—both the way the elements are arranged on the stage and the output.

Each of these examples looks at a different way to take the data handling techniques from the first half of the chapter and put them together into a full data-driven site for the fictitious newspaper "The Sticksville Star."

Sections on the Timeline of One Big SWF

This monstrosity is included as a cautionary example of what *not* to do. Sadly, this is by far the most common architecture used for this type of site. Look at the following image and try to imagine what it would be like to maintain a site like this. (That shouldn't be hard—chances are you have built a site with this kind of architecture.)

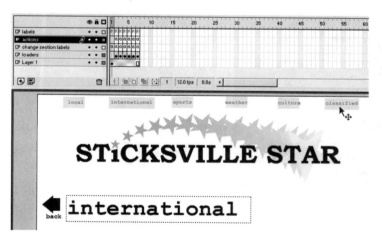

The *idea* behind this kind of site is actually good: divide the site into sections, one section per frame on the timeline. While this sounds good initially—this conceptual framework divides elements by function—there are several problems with it.

First, it is too easy to lose track of where things are located on the timeline. When I built this example, I constantly found myself going back and forth between the timeline and the instance palette to see if I was in the right frame. You could make the frames in the timeline maximum size or even leave a few blank frames between keyframes so you can read the labels, but this just adds to the next big problem—file size. By adding extra frames and repeating code, our compiled SWF output has shot up to a size of 19K, versus the original 10K in the plain dynamic menu example.

The following code is in the main timeline, actions layer, third frame. One of the main reasons people design sites this way is because of the belief that a trip to the server *should* be made for every user navigation event. By extension of that idea, this type of site usually duplicates large blocks of code, changing only one identity for each section.

```
stop();

back();

function back(){
    article._x=-560;
    menuMaker();
}


function menuMaker(){
    counter=1;
    menuY=220;
    for(element in internationalHub.nameValPairs){
        //we only want to make a menu item for the headlines
        if(element.indexOf("headline") != -1){
            attachMovie("menuItem","menuItem_" + element, counter);
            _root["menuItem_" +
element].label=internationalHub.nameValPairs[element];
            //get the number of the headline (corresponds to the number of the story)
            _root["menuItem_" + element].articleID=element.substring( 8, 10 );
            //place the menu items in two columns
            if(counter % 2 ==0){
                _root["menuItem_" + element]._x=350;
                _root["menuItem_" + element]._y=menuY;
            }else{
                menuY += 30;
                _root["menuItem_" + element]._x=55;
                _root["menuItem_" + element]._y=menuY;

            }
            counter++;
        }
    }
}
```

```
    }


function showArticle(ID,headline){
    for(MC in _root){
        if(MC.indexOf("menuItem") != -1){
            _root[MC].removeMovieClip();
        }
    }

    article.story=internationalHub.nameValPairs["story" + ID];
    article.label=headline;
    article._x=55;
}
```

This code is identical in each section, except for the name of the associative array.

It should be clear at this point that I don't like this style of architecture. The timeline is a tool for animators, not coders. While the idea seems good at first, this type of design typically duplicates elements unnecessarily, is messy, and makes the user wait for each data download.

Sections in MCs

This is a very fast, efficient—if forward looking—site architecture. It uses most of the same techniques already described in the chapter, with the addition of a function to load data from all five separate data sources. This function cycles through Movie clips in the library, each of which loads all the data for its corresponding section and forms an associative array for that section in a permanent hub. As each clip finishes loading, it is removed from the timeline (and hence memory), and the next one starts.

First look at the MC "hub" in the upper-left corner of the stage. It could not be simpler. This code creates the arrays that will hold all the data for the entire newspaper.

```
onClipEvent (load) {
    localPairs=new Array();
    internationalPairs=new Array();
    sportsPairs=new Array();
    weatherPairs=new Array();
    culturePairs=new Array();
    classifiedPairs=new Array();
}
```

You can see how a huge amount of data is neatly organized in the hub MC instance in the following image. The debugger shows a list of arrays, one for each section.

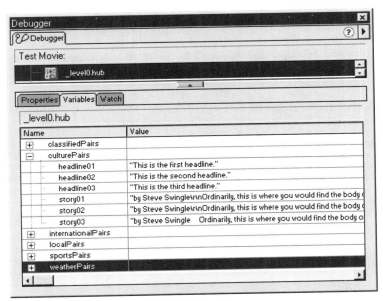

The functions on the main timeline are going to look familiar, but there are some important differences. Scan the following code for the changes.

```
sections=new
Array("local","international","sports","weather","culture","classified");
jCounter=0; //cycles through 'sections' array in function dataGetter()
dataGetter();

//------functions---------\\
function back(){
   article._x=-560;
   menuMaker(_root.section);
}

function menuMaker(section){
   article._x=-560;
   clearEmOut();
   counter=1;
   menuY=220;
```

```
    _root.section=section;
    _root.sectionHeading=section;
    for(element in hub[ section + "Pairs"]){
        //we only want to make a menu item for the headlines
        if(element.indexOf("headline") != -1){
            attachMovie("menuItem","menuItem_" + element, counter);
            _root["menuItem_" + element].label=hub[section + "Pairs"][element];
            //get the number of the headline (corresponds to the number of the story)
            _root["menuItem_" + element].articleID=element.substring( 8, 10 );
            _root["menuItem_" + element].section=section;
            //place the menu items in two columns
            if(counter % 2 ==0){
                _root["menuItem_" + element]._x=300;
                _root["menuItem_" + element]._y=menuY;
            }else{
                menuY += 30;
                _root["menuItem_" + element]._x=55;
                _root["menuItem_" + element]._y=menuY;
            }
            counter++;
        }
    }
}


function showArticle(ID,headline,section){
    clearEmOut();

    article.story=hub[section + "Pairs"]["story" + ID];
    article.label=headline;
    article._x=55;
}
```

First of all, the menuMaker() function now takes an argument, section. This is used throughout the function to identify which array in the hub MC instance will serve as the internal data source.

The next big difference is that there are more possibilities to contend with. The user may jump from an article to a different section. The easiest way to deal with this is to clear the stage before placing anything there. That is why you see the function clearEmOut() called from within each other function.

Finally, the object path to our associative array is getting very elaborate, owed to the variable identity of the array. This is a small price to pay for having all data available within the movie for instant access.

The function dataGetter below first removes the previous Movie clip, then attaches the next, as ordered in the array called "sections."

```
//pulls MC's from the library as the prev. one is done loading.
function dataGetter(){
    if(jCounter>0){
        _root[sections[jCounter-1]].removeMovieClip();
    }

    _root.attachMovie( sections[jCounter], sections[jCounter],jCounter+1 )
    jCounter++;
}
```

Finally, the buttons across the top of the page set the whole thing in motion once the data is loaded.

```
on(release,releaseOutside){
    _root.menuMaker("local");
}
```

To be thorough with this application, you probably wouldn't want to place the buttons on the stage until the data for the corresponding sections was loaded.

While I really like this architecture, there is a serious problem with it. IE is notorious for truncating larger data transfers into Flash from data sources. This application falls prey to this bug. In Chapter 18, all of these problems will be solved when we exchange data as discrete packets in the form of XML objects, so let's not worry about it too much right now. The application works fine in the authoring environment and in Netscape.

External SWFs or Shared Libraries—Why Not Both?

international.fla, external_SWF.fla, local.swf

When I first started tinkering with the beta of Flash, the idea of shared library items really got me excited. The idea of reusing elements in separate SWFs had been around in the Flash 4 days, but in a different form.

Previously, using placeholders for external SWFs, Flash developers could share compatible elements like a logo or a sound across an entire site. This type of framework is also beneficial for its simplifying effect. You get a kind of serenity from working in an FLA that has only one line of ActionScript. Open the example files, located in the folder 04external_SWF on the CD, and see what I mean.

In addition to the time-saving shared library elements used throughout the chapter, this iteration of our Sticksville leitmotiv uses placeholders for external SWFs, with the latter serving as the unit by which to divide the newspaper into sections.

The following code excerpt is from *international.fla*, the MC instance "hub" in the upper-left corner of the stage. The only new thing here is that the data is going into an object addressed as "_parent.article." This Flash movie really doesn't care where it ends up—it will be happy anywhere.

```
onClipEvent (load) {
    loadVariables ("international.txt", this);
}

onClipEvent (data) {
    _parent.article.label=headline;
    _parent.article.story=story;
}
```

Each of the buttons across the top of the stage in the main movie, *external_SWF.fla*, contains a script like the one shown here. This action replaces whatever was previously in the space of _root.ph with the new movie, *local.swf* in this case. The Movie clip instance ph is a blank placeholder on the stage (see the following image).

```
on(release,releaseOutside){
    loadMovie ("local.swf", "_root.ph");
}
```

local   international   sports

STiCKSVILLE STAR

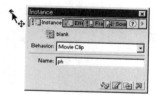

This version of our newspaper is obviously simplified from the full version with a number of articles in each section, but not drastically. You will notice that each of the external SWFs, in addition to the requisite data-loading function, contains a photograph. This was done to underscore some of the best uses for this type of architecture.

This type of structure is perfect for a site where you want to regularly update bitmap images, but don't want to mess with server-side applications that do this. By isolating the image in a very simple movie—even a movie by itself—it becomes very easy to make the changes without worrying about inadvertently breaking your ActionScript somewhere else in the application. Another scenario in which this is ideal is a team development environment where movies can be divided between animation or visual elements in one category and logical or ActionScript elements in the other. Graphic artists can go crazy on one set of Flash movies, while coders carefully craft streamlined scripts in others.

One Section per SWF/HTML Page

This example, found in the folder 01one_section_per_HTML_page on the CD, is the most obvious solution to a lot of usability and scripting problems, and you have to admit, it *is* effective.

The central concept of this solution is that there is one HTML page and one SWF for each section of the newspaper. The following code is from *local.fla*, the MC instance called "hub" in the upper-left corner of the stage.

```
onClipEvent (load) {
    loadVariables ("../../local.txt", this);
    nameValPairs=new Array();
}

onClipEvent (data) {
    //dump the newly acquired data into the array "nameValPairs"
    for(name in this){
        nameValPairs[name]=this[name];
    }
    _root.menuMaker();
}
```

The address of the data source in this code snippet ("../../local.txt") is one of two things that makes each of the FLAs in this example unique. The other is the

HTML-style text links at the top of each page. The link to the current section is disabled in each FLA.

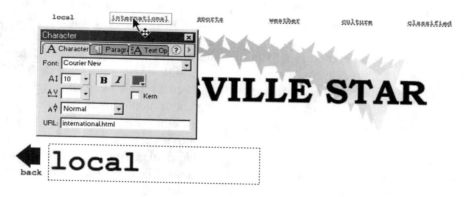

With a little creativity and even less effort, you could make one SWF work with the same functionality using the same model. Using the following code to embed the Flash Player in the HTML page, you can pass the value "culture" to a variable called "section" at the root level of the movie.

```
<OBJECT classid="clsid:D27CDB6E-AE6D-11cf-96B8-444553540000"
codebase="http://download.macromedia.com/pub/shockwave/cabs/flash/swflash.cab#
version=5,0,0,0"
 WIDTH=640 HEIGHT=800>
 <PARAM NAME=movie VALUE="culture.swf?section=culture">
 <PARAM NAME=quality VALUE=high>
 <PARAM NAME=bgcolor VALUE=#FFFFFF>
 <EMBED src="culture.swf?section=culture" quality=high bgcolor=#FFFFFF
WIDTH=640 HEIGHT=800 TYPE="application/x-shockwave-flash"
PLUGINSPAGE="http://www.macromedia.com/shockwave/download/index.cgi?P1_Prod_
Version=ShockwaveFlash"></EMBED>
```

Using the example as it appears on the CD, shared libraries become mandatory. For mundane functions like fronting a newspaper, Flash needs to take advantage of all of its strengths, and file size is one of them. Each of the individual HTML/SWF page combinations features extremely good file size—1K HTML + 12K SWF (99% of which is font outlines, so you could trim it down even more with a less intricate font).

In addition to better file size than you would expect on a similar HTML page, this solution features better navigation than is possible with an HTML of comparable amount of content. Usability experts say that users don't mind scrolling, but you have to wonder if "don't mind" really means "have learned to live with it" (the way people who suffer from horrific persecution learn to live with things). Because the scope of the page will never be outside the range of a quick fingerwheel flick, this navigation scheme is clearly superior to HTML.

What to Take Away from This Chapter

With pressure to provide usable designs on one side and efficient interfaces with data sources on the other, good data handling and site architecture are the keys to unifying divergent forces for a beneficial outcome. With the end user always in mind, always strive to structure your Flash movies with the elements separated by function.

Connectivity and Server-Side Processing

OBJECTIVES

▶ Review Basic Concepts of HTTP, Server-Client Model

▶ Explore Basic Configuration of PHP, MySQL, and Apache Web Server

▶ Learn How and Why to Use Regular Expressions

▶ Build a Flash Front End for PHP/MySQL Applications

▶ Create Flash Applications Using XML as a Data Source

▶ Discover Swift-Generator and Swift-Script Basics

Flash and the Web Server

IN THIS CHAPTER:

Understanding Servers

Installing Apache on Windows

Configuring and Running Apache

Minimal Apache Security

A s a preface to this part of the book, we should take a moment to talk about what role Web servers and server-side processing play in standard Flash development. If you have only tinkered with Flash as a hobby or if you have only worked as part of a large team of specialists, you may not even realize that it is necessary to understand how a Web server works.

The following list should illustrate how much easier your Flash application development could be—or perhaps how much more powerful your applications could be—with a few basic server skills. Each of the following tasks is something that is reiterated in discussion groups so frequently that I have added sorting rules to my email client to automatically delete as many as possible. The common thread among all these topics is trying to use client-side kludges to do something that could easily be done on the server. The worst thing about the conclusion of each of these threads is that they are usually temperamental kludges that do not translate well between browsers, versions, and platforms.

▶ Write to a text file.

▶ Handle large amounts of data.

▶ Organize data.

▶ Search a body of data.

▶ Email form results.

▶ Use pattern matching (like validating an email address so that it matches xxxx@xxxxxx.com, net, uk, ru, etc.).

▶ Track a user session.

▶ Make a Flash movie reload in a user's browser fresh every time.

▶ Detect user agent variables, like Flash Player version, browser version, and so on. This one has some advantages to using a client-side solution (like being cheap), but server-side solutions are definitely more comprehensive, reliable, and easier to maintain.

▶ Process image or load an image into a Flash movie on the fly.

If you have ever wondered how to execute any of these things, the answer is, simply: servers. This part of the book will first cover HTTP servers in general— what they do, how they work with your Web browser to render the output you see on your monitor, what kind of work is best for them, and how to set up and run the most popular Web server, Apache, on the computer where you do most of your work.

The remaining chapters will cover some easy but powerful applications of the server-side scripting language PHP, the almost-too-good-to-be-true database server MySQL, simple and intuitive data markup with XML, and finally, real-time SWF generation with the server component Swift-Generator.

Understanding Servers

All but a handful of Flash developers must at some time deal with issues related to serving documents and files via HTTP. Flash was built for the Web, so it makes sense that most Flash content ends up on the Web. Understanding what happens on the roundtrip from the Web browser to server, then back to the Web browser can help you to identify, explain, and correct unexpected behaviors you may find when you upload your Flash application to a Web server.

Client/Server Review

A fast, easy path to understanding how Web servers work is to simply trace the path of a typical HTTP request, from browser to server and back to browser. The following paragraphs will refer to Figure 15-1.

When a Web browser makes an HTTP request to a Web server, the header (and body, if there is one) of the request travels from the user's computer through any number of routers to the appropriate Web server (step 1 in Figure 15-1). For our purposes, let's assume that the Web server is one computer running the Apache Web server software, along with a couple other server applications.

These other applications could be anything. Two examples of server applications would be the PHP scripting language interpreter and the MySQL database server software. We will cover these in the next two chapters, respectively.

When the Apache Web server software—running on the computer we are also calling the Web server—receives an HTTP request that requires output from these other applications, it sets them in motion and waits for their output. This works like Photoshop filters in a way. Take Eye Candy or Power Tools, for example. When you apply one of these filters, it is obvious that you are running a completely separate process on your computer. The interface changes, the commands are different, and the options for output are different. But the output from these applications is used exclusively for Photoshop. So instead of telling a plug-in to apply a drop shadow to a selection, Apache might tell a PHP script to retrieve all database records pertaining to a selected word.

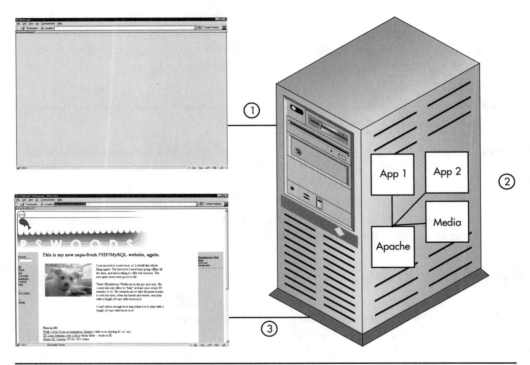

Figure 15.1   *The familiar client-server model*

This is what is happening in step 2 of Figure 15-1. Apache takes the output from two server-side applications, as well as media like JPEG, GIF, or SWF, and static HTML and sends it all back to the Web browser (step 3). In this model, the Web browser is the *client* and the Web server—the whole package including hardware and all software—is the *server*. The machine running the Web browser in this scenario is also referred to as a client, or *client machine*.

HTTP Review

In the previous chapter we reviewed some of the mundane technicalities of the GET and POST types of HTTP transaction requests. This is the kind of stuff you just have to learn by rote, and it certainly isn't fun or sexy, but understanding a little bit more about exactly what an HTTP server *is* may help the information stick better.

You may recall that our discussion in the last chapter included a screen shot of a telnet session in which I typed a GET HTTP request manually. What I didn't mention at that point is that you could type an HTTP header that didn't make sense to the Web server. The following image shows what happens in that instance.

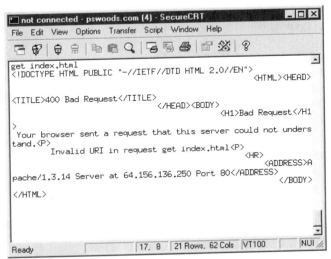

The main concept to be gleaned from this example is that Apache—along with all other HTTP Web servers—is a command line application, meaning that instead of using a mouse in a graphical interface, you feed it text commands. Its input is human-readable text, and its output is…anything you can imagine!

In your lifetime, you have probably sent hundreds, thousands, or even millions of this type of text command to Web servers. Of course, your browser helped you by translating button clicks and simple URLs into full HTTP headers. The following steps recap the course of a typical HTTP transaction.

1. User clicks on a link.

2. Browser sends GET request to appropriate URL.

3. The Web server (Apache running on the machine we call the Web server) determines which processes outside itself need to run and sets them in motion.

4. Apache collects the output from the other server applications, combines the output with static elements like HTML, pictures, and Flash movies, and then sends the output back to the client.

5. Apache closes the connection. The HTTP transaction is complete.

NOTE

In reality, there are some extra steps in there. The Internet infrastructure—stuff like DNS routers—makes sure HTTP requests point to the correct server machine. Most developers never have to worry about how this works. The client machine doesn't really connect directly to the server; there is a whole bunch of hardware in between, but knowledge of that hardware doesn't help us at this point.

Here's an interesting piece of Web trivia for you regarding the last step above. In the early days of the Web, when the hottest thing going was static, hard-coded text with no pictures, every separate medium in an HTML page required a separate HTTP transaction. This was no problem at first because there was only one medium—an HTML page. Later, when HTML pages started to embed pictures and even *multiple pictures* (ooooh, aaaaah!), it became obvious that 15 successive connections to the same server was not the way to go. Today Apache incorporates a feature called KeepAlive. KeepAlive does what it sounds like: it keeps the connection between the client and the server open until all the stuff for a given page has been sent. We will see a variable for this feature when we get to the configuration of Apache.

MIME Types

If you have ever spent any amount of time lurking or participating in a community "site check," you have probably seen a site that promised *rockin'* interactivity and *kewl* animation, but in reality offered that little broken image icon in the corner of the page. The culprit in these cases is the MIME type.

MIME, or the Multi-Purpose Internet Mail Extensions, was originally conceived as a standard by which files other than ASCII text could be exchanged via email. The idea was to supply a description of the file being emailed so that the email client (like Outlook and Eudora)—as well as the various email servers that passed the messages along—would know how to handle the file being sent.

It didn't take long for the idea to be extended to HTTP servers and clients. On a modern HTTP server, each response header includes a description of each separate media type embedded or otherwise included in the page. This helps the browser render the output smoothly by giving it advance warning. The browser begins initializing the respective players, plug-ins, or native classes to render each media type it is about to receive from the server.

The server software (Apache) has to be explicitly told which MIME type it should announce in the HTTP header for each type of file it might serve. The reason for the broken image on the numerous aborted site checks is that the Webmaster did not add the MIME type for Flash movies to the configuration of the Web server. When the server sent the page to your browser, there was no information in the header, so the browser didn't know to initialize the player. By the time the browser got to the <OBJECT> and <EMBED> tags, it was too late; so you get a broken image.

Another symptom you may have seen is getting a download dialog for MOV and PDF media instead of having them open in the Web browser. The difference between this outcome and the broken image is that the designer has linked to these files, as opposed to explicitly embedding them in an HTML page. Most HTTP servers with default configuration will allow you to download any document, even if it doesn't recognize that document.

Most of the common MIME types, like JPEG and GIF, are already set when you install the Apache server. Some types will require a manual entry in the server configuration, which we will cover later in this chapter.

Different Types of Servers

As soon as you venture from the cozy warmth (I hope) of our discussion out into the big, scary world, you are going to get hit with a million confusing phrases that include the word "server." We have already defined the two most common uses, the HTTP Web server software and the computer that runs it, but it is worth mentioning some other standard types of servers and their attendant buzzwords.

▶ **Web server**   Typically means two things simultaneously. People are usually talking about the machine that is designated to handle the HTTP requests sent to a particular domain, as well as the software (Apache) that makes it work. The machine is a Web server and the software is a Web server. Web server is synonymous with HTTP server.

▶ **Application server**   Is the first and foremost a buzzword used to make actors in commercials (the 24-year-old supposed CIO in the nonprescription glasses) seem intelligent and informed. The definition, in reality, is fuzzy at best. The most inclusive distillate I can concoct is *any program that executes as part of a larger Web application.* The biggest area of interest in the bigger category of application servers right now is database applications. For instance, several companies that sell primarily commercial database products are now offering application servers that publish content from a database on the Web. Another way to think of *application server* is as all the stuff in the middle—between the back-end applications (such as proprietary inventory software that never heard of the Web) and the HTTP server. In the olden days, we simple developers called this class of server applications *middleware.* Two very popular application servers are ColdFusion and Oracle.

▶ **FTP server**   Is something you have almost certainly already used. FTP, or File Transfer Protocol, is a separate Internet language for moving files across networks. It is entirely possible to transfer all files via HTTP, but that protocol does not include the built-in options available with FTP, like data integrity checks and security. In addition, FTP typically features much greater performance than HTTP transfers. An FTP server is an application, just like Apache, that runs on a Web server machine and listens patiently for incoming requests. There are special, separate clients made for moving files via FTP, as well as invisible clients built into most Web browsers that manage transfers in the background using default settings. An example of a very popular FTP server is Mojave.

An excellent resource for all things regarding servers is ServerWatch, part of the Internet.com family of sites for developers. You can find them at http://serverwatch. internet.com/. They have general information, tutorials, news, and reviews.

What Kind of Work Is Best Left to the Server?

There are three main advantages to executing code on the server side, as opposed to the client side, of an HTTP transaction. The most obvious is that data stored on the server can survive the transition between connections. In other words, once an HTTP transaction is completed and the connection is closed, there is nothing built into the protocol to link a new transaction to the old one. It is often said of this infrastructure design oversight that "the Web has no memory." The way to endow the Web with memory is to save information on the server. This can take many forms. In the following chapters we will learn how to save data using both text files and a database.

Another big advantage that server-side processing possesses is a little less obvious. It is really a fault in client-side processing, namely, compatibility. Web browsers feature wildly divergent implementations of standard scripting languages, every one of them broken. That, coupled with the fact that the same browser is fundamentally different between each platform and between each major version on each respective platform, makes truly compatible, complex scripting on the client side practically impossible. When you build a script for a server to run, be it PHP, Perl, or some manifestation of Java, you have to worry about exactly one interpreter and exactly one platform. That brings the difficulty rating from impossible down to easy in one step.

Finally we have the client-side scripting that we are *most* concerned with, ActionScript. It has limits. A common example is validating an email address. If

I had a nickel for every time I saw a thread about validating an email address in a Flash form, I'd be writing my memoirs instead of this book. The conversation usually centers around whether it is possible first, then how you might do it, and finally, a link to an FLA that someone has kludged out over the course of an afternoon that could have been better spent. In communities for server-side scripting languages like PHP, such conversations center on things like the rare-case implications of using the modifier *i*.

The difference in this matter is regular expressions. This is one of the many things that all server-side scripting languages were built to do quickly, efficiently, easily, and with a range of power that is well into the realm of overkill. Another type of function in this category is file I/O. All server-side languages have an extensive set of native tools for it, but Flash has none.

You don't necessarily have to learn a server-side language. You *do* have to learn where the boundary is between the capabilities of Flash and the fundamental strengths of server-side languages.

Why Apache?

In every reputable statistical survey over the past couple of years, Apache has occupied about 60% of the HTTP server market. Nothing else occupies more than a corner of Apache's shadow. This is a real phenomenon of the open source movement—much more so than Linux. From Microsoft's mammoth Hotmail site right down to my personal site for limericks and ribaldry unworthy of paper, everyone who uses the Web uses Apache at one end or the other.

In this and the next two chapters, I have chosen software that represents the best mix of popularity, ease of use, and free availability. If you learn the rudiments of these three server components—Apache, PHP, and MySQL—you will have no trouble understanding and even building a number of fast, scalable, and incredibly useful applications.

Because of Apache's overwhelming popularity, you will find that a lot of Flash applications you develop in a team environment will ultimately be served by Apache. In addition, you will be able to find an extremely inexpensive, reliable, professional host for your own applications running Apache.

Apache has a ton of features that make it attractive for organizations that want to build a Web server, including the ability to compile a wide variety of extensions with the server and ever-increasing scalability. These factors are beyond the scope of this book.

TIP

To see which server, OS, host, and even middleware that your favorite site is running, you can use the free service at http://netcraft.com/whats. Type in the domain you want to query in the box labeled "What's that site running?" You might be surprised where Apache pops up.

Installing Apache on Windows

Among that 60% majority of Web servers running Apache, most of them are some flavor of Unix. Linux, FreeBSD, Solaris—you name it. That's the mix Webmasters have found to be stable, reliable, and affordable. Which begs the question: "Why on earth would I ever want to take up disk space and resources on my desktop computer with this stuff?"

In my experience, the easiest way to predict the behavior of the server for which you are developing is to emulate it on your development workstation. In other words, you build it on your own machine using the closest approximation you can manage of the actual server's configuration. Then you upload everything as is.

If that doesn't convince you, consider this analogy. Suppose that Flash-compiled SWF output was interpreted by a server component instead of the Flash Player. You would have two choices for previewing your Flash movie. Choice one is uploading the new SWF to your remote host or to your company server on your LAN, emptying your browser cache, navigating to the HTML page, and previewing. Choice two would be using File | Publish Preview | HTML from Flash to view your movie on your locally installed server. This is precisely the type of advantage you will have in the next chapter when we start to deal with PHP.

Obtaining Apache for Windows PCs

If you have made it this far (deciding it is worthwhile to install Apache on your desktop machine), you have a nice downhill coast ahead of you. Obtaining, installing, and configuring Apache on Windows computers is easy. It doesn't get difficult until you try to get a server, a scripting language, and database server all working in harmony.

To get a compiled, guided installation of Apache Web server, go to http://www.apache.org/dyn/closer.cgi and select a mirror close to you. At this point you should be looking at a long list of directories and files compressed by and for the Unix Tape Archive (TAR) utility.

Select the directory called "binaries." This folder contains the precompiled versions of Apache, as opposed to the raw source code contained in the other directories and files.

The reason that this is a backwater of the Apache project and not the mainstream is that most Webmasters compile the applications to their tastes, including modules, custom extensions, and the like. It's not as if anyone benefits from hiding the source code, which is the primary reason commercial applications come precompiled.

Look for the directory called "Win32." Once inside, you could easily get confused. You are looking at three categories of things here: the newest stable release, usually with and without source code included; one or two previous versions; and finally, another folder, "old," containing even older versions.

Here is how I pick: I choose the oldest version installer package in the current directory, without source code. Being developed for *-nix systems and ported to Windows as an afterthought, the enhancements between one or two versions are all but entirely lost on Windows OSs. It's been like that all the way back to version 1.3.1, the first Windows port. Consumer Windows versions like 98 aren't meant to be production Web servers, anyway—that's what NT is for. The good thing about the older versions is that bugs have been discovered and ironed out, so you can be sure you are getting a stable application.

There are lots of cautions, disclaimers, and pointers to resources on the download page, so be sure to read them all to see which apply to your setup. All the information you need to pick a version is on this page. After you pick, simply download and install. It's that easy. The installation wizard is as effective, comprehensive, and comprehensible as with any commercial product.

NOTE

At the time of writing, Apache 1.2 is nearing its Alpha release. This release, when finished, promises a version implemented in the native Windows API. When it's released as a stable build, it might be worth your time to upgrade.

Because the goal of installing Apache on your desktop PC is to mirror the actual server environment in your development environment, you may want to install Apache in a directory path that mirrors the path on the server. To do that, figure out which folder on the server contains the directory "htdocs" and create that path on your local drive. For instance, I have Apache set up on my PC to mirror the configuration of my personal site, which is on a virtual host. The path to my lowest branch on the server is /home/htdocs/pswoods/. To match this path on my PC, I created the directory "home" and installed Apache there, as you can see in the following image. The Apache installer will let you pick the target directory.

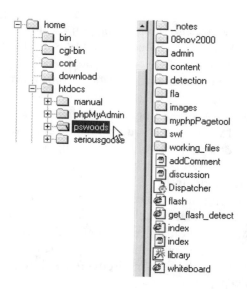

Is It Free?

Apache is one of the extremely rare instances of world-class software that is absolutely free, absolutely no strings attached. There are restrictions on distributing the software and building derivatives based on the Apache source code, but that's about it. Imagine—you can make millions on a commercial Web site running Apache, with your server software being a significant contributor to your success, and never pay a cent for it. If you do happen to make millions on a commercial Web site running Apache, you should probably send them some money. You can find out where to send it at http://www.apache.org/foundation/contributing.html.

Bundled Installation—PHPTriad

Before you suffer through the pain of installing, configuring, and otherwise wrestling with Apache, PHP, and MySQL on a Windows OS, you should know that at the time of writing, there is a free application at Download.com called PHPTriad. This brilliant little package is basically an installer for the aforementioned server components, plus a visual front end for the otherwise-command-line MySQL server called PHPMyAdmin.

In the case of MySQL, there is really no advantage to installing it yourself on Windows. In the end, we will only be using the client component of the MySQL package on our desktop computers, and that is just a self-installing application. No mystery. PHP and Apache, however, reveal some important insights into how they work in their configuration files. The Apache server and the PHP engine each read these files when they initialize.

Configuring and Running Apache

Before you get all excited about running a Web server on your machine, there are a few more details to savor. The minimum you will have to do is edit the main configuration file that Apache loads when it starts. This is easy, despite all the cryptic names on the exterior.

There are a few key differences between sending an HTTP request to a server on the same machine and sending that same request to a server on the Internet. The following list gives an overview of these factors.

▶ **Host name and URL**   When you send your browser looking for http://seriousgoose.com, there is nothing on your own computer that tells the browser which Web server hosts this site. Finding the exact computer that serves the content for Serious Goose is a matter of passing your request from your ISP to the big, mysterious DNS routers that direct all Internet traffic, and we already said that we're not interested in that. You don't have a registered domain that points to your home or office PC, so we can't use a made-up domain name to find the server on our machine. Luckily, there is a standard namespace and IP reserved as a shorthand for "the local machine." The domain for a local host is simply "localhost," and the IP is 127.0.0.1. Once we get Apache configured, you can simply point your browser to either http://localhost or http://127.0.0.1.

▶ **Port**   The world standard port on which any Web server listens for incoming HTTP requests is 80. If you should change the default configuration of the Apache server so that the port was something else—180, for instance—you would have to point your browser to http://localhost:180 in order to get to the root Web directory of the server.

▶ **Funny paths**   When you use server-side applications (like PHP and Swift-Generator), you will notice paths in your browser's address bar that don't exist, like http://localhost/php/php.exe/test/test.php?path=funny. This is simply a side effect of mimicking a Unix-oriented environment in Windows. Do not be alarmed. You will find that everything will still work on your local server, and your applications will continue to work when you upload them to the identical directory structure on your host's Web server.

httpd.conf

In the directory where you installed Apache, you will find a folder called "conf," which contains every file Apache looks at when it starts, plus a whole bunch of files it doesn't use. Each file with the *default* suffix is there just as a backup for you, should you ever bungle the real configurations so badly that you would be better off starting over from square one.

Then you have *access.conf* and *srm.conf*, vestiges of a bygone era of Apache. These are included for people who are upgrading from an older version and have a lot of time and tweaking invested in these files from their old installation. You are not one of these people.

You will notice a file named simply *magic*, which is a configuration for the mod_mime_magic Apache module. This module is for sites that need to determine the MIME type of files dynamically by reading a little bit of the file at run time. This is not you, either.

Depending on your installation, there may be a few other peripheral interests represented in this folder, and finally we come to *httpd.conf* and *mime.types*. These are the only two files we (and most Webmasters) are ever going to be concerned with. By now the task of configuring Apache should be approximately 1/5 as daunting as when we started.

Open *httpd.conf* in your favorite text editor and read it. It is a model for anyone who writes code and doubts the value of comments. As the head of the document says, it is divided into three main parts: Global Environment, Main or Default Server Parameters, and Virtual Hosts.

The last section is only used if you host multiple domains at the same IP. This certainly doesn't apply to our desktop installation, but it can be helpful to be familiar with these settings. At some point you may have to communicate intelligently with an ISP for a small business (or even your own homepage) about the settings for your site. These settings will be found in the Virtual Hosts section of this document.

httpd.conf documents itself so well that I can hardly add value to it by commenting on the commentary. I will, however, point you toward the settings you will definitely want to change before you start. Remember that you are trying to mimic the behavior of your production server as closely as possible.

▶ **ServerRoot**   This is the directory where you installed Apache. On my machine, it's ServerRoot "c:/home."

▶ **ServerAdmin**   This is technically not critical, but it reduces the anxiety created when you test your app and get a 404 (page not found) error. This is the email address of the server admin. Hopefully no one will see this but you.

▶ **ServerName**   This will be "localhost," in order to meet the incoming requests from your browser.

▶ **DocumentRoot**   This is where you want Apache to point as the root Web directory. On my machine it's "C:/home/htdocs/pswoods," but it could be any arbitrary directory outside of the installation directory. For instance, you could just have as your root "C:/www/inetpub." Notice that there is no ending slash on these paths.

▶ **<Directory>**   This should be the same as DocumentRoot.

▶ **DirectoryIndex**   You can have multiple entries for this variable. This indicates the possible document names that can serve as a substitute for the default Apache directory index. The most familiar function of a directory index is the front door of any Web site, usually *index.html*. Copy one of these lines and change the copied line to **DirectoryIndex index.php**. That will allow us to use a PHP script as a directory index in the next chapter.

▶ **ScriptAlias**   If you plan to install Perl, you will want to define a cgi-bin. This type of server-side programming, while still effective and still in use everywhere on the Web, is falling out of fashion quickly. I still use a lot of my old Perl scripts at my personal site, so I added the following line to my *httpd.conf*: ScriptAlias /cgi-bin/ "C:/home/htdocs/pswoods/domaincgi/". We will have to add a line for PHP when we install the interpreter in the next chapter.

That's all we have to do for now. We will come back to this file in the next chapter when we install PHP. This file initializes the way Apache interacts with other applications on the server, so it is important to get everything right. The settings that we just adjusted/added are a little less finicky than the settings we will add to accommodate PHP.

CAUTION

Some directory paths that you type into httpd.conf require ending slashes and others require that you don't add ending slashes. Read the description for each setting carefully before you change anything to see which rule applies to that setting.

mime.types

This configuration file is even easier to deal with than *httpd.conf*. You simply have to make sure the following line appears somewhere in the file:

```
application/x-shockwave-flash    swf
```

You used to have to add this manually, but it seems to be included in the defaults nowadays.

DOS Commands

Some Apache installations for Windows create a shortcut to start the server, but not one to stop it. This seems backward, since the command to start Apache is much more obvious.

The command to start Apache is simply the path to *Apache.exe*. On my system, it's simply "home\apache." If you don't already have one, you can create a shortcut to *Apache.exe* the same as you would for any other application, and it will start running in a DOS shell.

What most people find unfamiliar about running Apache on Windows is that you can't exit the application from the same DOS window in which you started it. In order to stop Apache, you have to open a separate DOS shell and type the path to Apache, plus the command line parameter -k shutdown. For example, on my machine, it looks like this: home\apache -k shutdown. The easiest way to get this done is to make a DOS shortcut, shown here:

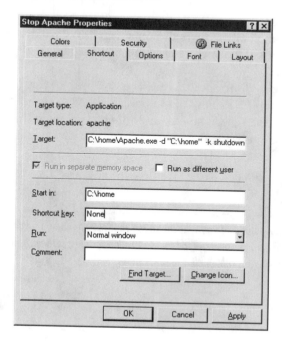

Minimal Apache Security

Your desktop installation of Apache is a good place to start learning some security measures that are quick and easy to implement. This is by no means a comprehensive look at Web server security. Rather, this is a warning to help you avoid the most common security blunders.

Configuration

This aspect of Apache security is going to be in the hands of someone else for the production server, but it never hurts to keep your eyes peeled for common disasters waiting to happen. Some things to watch for:

- ▶ Your Perl scripts will run outside your cgi-bin.

- ▶ You can look at other directories outside your own with an FTP client or through telnet with your shell account.

- ▶ You can use the <#!include> tag in the input field of your guestbook script.

If you notice things like this on a hosted site you are working on, you might want to mention them to the admin. Holes like these will be exploited on any server that attracts any traffic whatsoever.

Index File in Every Directory

Apache allows you to configure the server to generate dynamically an index of any directory. You have probably seen this at some point. It is just a linked list of all the file and subdirectories contained within that folder. This option is turned on when the word "Indexes" appears anywhere in the line that begins with "Options" in *httpd.conf*.

This is generally a security risk, especially for the type of server-side script development we will be discussing in the next two chapters. Since PHP is often used as an administrative front end for a MySQL database server, there are almost always going to be links on a site that are meant for administrative eyes only. Turning on dynamic index generation just invites bored teenagers to wander through your site looking for trouble.

While you can't always persuade an admin to turn this feature off, you can take one simple precaution to negate the liability it creates: put an index file in every directory. I usually concoct a file that uses the same template or style sheet as the rest of the site—like a custom 404 page—that has some message about either going to the site front door or back to the referring page (using the JavaScript history() object).

.htaccess

There is a positively brilliant little feature included in most Unix-oriented HTTP servers. It takes the form of two simple text files, *.htaccess* and *.htpasswd*, and allows you to require a password for access to a directory. The first of these files sets the basic criteria for the authentication process: the protected directory (the file must be in this directory), the message to show in the pop-up box (see the following image), and lots of optional additional parameters. Following is the template I use for all applications of *.htaccess*.

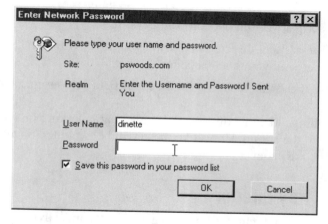

```
AuthUserFile /home/htdocs/pswoods/security_demo/.htpasswd
AuthName blahBlahBlah
AuthType Basic
<Limit GET>
require valid-user
</Limit>
```

Once you fill in the correct directory and upload *.htaccess*, you are ready to add *.htpasswd*. This feature uses the Unix crypt() function, so you have to do it on the server through telnet. Navigate to the directory you want to password-protect and type **htpasswd -c .htpasswd username**, where username is any username you choose. The server will prompt you for a password. Using the parameter -c creates the file *.htpasswd* the first time you add a user. To add users, simply type **htpasswd.htpasswd username**.

What to Take Away from This Chapter

This has been a 100-level class in the big issues surrounding HTTP servers—an overview. We have covered the basic concept, installation, and configuration of the world's most popular Web server, Apache. At this point you have a development environment that mirrors most Apache servers, allowing you to cut development time by testing your Flash applications locally. For more information on the Apache Web server, see http://httpd.apache.org.

Introduction to PHP

IN THIS CHAPTER:

I love PHP—there is no point in trying to hide it. After struggling to learn Perl, tackling concepts like interpreter path (different on every machine), placing and including external libraries, dealing with fussy syntax and the Unix command line text editor Vi (there was no practical Windows port of Perl in the Stone Age), PHP3 was like a miracle. It is easy to use, portable between platforms, and now, in version 4, unbelievably fast with some types of installation.

Background

First, a little history is in order. PHP was originally conceived in 1994 by Rasmus Lerdorf as Personal Home Page Tools, a pet project. Lerdorf added form interpretation tools, one of the most common and important burdens of Web scripting, and PHP/FI started to be adopted by other Webmasters looking for an effective, easy-to-script form handler. It was not until the parsing engine was rewritten by Zeev Suraski and Andi Gutmans that PHP, now called version 3.0, became a worldwide phenomenon. That engine was later rewritten from scratch *again*, to the current version 4, in favor of numerous performance enhancements. (Version 4 introduced new functions but did not *require* PHP hackers to learn any new syntax or vocabulary, and almost all PHP3 scripts run on PHP4 without any editing.)

It is easy for anyone with a little scripting experience to learn the basic skills of PHP. Because of its ease of use, powerful functionality, prevalence, and price (free), PHP is an ideal tool for most jobs you might want to complete on the server side of your Flash applications. The following list demonstrates how PHP is a parallel of and a good match for Flash:

- ► Large, enthusiastic community that shares code
- ► Large user base still growing
- ► Compiled with about 40% of Apache servers, according to the current Netcraft survey at http://netcraft.com
- ► Widely supported
- ► Runs on both Win and *-nix platforms without translating scripts
- ► Very easy to learn
- ► 99 percent of syntax *concepts* will be familiar
- ► Current version (4) is a complete rewrite with numerous, revolutionary (performance) enhancements

▶ Supports extremely wide range of databases, and switching between databases is very easy; ODBC not typically required, but supported

▶ Large, efficient set of string functions to complement Flash 5

If you have ever wondered how to add functions to your Flash applications, such as a high-score feature, a page counter, a simple guestbook that does not require a database, a form mailer that does not require HTML, a separate *.accesslog* to track Flash usage, or a no-cost server-side user agent detection scheme, PHP may be the answer. Chances are, if you start with a specific goal in mind, you can learn enough PHP in an afternoon to build a simple solution (or at least find and install a script with a more comprehensive solution). This chapter serves as an introduction to PHP and some of the basic features I feel are most useful to Flash developers who need a fast and easy way to build a server-side application.

Installation and Configuration

If you chose to install PHPTriad in the previous chapter, you are done with installation. You can skip ahead to the next section. Mac users: at the time of writing, there seems to be great promise in the idea of OS X in the area of supporting Unix-centric Web standards like PHP. On the other hand, if you want something you can install on your G4 today, the only option I found in my brief inquiry into the subject was WebTen (http://www.tenon.com/products/webten/).

For the rest of us, this installation will be as easy as Apache was. We are going to install the CGI version of PHP. There *is* an ISAPI version available, as well as various hackers' extensions of the core language specifically for Windows and the source code for you to tweak and compile as you like; but if these other options appeal to you, you would not benefit from the info in this section. We are looking for the easiest, most trouble-free installation for Windows. The goal is to create a development environment that simply has the ability to execute PHP scripts, without worrying about performance.

1. Go to the "downloads" section of http://php.net. You will find a prominent section that links to and explains a few of the most recent stable versions of "Win32 Binaries." Locate the one that is packaged as a Windows installer and download it.

2. Run the standard installation. First it will ask you where to install PHP. This is totally arbitrary. We will add the path to the PHP interpreter to Apache's *httpd.conf* later, so just choose by your personal preferences. The installer will

also ask you for information about your outgoing email server (SMTP) and your email address. This is for PHP's built-in mail feature. Finally, the installer will ask you which server you will be using with PHP. Click Apache. Finish the installation.

3. Open *httpd.conf* in the conf directory of your Apache installation. We worked on this file in the previous chapter.

4. The first thing you will want to add is a DirectoryIndex. Go to the line that probably reads "DirectoryIndex index.html" and add a new line right below it: **DirectoryIndex index.php**. This will allow you to use a PHP script as an index directory.

5. Next add the path to the PHP installation. You do this with the ScriptAlias setting. Add the line **ScriptAlias /php/ "C:/PHP4/"**, including the ending slash and double quotes, where C:/PHP4/ is the directory into which you installed PHP. This is the directory in which the server will execute PHP scripts.

6. Next we need to add the MIME type for PHP scripts. You can do this either in the *mime.types* configuration file in the conf directory or by simply adding the following line to the same file we have been working on, *httpd.conf*: **AddType application/x-httpd-php .php**.

7. Finally, Apache needs to know exactly which program will execute scripts of the PHP MIME type. You do this with the Action parameter:**Action application/ x-httpd-php "C:/PHP4/php.exe"**. In this example, C:/PHP4/php.exe is the path to the PHP interpreter on your machine. You need to include the double quotes.

8. Open *php.ini* in your Windows directory. The installer will have placed it there automatically. Not only that, but the installer also set all the critical variables for you so that you don't *have* to change anything. There is one particularly annoying feature you should disable, though. If you leave the defaults as is, you will get all kinds of cautionary notices from the built-in debugger. You will get these warnings for things as anal as not using the currently recommended syntax, and whatnot. This is something like the use of strict designation in Perl. To change this so that you only see fatal run-time errors, change the error_reporting line to look like this:

```
error_reporting    = E_ERROR;
```

A complete list of options for this parameter can be found at http://www.php.net/manual/en/features.error-handling.php. The *php.ini* file exists primarily for installations like ours on Windows systems. If you use PHP on a hosted production server, all of these things will be set for you, along with all the variables in Apache's *httpd.conf*. If your situation should call for dedicated, nonvirtual servers, either hire a professional Apache guru or plan on spending months reading about and experimenting with configuration. These little files make a big difference in how well a production server performs.

You should now have PHP running on your Apache Web server.

PHP Basics

Before we go any further, it would be a good idea to make sure that your installation works. Copy the following code into your favorite HTML or text editor.

```
<html>
<body>
<?php
phpinfo();
?>
</body>
</html>
```

Save this code as any file with a PHP extension (for example, *information.php*), and check it in your browser. There are several things worth mentioning here that may seem obvious, but you would be surprised how many people get tripped up on these issues.

► Apache must be running.

► If Apache was running when you added lines to *httpd.conf*, you will have to restart Apache before the changes take effect. In other words, you have to shut down the Apache application (not your PC) and start it again.

► You must access this file by means of an HTTP request to the server. (You can't just open the file in your browser from the hard drive.) The easiest way to do this with your standalone browser is to type its address into the location bar (for example, **http://localhost/information.php**).

► Many text and HTML editors allow you to preview documents by way of your local Web server—some of them within a tabbed document window within the development environment. Figure 16-1 shows one such editor, EditPlus (http://editplus.com), with our test file previewed in the built-in browser. I have come to consider this type of feature indispensable when writing scripts. It not only saves time by starting quickly and managing the browser's cache (so you know you are viewing the effects of the last changes you made), but also helps you keep your train of thought because you don't have to switch between applications.

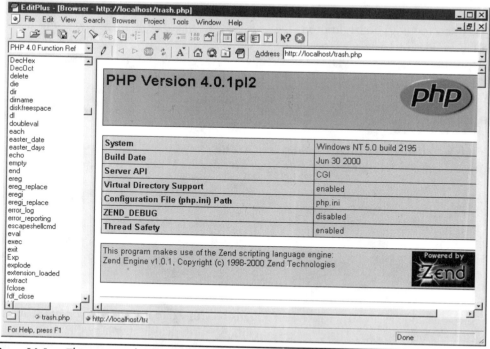

Figure 16.1 *This text and HTML editor showing a preview of our test file*

If you have done all those things and PHP still isn't working, your best option is to go online and search for information on the errors you are seeing. Zend.com and phpbuilder.com both have active open forums with answers to lots of questions that are likely to cover any beginner situation. Your next best option is to download and install PHPTriad, taking solace in the fact that at least you tried.

PHP + HTML

PHP code can be mixed with HTML, as in our first example, or it can be a standalone script with any type of markup. Obviously, when you use PHP as a middle tier between Flash and some data source, you don't need any special HTML markup. In that case, you can omit any HTML, since no browser will need to process the output. For example, if our first example had been meant to produce output for Flash, it could have been written as follows:

```
<?php
phpinfo();
?>
```

As you can see, PHP is always contained within the tags <?php ?>. The function phpinfo() is a special function that returns a lot of handy information about your server environment. If you look at the output from this example in your browser, you will find the values of some of the variables from *php.ini* and Apache's *httpd.conf*, plus information about your machine.

Syntax

PHP is case sensitive, so I suggest picking one variable-naming scheme and sticking to it religiously. For instance, if you create a variable called $monkeySee, and then try to call it with $MonkeySee, you will get unexpected results.

You will find that the syntax of PHP is familiar and easy after working in the ECMA-286-based ActionScript. Functions, statements, and most of the control structures work exactly as they do in ActionScript.

There is basically one big adjustment you will have to make if you haven't worked in a language like this before. There is no dot-delimited object structure. Objects take the form of a prefix, usually followed by an underscore, then the various methods. The instance of such objects is either designated as an argument to a generic method or created with a constructor. For instance, compare the following code as it would appear in JavaScript or Flash to how it would appear in PHP.

```
//the Flash way
var myList=new Array("milk","eggs","flour");
myList.pop();

//the PHP way
array_pop($myList);
```

Variables

All variables in PHP are identified as such by the dollar sign ($). PHP has a neat trick similar to Flash's eval() function that lets you point to variable identifiers dynamically. The following example shows how.

```
$animal="dog";
$$animal="terrier";
```

The second line of this example uses the *dynamic variable* $$animal, which is the equivalent of $dog. An easy way to conceptualize how this works is this: PHP evaluates all the consecutive dollar signs, starting at the right and moving left, evaluating each step. In this example, when PHP evaluates $animal, it gets "dog," so the dynamic variable $$animal is the same as the variable $dog. You can stack these up as high as you like, but the utility of this trick wears thin very quickly as things get more complex.

Type

PHP, like Flash, is *not* a strongly typed language. In other words, you don't have to designate a variable as a number, string, array, or object. For instance, you can convert a number to a string just as you would in Flash, using the dot instead of the plus sign to concatenate:

```
$roundNumber="The total is " . $roundNumber . "\.00 USDollars";
```

Output

So far we haven't seen how to return strings or numbers to the Web browser. Luckily, this is easy. There are two main methods for output—unformatted and formatted.

Echo

When you simply want to output a variable value, number, or string, use echo. You've probably been dying to know how to output "Hello World," so here it is:

```
echo "Hello World<BR>\n";
//outputs Hello World
$goodwillMessage="Hello World<BR>\n";
echo $goodwillMessage;
//same thing
echo "$goodwillMessage";
//still the same thing
```

You should notice a few things in this code. First of all, comments work the same as in Flash. There is one other comment notation available—the pound or number sign (#), which hides everything from the interpreter that comes after itself on the same line.

In the example, you see that string literals work the same way as in Flash. If you have a string in quotes, it is output literally, while a variable identifier outside of quotes is interpreted. The only thing that may throw you is the fact that variables are still interpreted when they are inside quotes.

Obviously, the <BR> tags give us a line break in the HTML output, but the importance of the newline character might not be obvious. When you use PHP for HTML output, it is entirely possible that you will want to look at the HTML source code if you have formatting problems. When that happens, it is much easier to look at the source when each line of markup is on its own line.

Printf

Suppose you wanted to print a nicely formatted HTML table that showed the double and the square of every number from 1 to 12. The doubles and squares of small numbers will become columns in a database entry in the next chapter, so be careful before you snort at the simplicity of this exercise.

You could use echo for this, but you would have a big, ugly line in the middle of your for loop. While we Flashers might be perfectly accustomed to big, ugly lines of code, it is not the norm in older, more elegant scripting languages. Here is how you could do it elegantly with printf:

```
echo "<table>\n";
echo "<tr><td>Number</td><td>Double</td><td>Square</tr>\n";
for($i=1;$i<=12;$i++){
    printf("<tr><td>%s</td><td>%s</td><td>%s</td></tr>\n",
    $i, $i*2, $i*$i);
}
echo "</table>\n";
```

The printf function uses any number of instances of the placeholder %s in the first argument, combined with any string in any format. The number of remaining arguments must match the number of placeholders used in the first argument, since these arguments are used to fill in the values for the placeholders, in order. In other words, when PHP gets to the first %s, it goes to the next arguments—in the case of the example, $i. When the next %s comes up, the value to plug into the placeholder comes from the next argument—in this case $i*2.

This function is very handy for HTML output, as you can see even in this simple example. By separating the dynamic data from the output format, printf makes it easy to make changes to a heavily formatted page.

Control Structures

Most of the basic control structures in PHP look exactly like those we have examined in JavaScript and ActionScript. There are a few differences, however, as well as a few extras. The first difference you are likely to run into is the if…else if control structure.

```
if($stuff="kewl"){
    goToSchool();
} elseif($stuff="nachos"){
    goToStore();
}
```

The big difference? There is no space between else and if. There is another difference that you probably didn't even notice. PHP uses one equal sign as a comparison operator instead of two.

Another handy control structure is PHP's version of ActionScript for…in. PHP, like Perl before it, calls this type of loop *foreach*. The following code shows first how we are accustomed to doing this in Flash, followed by the PHP equivalent.

```
//the Flash way
for(ingredient in myList){
    trace(myList[ingredient] + "\n");
}


//the PHP way
foreach ($myList as $ingredient){
    echo "$ingredient<BR>\n";
}
```

In this example, we loop through the array myList and output the *value* of each element using the placeholder. There is also a shorthand for dumping the identifier of each array element into a placeholder while you loop through an array. For a plain array, this would be just a series of numbers, but for an associative array, this is the name part of the name-value pairs. This will be important when we get to extracting the name-value pairs from form input.

```
foreach($myList as $ingredient => $brand){
    printf("%s:    %s<BR>\n",$ingredient,$brand);
}
```

In this example, $ingredient is the placeholder for the identifier (name) of each array element and $brand holds the value of each element. Often you will see the variables $key => $value used simply because they remind you which placeholder is which in terms of array structure. I prefer to give them descriptive names suitable to the occasion.

The switch control structure works exactly as it does in JavaScript. In fact, the example from Chapter 6 in the code shown next will work in PHP without any changes to the control structure itself, save a dollar sign in front of the variable name.

```
switch ($usrPassword){
case 'TNPRock':
      echo "Kyles_Home_Page";
      break;
case 'SPRocks':
      echo "Stans_Home_Page";
      break;
default:
      echo "forgot your password?";
      break;
}
```

A Few Useful Built-in Features

One of the things I love about PHP is the way common, mundane tasks are boiled down to an easy shorthand or special function. It seems that the designers of the language were attuned to all the tasks developers need to do most often and simplified each task to a single word or function. In this part of the chapter we will look at a few of the most amazing, useful functions.

$HTTP_USER_AGENT

We touched on the Navigator object in JavaScript briefly in Chapter 7. This object contains detailed information about the user's browser, including type and version. It is often used as the basis for a client-side browser or even plug-in detection scheme. While it is an extremely handy object within any given browser DOM, the problem is that every major browser's implementation of JavaScript is abysmal in terms of standards. So you are left with the choice of either supporting only certain browsers or writing an endless string of spaghetti code to try to accommodate everyone (which you never will).

An easy solution for simple jobs like detecting browser version is PHP's built-in $HTTP_USER_AGENT. This is a built-in *global* variable, so you'll always know where to find it. It is always accessible and always has a value when your script is called by a browser.

CAUTION

The examples in this chapter need to be in a public directory on your Apache server in order to run. I recommend copying the entire contents of the chapter folder to your htdocs directory. When it is time to view a particular example, you can point your browser to http://localhost/examples/file.name.

$HTTP_POST_VARS and $HTTP_GET_VARS

echoVarsFromURLString.php, echoVarsFromHTMLForm.php, genericForm.html, submitInRecursiveForm.fla, submit.html, submit.fla

Form handling was one of the first big selling points for PHP, and it only got better in its modern incarnation. The following code, from *echoVarsFromURLString.php* on the CD, is all it takes to parse through the variables submitted as a URL string and return them as a formatted series, one pair to a line. Put this file in your htdocs directory in your Apache application folder and send it an HTTP request including some variables—for instance:

http://localhost/echoVarsFromURLString.php?myname=joey&myjob=okay.

```
foreach($HTTP_GET_VARS as $key => $value){
    printf("%s:    %s<BR>\n",$key,$value);
    }
```

We have already seen everything here except PHP's built-in $HTTP_GET_VARS. This is an array with global scope, just like $HTTP_USER_AGENT.

The only thing that could possibly trip you up using the *environmental variable* $HTTP_GET_VARS is that it has to match the HTTP request method. In other words, if you called this script with an HTML form using a POST action, it would not work.

There is a separate environmental variable for handling name-value pairs from POST HTTP requests. To see this variable, $HTTP_POST_VARS, in action, open *genericForm.html* (you will also need to move *echoVarsFromHTMLForm.php* to the same directory), again from your htdocs directory and through your Web browser (http://localhost/ genericForm.html).

```
foreach($HTTP_POST_VARS as $key => $value){
    printf("%s:    %s<BR>\n",$key,$value);
}
```

When you fill out the form and submit it, it calls the PHP script *echoVarsFromHTMLForm.php,* using the HTML <FORM> tag: <form method="post" action="echoVarsFromHTMLForm.php">. You should see the same type of formatted output as in the example using the GET HTTP request method.

The next example, *submit.html*, is the same concept, executed in Flash. The following code is from *submit.fla*, the source for the movie embedded in *submit.html*.

The following code has been stripped of escape() functions for the sake of clarity. This would cause problems for some browsers if the user input special characters and spaces into the form fields. Another example in this chapter, *submitInRecursiveForm.fla*, addresses this problem. You can see the code in that example if you are interested.

```
on (release, releaseOutside, keyPress "<Enter>") {
   bigURLString =
"echoVarsFromURLString.php?submit=ohYes&variable01="+variable01+
"&variable02="+variable02+"&variable03="+variable03+
"&variable04="+variable04+"&variable05="+variable05;
   getURL (bigURLString);
}
```

Since this code uses the getURL action (a GET HTTP request, just like a browser sends), it uses the PHP script that echoes variables from the $HTTP_GET_VARS array. This script is *echoVarsFromURLString.php*.

This type of interaction with server-side scripts is less common than using the LoadVariable action, probably because handling the front end of the application entirely within Flash gives you a visually pleasing user experience without the interruption of page loads. However, using GET for simple jobs like passing a few variables in a URL string has numerous advantages, including easier error handling (on the server) and more control placed in the hands of the user (ability to go back). We will see in a subsequent example how this method can be used to dynamically pick different Flash movies to embed in the page.

$PHP_SELF and "Here" Documents

recursiveForm.php

The next logical step is to combine the form with the PHP script. Put *recursiveForm.php* in your htdocs directory and load it from your server. The following code is the beginning of the logic that drives this example.

```
if($submit){
     foreach($HTTP_POST_VARS as $key => $value){
          printf("%s:    %s<BR>\n",$key,$value);
     }
//otherwise, print the form
}else{...
```

NOTE

If you do not have nonfatal error reporting turned off, you will get a little nastygram regarding the first line of the preceding code . If you are concerned about this or if you are using a production server that does not have error reporting turned off (this is rare), simply initialize the variable ($submit = ""). Then you will have to change the test to if($submit != "")...or something to that effect.

Now the script will only regurgitate the variables in the POST HTTP request if the variable $submit has a value. This variable comes from the submit button in the form, to which we added a name attribute: <input type="submit" name="submit" value="Post to PHP">.

If there is a value assigned to the variable $submit, it means that the script was reached by the user clicking on the submit button. To see the circumstances in which this happens, we have to look at the rest of the code in this example. Picking up where we left off...

```
...}else{
    echo<<<ENDPAGE
        <form method="post" action="$PHP_SELF">
        <input type="text" name="variable01" value="variable01">
        <input type="text" name="variable02" value="variable02">
        <input type="text" name="variable03" value="variable03">
        <input type="text" name="variable04" value="variable04">
        <input type="text" name="variable05" value="variable05">
        <input type="submit" name="submit" value="Post to PHP"
    </form>
ENDPAGE;
}
```

The action listed in this form is $PHP_SELF, which is a PHP shorthand meaning "send the POST HTTP request back to the current script." In this example, the end result is the same as if the action attribute had been "recursiveForm.php" or "http://localhost/recursiveForm.php."

The other new item in this code is the way the argument to the echo function is delimited. When echo is followed by three consecutive less-than signs (<<<), the string that follows replaces the quotation mark as the delimiter for the echo function. Such a function is called a *here document*. Looking at the quotation-filled string that needs to be output in this example, it is easy to see why this is valuable. There are a few tricks that can catch you up when you use here documents this way, as follows:

▶ The delimiter starts immediately after the last less-than sign (<), spaces included.

▶ The end delimiter must be on its own line, terminated with a semicolon. (It is the end of the echo function started so many lines ago.)

▶ The delimiters must match *exactly* and are case sensitive.

▶ The delimiter is not a variable (no dollar sign).

▶ If you pick as a delimiter a word that might come up in the encompassed string, the echo function could terminate at that point, yielding unexpected results. Pick a word that is unlikely to show up in the string.

Now that you have enough background for each of the individual parts, take another look at the whole script in your text editor to get a feel for the flow of logic. When a user first loads the page, $submit is not defined, so the script moves to the second half of the control structure, which prints the form. If you look at the HTML source at this point using your browser's view source function, you will see that the $PHP_SELF variable has already been interpreted and replaced with the path to the script. After the user fills out the form and clicks the submit button, the form data is passed back to the same script. The $submit variable now has a value, so the first half of the control structure will execute, printing the formatted name-value pairs.

Include() and Assign Flash Variables Without ActionScript

 recursiveForm-SWF.php, SWFform.inc, submitInRecursiveForm.swf, SWFDisplay.inc

The next example, *recursiveForm-SWF.php*, duplicates the functionality of the previous example, only with Flash as a front end. The code in this script, included in its entirety below, is noticeably more streamlined.

> **NOTE**
>
> *The examples in this chapter are optimized for legibility and simplicity. Many HTML tags have been stripped for the sake of keeping the code uncluttered, and it is only because of today's code-tolerant browsers that you can view these files without errors. When serving content in a production PHP application, you should always serve the correct HTML tags for the browser(s) you are trying to reach.*

```
//if the $submit variable has a value (user has submitted form)
if($submit){
        foreach($HTTP_GET_VARS as $key => $value){
          $nameValPairs.=("$key=$value&");
```

```
    }
  include ("SWFDisplay.inc");

//otherwise, print the form
}else{
  include ("SWFform.inc");
}
```

NOTE

The INC files must be in the same directory as the PHP script in order for this code to execute properly. If for some reason you want to put them in a different directory, just make sure to note the directory path in the include() argument.

Everything is the same, except that in place of the HTML form and the foreach loop that prints the name-value pairs, there is a function called "include." This function takes one argument—the name of a file. The script opens the named file at run time and includes it in the output. This example uses separate files to hold the big blob of code generated by Flash upon publishing the two SWFs used in this example. There is nothing special about the file extension *.inc*—you can include HTML, TXT, and even other PHP. There is nothing interesting contained in the file *SWFform.inc*. It is simply the code to embed the movie *submitInRecursiveForm.swf* in the HTML page generated by the script. This movie uses the GET HTTP request method, just as in the previous SWF example.

The really interesting part of this example is in *SWFDisplay.inc*. This code is inconspicuously tucked away in the midst of the great blob.

```
<PARAM NAME=movie VALUE="echoVars.swf?<?php echo $nameValPairs ?>">
```

You will recognize most of it as one of the <PARAM> tags nested within the <OBJECT> tag. There is, however, a snippet of PHP embedded right in the attribute of this tag. This code is executed when the main script pulls this file for output. It interprets it as HTML, and because there is PHP embedded within the HTML, it executes that code. As sneaky as this seems, it is a very common scenario (at least in the world outside Flash).

The variable $nameValPairs is given a value in the foreach control structure. It is formatted as a URL encoded string that Flash can understand (for example, echoVars.swf?variable01=stuff&variable02=nachos...).

The power of this extremely simple example might not be immediately obvious. Consider the following list of accomplishments of these eight lines of interpreted code:

▶ Dynamically serves different Flash movies based on user input.

▶ Dynamically assigns variable values to Flash at the _root level using a URL encoded string in the <OBJECT> tag. This is done without using error-prone, incompatible JavaScript.

▶ Processes form data from Flash without the LoadVariables action.

As silly as this example is, it drives home the whole point of using PHP as a simple tool for simple jobs. It is entirely possible to pass variables this way using nothing more than JavaScript on the client side. However, it requires a lot of skill and attention to detail. Threads discussing how to do it go on for days when they start in the popular forums. Even then, because of browser differences, combined with the fact that some browsers are not JavaScript enabled, you are talking about completing this job successfully for a *percentage* of users. Using this tiny, easy, server-side script, your percentage will always be 100%, *ceteris paribus*. This is because you are not relying on the client to have technology that is compatible with your application.

TIP

PHP.net and Zend.com have extensive documentation on their respective sites, and their sites are fast enough—thanks to PHP—that you can easily use them as your official bookshelf reference. Most functions in PHP have similar alternatives whose differences range from nuance to critical. Include() is one such function. As a research project to get you familiar with these valuable resource sites, go to both of them and search for the function include(). Find the three other similar functions and read about the differences between them.

Pattern Matching

PHP is a language that can do a lot with a few lines of code. Pattern matching is one area where this is especially true. A single line of PHP using regular expressions to match a pattern in a string can accomplish what would take Flash a hundred lines of code to do.

Regular Expressions

A *regular expression* is nothing more than a pattern used to compare against a string. It can be as simple as a single letter, testing to see whether that letter is contained within a string.

The advantage of regular expressions over simple string methods like indexOf() is that you can use more general criteria than the exact spelling of a specific string. For instance, you can use a *wildcard* expression that matches any character, a modifier expression that matches only the string you are looking for if it is preceded by whitespace, or a group of characters in brackets that will match any character identified by that group. These are just a few very common examples of the huge array of capabilities found in regular expressions.

With a bit of genius, a lot of time, and a big gob of spaghetti code, you can match the function of most common regular expressions in Flash. However, doing this is so unbelievably cumbersome for the developer and inefficient that it should be considered a waste of time. You may spend an afternoon and a hundred lines of code to match the functionality of 10 characters in a language like PHP that supports regular expressions.

Match

Checking to see whether a pattern is found within a string is a common task. PHP makes this very easy. Consider the following example:

```
if (ereg("PSWoods", $name)){...
```

This expression returns true if the variable $name contains "PSWoods" or "PSWoods, Esq.". It will return false if the case does not match, as in "pswoods". There is another function, eregi, which addresses case sensitivity:

```
if (eregi("PSWoods", $name)){...
```

This expression will return true if $name contains any case combination of the letters that make up "PSWoods"—for instance, "psWoods", "pswoodS", or "pSwOoDs".

Beginning and End of a String

The PHP regular expression toolset includes lots of modifiers to handle every special circumstance you might want to test. For instance, you might want to see if a certain letter or pattern came at the beginning of the string against which you are matching:

```
if (eregi("^Once upon a time", $storyText)){...
```

This expression returns true if the string begins with "Once upon a time, there were three bears…" It will return false if the pattern is not at the beginning of the string, as in "There were three bears once upon a time…" The caret (^) signifies the beginning boundary of the string.

The next expression returns true for any case combination of "the end." at the end of the string.

```
if (eregi("The End\.$", $storyText)){…
```

The dollar sign ($) is a special character meaning the ending boundary of the string contained in $storyText. The backslash is required to escape the period because it has a special function, as you will see. But what if you want to match any punctuation? For instance, suppose you want to match any of the following: "The End!" "The End?" or "~The End~".

Placeholders

In order to match the "The End" followed by any single punctuation mark, use a placeholder to signify that any character can go in that spot, as follows:

```
if (eregi("The End.$", $storyText)){…
```

The dot (.) is the special character in PHP that serves as a placeholder for any character. So now our regular expression will return true for any of the clever punctuation alternatives we mentioned before.

Now suppose we wanted to see if the story had been written by the one person who seems to write all spam emails worldwide: "THE END!!!!!"

```
if(eregi("The End!+$", $storyText)){…
```

This will return true if any number greater than zero exclamation points follows "The End" (case insensitive) at the very end of the string. This is not going to be the final solution, though, as you may have already guessed. There is another possible scenario. The regular expression still hasn't accounted for the possibility that there could be multiple instances of any kind of punctuation at the end of the $storyText variable—for instance, "The End???" The most obvious first try might be something like this:

```
if(eregi("The End.*$", $storyText)){…
```

This should be familiar by now, except for *. This means the same thing as +, except that it will match zero or more of the preceding character or expression. If you really think about this expression, you will see that it doesn't quite work. It will match the string "The End"(case insensitive) followed by any number of any character. It wouldn't make sense in the context of a good story, but it is conceivable that someone could write, "The Endxxxxxxxxxxxxxxxxxxxxxxxxxxxxxxxx"; our expression would still match. Clearly we are ready for another tool in the regular expressions toolbox.

Grouping

You can use a set of square brackets to group an assortment of characters against which you would like to match. This is where the power of regular expressions should begin to become apparent.

```
if(eregi("The End[?!.,;:]*$", $storyText)){
```

This is more like what we were looking for. We are now checking to see if the string value of $storyText ends with "The End"(case insensitive) followed by zero or more repetitions of any of the punctuation marks inside the brackets. This is an extremely handy trick. It works with any class of characters. For instance, suppose you want to match against the word "stationary," not giving the user the benefit of the doubt that he would spell it correctly. You could check for either spelling:

```
if(eregi("station[ae]ry", $storyText)){…
```

Ranges of alpha characters and numbers can be designated using shorthand. For instance, the following example checks to see if the value of the variable $surname begins with a letter in the first half of the alphabet.

```
if(eregi("^[a-m]+", $surname)){…
```

You can also designate what you *don't* want to match by negating characters within the brackets. When you use the caret (^) inside the braces, it means to match *anything but* the following character. For example, if you wanted to search a string for "dates", "mates", "hates", and "rates", but not "fates", you might write an expression like this:

```
if(eregi("[^f]ates", $storyText)){…
```

Classes

We still have a problem with the expression that checks to see if $storyText ends in some variant form of "The End" followed by any repeated punctuation. I didn't include *all* punctuation. Some could still conceivably type "The End'''".

The solution lies in classes. *Classes* are predefined shorthand for large groups of characters. For instance, the class for punctuation looks like this:

```
if(eregi("The End[[:punct:]]*$", $storyText)){...
```

The following table shows some other useful classes of characters that can save you a lot of typing.

Class	Description
[:digit:]	digits
[:space:]	any whitespace character
[:blank:]	space and tab
[:alnum:]	alphanumeric characters
[:alpha:]	alpha characters, case insensitive
[:lower:]	lowercase alpha characters
[:upper:]	uppercase alpha characters

Take a look at the following line of code. This regular expression will match if the variable $storeName is either "Nordstrom" or "Nordstrom's". There are two new elements in this line. First, the parentheses, as you would expect, group the apostrophe and the *s* so that they act as one component of the expression. Second, the question mark means that the string can either contain "'s" or not. It will match either way.

```
if(eregi("^PriceMax('s)?$", $storeName)){...
```

Replace
searchResult.php

Just as you can easily find complex patterns within a string, you can easily replace these patterns with a new string fragment. For example, if you wanted to filter an objectionable word, "potty", from all user input in a guestbook application, you could use something like the following:

```
$userInput = ereg_replace("pott[yi]","p****",$userInput);
$userInput = eregi_replace("pott[yi]","p****",$userInput);
    //same, only case insensitive
```

These functions return the modified value to the variable on the left side of the equal sign. For instance, if $userInput contained the string "He has a potty mouth. Potti, I say.\n", this expression would return "He has a p**** mouth. p****, I say."

The script *searchResult.php* is a practical example of this type of string pattern replacement. The code from this example follows.

```
$searchResults='<a href="http://bigco.com">BigCo</a>, the makers of
Flash-O-Matic.<br>
<a href="http://sdfj.com">SDFJ</a> has some Flash tutorials.<br>
<a href="http://quack-a-nator.com">Quack-A-Nator</a>
    will make you laugh in a flash.';

$searchTerm="Flash";

$searchResults=eregi_replace( $searchTerm,
   "<B><I>".$searchTerm."</I></B>" , $searchResults);
echo $searchResults;
```

The variable $searchTerm would ordinarily be from user input, and $searchResults would be the result of a database query, such as we will discuss in the next chapter. This example compares the pattern defined in $searchTerm to the string generated by the query, $searchResults, and appends a bold and italics tag to each instance of the word. This is a very common application of regular expressions.

Validate Email

validator.php

The Holy Grail of fill-out forms in Flash seems to be validating email. At any given moment, it seems, someone somewhere in the world is at a workstation writing post for a discussion group or bulletin board about how to do this inside Flash. As I have alluded to at least once already, I don't think this is an appropriate job for Flash. Look at the following code, which is from *validator.php*. This script is another recursive form. This time the first half of the script uses a simple, one-line regular expression to validate the email address.

```
//if the $submit variable has a value (user has submitted form)...
if($userEmail){

    $emailPiece="[[:alnum:]]+";
    if (eregi("^$emailPiece([-_.]?$emailPiece)*@
```

```
$emailPiece([-_.]?$emailPiece)*$", $userEmail)) {
        echo "Looks Good<p>\n";
    }else{
        echo "That is not a valid email address.<p>\n";
    }
}
//print the form no matter what
    echo<<<ENDPAGE
        <form method="post" action="$PHP_SELF">
            <input type="text" name="userEmail" value="$userEmail">
            <input type="submit" value="Post to PHP">
        </form>
ENDPAGE;
```

Everything in this example is familiar except the regular expression itself. It may look like an incomprehensible jumble if you haven't become accustomed to regular expressions yet, but if you break it down into bite-sized chunks, it is easy to understand.

The basic unit of our regular expression is going to be the variable $emailPiece. This is the class of characters that includes anything alphanumeric. This is the basic unit of an email address. For instance, in the fictitious email "s.harlenhopp_sales39840@main-street.sticksville.ok.us.widgets-r-us.com," each part that is not a dash, underscore, dot, or at sign falls into this category. Everything is either a number or a letter.

First notice that the regular expression defines the initial and final boundaries of the string with the caret and the dollar sign. This is to guard against someone accidentally (or otherwise) running her email together with other words. For instance, these modifiers catch mistakes like "my email is pswoods@danube.com," where some joker has written her email in prose instead of just filling in the blank.

Next is our $emailPiece, followed by the ([-_.]?$emailPiece)* pattern. This pattern allows for the possibility that there is another group of alphanumeric characters, separated from the first by a dash, an underscore, or a period. The question mark after the punctuation group means that this group can exist or not—it doesn't matter either way. The whole point of this part of the pattern is to allow these three punctuation marks in the first half of the email address. Notice that the whole regular expression would return false if this punctuation were at the beginning or the end of the part of $userEmail before the "at" sign.

Next is the at sign, and finally a repeat of the first half of the pattern. You could remove the underscore from this iteration of the [-_.]? pattern, since domains may not contain this punctuation.

This is by no means the most comprehensive method that PHP has to offer for checking the validity of an email address. If you are interested in validating form input, the list of PHP resources runs deep, including custom modules. The point is that with a single line, we have created a *pretty good* email validation scheme. The main weakness of this particular scheme is that we have not checked the top-level domain (com, net, org, etc.) of the user's email address. Not bad for one line of code.

PHP also supports Perl-style pattern matching, which is very similar, except that it uses forward slashes as delimiters for the regular expression. Adding this type of regular expression in addition to the style we have already discussed gives you access to an even larger gamut of matching possibilities, including word boundaries, beginning and end of lines in a file, and on and on.

If you are interested in harnessing the amazing power of regular expressions, old Perl books seem to be the best resource. O'Reilly's holy canon of Perl, including *The Camel Book*, have explanations and examples. The ultimate resource—not surprisingly, also from O'Reilly—is *Mastering Regular Expressions*. The style of regular expressions taught in these resources is directly compatible with Perl, PHP, and JavaScript.

File Handling
mailingList.php

There are a lot of quick, easy, useful things you can do with a small text file on a server. For example, you can use PHP to create small data sources, personalized settings, or scripts for other programs (like Swift-Generator) quickly and easily. That said, I should give two considerable qualifications.

The biggest risk involved in using PHP to write to files lies in the possibility of two users simultaneously writing to a file. In other words, two users might submit a form to the same script at *exactly* the same time, causing the data written to the file to get jumbled. There is a built-in precaution against this, flock(), but this feature is negated by PHP's new ability for multi-threading, which is implemented on many production servers. Because of this issue, use of this technique is best left for jobs in which it is extremely unlikely or impossible that two users would be operating on the same file simultaneously. This type of situation is true when there is only one user for the script (like an admin for a site with a Flash front end using text files as a data source) or when a unique file is created for each user.

The next biggest issue is performance, but this will not be as important in the kind of applications we mentioned. Writing a file to a disk is going to be many times slower than using a database, simply because a database server typically operates with the host computer's primary memory, while writing a file relies on the hard drive to write the file as fast as it can spin and wiggle.

The following example code is selected (and simplified) from *mailingList.php*. This script makes use of the directory "files," which must be contained in the same folder in which you run the script.

```
$fp = fopen ("files/list.txt", "a+" );
$existingList = fread($fp,10000000);
   fputs ( $fp, $userEmail."|" );
fclose ( $fp );
```

This is a typical scenario when dealing with external data in PHP: you create an object to handle the connection to the external source—in our case $fp (for "file pointer," but the identifier is arbitrary)—manipulate the data using the object and then close the connection—in this case close the file.

The function fopen() is the most elastic of the functions used here. It takes as its arguments first the path to the file to open, then a special modifier called the mode. The possible values of mode are shown in the following list, which is adapted from the PHP manual at Zend.com.

- ▶ **r**   Read only. File pointer is at the beginning of the file by default.

- ▶ **r+**   Read *and* write. File pointer is at the beginning of the file by default.

- ▶ **w**   Write only. File pointer is at the beginning of the file by default. Erase any data in the existing file. If the file does not exist in the given directory, create it.

- ▶ **w+**   Read *and* write. File pointer is at the beginning of the file by default. Erase any data in the existing file. If the file does not exist in the given directory, create it.

- ▶ **a**   Write only. File pointer is at the end of the file by default. If the file does not exist in the given directory, create it.

- ▶ **a+**   Read *and* write. File pointer is at the end of the file by default. If the file does not exist in the given directory, create it.

The function fread() uses the file handle $fp that we created in the first line and reads the number of bytes designated in the second argument. If the end of the file occurs before this amount of data is read, it stops there without generating an error.

The function fputs() writes new data to the file. In this example, everything in the variable $userEmail will be written to the file, followed by the pipe character, which is used as a delimiter. The delimiter has no immediate use in this example; it is included because this is a typical way to handle data stored in a flat (text) file.

Finally, fclose() closes the file. The new information will be written to the file, and the variables loaded from the file—in this case $existingList—will remain in memory for use elsewhere in the script.

Putting It Together: A Mailing List Signup

mailingList-SWF.php, mailingList.php, list.txt, subscribe.html, subcribe.fla

The final example for this chapter is *mailingList-SWF.php*. This example uses everything we have covered so far, plus the long-awaited loadVariables action in the Flash movie. It is an application to add users' email addresses to an opt-in mailing list. It takes the address and adds it to a pipe-delimited text file. Before we delve into the simple ActionScript that makes the movie work, first look at *mailingList.php*, the HTML-only version of this application.

Everything should be familiar in the following code. I will briefly describe the flow of events.

```
$emailPiece="[[:alnum:]]+";
if (eregi("^$emailPiece([-_.]?$emailPiece)*@$emailPiece
   ([-_.]?$emailPiece)*$", $userEmail)) {
//----------open the file, check for dupes,
  and write to the list----------\\
  $fp = fopen ("files/list.txt", "a+" );
  $existingList = fread($fp,10000000);
  //check to see if the user is on the list already
  if (eregi($userEmail,$existingList)){
     $errorMsg="You were already subscribed.";
     //if not, write to the file
  }else{
     fputs ( $fp, $userEmail."|" );
     $errorMsg="You are now on the list.\n";
  }
```

```
fclose ( $fp );
echo $subAction;
```

The two worst things that could happen in terms of handling data for a mailing list are invalid email addresses and duplicates on the list. This script uses simple regular expressions to guard against each. The first section of code in this example is the same email validation regular expression used earlier.

If the email address checks out, the file containing the list is opened, and the contents are loaded into the variable $existing list. At this point another regular expression is used to match the user input, $userEmail, to the new string $existingList. A match would mean that the user is already subscribed to the list, so the variable $errorMsg is set to reflect this.

If there is no match—the else section of the control structure—the user's input and the delimiter are written to the end of the file, and $errorMsg is given a value to confirm this to the user. Finally, the script exits the control structure and closes the file, whether or not anything was added.

Try this script in your browser and confirm that it works. Open *list.txt* in the files directory and see the email addresses you entered. Next try the Flash version, *subscribe.html*. This is nothing more than a Flash front end for the same script, save the form output and the Flash-friendly format of the $errorMsg variable. The script used for the Flash version is *mailingList-SWF.php*.

If you open *subcribe.fla*, you may be disappointed to find very little ActionScript. This is all there is:

```
on (release, releaseOutside, keyPress "<Enter>") {
    loadVariables ("mailingList-SWF.php", this, "GET");
}
```

This code is attached to the button inside the MC instance named "hub." When the user submits the form, the Flash player takes care of feeding the variable userEmail into the URL string, just like in an HTML form using the GET method. You could also use POST for this example, but you would be sending extra information unnecessarily.

Nothing else happens within this movie, except that the dynamic text field displaying the variable errorMsg will update after the script executes. If you were to use this scenario for a production Flash application, you would want to use some kind of timer to declare a value for errorMsg internally—within the Flash movie—in case the script crashes for any reason.

What to Take Away from This Chapter

If you have ever had a favorite Swiss Army knife, all-in-one tool, or even an electronic PDA you found especially handy, you can relate to the idea of using PHP as a handy tool in your Flash applications. It doesn't have to be your primary focus—or even something you spend a lot of time on—to be useful to you. You can easily learn enough PHP in a few afternoons to save countless hours of development time down the road. And by leaving server-side jobs to the server, you let Flash operate within the realm of its built-in strengths. This can only make for better Flash applications.

Introduction to MySQL

This chapter is a rough-and-dirty introduction to the wonderful world of MySQL, where everything is fast, free, and packed to the roof with useful functions. The discussions and examples provide you with just enough knowledge to get data-backed Flash Web applications up and running.

The examples in this chapter revolve around the fictitious delicatessen El Deli Hermanos, including a Flash front end for reading daily specials from a MySQL database, an application to maintain this database, and a postcard application with a 100 percent Flash front end.

History and Introduction

In order to fully appreciate what a marvelous and revolutionary windfall MySQL is for the Web developer, a small dose of history is in order. The idea of indexing data probably goes back as far as recorded data. You can find hundreds, if not thousands, of papers, books, and online articles describing various systems throughout history as "the first database." While it is probably not productive to consider what was *really* a database before electronic computers, it is interesting that there always seems to have been in man a deep, built-in yearning to organize data.

My personal submission for consideration as the world's first database is the invention of one Herman Hollerith, a German immigrant who worked at the U.S. Census Bureau in the late 1800's. Hollerith's machine kept a running total of the columns selected in multiple rows on punchcards. Though the name came later, Hollerith's invention, funded by the U.S. Census Bureau and used as a provider of automated data handling, became the kernel that spawned IT giant IBM *in the late nineteenth century*. You can find the whole story, along with pictures of these machines, at http://www.ibm.com/ibm/history/story/.

The term *database* came about in the 1960s, paralleling the rise of practical electronic computing. These databases were an unbelievable technological revolution at the time, and are of course laughably simplistic and slow by today's standards.

The first boon to databases was the disk drive, which had the advantage of random access over the preceding tape drive. This allowed for the machine holding the data to go immediately to the area of the storage medium that held the desired data, instead of cycling through a big spool of magnetic tape.

At this point in database history, state-of-the-art data applications took the form of *navigational databases*—collections of data in which you had to know where data was to find it. In other words, to use the database, you had to navigate through a hierarchy using a low-level language.

The technology of navigational databases was thought to be the destination along the road of data application development; so it is not surprising that E. F. Codd's seminal 1970 paper, "A Relational Model of Data for Large Shared Data Banks," was not originally warmly received by his employer, IBM. Codd's ideas, using a high-level language to act upon data, without the need for the user/programmer to know the exact hierarchy of the data, was the impetus for the relational database as we know it today. Modern examples of relational databases include Microsoft Access on the desktop and Oracle on the server.

MySQL was born from the work of Michael "Monty" Widenius while in the employ of the Swedish company, TcX. Although building a high-performance database system in-house is not unheard of, MySQL was different in that it was adapted to be acquired, compiled, and used by anyone with an Internet connection.

In a modern database industry generating billions in annual revenue, MySQL has little company as a high-performance relational database server that is free. As you may know—or as you may have inferred from the prominence of "big" names in the history of databases—industrial-strength database applications have traditionally been very expensive. Combined with the cost of MySQL's natural *-nix habitat (also free), MySQL is an attractive solution for anyone who needs a fast and powerful database application. Together with PHP and Apache, MySQL is considered by many (including Netcraft, the people who make a living from examining Web sites' back ends) to be the standard for Linux Web servers.

How Does MySQL Measure Up?

Database people are given to comparing things, and databases themselves do not escape their scrutiny. MySQL is often compared to both commercial database solutions and other free/open source databases like PostgreSQL. Without getting mired in benchmarks and details that are of interest only to database specialists, let's take a look at some key areas of comparison.

▶   **Performance**   MySQL compares favorably in terms of speed against any database, commercial or free. While it is probably impossible to determine which is the absolute fastest database server on the Web, MySQL is generally accepted to be faster than its primary free competitor, PostgreSQL. The MySQL developers have published the results of their own benchmark tests at http://www.mysql.com/information/benchmarks.html.

▶ **Stability**   If you use a database just for dynamic content or similar applications that do not handle data that *is* the central component of your business, you will probably never experience stability issues with MySQL, either on a professionally configured production server or on your limited Windows/Apache server, as described in this part of the book. You should be aware, however, that there are enhancements (collectively called ACID) built into commercial database packages like Oracle that are not included in MySQL. These enhancements ensure that data transactions are more or less bulletproof, surviving even hardware failures. For a full explanation, see http://philip.greenspun.com/wtr/aolserver/introduction-2.html.

▶ **SQL compliance**   MySQL compares favorably in this area. One nice feature of the MySQL/PHP combination is that porting a script to a different database server is often as easy as changing the prefix on your database functions. The concepts and basic syntax of any good SQL resource will apply in MySQL.

▶ **Server-side scripting interfaces**   If this part of the book has been helpful to you, you will probably never find a programming or scripting language with Web server features that doesn't support MySQL. Some examples of languages with support are PHP, Perl, Java, Visual Basic, and Visual C++.

▶ **Features**   MySQL does have a smaller feature set than Oracle or even PostgreSQL, but it is perfectly suitable for most applications that concern Flash developers. The fact that it is lighter on advanced features like fail-safe transactions (which ordinary schmoes like you and me will never require) allows MySQL to consume far less system resources than other databases, which in itself is an attractive feature, especially since we are mirroring a server installation on our desktop machine.

▶ **Ease of installation/use**   As the next section of this chapter outlines, MySQL is more or less self-installing on Windows. Similarly, it is easy to compile and install on a *-nix/Apache production server for experienced Webmasters. In addition, the MySQL client component(s) is simple and easy to use.

MySQL Client-Server Model
index.php

There are two basic components to the MySQL database software: the server and the client. The server is the part that does all the actual work, creating and manipulating data. This is the only part that is in use when you are not creating or editing your databases with the client. Server-side scripts can interact with the server to get data out of the databases without use of the client.

The client is the command line application you use to create and edit databases. It is the default interface with your databases. At the time of writing, the MySQL client is a great source of interest. An increasing number of PHP scripts can serve as a replacement for the client by using forms to input data and queries visually. One such application is PHPMyAdmin, which will be accessible from your htdocs directory as *index.php* if you installed PHPTriad in Chapter 15. This is the PHPMyAdmin interface:

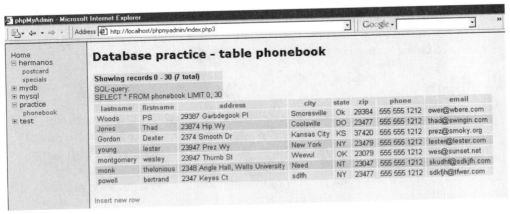

Another interesting development in this area is the release of the beta official MySQL GUI. This application is being developed as a visual alternative to the old command line client that we will use in this chapter. At the time of writing, this application isn't done yet, but the application is planned to support the features of the command line client, such as creating tables and inputting SQL queries, as well as new features like directly editing entities in a table as users of desktop databases are accustomed to.

Installation

Installing MySQL on any version of Windows consists of running an installer, which does little more than unzip the compiled program into the directory you choose. The newest component of the MySQL package, the GUI, comes with a similarly easy installer.

If you want to use MySQL as a service on NT/2000, using an actual Web server, you can do that, too. We are not going to outline this process, but it is covered in detail in the documentation section of the MySQL Web site. If you installed PHPTriad, you will already have MySQL installed in c:\apache\mysql.

Obtaining and Installing MySQL

Go to http://mysql.com/downloads/mirrors.html and find a mirror close to you. Go to the "downloads" section. Choose the latest version listed as stable and download it.

Run the installer. It will install everything to c:\mysql by default, which is as good a place as any for our purposes. If you change the directory, keep in mind that you will either need to navigate to that directory from a DOS command line or create a shortcut to start a DOS shell in that directory.

Next, download the GUI in the Graphical Clients section and install it. At present, you have to create a shortcut manually for your desktop or Start menu.

Mysqlshow

To see the default databases and tables included in the MySQL installation, we are going to fire up the included mysqlshow application. Open a DOS window (usually somewhere in Start | Programs | Accessories by default) and navigate to the directory that holds your MySQL executables (c:\mysql\bin by default). If you look at the directory listing, you will see a number of executables. The main ones we will use are mysqld (the server), mysql (the client), mysqladmin, and mysqlshow. Mysqlshow, as the name says, shows you what is in the database or table you designate in the command line. For instance, try the following commands:

```
mysqlshow mysql
mysqlshow mysql user
mysqlshow mysql user user
```

The first example should give you something like what you see here:

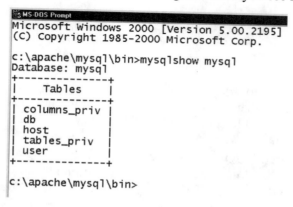

The meaning of these commands may not become clear until you see a database with more transparent names, but this is the only populated database that comes preinstalled. The first argument is the database name, followed by the name of the table, and finally the name of a particular field in that table. When you just give mysqlshow one parameter (mysql), it shows you the tables in that database. With two parameters you see a list of the fields in that table, complete with detailed information about the column type. Giving it three parameters lists only the designated field with all the information about its column type.

License

A quick, casual survey of the MySQL landscape would lead you to believe that this database software is open source and entirely free. This is not exactly right. MySQL is technically not considered open source, because it does require a license and a fee in certain situations. For full, current details, see http://www.mysql.com/support/arrangements/mypl.html. It just happens that one of those situations is using the MySQL server on Windows.

Don't worry, though; there are several consolations. First of all, at the time of writing, you are free to use the Windows version of the server for 30 days. That is more than enough time to learn how to use the software, after which you can begin using the MySQL server on your production *-nix server. Since the client is free on any platform, you can connect directly with the remote MySQL server and work directly with the live database, provided that your server admin is willing to add permissions to facilitate this. Finally, the Windows license is very inexpensive. Chances are, you've spent more on frivolous software like games than you will spend on this amazing tool.

SQL Crash Course

The Structured Query Language is the lingua franca of databases. Practically everything you will do in MySQL will be expressed in SQL. This part of the chapter will give just enough background to get up and running with some practical, if simple, MySQL applications using PHP as the middleware and Flash as the front end.

Getting Started

practice.sql

The first thing you will need is some data with which to practice. On the CD, you will find a file called *practice.sql*, which can be used to dump a complete, populated table into a practice database.

First copy *practice.sql* to the directory in which your MySQL database server resides (for example, c:\mysql\bin or c:\apache\mysql\bin). Next open an MS-DOS prompt and navigate to that directory. If you are not sure how to navigate in DOS, just type **CD**, then the path where you want to go (for example, **CD c:\apache\mysql\bin**).

Once you are there, make sure mysqld.exe is running and type the following commands.

```
mysqladmin create practice
mysql -u root practice < practice.sql
```

The first line creates the database "practice" using the mysqladmin program. This application is usually used primarily by the database administrator, so you don't have to worry about learning a lot of commands for it. The second line is extremely useful, and commonly used, so you should make sure you remember it somehow.

This instruction to MySQL executes the contents of *practice.sql* as if you typed everything contained in it from the command line. This is a necessity when you deal with more complex databases or larger amounts of data, since it is just too cumbersome to type everything from the command line. You can export a file formatted like *practice.sql* directly from some programs. This file was created using the PHP script PHPMyAdmin.

Use mysqlshow to see if the data is in the database. You should see something like the following image, showing the table "phonebook."

```
mysqlshow practice
```

```
MS-DOS Prompt
Microsoft Windows 2000 [Version 5.00.2195]
(C) Copyright 1985-2000 Microsoft Corp.

c:\apache\mysql\bin>mysqlshow practice
Database: practice
+-----------+
| Tables    |
+-----------+
| phonebook |
+-----------+

c:\apache\mysql\bin>_
```

Logging in to MySQL

Once the phonebook table has been created and populated, you are ready to try some commands from the MySQL command line. The following command will get MySQL running for you so you can try some SQL queries.

```
mysql -u root practice
```

The command syntax is as follows:

```
mysql -u username (-p) (-h hostName) (databaseName)
//example: mysql -u pswoods -p -h 255.255.255.255 wwwPages
```

The variables in parentheses are optional. The -p combination tells MySQL to prompt you for a password, as you will see in the next image. This chapter does not make use of passwords, simply to increase compatibility and decrease the amount of manual changes you have to make to your MySQL setup before you can do some real examples. The default setup when you install MySQL is for one user, root, and no password set.

```
MS-DOS Prompt - mysql -u pswoods -p
Microsoft Windows 2000 [Version 5.00.2195]
(C) Copyright 1985-2000 Microsoft Corp.

c:\apache\mysql\bin>mysql -u pswoods -p
Enter password: _
```

The -h parameter and the hostName that follows it tell MySQL which host it should ping for queries. This is one of the big strengths of this database server. You can have the MySQL server component running on your superfast, souped-up Linux Apache server, and use the client component or PHP scripts on your desktop PC to send queries to the server. It is very common for hosting companies to have separate machines dedicated to running the MySQL server, with an HTTP server running on another machine. In this scenario, using -h hostName is necessary.

Finally, the databaseName parameter tells MySQL which database to use for the queries that will follow. If you don't type this on the command line when you first invoke MySQL, you will have to type "use databaseName" once you are running MySQL. When you are done messing around in the MySQL command line client, simply type \q and press ENTER to exit the program.

CAUTION

The examples throughout the chapter assume that you are the root user (the database administrator) and that no password is required to log in as this user. There are exactly zero chances in a billion that this will reflect the settings on your production server; it is done for the sake of simplicity, so that all the examples will be sure to run on your system without having to alter them. The best practice for locally testing your own scripts is to reflect on your workstation the same username/password combination provided to you by the database admin on your production server. That way, you can simply move the script to the server and it will work.

Useful Commands

This chapter barely scratches the surface of MySQL, and SQL is another subject entirely. The following sections are meant to serve as a quick cheat sheet for the SQL commands we will use in this chapter, as well as some of the most common commands that you will use every day.

CREATE

One nice thing about SQL is that, like ActionScript and JavaScript, code sounds like what it does. CREATE as we will use it is a function to create a table. The following example is the SQL statement used to create a table in the example used for most of the chapter.

```
CREATE TABLE specials (
pkey INT (10) not null AUTO_INCREMENT,
name VARCHAR (50) not null ,
description VARCHAR (200) not null ,
price VARCHAR (10) not null ,
PRIMARY KEY (pkey)
);
```

This statement creates a table called "specials" with the field's pkey, name, description, and price. The field pkey is designated as the *primary key* (the column by which the table is indexed). If you are familiar with another database, or just database concepts in general, you know that an indexed primary key is what makes a database fast and powerful. It is not generally necessary to create a primary key in MySQL manually, since it will create one for you if you do not designate a column you define to be the primary key. Our example uses a primary key that accepts values created in Flash in order to demonstrate a particular flow of data that is common in Flash Web applications.

The basic syntax of the CREATE function is as follows:

```
CREATE TABLE tablename(
columnName COLUMNTYPE (length) [options],
columnName COLUMNTYPE (length) [options],
...and so on...
GENERAL TABLE FUNCTIONS
);
```

For the simple applications discussed in this chapter, you could easily use the column type VARCHAR for every column in every table. This type holds anywhere from 1 to 255 characters, or as many as you specify. A string that is longer than the designated length will be truncated to that length. For instance, if you create a column of type VARCHAR and give it a length of 10, then try to input the string "the quick brown fox", you will end up storing the string "the quick"—the first 10 characters.

The other common column type we will use extensively in this chapter is INT. This is simply an integer with a possible range of values from 0 to 4294967295, or having the number of digits you designate.

Try to add a table to your practice database using the VARCHAR and INT column types. Observe the syntax shown above, remembering to put a semicolon at the end. It is easy to get lost typing one long SQL statement into a command line that wraps inside a DOS window (or a Unix command line). The easy solution is to type one idea per line, as shown in the examples above. MySQL will not try to interpret the statement until you type the semicolon and press ENTER, as shown here:

```
MS-DOS Prompt - mysql -u root
Microsoft Windows 2000 [Version 5.00.2195]
(C) Copyright 1985-2000 Microsoft Corp.

c:\apache\mysql\bin>mysql -u root
Welcome to the MySQL monitor.  Commands end with ; or \g.
Your MySQL connection id is 93 to server version: 3.23.22-beta-debug

Type 'help' for help.

mysql> use practice
Database changed
mysql> CREATE TABLE waterQuality(
    -> tds INT,
    -> turbidity INT,
    -> bioLoad INT,
    -> taste VARCHAR (50)
    -> );
Query OK, 0 rows affected (0.08 sec)

mysql>
```

TIP

The all-caps syntax for predefined SQL identities is not necessary in MySQL. It is, however, strongly recommended. By using uppercase for SQL and lowercase for column names and other variables, your query strings will be much easier for you to read because this allows your eyes to go directly to either the functions or the variables on which the functions operate. In addition, this syntax ensures compatibility with all SQL-compliant databases.

So far, we have only talked about two column types. In the interest of keeping the examples simple and focused, these are the only types used in the Flash Web applications in this chapter. Table 17-1 lists a few of the other very common, useful column types, for which you may find immediate use.

Knowing how to create tables is useful, in case you ever want to do it dynamically using a server-side script. On the other hand, the number of visual front ends available for MySQL is growing. In addition, there are PHP scripts and the official MySQL GUI that will do this for you.

Whether or not you decide to commit the syntax of CREATE to memory, you should definitely spend some time practicing the remaining SQL statements, as you will use most or all of them in every data-driven application you build.

Column Type	Default Range	Description
BIGINT	0 to 18446744073709551615	A really big integer.
FLOAT[(M,D)] ex: price FLOAT (5,2)	−3.402823466E+38 to 3.402823466E+38	Floating point number, where M is the total number of digits and D is the number of decimal places.
DATE	1000-01-01 to 9999-12-31	
TIMESTAMP [(M)] ex: tstamp TIMESTAMP (120)	1970-01-01 00:00:00 to the year 2037	Displays TIMESTAMP values in YYYYMMDDHHMMSS if M is 14, YYMMDDHHMMSS if M is 12, YYYYMMDD if M is 8, or YYMMDD format if M is 6. Use this field to sort entries in guestbooks and bulletin boards.
TEXT	0 to 65535	Giant string.
LONGTEXT	0 to 16777215	Unbelievably huge string.

Table 17.1   *Useful Column Types*

SELECT

SELECT is the function used most in the examples in this chapter, and perhaps used most in general. You use SELECT to get data out of your database, using the parameters you designate. The following SQL statements will return all fields from each entry in practice.phonebook (the first one), and the lastname and firstname fields in practice.phonebook (the second one).

```
SELECT * FROM phonebook ;
SELECT lastname, firstname FROM phonebook;
```

WHERE is a parameter used in conjunction with SELECT, as well as a lot of other SQL functions. It modifies the statement to make it more specific. In the following example, the query returns all fields from any entry where the field lastname is equal to "monk."

```
SELECT * FROM phonebook WHERE lastname='monk' ;
```

LIKE allows you to use wildcards, as in the following example. The percent sign is used as a placeholder for any number of any character(s). This particular SQL query will return all the fields from practice.phonebook where the lastname column begins with the letter *m*.

```
SELECT * FROM phonebook WHERE lastname LIKE 'm%' ;
```

ORDER BY does what it sounds like. It orders the results of your query by the column you designate. Use the additional parameter DESC for descending order and ASC for ascending order. The following example returns a list of last names, first names, and phone numbers, ordered by lastname in ascending order, where the area code (the first three numbers) of the phone number is 555.

```
SELECT firstname,lastname,phone FROM phonebook WHERE phone LIKE
'555%' ORDER BY lastname ASC;
```

These few simple variations on the SELECT function will perform an amazing array of data handling for you. At this point, you already have enough background to get data out of a very simple database in any order you choose.

INSERT

INSERT is the function you use to put data into the database, one row at a time. You can either tell MySQL which fields you want to write to (some fields can be left blank or can be automatically populated), as shown in the first example code shown here. Otherwise, you can simply give MySQL the values you want to insert and it will use the default order of columns you set when you created the table as a guide, as in the second example here.

```
INSERT INTO phonebook (lastname,firstname,address,city,state,zip,email)
VALUES ('smith','john','2347 Fondue Circle','Squaresville' ,'CA','90210',
'jsmith@email.com') ;
//...or simply:
INSERT INTO phonebook VALUES
('smith','john','2347 Fondue Circle','Squaresville' ,'CA','90210',
'jsmith@email.com') ;
```

UPDATE

UPDATE is like INSERT, except that it changes the values of existing entries' columns. UPDATE must be given some criteria by which to match an existing entry, so it is usually used in conjunction with WHERE, as shown here:

```
UPDATE phonebook SET lastname='Jingleheimer-Schmidt', firstname='John' WHERE
lastname='Woods' ;
```

DELETE

DELETE does what it sounds like. It deletes the entry or entries you designate. The following example deletes any entry from practice.phonebook where the lastname column has the value "jones."

```
DELETE FROM phonebook WHERE lastname = 'jones' ;
```

DROP

DROP is a special keyword used for entities larger in scope than table entries—tables, for instance. The following SQL statement will drop the phonebook table from the database.

```
DROP TABLE phonebook;
```

Retrieving Records Using PHP

If you retained the basics of PHP from the previous chapter, this is going to be a walk in the park. PHP was still developing during the advent of data-driven Web development, so there is extensive, easy-to-use, built-in support for databases.

NOTE

The database we will use in these examples has been reduced to the most simplistic design possible in order to avoid too long a diversion into that field. If you plan to design the database with which you will exchange data, some additional study is required. Database design is a huge field, complete with thick layers of geek esoterica. To suggest that we so much as glance at the surface of this field would be an insult to the people who understand and practice it well.

HTML Output

specials.sql, specialsHTMLOnly.php

To begin the first example, the database "hermanos" needs to be created. We will also need a populated table called "specials." The file *specials.sql* will create the table and fill it out with the following commands. Copy *specials.sql* to your mysql/bin directory and execute the following commands, just as we did with the practice database.

```
mysqladmin create hermanos
mysql -u root hermanos < specials.sql
```

This example, *specialsHTMLOnly.php*, sends a simple SQL query to the hermanos database and prints the results in an HTML table. This is a component of our Web site for the imaginary establishment El Deli Hermanos—the daily specials listing. The following code shows the script connecting to the database and executing the query.

```
<HTML>
<BODY>
<?php

$db = mysql_connect("localhost", "root");
mysql_select_db("hermanos",$db);
$result = mysql_query("SELECT * FROM specials",$db);
```

The first MySQL function, mysql_connect(), establishes a connection with the database server using the same parameters as we used with the command line client component. In this example, "localhost" is the domain and "root" is the username. If there were a password argument for this function, it would follow the username. The object $db (arbitrarily named) is created to refer to this connection in subsequent commands.

Next the function mysql_select_db() designates the database hermanos as the current or selected database, using the object $db as the second argument. Finally, a special type of object is assigned to $result by the mysql_query() function, which takes any valid SQL statement as its first argument and the name of the connection object as its second argument. When you have a long, complex SQL query to feed into the mysql_query() function, it is easier to save your query as a string variable.

```
$sql="SELECT * FROM specials";
$result = mysql_query($sql, $db);
```

This way, your SQL is on its own line, which makes it easier to read and find problems. It also makes it easier to copy your query into the GUI and check to make sure your SQL is valid, as shown here:

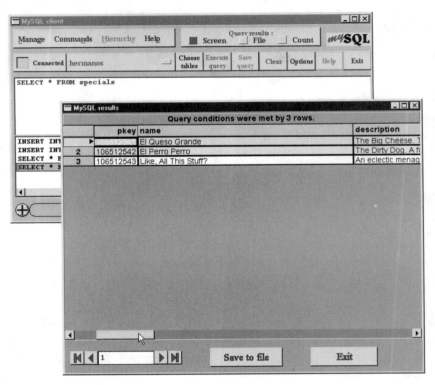

At this point in the script, there is an object, $result, that contains the result of the MySQL query. It is not yet formatted for output, so another step is required. There are several methods for doing this, but the following code demonstrates one of the handiest tools for this job.

```
echo "<table cellpadding=10> ";
echo
"<tr><td><b>Specials</b></td><td><b>Description</b></td><td><b>Price</b></td></tr>\n";

while ($myrow = mysql_fetch_array($result)) {
    printf("<tr><td>%s</td><td>%s</td><td>%s</td><tr>",
$myrow["name"],$myrow["description"],$myrow["price"]);
}

echo "</table>\n";
?>
</BODY>
</HTML>
```

The function mysql_fetch_array() cycles through each row contained in $result and creates an associative array for each, where the column names are the keys. Within each iteration of the while control structure the script prints a formatted string, an HTML table, containing the selected elements from these arrays.

The final result is a tidy little rendition of the information contained in the specials table. This is done with less than 10 lines of executable code. This example really should have some kind of if control structure to handle the possibility that the mysql_fetch_array() function is not able to execute. This was omitted for the sake of clarity.

Flash Output

specials.fla, specials.html, specialsSWF.php

Now we are going to do the same thing, only with Flash as a front end instead of HTML. This example is *specials.fla* and the following code is from the main timeline, first frame. You can preview this movie in *specials.html*.

```
loadVariables ("specialsSWF.php", "hub", "GET");
```

The call to *specialsSWF.php* is made, using GET. The data returned from this script will load into the MC instance hub. You can verify that the variables are being loaded into this blank Movie clip using the debugger:

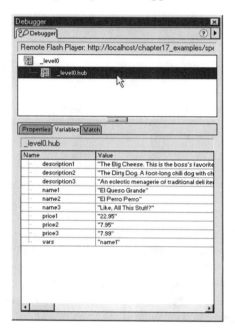

The following code is from *specialsSWF.php*, which is essentially the same as the previous example, except that the output is specially formatted for Flash.

```php
<?php

$db = mysql_connect("localhost", "root");
mysql_select_db("hermanos",$db);
$result = mysql_query("SELECT * FROM specials",$db);

$counter=1;
while ($myrow = mysql_fetch_array($result)) {
    printf("&name$counter=%s&description$counter=%s&price$counter=%s",
rawurlencode($myrow["name"]),rawurlencode($myrow["description"]),rawurlencode(
$myrow["price"]));
    $counter++;
}

?>
```

No HTML is required, since this page will never be directly rendered by the browser. The function rawurlencode() is used to format the output in URL encoded syntax, which is more likely to make it into Flash intact.

The following code is in the MC instance "hub," which is in the upper-left corner of the stage. This is what executes when the data is returned from the PHP script.

```
onClipEvent (data) {
   for (vars in this) {
      _root[vars] = this[vars];
   }
}
```

When the script sends the variables back to Flash in a format it likes—onClipEvent(data)—the for...in loop cycles through the variables and copies them to the _root level of the movie. This works because the dynamic text fields that display the output are on the main timeline—that is, at the _root level, as illustrated here. That's all the code there is to this application. Very simple.

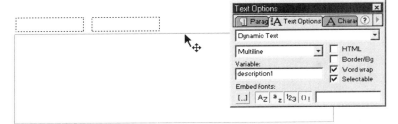

Modifying Records—Admin Application

specialsAdmin.php

Before you examine the code in the next example, take a look at it on your local Web server. Use it a few times and make sure you really understand how it is intended to be used. The example is *specialsAdmin.php*. This app is designed to allow the owner of our model Web site—possibly Senor Hermanos himself—to update the fields of his specials database table without any technical knowledge.

NOTE

As with the example recursiveForm.php in the previous chapter, this script will generate an error if nonfatal error reporting is not suppressed. As before, if this presents a problem for you, simply initialize the variable ($submit = ""). Then you will have to change the test to if($submit != "")...or something to that effect.

Click on edit in any row and change something in the entry using the HTML form. Once you are satisfied with the changes, submit the form and observe the changes being made. The script is not merely echoing variables from the $HTTP_POST_VARS array; it is actually changing the database entries. If you need to satisfy yourself that this is the case, close your browser, reopen it, and go back to the script. The changed values are still there.

When you enter the script for the first time, without variables in the URL string, you will come to this section of the control structure. This merely prints out the table containing the specials listings, as before, along with a link to edit each listing.

```
//admin is returning calling the script with no variables in the URL string/POST
request body
}else{
    drawTable();
}

//draw the table that lists the specials
function drawTable(){
    $db = mysql_connect("localhost", "root");
    mysql_select_db("hermanos",$db);
    $result = mysql_query("SELECT * FROM specials",$db);

    echo "<table cellpadding=10> ";
    echo
"<tr><td><b>Specials</b></td><td><b>Description</b></td><td><b>Price</b></td>
</tr><td></td>\n";

    while ($myrow = mysql_fetch_array($result)) {
        $id=$myrow["pkey"];
        printf("<tr><td>%s</td><td>%s</td><td>%s</td><td>%s</td></tr>",
$myrow["name"],$myrow["description"],$myrow["price"],"<a
href=\"$PHP_SELF?edit=$id\">edit</a>");
    }
    echo "</table>\n";
}
?>
</BODY>
</HTML>
```

The first new thing we encounter is the function drawTable(). This is a custom function. As you can see, the syntax for functions is the same as in JavaScript and ActionScript.

The function contains the same stuff as in the previous examples, with the exception of the link. The field pkey serves as the primary key for the specials table. This column contains a unique value in every row that is used by the database to sort the entries quickly. By using the primary key to identify table entries, we ensure that we will get the exact entry we are looking for. This value is appended to the URL string in the variable called "edit."

The next logical step is the edit portion of the script, which prints the table containing the current values of the database entry. Again, we start in familiar territory, except that the SQL query in the mysql_query() function now matches the particular entry we want to edit.

```
if($edit){
    $db = mysql_connect("localhost", "root");
    mysql_select_db("hermanos",$db);
    $result = mysql_query("SELECT * FROM specials WHERE pkey='$edit'",$db);
    $myrow = mysql_fetch_array($result);
?>

<!--switch out of PHP mode to avoid manually escaping all those quotes -->
<form method="post" action="<?php echo $PHP_SELF ?>">
    <input type="text" name="name" value="<?php echo $myrow["name"] ?>">
    <input type="text" name="price" value="<?php echo $myrow["price"] ?>">
    <br>
    <textarea name="description" cols="45" rows="5"><?php echo
$myrow["description"]?></textarea>
    <br>
    <input type="hidden" name="id" value="<?php echo $myrow["pkey"] ?>">
    <input type="submit" name="update" value="update">
</form>
<?php
```

While it looks like there is a lot of code here, it is actually very simplistic. We have exited the first PHP script and switched to HTML. It is not practical to use a here document in this situation, since the quotes in the array identifiers like $myrow["name"] are a required part of the syntax, and must be interpreted. Instead, we use lots of tiny PHP snippets to invoke the interpreter and place the current values into the HTML form. Notice that the primary key is still passed to the next phase of the script as a hidden variable in the form, id.

Finally, after the user submits the form, the update section of the script writes the new HTML form data sent via POST, using the UPDATE function in the SQL query.

```
//admin has just typed in new values for a particular special
}elseif($update){

    $db = mysql_connect("localhost", "root");
    mysql_select_db("hermanos",$db);
    $sql = "UPDATE specials SET name='$name', price='$price',
description='$description' WHERE pkey='$id'";
    $result = mysql_query($sql, $db );
    drawTable();
```

Despite the eye-straining HTML in the middle of the script and the needless repetition of the mysql_* functions, this script is very simple. If you wanted the code to be more streamlined, you could break the mysql_* functions out into a custom function using the SQL statement as an argument. You could also put the HTML in a separate file and include it.

This type of application is very valuable to users because it gives them an easy way to manage data. This is always an issue when building a data-driven site: how will the data be entered and updated? In general, the more people are willing to pay, the less they are willing to learn.

Putting It All Together—Postcard App

postcard.fla, postcard.swf, postcard.php, pickup.swf, pickup.php, retrieve.php, postcard.sql

The last application uses concepts from this and the previous chapter to build a postcard application in Flash. The application consists of six components:

▶ The table "postcard" within the hermanos database.

▶ The Flash movie used by the sender of the postcard to select a background image and type a message. This is *postcard.fla*.

▶ The PHP script that writes the input from *postcard.swf* to the postcard table in the database. This is *postcard.php*.

▶ The Flash movie used by the recipient of the postcard to view the message and image from the sender. This is *pickup.fla*.

▶ The PHP script that takes the primary key variable included in the URL string and passes it to *pickup.swf*. This is *pickup.php*.

▶   The PHP script that feeds data to *pickup.swf*. This is *retrieve.php*.

You will have to copy all the files somewhere in your htdocs directory, as usual, plus create the postcard table in our typical style.

```
mysqladmin create postcard
mysql -u root hermanos < postcard.sql
```

The last thing you will have to do in preparation to use this app is set your SMTP settings in your *PHP.ini* file. Open this file and find two lines that look approximately like the following. Edit them to reflect the address of your SMTP server (look at your email client's settings if you don't know) and your return email address. Of course, you only have to do this if you really want to send email with your application.

```
SMTP               = smtp-server ; for Win32 only
sendmail_from      = pswoods@email.com ; for Win32 only
```

This is what allows you to use the mail feature in PHP, which informs the recipient that a postcard is waiting for him. If you elect not to use this option, or if you have trouble with it, you can see how a finished postcard looks at the address http://localhost/postcard/pickup.php?id=982033627541th, where postcard is the directory in your htdocs folder in which you placed this example. There is one entry in the postcard table as it is created with *postcard.sql*.

Start from the End—Output

pickup.php, SWFDisplay.inc, pickup.swf, specials.fla, retrieve.php, specialsAdmin.php

We'll start backward, following the flow of events from the recipient's perspective, since that will be the most familiar territory in this application. The following code is from *pickup.php*.

```
<HTML>
<BODY>
<?php

//if the $submit variable has a value (user has submitted form)...
if($id){
   foreach($HTTP_GET_VARS as $key => $value){
      $nameValPairs.=("$key=$value&");
      }
   include ("SWFDisplay.inc");

//otherwise, print the form
```

```
}else{
   echo"it looks like this is not a valid pickup address.";
}

?>
</BODY>
</HTML>
```

This is a rehash of a trick we learned in Chapter 16, where we append the name-value pairs in the URL string to the code that embeds the Flash movie in the page. The following code is a small selection from the messy *SWFDisplay.inc*, which should illumine you if you don't remember.

```
...< PARAM NAME=movie VALUE="pickup.swf?<?php echo $nameValPairs ?>">...
...<EMBED src="pickup.swf?<?php echo $nameValPairs ?>"...
```

The little PHP snippets grab the variable values from $nameValPairs and feed them into the Flash movie. $nameValPairs was built in the main part of the script using the foreach...as control structure.

The next step is for *pickup.swf* to act on the information it received from the PHP script we just examined. The URL string will be in the form of http://host.com/postcard/pickpup.php?id=23094234098xx. The only variable to consider is id, which holds the primary key value for the card's database entry.

The following code, from *pickup.fla*, main timeline, first frame, shows how this process starts. This movie is very similar to *specials.fla*, in which the hub is used as a container for the incoming data.

```
loadVariables ("retrieve.php?id=" add id, "hub");
```

When *retrieve.php* is invoked with the variable id in the URL string, it executes the following code. This is similar to the update section of *specialsAdmin.php* that we looked at earlier, except that we are just displaying the matching MySQL table entry, instead of changing its contents.

```
<?php

//if the $submit variable has a value (user has submitted form)...
if($id){
   $db = mysql_connect("localhost", "root");
   mysql_select_db("hermanos",$db);
   $result = mysql_query("SELECT * FROM postcard WHERE id='$id'",$db);

   if ($myrow = mysql_fetch_array($result)) {
   printf("%s=%s&%s=%s&%s=%s&%s=%s&",
"sender", rawurlencode($myrow["sender"]),
"recipient", rawurlencode($myrow["recipient"]),
```

```
"message", rawurlencode($myrow["message"]),
"mc", rawurlencode($myrow["mc"]));
   echo "errorMsg=here is your card.";
   } else {
   echo "errorMsg=sorry - i couldn't find your card";
   }

//no $id was specified. give error message
}else{
   echo"errorMsg=sorry - your card is missing";
}

?>
```

Notice that we have introduced some modest error handling. If no id is specified—or if no database entry is found—an error message is returned. Otherwise, the script returns the data entered by the sender, along with the message "here is your card."

Once the data has been output to Flash, the following code, attached to the MC instance "hub" in the upper-left corner of the stage, will execute.

```
onClipEvent (data) {
   for (vars in this) {
      _root[vars] = this[vars];
   }
   loadMovie (mc + ".swf", "_root.ph");
   _root.ph._alpha=40;
}
```

This is the same code we saw in *specials.fla*, except that we added a routine to load the external SWF selected by the sender of the postcard. Just as in *specials.fla*, the dynamic text fields are directly on the stage (the _root level). The external SWF that is loaded into the MC instance ph is not in danger of overlapping the text only because it is on a lower layer on the timeline, as shown here:

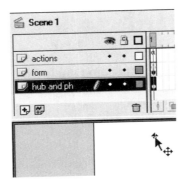

Input

postcard.php, pickup.php, genericForm.html

Now we are going to look at how the data gets into the hermanos.postcard table to begin with. The next piece of the puzzle, *postcard.php*, is a new mix of familiar concepts (and recycled code). The input for this script from the Flash movie will be the variables sender, recipient, message, and email.

```php
<?php

//validate sender variable (must begin with 2 alphanumeric chars
if (eregi("^[[:alnum:]]{2,}", $sender)) {

    //validate email and send message
    $emailPiece="[[:alnum:]]+";
    if (eregi("^$emailPiece([-_.]?$emailPiece)*@$emailPiece([-_.]?$emailPiece)*$",
$email)) {
```

Up to this point, we have simply validated the email address and sender name provided by the sender of the postcard. The reason we want to make sure the sender's name starts with two alphanumeric characters is that we use these two characters as part of the primary key in the database entry. To review regular expressions, see Chapter 16.

```php
        $body="click here to pick up your card \n\n
http://localhost/chapter17_examples/postcard/pickup.php?id=$id";
        mail("$email","a postcard from $sender", "$body");
        echo "errorMsg=your postcard has been sent.";
    }else{
        echo "errorMsg=invalid email";
    }

//skip to here if $sender does not start with 2 alphanumeric chars
}else{
    echo "errorMsg=invalid sender name";
}
```

The mail() function is new. This function sends the email message designated in the last argument to the recipients in the first argument with the subject line in the middle argument. Here we are using the syntax mail(address, subject line, body text). The body of this outgoing email is a simple instruction to click on the link to the page we already reviewed, *pickup.php*.

```
$db = mysql_connect("localhost", "root");
mysql_select_db("hermanos",$db);
$result = mysql_query("INSERT INTO postcard VALUES
('$id','$sender','$recipient','$email','$message','$mc')",$db);

?>
```

Finally, if the user's input passes the tests applied by regular expressions, the data is added to the database using the INSERT SQL function. A funny thing about inserting variable values in a SQL statement like this is that the variables must be in single quotes.

Before diving headlong into *postcard.fla*, the Flash front end for our application, look at *genericForm.html* and try it a few times. The following form is from this simple HTML page.

```
<form name="form1" method="post" action="postcard.php">
    <input type="text" name="id" value="id">
    <input type="text" name="mc" value="mc">
    <input type="text" name="sender" value="sender">
    <input type="text" name="recipient" value="recipient">
    <textarea name="message">message</textarea>
    <input type="text" name="email" value="email">
    <input type="submit" name="Submit" value="Submit">
</form>
```

This example is not part of the application. Not only that, it is baby-simple. You must be wondering why I've included this simple form in this chapter, especially right before we get to the really juicy stuff—the Flash front end for entering the MySQL data. The point is this: as complicated as the following Flash movie may appear, our goal is, in fact, to duplicate the functionality of this simple form.

Open *postcard.fla* and look around for a moment before we dive into the code. The guiding concept in this movie, as with any good application, is that objects, including Movie clips, are divided by function. That being the case, and because there are several separate stages to this part of the application (selecting an image, filling out the card, sending the data, and receiving a response), all library items except blank and hub are pulled out dynamically at run time.

As you can see in the following image, the stage is empty of graphical elements when the movie starts. Most of the code in this movie pertains to the transitions between stages and the movement of the Movie clips that goes along with those transitions.

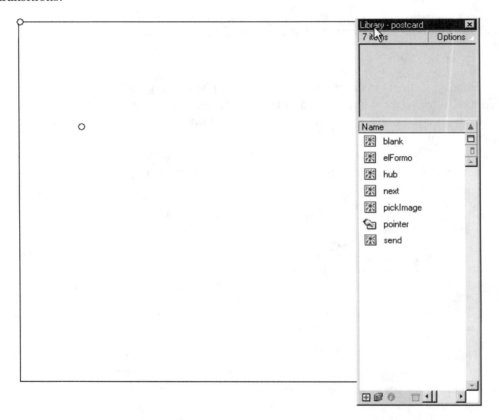

The first code we need to look at is on the main timeline, in the first frame.

```
mcNames = new Array("dog", "sandwich");
loadMovie (mcNames[0]+".swf", "ph");
hub.mc = mcNames[0];

// attach SWF picker
attachMovie("pickImage", "pickImage", 1);
pickImage._x = 175;
pickImage._y = 50;
```

```
// attach next MC
attachMovie("next", "next", 9);
next._x = 480;
next._y = 430;
```

Besides the obvious placement of the Movie clips pickImage and next, this section of ActionScript initializes the array mcNames, which lists the external SWFs available as background images. The variable hub.mc is given an initial value, in case the user decides not to change the original background. If you wanted to be really slick, you could load this array dynamically from a PHP script, which would read the contents of a directory used only for available background SWFs.

The first thing a user will have to do is pick a background image. This is done in the pickImage MC. The following code is on the timeline of pickImage.

```
this.i=0;
```

The buttons nested within pickImage have the following code attached. This is the ActionScript that changes the background image as the user clicks on the left and right arrow buttons.

```
//button pointing left
on (release, releaseOutside) {
    i--;
    if (i== -1){
       i=_root.mcNames.length-1;
    }
    loadMovie (_root.mcNames[i] + ".swf", "_root.ph");
    _root.hub.mc=_root.mcNames[i];
}
//button pointing right
on (release, releaseOutside) {
    i++;
    if (i==_root.mcNames.length){
       i=0;
    }
    loadMovie (_root.mcNames[i] + ".swf", "_root.ph");
    _root.hub.mc=_root.mcNames[i];
}
```

As the user clicks on either button, the counter variable, i, in the parent MC, pickImage, is incremented or decremented, and the corresponding external SWF listed in the_root.mcNames array is loaded in the MC instance _root.ph.

The Movie clip next contains the following action. This sets the custom function switchMode() in motion on the main timeline.

```
on (release, releaseOutside) {
  _root.switchMode();
}
```

The function switchMode on the main timeline appears as follows. This code simply gets rid of the Movie clips associated with the background-selection stage of this movie, next and pickImage. The background SWF is lightened so that it does not visually conflict with the overlying form (_alpha=30), and the MC that encompasses the next stage, elFormo, is attached.

```
//segue from image selection to user form
function switchMode () {
   next.removeMovieClip();
   pickImage.removeMovieClip();
   ph._alpha = 30;

   // attach elFormo MC
   attachMovie("elFormo", "elFormo", 9);
   elFormo._x = 125;
   elFormo._y = 70;
}
```

The following actions are on the timeline of the MC elFormo.

```
function attachSend(){
this.attachMovie( "send", "send", 1 );
send._x=265;
send._y=280;
}
attachSend();
```

It is especially important for the presence of Send MC on the stage to be variable, since there are times when you will not want the user clicking the button it contains. Since attaching the button is broken out into a function, it can be easily called from anywhere in the movie while elFormo is on the stage.

Once the user has filled out the input text fields in elFormo, the next logical step is to click on the button in Send MC. This is the button that sets the whole data process in motion. The following code is attached to this button.

```
on (release, releaseOutside, keyPress "<Enter>") {
  _root.sender();
}
```

The first thing to happen in the function sender() is the now-familiar migration of data from one object path to another.

```
// send form variables hub
function sender () {
   elFormo.errorMsg = "adding your postcard to the database...";
   for (vars in elFormo) {
      // get rid of unnamed instances (the "send" button)
      if (vars.indexOf("instance") == -1 && vars.indexOf("errorMsg")== -1) {
         hub[vars] = elFormo[vars];
      }
   }
```

The meaning of the for…in control structure should be transparent and immediate by now. We are moving the variables contained in elFormo to the MC instance called "hub." The control structure inside the for…in loop filters out unnamed instances (the button) and the value of the errorMsg variable. Since we do not need to send these variables to the PHP script, there is no need to load them into the hub.

```
// create a unique ID
   elDato = new Date();
   hub.id = elDato.getTime()+hub.sender.substring( 0, 2)
   elFormo.send.removeMovieClip();
   hub.dataLoader();
}
```

Finally we create a unique id for this postcard submission, remove the send button in elFormo, and set the dataLoader() function in motion in the hub MC instance. The interesting thing about the id variable is that this will become the primary key for our database entry. Although MySQL contains much more adept tools for creating unique primary key values, building this number in Flash saves a trip to the server, lines of code, and general pedagogical confusion in the *postcard.php* script. The id variable is assigned a value by combining Date.getTime() (the exact time in milliseconds measured since the "Unix epoch"—Jan 1, 1970) and the first two alphanumeric characters in the sender's name.

The MC instance "hub," in the upper-left corner of the stage, contains the code for the function dataLoader() in its timeline. This is a simple loadVariables statement, as seen in all the previous examples.

```
function dataLoader () {
   loadVariables ("postcard.php", this, "GET");
}
```

Finally, the code attached to the hub MC is as follows:

```
onClipEvent(data){
   _root.elFormo.errorMsg=this.errorMsg;
   if(this.errorMsg.indexOf("invalid") != -1){
      _root.elFormo.attachSend();
   }
}
```

The first order of business when the script returns the errorMsg variable's value is to output this value via elFormo (the red letters at the bottom). Next, if there is a problem with either the email address or the sender's name, the send button MC is reattached to elFormo so that the user can try to send the data again.

What to Take Away from This Chapter

Databases and database design are not light subjects by any stretch of the imagination, but databases can be extremely handy in light doses. In general, the more you learn about dynamic data sources, the more you will want to use them. While MySQL is not an absolutely perfect database, it is a particularly good fit for simple data-driven Flash applications.

Introduction to XML

IN THIS CHAPTER:

General XML

Flash XML

This chapter is an introduction to the wonderful world of data that is organized by a standardized structure, with a sharp focus on a few specific applications of XML in Flash. We will cover some of the general topics surrounding XML as it is currently developing, then dive right into the Flash applications.

General XML

Somewhere in the world about two years ago, a developer was standing in the wrong place at the wrong time—sort of like the infamous car ride of Archduke Franz Ferdinand that touched off that *other* big movement. This developer was in earshot of some kind of reporter or marketing type when he said something to the effect that "XML is the biggest thing since the Web itself…"; and the buzz hasn't stopped gaining momentum since.

The Buzz Versus the Promise

You have probably learned by now to ignore hilariously over-hyped trends— e-commerce, B2B, and WAP, to name a few—but XML really has some substance. The thing that the Web has needed since its introduction to the public finally looms on the horizon, and it looks like it may actually come true. I am of course talking about the separation of data and formatting.

Structured Data on the Web Client

The first big question that always comes to mind when talking about XML is "What need is there for XML when it is so easy to output database queries to Web pages?" Certainly an old-fashioned relational database is a good source of structured data?

Database integration is handy, but, as we saw in previous chapters, re-creating the relationships between data as they exist in a database is a tricky business on the client side, whether it be Flash or just a vanilla HTML page. XML is by definition a client-side structured data set. While originally conceived as a markup that would be viewed directly in a client (such as a Web browser), XML is probably more likely to become a standard structured data set that gets loaded into a wide variety of clients, where it will be manipulated.

Flash already supports this type of loading—data, structure and all. It is also possible with client-side scripting languages like JavaScript. The allure of this type of direct translation between the structure of the data source and the document for the client is as follows: if you can make one trip to the server and obtain a big set of data, which contains a lot of additional information simply in the order in which the data is organized, you can use an XML-enabled scripting language to perform more of the user's required tasks without making additional trips to the data source. Additional trips to the server cause the delay due to download, loss of time from page reloads (you have to find your spot, refocus the section you are using, etc.), and greater frequency of errors.

Easy, Standardized Communication

While it is nothing new for businesses to use a shared language or format to communicate electronically, it *is* new to use a standard markup and document structure in a human-readable text file. In the past, businesses would spend lots of money hiring a team of *real* programmers to build a link between proprietary systems. A classic example of this is the 14 bazillion cash register and credit card processing systems. It should tell you something to know that most property-level managers in retail and hospitality have worked directly with software engineers at some point in their careers.

The promise of XML is that any two applications can communicate without having to know anything more than the XML structure being used. Structures are being standardized in the form of DTDs and schemas, which will be discussed shortly.

Worldwide Index Versus the Magical Voodoo Search

Think about trying to find something on the Web. If you are really intent on finding something, such as a Web site you saw once and liked, but can't find, you will at some point try Yahoo to find what you are looking for. The reason that this particular search engine is so successful is that it is not really a search engine; it is an intelligently composed index.

Typical search engines follow a workflow that is something like the following. A program, called a *spider*, *crawler*, or some other such name, follows every link on every page it can find. On each page it finds, in addition to cataloging links and following them, it reads the page for key words. This is how it knows to match certain pages with certain words. The problem with this is that there is no sure means of discerning the meaning of any of the data in the page; it's pretty much just a blob of meaningless text.

Yahoo, on the other hand, employs real people (the ultimate program) to make decisions about how a site should be cataloged, based on their perception of the content as they view it through a browser. (Vision and reasoning; try to write software for *that*!)

The promise of XML is that all Web data will be indexed within itself. That is, *metadata* contained in the XML document—its document type, which tags contain which values, and generally, information about the information—will provide all the information needed for a comprehensive search. If the Web somehow magically transformed from HTML to 100 percent XML documents overnight, you would likely be able to search the Web with as much certainty as doing a database query.

Nuts and Bolts

The next few sections give a broad overview of a few of the standards most intimately related to XML. These are the standards that will be most useful to you if you venture outside Flash in the area of XML. I have chosen topics that seem the most promising at the time of writing, but keep in mind that XML is very new, is the focus of a lot of excitement, and is changing extremely rapidly. Some of these standards will doubtless have fallen out of vogue within a few years.

The XML Standard
news.xml

XML documents do not have very many requirements to be considered *well-formed*. Being well-formed means that the document meets the following criteria:

- ► It contains a unique root element.
- ► Elements have end tags.
- ► Elements do not overlap (they are embedded in the correct order).
- ► Cases match between beginning and end tags.

Aside from these simple criteria, you are more or less free to compose an XML document as you see fit. The following example, *news.xml*, shows a very simple XML document.

```
<newsItem>
<category name="Classified">

<article>
<author></author>
<headline>Clean Fill Wanted</headline>
<date>July 4,2001</date>
<text>No Gravel. Not willing to pay. Call Sam Barnes at 555-3948</text>
</article>
```

```
<article>
<author></author>
<headline>Free to Bad Home</headline>
<date>July 4,2001</date>
<text>Litter of 12 English Long-Ear Rabbits.
   For snake food only. Dora 555-2348</text>
</article>

</category>
</newsItem>
```

Schema and DTDs
newsSchema.xml

The idea behind both schema and DTDs (Document Type Definitions) is simple: provide an outline of the structure of an XML document in a form that parsing engines can understand. In other words, schema and DTDs tell the program that interprets XML markup what the structure of the document is, which elements are allowed at any point in the structure, and how many of each element is allowed. The value of these instructions to developers lies in ensuring that every XML document is 100 percent compliant with the schema or DTD it claims as its model. In other words, XML is validated by DTDs and schemas.

Unless you were around for the entire course of the bastardization of HTML, it probably will not be immediately obvious why anyone would care whether an XML document is pure in form, but a short look at Internet history should give us some clues. When a few visionary companies realized the commercial potential of the Web way back in the Stone Age (the mid-1990s), one of their first wishes was to extend the capabilities of Web browsers to include other media. The first giant breakthrough was the image tag. Images have nothing intrinsically to do with the structure of a document, so no one thought to place any kind of restriction on how this tag should fit into a document. You just drop it any old place inside the <BODY> tag, if you choose to close your <BODY> tag. That's another thing that went wrong with HTML: browsers were designed to be fault tolerant to a fault. Since HTML was deemed to be too hard to learn for the masses (this was in the days before WYSIWYG), it was thought necessary to code browsers to be prepared for pretty much any misuse of HTML syntax. Over time, hacks, extensions, proprietary browser instructions, wrong syntax, and every kludge that a marketing crony at a browser company thought was *kewl* became part of the public conception of HTML. I knew better, but even I stopped using closing </P> tags back when Notepad was *the* HTML editor.

That's where we are today. Though it hasn't caused the uproar in the development community that it probably intended, HTML has been unconditionally abandoned by the World Wide Web Consortium, or W3C, the international committee that recommends standards for the Web. HTML in its popular implementation has become useless, except as a proprietary set of instructions for the current harvest of feature-bloated browsers. All the tags that have been added in the interest of making individual browsers more attractive—<BLINK>, for instance—have already become historical curiosities, like the code that made the beep on the first digital microwave.

You really see this when you try to build an application that parses through HTML Web pages sight unseen, looking for meaningful data. I once built a Perl application for myself that was designed to grab the contents of a <FRAMESET> tag from my favorite entertainment site, find the URL of the page with the nonadvertising content, read it using LWP, and regurgitate the contents. The original version was working within minutes and a few lines of code, but it seemed to require adjustments accounting for little human touches every day for weeks before it became reliable.

Schema and DTDs prescribe the structure that an XML document must follow. If a validating parser—a modern Web browser, for instance—loads an XML document and finds that it does not comply with its attached DTD or schema, it will not render the document; it will give an error message. This is to ensure that people using XML to exchange *data*—not just mark up fancy, dancing <BLINK> tagged "Under Construction" pages—have a common ground upon which they may rely. If you share a DTD or schema with another developer, your XML documents will be 100 percent compatible.

The primary difference between a DTD and a schema is that a schema is itself an XML document, while a DTD is a specialized syntax left over from its progenitor, SGML. An example of an XML DTD included within an XML file follows. The DTD is everything within the <!DOCTYPE> tag.

```
<!DOCTYPE newsItem [
<!ELEMENT date    (#PCDATA )>
<!ATTLIST date    e-dtype NMTOKEN   #FIXED 'date' >
<!ELEMENT author  (#PCDATA )>
<!ELEMENT text    (#PCDATA )>
<!ELEMENT headline   (#PCDATA )>
<!ELEMENT article  (author , date , headline , text )>
<!ELEMENT category  (#PCDATA )>
<!ELEMENT newsItem  (category , article )+>
]>

<newsItem>
<category name="Classified">
```

```
<article>
<author>Stevie Ray Jones</author>
<headline>Clean Fill Wanted</headline>
<date>July 4,2001</date>
<text>No Gravel. Not willing to pay.
   Call Sam Barnes at 555-3948</text>
</article>

<article>
<author>Stevie Ray Jones</author>
<headline>Free to Bad Home</headline>
<date>July 4,2001</date>
<text>Litter of 12 English Long-Ear Rabbits.
   For snake food only. Dora 555-2348</text>
</article>

</category>
</newsItem>
```

By including the DTD, you ensure that the document is not only well-formed (contains an end tag for every element, doesn't break any XML rules within itself), but also valid (conforms to the agreed-upon structure). Validating is widely considered a necessary step at some point in the XML publishing process. For the sake of this chapter, we are going to assume that this is already done before we bring data into Flash, since that is the assumption that Flash makes. There is no validation performed on incoming XML documents.

An example of the same document definition, this time defined as a schema, follows. This code is in the schema only. In a publishing situation in which XML documents were validated according to this schema, each XML file would link to this external file, *newsSchema.xml*, in the processing instructions at the beginning of the document.

```
<?xml version ="1.0"?>
<Schema name = "SVilleStarSchema.xml"
   xmlns = "urn:schemas-microsoft-com:xml-data"
   xmlns:dt = "urn:schemas-microsoft-com:datatypes">
   <ElementType name = "date" content = "textOnly" dt:type = "date"/>
   <AttributeType name = "series" dt:type = "string"/>
   <ElementType name = "author" content = "textOnly"/>
   <ElementType name = "text" content = "textOnly"/>
   <ElementType name = "headline" content = "textOnly"/>
   <ElementType name = "article" content = "eltOnly" order = "seq">
```

```
<element type = "author"/>
<element type = "date"/>
<element type = "headline"/>
<element type = "text"/>
</ElementType>
<ElementType name = "category" content = "textOnly"/>
<ElementType name = "newsItem" content = "eltOnly">
    <group order = "seq" minOccurs = "1" maxOccurs = "*">
    <element type = "category"/>
    <element type = "article"/>
    </group>
</ElementType>
</Schema>
```

At the time of writing, it appears that DTDs are gaining prominence as the standard way to validate XML documents. In addition, public databases of standards for different industries are popping up, lending to the optimism that standards may one day rule the Web. One good resource for public DTDs is http://www.schema.net/. For more information on DTDs and schema in general, including tutorials, see http://w3.org/XML and http://xml.com.

XSL and CSS

news.xsl, news.xml

Cascading Style Sheets (CSS), with which you should already be familiar, and the Extensible Stylesheet Language (XSL) are used to render XML. The goal of XML being to separate data from layout, these standards handle the layout. While CSS works with XML pretty much the same as it works with HTML, applying formatting to specified nodes, XSL can actually transform XML documents. This is especially useful for server-side applications that render XML into backward-compatible HTML content.

The following example, *news.xsl*, shows a simple scenario in which the contents of *news.xml* are formatted in a table. Open *news.xml* in a current-version browser to see how this XSL renders the document.

```
<?xml version='1.0'?>
<xsl:stylesheet xmlns:xsl="http://www.w3.org/TR/WD-xsl">
<xsl:template match="/">
<html>
<body>
    <table cellpadding="10">
```

```
    <tr>
        <td>Headline</td>
        <td>Story</td>
        <td>Date</td>
    </tr>
    <xsl:for-each select="newsItem/category/article">
    <tr>
        <td><xsl:value-of select="headline"/></td>
        <td><xsl:value-of select="date"/></td>
        <td><xsl:value-of select="text"/></td>
    </tr>
    </xsl:for-each>
  </table>
</body>
</html>
</xsl:template>
</xsl:stylesheet>
```

The most important thing to realize about this type of formatting transformation is that it is not currently practical to deploy content on the Web this way. No browsers before the 5.5 level had complete support for the W3C spec for XSL, so trying to render your data using these standards alone would alienate most users.

Flash XML

After wrestling with data in Chapter 14, you will be relieved to find that Flash's XML implementation makes it very easy to work with Web data. At this point, the only really big problem with XML in Flash—the mishandling of whitespace characters—has been fixed. In addition to everything working as designed, there are lots of built-in methods, handlers, and properties to make working with data much easier within an XML object.

The General Idea

There are two objects in Flash 5 ActionScript designed to work with XML data. The first one is the XML object. This is the object we will concentrate on the most in the examples. The other object, XMLSocket, is used specifically to send and receive XML data packets over an open socket connection.

Nonvalidating Parser

Flash assumes that you are satisfied with the design of the data structure in an XML document at some point before it is loaded. Flash does not compare XML documents to their DTDs or schemas, even if they are linked in the processing instructions. Since no validation is performed, Flash's XML parser is said to be *nonvalidating*. Validation can easily be handled either on the server at run time or with the authoring tool that creates the XML document.

Instant Data Structure

When Flash loads an external XML document into a native Flash XML object, the structure of the document is preserved within the object. In other words, you do not have to perform any manipulations to form associations between the different bits of information. Everything that was in the original file, from the <!DOCTYPE> declaration to the bottom-most node, is in the same order in the Flash XML object. The only thing left to do after you load an XML document is to move about the document tree and find the information you want.

Lost in Whitespace

You should be aware that there was a serious bug in the Flash 5.0.0.0 player that caused certain whitespace characters to be interpreted as XML nodes, which could either give you undesirable results or cause your Flash application to run very slowly, depending on how vigorously you tried to solve the problem. This bug was fixed in the r41+ Flash Players.

The Web—Now Featuring Memory!

Persistent connections, enabled by Flash's new XMLSocket object, are an answer to the old saying "the Web has no memory." This saying refers to the nature of HTTP transactions, where a request is answered, and then the server forgets that the client ever existed. Socket connections in Flash 5 make it possible to build real-time multiuser interactivity, such as multiplayer games and chat.

Static XML Documents

The trick to doing something with XML data inside Flash is being able to parse through the entire tree, even if you aren't 100 percent sure of its exact structure. For instance, we have already seen that many (most?) XML documents can have repeating elements, which change in number, depending on the circumstance. When you compound that aspect with the infamous whitespace bug and nodes in the Flash XML tree for processing instructions, things become very uncertain. To see how this works out, let's consider a very simple example with no ActionScript parsing routine.

Simple Example
simpleNoParse.fla, Classified.xml, simpleRead.fla

The following example is *simpleNoParse.fla*. This movie simply loads an XML document and outputs a message telling whether the load was successful.

At the time of this writing, no patch has been issued to update the player embedded in the Flash IDE to include the ignoreWhite property. To take advantage of this property, included in r41 and later players, first make sure your primary browser on the machine you use for development has an updated debug player, version 5r41 or higher. You can find an updated debug player by going to http://www.macromedia.com/support/flash/ and searching for "debug player." Then, when you want to preview a Flash movie, instead of using Debug Movie (CTRL-SHIFT-ENTER) or Test Movie (CTRL-ENTER), use Publish Preview (F12). You can use the debugger if you have checked Debugging Permitted in your Publish Settings (CTRL-SHIFT-F12).

Test this movie using Publish Preview (F12) instead of Test Movie or Debug Movie. In your browser, use the Flash Player context menu to open the debugger:

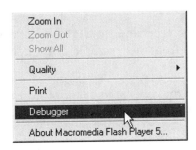

You should see the XML document *Classified.xml* parsed into an accurate representation of its structure:

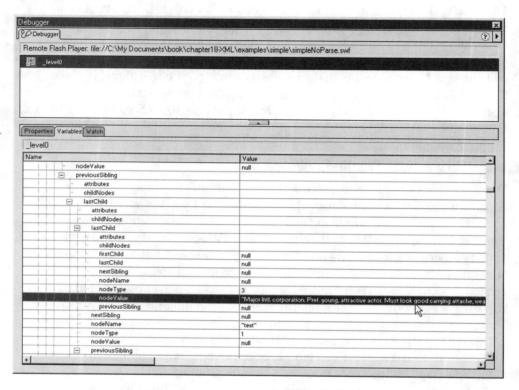

For my money, this is the single most attractive feature of the Flash XML toolset. This automatic parsing takes an entire XML document and converts it into one big native ActionScript object. This takes care of what we were trying to do in Chapter 14 with the hub Movie clip, namely, create a structured object of data with clear boundaries.

The following is the code from this example. It is on the main timeline, in the first frame.

```
//------------------communicates whether the load was successful
function myOnLoad (success) {
   if (success) {
      output = "finished loading the XML document.\n";;
   }else{
      output = "there was an error loading the XML document.\n";
   }
}
```

```
//-----------------first code executed
xmlObject = new XML();
xmlObject.ignoreWhite = true;
xmlObject.onLoad = myOnLoad;
xmlObject.load("Classified.xml");
```

This whole blob of code is a preparation of the XML object. We will use this same structure throughout the examples in this chapter. The first thing to execute is the constructor for a new XML object, which is required. The identifier xmlObject is arbitrary.

Next is the property ignoreWhite, the recent addition to the XML object. This must be set to true *before* you load the XML object if you are to take advantage of it. Remember that only users with a Flash Player 5r41 or higher can recognize this property, so if your application relies on this property (as all of the examples in this chapter do), you will need a comprehensive detection/redirection scheme.

Next we override the default onLoad callback method with the function myOnload(). This function feeds a message to the only text field on the stage, output. The default syntax of the onLoad method is as follows:

```
xmlObject.onLoad(success);
```

This method executes automatically when an XML document is received. If there were no problems with the load() method, success will return true once the document is loaded. Otherwise, success will be false. By extending this method, you can select which code you would like to execute, based on whether you successfully loaded the XML document.

Finally, once everything else is in place—object created, ignoreWhite parameter set, and onLoad() function defined—we load the document. In this case, it is *Classified.xml*. This XML file happens to be in the same directory as the movie. Otherwise, we would have to specify either a directory or a URL, just as we would for loadVariables().

Now that we have an XML object loaded (you can think of the stationary XML file as the object—it has the same structure, hence the value of using XML as a data source), we can begin to do some meaningful work with the data. But before we do, take a look at what we will be reading, *Classified.xml*, which is included here.

```
<?xml version='1.0'?>
<newsItem>
<category name="Classified">

<article>
```

```
<author>Billy Ray Halleldorf</author>
<headline>Clean Fill Wanted</headline>
<date>July 4,2001</date>
<text>No Gravel. Not willing to pay.
    Call Sam Barnes at 555-3948</text>
</article>

<article>
<author>Stevie Joe Cyrus</author>
<headline>Free to Bad Home</headline>
<date>July 4,2001</date>
<text>Litter of 12 English Long-Ear Rabbits.
    For snake food only. Dora 555-2348</text>
</article>...and so on
```

Because this example, *simpleHardCoded.fla*, is specifically designed to read through this rigid structure, it is important to understand the structure. Take a moment to make sure you understand how this XML document is organized.

The code for *simpleHardCoded.fla* follows. As you can see, there is a lot of repetitive code, so this is obviously not going to be our final solution. The first part should be familiar.

```
//-----------------decide whether to continue
function myOnLoad (success) {
    if (success) {
        output = "\n";
        parser(xmlObject.firstChild.firstChild.firstChild);
    }else{
        output = "there was an error loading the XML document.\n";
    }
}


//-----------------first code executed
xmlObject = new XML();
xmlObject.ignoreWhite = true;
xmlObject.onLoad = myOnLoad;
xmlObject.load("Classified.xml");
```

The only new thing here is that we have called a function from within the myOnLoad function. This is the way we start any function that reads through the XML tree for the rest of the chapter.

Notice the XML object method we use (repeatedly) to feed into the parser() function, firstChild. This method moves the pointer in the XML tree to the first child node under the current node. If you hard-code a function this way, you have to figure out where you want to start by looking at the debugger, as in the previous example. The next block of code is entirely new.

```
//------------------
function parser(branch){
    while (branch){
        output += branch.firstChild.nodeName + ":    ";
        output += branch.firstChild.firstChild.nodeValue + "\n";
        output += "    " + branch.firstChild.nextSibling.nodeName + ":    ";
        output += "    "
     +branch.firstChild.nextSibling.firstChild.nodeValue + "\n";
        output += "    "
     +branch.firstChild.nextSibling.nextSibling.nodeName + ":    ";
        output += "    "
     +branch.firstChild.nextSibling.nextSibling.firstChild.nodeValue + "\n";
        output += "    "
     +branch.firstChild.nextSibling.nextSibling.nextSibling.nodeName + ":    ";
        output += "    "
     +branch.firstChild.nextSibling.nextSibling
     .nextSibling.firstChild.nodeValue + "\n";
        branch = branch.nextSibling;
    }
}
```

The argument branch represents the xmlObject object, with the pointer at the first <article> node in the tree. The first line of code within the while control structure adds the name (via the nodeName property) of the first child node within <article> to the output text field. If you look at the XML code above, you will see that this should be "author"; and this is consistent with what you will see when you publish the movie.

The function methodically trudges through each node inside each article tag until it reaches the end of the while structure. The nextSibling method moves the pointer to the next node on the same level; so from the <author> node, nextSibling moves you to <headline>. At the end of the while loop, branch, which is the xmlObject object at the first <article> node, is promoted to its next sibling. This will be the next <article> node as long as there is an article node, or as long as branch has a value—hence, while(branch){...

This method of traversing the XML object tree is crude, to say the least. Besides being boring to type and read, it does not allow for any deviation from this simple XML structure. This type of XML object handling is best reserved for cases when you can be certain that the structure of the original XML document will never vary. One such case is the last example in this chapter, the Flash chat client. Even this example is severely weakened by this form of object handling, because it can be broken by typing an XML object within the user input line.

In the next example, *simpleRead.fla*, we will use a recursive function to swing from branch to branch on the tree created by the native Flash XML parser. The primary difference between this example and the previous one is that this movie will read through any XML structure, regardless of its shape, and reproduce it in the output text field. The first block of code should look 100 percent familiar this time.

```
//----------------decides whether to proceed
function myOnLoad (success) {
    if (success) {
        treeClimber(xmlObject.firstChild);
    }else{
        output = "there was an error loading the XML document.\n";
    }
}

//----------------first code executed
xmlObject = new XML();
xmlObject.ignoreWhite = true;
xmlObject.onLoad = myOnLoad;
xmlObject.load("Classified.xml");
```

We create the XML object, set its parameters and handlers, and load the XML document. The extended onLoad handler sets the new version of the parser function in motion. The code for treeClimber() follows.

```
////----------------the function that moves through the XML tree

function treeClimber(branch){
    if(branch.nodeValue != null){
        output += branch.nodeValue + "\n";
    }

    if(branch.hasChildNodes()){
```

```
        branch = branch.firstChild;
        treeClimber(branch);
    }

    while (branch.nextSibling != null){
        branch = branch.nextSibling;
        treeClimber(branch);
    }
}
```

To get a feel for how this function flows, I will trace the execution of this code on xmlObject as it appears in this example, with *Classified.xml* as the source. The initial value of the branch argument is xmlObject.firstChild, which corresponds to <newsItem> in *Classified.xml*. The initial value of depth is 0. Since this node does have a value for nodeName, it will return true for the first if control structure.

The next if control structure tests the property hasChildNodes, which will return true if the node contains any nodes lower than itself in the XML structure. This is true for <newsItem>, so the code inside the control structure executes.

The value of branch is changed to the first child node inside branch—in this case <category>—and the function starts over with this new value. This is the point at which the rabbit ducks into the magical hole of the recursive function. Mentally mark this spot, because this is the point at which the next iteration of treeClimber() will exit when it returns false.

The next iteration works exactly as the first did, only with the node corresponding to <article> and depth value of 1. This time, when the code goes back to the top with the first child node of the first article node, it will not find any children. The new value of branch, <author>, does not have an XML node lower than itself in the hierarchy; so it will return false and exit to the middle of the if control structure that tests for child nodes.

At this point, the new value of branch is changed to the next sibling to <author>, which is <headline>, and the function enters the while control structure. This loop goes through the whole function for each node at this level of the XML hierarchy in this branch. When that possibility is fully exhausted (the function has explored the <text> node in the first <article> branch), the function exits to its previous place— the place I said to mentally mark. Don't worry if you got lost. The first time I saw a *recursive* function like this—a post by Flash guru Branden Hall on the Flash 5 beta discussion list—I had to print it out on paper and mark spots with my fingers to follow it all the way through. If you will recall, we covered recursive functions way back in Chapter 7, our introduction to JavaScript.

Read Headlines from a Dynamic Source
readHeadlines.fla

Now that we have a slick recursive function to read through an XML structure, we are going to add some format-specific elements and read some different documents that all have the same structure. The example is *readHeadlines.fla*, in the sticksvilleStar folder, and the documents are dynamically generated XML news headlines from the very-cool resource Moreover.com. Moreover provides XML news feeds from a bazillion categories, and it is free to use them under certain conditions. (See their site for terms and conditions at http://w.moreover.com/site/about/termsand conditions.html.)

This application is the little pop-up you get when you click on the "Headlines from Moreover.com" link at the bottom of the main page of the Sticksville Star. When you click on the buttons across the top of the stage, you set a function in motion like the one we just reviewed. These buttons all contain code like the following. Only the argument to the getNews() function call differs in each.

```
on (release, releaseOutside) {

getNews("http://p.moreover.com/cgi-local/page?c=Graphics%20industry%20news&o=xml");
}
```

These buttons refer to getNews() on the main timeline. Since the scope of the buttons is also _root, also known as _level0, we do not have to define an absolute object path for getNews(). The getNews() function on the main timeline is as follows:

```
//------------load the designated XML file
function getNews(newsURL){
HLCounter=0;
xmlObj=new XML();
xmlObj.ignoreWhite=true;
xmlObj.load(newsURL);
xmlObj.onLoad=myOnLoad;
}
```

This and the myOnLoad() function below are the same as before, except that the argument to xmlObj.load() is a variable. This allows us to reuse the code in parser(). In other words, we use the same function for each button and each XML news feed.

```
//------------decide whether to continue
function myOnLoad(success){
    if(success){
```

```
        parser(xmlObj.firstChild);
    }
}
```

The treeClimber() function is similar to the previous example, but there are some additional lines that have a bearing on this specific document structure. Since we are no longer interested in regurgitating the entire XML tree, we only perform specific code for specific instances, extracting only the parts of the XML data structure that are useful for this application.

```
function treeClimber(branch){
    if(branch.nodeName == "url"){
        deadSeaScroller.document.document.attachMovie
    ("headline","headline" + HLCounter, HLCounter+5);
        with(deadSeaScroller.document.document["headline" + HLCounter]){
            _x=0;
            _y=HLCounter * 38;
            headline=branch.nextSibling.firstChild.nodeValue;
            sourceCredit= " (from "
    + branch.nextSibling.nextSibling.firstChild.nodeValue + " ).";
            headline += sourceCredit;
            storyURL=branch.firstChild.nodeValue;
        }
        HLCounter ++;
    }
    if(branch.hasChildNodes()){
        branch = branch.firstChild;
        treeClimber(branch);
    }

    while (branch.nextSibling != null){
        branch = branch.nextSibling;
        treeClimber(branch);
    }
}
```

If you look at one of the XML news feeds at Moreover.com, you will see that there isn't any information we will use before we get to the <url> branch. When treeClimber() comes to one of these nodes, it begins by attaching an instance of the headline MC to the document MC instance, buried deep inside the scrolling mechanism. We touched on this scrolling SmartClip briefly in Chapter 10, so we are not going to go over it here.

The headline Movie clip is placed, and values are assigned to it. These values will be used later to launch the appropriate URL.

Finally, the button inside headline MC contains the following code. This is what launches a separate Web browser window for the story content.

```
on (release, releaseOutside) {
    getURL (this.storyURL, "_blank");
}
```

The variable storyURL is assigned a value for each Movie clip as it is placed. This value comes from the value inside the <url> tag in the original XML file.

This application is obviously not industrial strength. It could easily do with a "loading" indication while the XML files are being downloaded and parsed. It also wouldn't hurt to include a more comprehensive error handling scheme, such as a dialog in the event of onLoad returning false. We covered this in the first example.

A Whole Truckload of Data
sticksvilleStar.fla

The final example using static XML files is the realization of our vision of a data-laden Flash Player that we first talked about in Chapter 14. Have you noticed that previous chapters come up a lot in this chapter? That seems to be one of the core characteristics of XML—making long-sought-after things possible. In this case, we jumped through a lot of hoops to build an object (the hub MC) containing structured data, only to decide that it wasn't an optimal solution, owing to the limitations on the loadVariables() method when embedded in some browsers.

The central concept behind the current remix of the Sticksville Star is a discrete, structured data object within each main menu item. This object will of course be an XML object. The way this is achieved is deliberately simplistic. We will re-create the functions used in the previous example within every section's Movie clip. To further simplify things, these Movie clips are not dynamically reproduced; they are duplicated within the library, so that the function is hard-coded within each section. This application is built this way to underscore the simplicity that XML can bring to a potentially treacherous application like the Sticksville Star. When I built this movie, I first made a Movie clip for the Classified section, worked the kinks out, and then duplicated it for each of the other sections.

Open *sticksvilleStar.fla* and have a look around. Almost all of the elements of the movie are on the stage already. The most radically different piece of this application is the mechanism used to hide the DHTML-style submenus, so we will look at that first. This is an old-fashioned hierarchical menu, using invisible buttons around the perimeter of the flyout to hide the submenu when the user rolls off it. These invisible buttons are contained in the library item Headlines PH, as you can see in the next image. Each button in this MC contains the following action.

```
on(rollOver, dragOver){
      _parent.hideHeadlines();
}
```

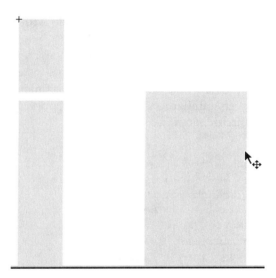

This Movie clip gets dynamically loaded into each section MC (for example, Local, Sports, Classified) at run time. Each of these MCs contains the following functions.

```
function showHeadlines(){
   // hide headlines
   ph._visible=true;
}

function hideHeadlines(){
   // hide headlines
   ph._visible=false;
}
```

When the user rolls off the submenu, which will be dynamically created in the vertical space between the invisible buttons, hideHeadlines() executes, and the submenu goes away. The next block of code, contained in the button in each section MC, activates showHeadlines() and makes the submenus appear. Each category MC contains the following code, more or less...

```
on (rollOver, dragOver) {
    showHeadlines();
}
```

This is one of the few instances of a trick I prefer to do with old-fashioned timeline layers and buttons over a purely scripting option. You could just as effectively use hitTest, mouse coordinate tests, and for...in control structures to do the same thing, but this way is just easier and performs faster on slow PCs.

The following code is the new face of our treeClimber function, now called "parser." This version is very similar to the headlines example, only we are handling a slightly different structure than before.

```
function parser(branch){
    if(branch.nodeName == "category"){
        this.section = branch.attributes["name"];
    }else if(branch.nodeName == "headline"){
        this.ph.attachMovie("headline","headline"
    + HLCounter, HLCounter+5);
        with(this.ph["headline" + HLCounter]){
            _x=130;
            _y=215 + HLCounter * 30;
            headline=branch.firstChild.nodeValue;
            storyText=branch.firstChild.nodeValue;
        }
    }else if(branch.nodeName == "text"){

        HLCounter ++;
    }
treeClimber(branch);
}

//-------------------------
function treeClimber(branch){
if(branch.nodeName != null){
    }
    if(branch.hasChildNodes()){
    branch = branch.firstChild;
```

```
        parser(branch);
        branch=branch.nextSibling;
        while(branch != null){
            parser(branch, tier+1);
            branch=branch.nextSibling;
        }
    }
}
}
//-----------------------
function myOnLoad(success){
    if(success){
        parser(xmlObj.firstChild);
    }
}

//-----------------------
HLCounter=0;
this.attachMovie("ph","ph",10);
xmlObj=new XML();
xmlObj.ignoreWhite=true;
xmlObj.load("xml/Classified.xml");
xmlObj.onLoad=myOnLoad;
hideHeadlines();
```

In addition to the new structure, we are also loading the entire text of each story into the submenu items, identified here as the headline MC. This is the storyText variable.

And thus our vision of a Flash-fronted Web is realized (at least in our little experiments). We finally built our little newspaper site so that it loads every bit of data for users to peruse at their leisure, with no further downloads required. The total size of the movie is not too heavy—30K, and you could easily cut this in half by using a single symbol for the star in the logo and choosing font outlines carefully. The following list outlines some of the more obvious, revolutionary features of the Flash XML toolset that make it superior to the previously described (in Chapter 14) methods using loadVariables.

▶ **Built-in handler (onLoad) for receiving data**   This frees you from the constraint of having to use a Movie clip or (much worse) a two-frame loop to determine when data is loaded. This handler also sports the feature of automatically knowing whether the load was successful.

▶ **Automatic structuring of data**   You may recall the lengths to which we went just to get a one-dimensional associative array inside a Movie clip, and that didn't even tell us anything *about* the data beyond a list of name-value pairs.

▶ **Built-in mechanism for navigating the data**   When we used the for...in loop to build associative arrays from data obtained with loadVariables() in Chapter 14, we were effectively gathering data about the data just received. Not only that, we still either had to know which variables we were looking for or list them all. With properties like firstChild and nextSibling, the XML object allows us to discover relationships in the data structure at run time.

▶ **General ruggedness**   Bugs that crop up when the loadVariables action is used have been known since Flash 4 first saw the light of day. If you don't believe me, look at any discussion or bulletin board archive and search for POST and GET. The fact is that using loadVariables has never been a confidence-inspiring endeavor. Using XML does inspire confidence. It works well, as evidenced in our newspaper example. It behaves predictably and can handle much larger amounts of data reliably. Plus, it has the aforementioned error handling features built in. In contrast to the loadVariables() function, the XML object was built for the big time.

XML Socket Connections

leChat.fla, leChat.swf

This example covers *leChat.fla*, a simple chat application. To use this example, you will need to obtain a chat server to run on your local server in order to echo the incoming XML data.

TCP/IP

The concept of Transmission Control Protocol/Internet Protocol should be familiar to anyone who has ever connected to the Internet or a LAN. It is the means by which many computer networks communicate. While TCP/IP consists of a whole array of protocols, from IP to telnet, one thing ties them all together. The central concept and goal of TCP/IP is to send packets of data back and forth between remote computers.

The main difference between the HTTP request methods used in previous chapters, activated by loadVariables(), and TCP/IP is as follows: When you send an HTTP request, you typically send a predefined message in a known format to port 80 on a

Web server. With TCP/IP, by contrast, you have access to the nuts and bolts of the data exchange, choosing the port of the computer you want to use and the type of data you want to send.

NOTE

It is possible to set up an HTTP service on a server to answer on a different port, but this is not commonly done.

Simple Chat Example

The final example in this chapter, *leChat.fla*, requires an additional server component in order to work. Luckily, there are plenty available for free, at least for your education. Your first step in this exercise is acquiring one of these and getting it running on your server. The following list should point you in the right direction.

▶ Get a free, light-duty Java chat server from the Flash community. At the time of writing, at least three are available with no restrictions on educational use. There is one at http://moock.com, one at the Macromedia exchange http://exchange.macromedia.com, and one at http://www.shovemedia.com/multi/. I believe any one of these will work for this example, but the one at Colin Moock's site is the one I used. If you use this option, the installation instructions will direct you to install the Java Runtime Environment. You can get this from Sun at http://java.sun.com. Don't skip this step; it won't work without it!

▶ Find any free server that echoes incoming XML packets to all connected clients.

▶ Write your own. Whatever your preferred server-side language, there is probably a tutorial online or a book on how to write a chat server with it. There is even an online tutorial showing you how to write a chat server in Perl at http://hotwired.lycos.com/webmonkey/97/18/index2a.html.

The first thing you see when you run *leChat.swf* is the login MC. This contains two items of interest—a send button, with the following code attached, and an input text field for the variable login.

```
on (release, releaseOutside, keyPress "<Enter>") {
    _root.login(login);
}
```

This action starts the process that results in the TCP/IP server connection, which we will examine in a moment. Once the user is connected, the loginMC clip is removed, and chatMC is pulled from the library in its place. The only action in this Movie clip is in the hidden button to the right of the stage, as seen in the next image.

```
on (keyPress "<Enter>") {
    _root.sender(input);
}
```

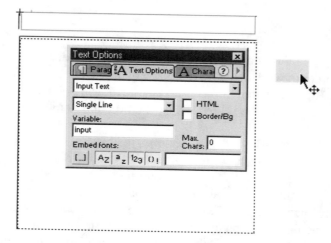

If you thought the chat application was going to be more complicated just because it is more fun, you are going to be disappointed. The remainder of the ActionScript in this application is shown here. This code is found in the main timeline, first frame.

```
///--------------------
function login(name){
    user=name;
    loginMC.removeMovieClip();
    _root.attachMovie("chatMC","chatMC",10);
    chatMC._x=7;
    chatMC._y=107;
    mySock = new XMLSocket();
    mySock.onConnect=myOnConnect;
    mySock.onXML=myOnXML;
    mySock.connect("localhost", 1998);
}

///--------------------
```

```
function myOnConnect(success){
      if(success){
            chatMC.output="connected\n";
      }else{
            chatMC.output="connection failed...\n";
      }
}


///--------------------
function myOnXML(doc){
      tempVar="";
      message = doc.firstChild.firstChild.nodeValue;
      userName = doc.firstChild.attributes["user"];
      tempVar= userName + ">>>" + message;
      chatMC.output=tempVar + "\n" + chatMC.output;
}


///--------------------
function sender(input){
      xmlString="<message user=\"" + user + "\">" + input + "</message>";
      newXMLObj=new XML();
      newXMLObj.parseXML(xmlString);
      mySock.send(newXMLObj);
      chatMC.input="";
}


///--------------------
_root.attachMovie("loginMC","loginMC",10);
loginMC._x=60;
loginMC._y=140;
```

The first thing you will notice is that there is a separate object class for XML socket functions, XMLSocket. We create the mySock object using a standard constructor and use it to connect using the connect() method, with arguments host name/url and port number. If you used one of the three similar Java chat servers mentioned at the beginning of this example, you will have to designate a port number when you start the app on which the server will listen for connections.

The methods onConnect and onXML are handlers similar to onLoad in the XML object. The onConnect(success) function executes when the process of trying to connect is completed, with (success) being the Boolean outcome of the endeavor, good or bad. The onXML(objectName) function executes when an XML data packet is received over this connection.

The sender() function is the code that creates and sends the XML object to the chat server. The basic structure of our XML object used in this application is as follows:

```
<message user="userName">message content</message>
```

After the new XML object, newXMLObj, is created, the method parseXML() is used to populate the object using the string we concatenated with user input and the necessary tags. This method is a method of the XML object, not the XMLSocket object. You could also use the createElement() and appendChild() methods in the following manner; but building the object manually from a string is easier for small, predictably structured jobs like ours.

```
newNode = new XML();
newElement = newNode.createElement("message");
myXML.appendChild(newElement); //and so on...
```

Finally, the socket method send() sends this object over the TCP/IP connection. The server receives it, and if all goes well, the server echoes the object to all connected clients.

The extended function of onXML, myOnXML(), is the handler for incoming XML data packets. This is the simplest implementation possible, using the assumption that we know the exact shape of the XML object, which may not be reliable. If you were to use this type of application for a live Web site, you would want to add a recursive function to seek out the specific nodes you need, as in the previous examples, plus error handling.

What to Take Away from This Chapter

While XML as a widely deployed client-side markup is still in pie-in-the-sky territory, Flash's implementation of XML and XMLSocket is ready for practical use. The value of having data that is automatically structured is by itself attractive enough to make you think twice about loading name-value pairs directly from a database. Combined with the built-in, datacentric methods and properties available in the native XML objects, Flash is a serious contender for any data-driven Web application front end.

Introduction to Swift-Generator

Swift-Generator is one of my all-time favorite Flash tools in any category. It is a free server application that creates SWF movies on the fly. In apparent contrast with its amazing power to create SWF content on the fly, the license is extremely attractive: the cost of using the application is including the Swift-Generator logo on your site. A very inexpensive fee buys you the privilege of dropping the logo. In this chapter, we will cover the basics of using this tool, as well as a few examples that best demonstrate its most useful functions.

Why on the Fly?

If this book is your first exposure to advanced ActionScript and integrating Flash with server-side scripting, you may wonder why you would ever need another application. After all, we've already talked about three different languages in this book (four if you count our incidental treatment of SQL).

Flash 3 and Dynamic Data

To give you an idea of how this type of tool came about, let's take a look back at the circumstances that gave birth to the idea of dynamic SWF generation. In the early days of Flash, there wasn't any scripting that was exposed to the developer. There were a few actions that could be applied, with a few fill-in boxes for parameters, but no wide open space where the developer could just type code. The only way to make complex actions in Flash 3 was to use JavaScript as the source of logic, using methods of the Flash Player object like we did in Chapter 8.

It was during this time that Macromedia introduced Generator. Since there was no way to interact with server-side scripts in a simple, practical way that a novice could figure out in an afternoon, a special tool was almost an absolute requirement.

As you know by this point in the book, anyone with a $3.99 Linux/Apache hosting plan that offers PHP and MySQL can build Flash-fronted data-driven applications, given a little ambition and time to tinker, but there are still some things that Flash can't do. Today, Macromedia generator still stands alone as a scalable, feature-rich server application for creating all kinds of content—not just Flash—but there are a few key tasks that Swift-Generator can do for you for a very nice price.

Image and Sound Replacement

At present, Flash 5 does not allow you to bring in raster images or sound files that have not been through the Flash authoring environment and compiled as an SWF. In other words, you can't just load a PNG or an MP3 from a directory on your server directly into a SWF at run time. You either have to import them into Flash and publish them as some form of SWF or look to another tool.

Swift-Generator can take bitmap images and sounds and compile them into SWFs on the fly, using parameters in both the URL string and a proprietary script that resides on the server. These abilities, combined with good old ActionScript and server-side scripting like PHP, give you a range of possibilities with broad horizons.

Swift-Generator Basics

The first thing you'll have to do to start using Swift-Generator is obtain it. Go to http://swift-tools.com and download the version for your platform. Unfortunately, there is no version available for the Mac. This chapter follows in the pattern of the previous chapters, assuming that we are working in a Windows environment that mirrors a typical *-nix/Apache server.

There's also a manual in PDF available on the download page. This should be your primary source of information for Swift-Generator. The manual covers many details that we will not cover this chapter.

The application as we are going to use it is by itself very simple to install, but in order to have all of the sample files on the Flash 5 Developer's Guide CD work without changing paths, you will have to duplicate the directory structure depicted here:

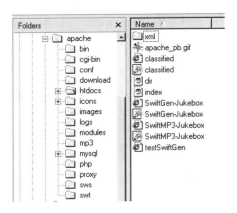

The hierarchy above the Apache installation, including the name of a folder in which Apache is installed, is not important. I have set up the examples in a way that you might set them up on a production server—with a directory designated for each type of component. If you are anxious to get going, and not mindful of organization or security, the temptation would be to install everything into CGI-BIN. The following is a list of considerations for where to place the example files for this chapter.

▶   All types of documents that we have worked with already (HTML, PHP, SWF) should go in the htdocs directory, and not a subdirectory of htdocs.

▶   The Swift-Generator executable, *swiftgen.exe*, will go in the CGI-BIN. You might as well download and place SwiftMP3 in this CGI-BIN at this time. We will be using this application in the last example.

▶   Copy the rest of the directories to match the illustration above.

What Is It?

Swift-Generator can be generalized as having a single function: combining outside media and data sources with a Flash template to create an SWF dynamically. This powerful function is commonly applied to two main categories of utility: a CGI application that outputs to a client through a Web server, and a command line, standalone application that is used to update Flash content with new media and data on a hard drive.

SWT Templates

Although Swift-Generator can use a SWF as a template for a new Flash movie with dynamic content and media, it is easier by far to use a SWT template. This file format, created for Macromedia generator, is one of the output options in your Publish Settings (CTRL-SHIFT-F12) in the Flash authoring environment. This is the type of template we will use for the examples in this chapter.

SWS Files—Swift-Script

Swift-Generator uses its own proprietary scripting language called Swift-Script, which is typically stored in a file with an *.sws* extension. These external scripts are read at run time. The information in these scripts may contain any of the following types of information, plus others not listed. See the manual for the full list and the syntax of each.

▶   Directory paths to the different media and data sources to be used for compiling the SWF output, including the path to the SWT template

▶   Type of output: file or CGI

- ► The cache expiration of the output
- ► If the output is to be file, the path in which to save it
- ► Instructions on how to process media
- ► Font replacement
- ► MySQL and ODBC connections and queries
- ► Commands to the native operating system, including the execution of scripts

We will only cover the basic commands associated with CGI output and image and sound replacement.

Swift-Script

The syntax of Swift-Script is a little different from anything else we've covered in the book so far, but it is very easy to learn. In addition, Swift-Generator will create a model script for any SWT template for you, so you can practically fill in the blanks to get the functionality you want.

Dump a Script
firstTry.fla, firstTry.swt, swiftgen.exe

Let's create a simple Swift-Script. The following steps will guide you through the process of making an SWT template and a SWS script.

1. Create a new Flash file with three bits of static text and a bitmap image on the stage; it absolutely does not matter what you use. Save the file as *firstTry.fla*. It doesn't matter where you save it. If you prefer, my version of *firstTry.fla* is included on the CD.

2. Publish your creation as a template. To do this, go to your Publish Settings (CTRL-SHIFT-F12) and select the check box for Generator Template.

NOTE
If for some reason you do not have this option in your Publish Settings, you can always export (CTRL-ALT-SHIFT-S) your current movie as an SWT template.

3. Move the resultant SWT to your swt folder in your Apache installation. (You should have already moved your example files there, including this folder.)

4. Open a command prompt (aka DOS shell) and navigate to your swt folder.

5. When you are certain that you are in the correct directory and that *firstTry.swt* and *swiftgen.exe* are both in that directory, type the following command exactly as shown: **swiftgen -d ../swt/firstTry.swt > ../sws/firstTry.sws**. This command dumps (-d) the extra information in the Flash template (../swt/firstTry.swt) into a new file (> ../sws/firstTry.sws). If you want to avoid typing extra paths, you could place the template into CGI-BIN to begin with, then simply type **swiftgen -d firstTry.swt > firstTry.sws**. However, by doing it as shown, you save yourself the trouble of having to type manually the paths to the different directories within the script that results from this command.

6. Open this new file in your favorite text editor and have a look. It should look something like the following:

```
% Script template from Template file firstTry.swt
INPUT "../swt/firstTry.swt"
% Output for testing
OUTPUT "export.swf"
% Output for CGI
%OUTPUT -cgi "-"

% Font definitions
% FONT 1  is  Arial
% FONT 4  is  Arial Bold

DEFINE IMAGE "06541331.jpg" {
    FILE "new.jpg or new.png"
    QUALITY 50
    WIDTH 180
    HEIGHT 362
    KEEPRATIO
}

SUBSTITUTE TEXT 2 {
    FONT 1 HEIGHT 12 KERNING 0.98 COLOR #000000
    STRING "Swift-Generator is great!"
}
SUBSTITUTE TEXT 3 {
    FONT 1 HEIGHT 11 KERNING 2.58 COLOR #000000
    STRING "This is fun."
}
SUBSTITUTE TEXT 5 {
    FONT 4 HEIGHT 29 KERNING 0.98 COLOR #000000
    STRING "I like words."
}
```

INPUT and OUTPUT

export.swf, testSwiftGen.html

First we're going to look at the options for input and output. The meaning of the input line should be obvious. It is merely the SWT template from which the script was derived. You should leave this alone unless you change the location of the input file.

The output option in the template file defaults to file output, such as you would use if you wanted to automate the publishing of your SWF content offline. In other words, using this script with this option results in a file called *export.swf* being written to your hard drive. This chapter focuses mainly on CGI output, so we are going to uncomment (the % is the comment symbol in Swift-Script) the line that reads %OUTPUT -cgi "-" and comment the default output line. Your script should now look like the following:

```
% Output for testing
%OUTPUT "export.swf"
% Output for CGI
OUTPUT -cgi "-"
```

You are now ready to use the script to regurgitate the original content of the SWT template. You have three options here, as follows:

▶   Type the URL string directly into the address bar of Netscape Navigator. This is handy for finding out whether the script performs as expected.

▶   Type the URL string directly into the address bar of Internet Explorer. This can yield unexpected results. This is generally not a good indicator of whether the script works or not.

▶   Create an HTML file with the proper <OBJECT> and <EMBED> tags, using the URL string as the source.

Select your method and try the following URL(s). The first line is the URL by itself, as you would type it into the address bar on your browser. The second line is a sample <PARAM> tag as you would alter it to see this Swift-Generator output properly embedded in an HTML page. (Don't forget to change the SRC attribute of the <EMBED> tag, too.) The file *testSwiftGen.html* on the CD demonstrates this method.

```
http://localhost/cgi-bin/swiftgen?sws=../sws/firstTry.sws
```

```
<PARAM NAME=movie
VALUE="http://localhost/cgi-bin/swiftgen?sws=../sws/firstTry.sws">
```

SET Variables

The way you handle variables in Swift-Script can throw you off if you aren't used to it; so we'll start with the easy way—reading them in from the URL string, just as we did with PHP. Change the string definitions in each of the three so that the string literals are now variable names. Follow the example set shown here:

```
SUBSTITUTE TEXT 2 {
    FONT 1 HEIGHT 12 KERNING 0.98 COLOR #000000
    STRING $text01
}
SUBSTITUTE TEXT 3 {
    FONT 1 HEIGHT 11 KERNING 2.58 COLOR #000000
    STRING $text02
}
SUBSTITUTE TEXT 5 {
    FONT 4 HEIGHT 29 KERNING 0.98 COLOR #000000
    STRING $text03
}
```

Now you are ready to generate some honest-to-goodness dynamic content. Try your URL string again, only this time add values for the variables. For example, you could try something like this:

```
http://localhost/cgi-bin/swiftgen?sws=../sws/firstTry.sws&text01=kewe
lla&text02=shake%20it%20up&text03=words%20rock
```

The text is updated in the SWF output from Swift-Generator, but the text fields are not dynamic text fields. The content has been generated on the fly.

This simple implementation will doubtless seem weak after we have worked with all manner of scripting; but we have begun. The next step is to set a variable value inside the SWS using a Swift-Script SET command. This is slightly reminiscent of the old Flash 4 ActionScript, if you remember that. The following example shows how you could get the same output by setting the variables within the script.

```
SET text01 "kewella"
SET text02 "shake it up."
SET text03 "words rock"
```

This type of definition parses through the text within the SWT template, looking for the identities listed within curly braces. In other words, this script will match "{text01}" and replace it with "kewella," regardless of its location. It can be in a glob of static text, in the middle of a sentence, or even within ActionScript.

Anywhere these identities occur in the SWT template, enclosed in curly braces, they will be replaced. If you use this method, as we will for a subsequent example, you will have to change the three text fields in *firstTry.swt* so that the variable identities {text01}, {text02}, and {text03} are contained somewhere.

Image Replacement
firstTry.sws, firstTry.swt

Simple text replacement could be useful for some occasions, but for my money, the real power of Swift-Generator is the ability to bring any bitmap image into a movie, even if it hasn't been imported through the Flash authoring tool.

To make *firstTry.sws* so that it can dynamically replace the image contained in *firstTry.swt*, append the line beginning with FILE as follows. This gives you the ability to change the image to the value of the $img variable in the URL string.

```
DEFINE IMAGE "06541331.jpg" {
    FILE $img + ".jpg"
    QUALITY 50
    WIDTH 180
    HEIGHT 362
    KEEPRATIO
}
```

To try this new functionality in our script, you have to designate the path to the image that you want to insert in place of the original. If you copied the example files into the directory structure I suggested, you should be able to see the updated image using the following URL.

```
http://localhost/cgi-bin/swiftgen?
    sws=../sws/firstTry.sws&img=../images/06541324
```

There are a few very important points to savor here. First, we designated the extension ".jpg" in the Swift-Script file, so it is automatically appended to the $img variable value. This is strictly a matter of preference. You could just as easily leave off the extension in *firstTry.sws* and include it in the URL string.

You should take note of each of the parameters present in any image definition in Swift-Script. QUALITY is simply the image quality setting—the same as in the Publish dialog or symbol properties dialog in the Flash development environment.

The proportions define the maximum dimension that the replacement image may span on each axis. The most important item in the parameters for situations in which you may have images of different sizes is KEEPRATIO. Including this parameter tells Swift-Generator to scale the replacement image to its largest possible size, given the dimension constraints WIDTH and HEIGHT, keeping its original aspect ratio. If you don't use this property and you replace an image with one that is smaller in one dimension, the last line of pixels will repeat to the edge of the designated area, giving the impression of an ugly blur. To see this effect, try changing the image definition to the following; then try a few images with different dimensions.

```
DEFINE IMAGE "06541331.jpg" FILE $img + ".jpg"
```

This is the most basic image definition that allows you to change the picture dynamically. This is perfectly suitable for a series of images of known dimensions that are all the same.

Sound Replacement

The syntax to define a sound is very simple. The following example is from *mp3.sws*. We will use this Swift-Script for our MP3 jukebox application later in the chapter.

```
INPUT "../swt/mp3.swt"

OUTPUT -cgi "-"

DEFINE SOUND "drip" $song
```

Before you get too excited about Swift-Generator's ability to replace sounds dynamically, you should be aware that there is a more suitable tool for replacing long, streaming MP3 files, also made by Oliver Debon, called Swift-MP3. You will be able to see a comparison of these tools in this respect in the MP3 jukebox application, as we will build a version using each app to compile the MP3 files as SWF. However, combined with its other features, being able to replace short event sounds is very handy.

Execute Commands
directory.sws, directory.swt

The following code is from *directory.sws*. This illustrates how you can execute a command as you would from a shell. If you place a high value on being able to develop your scripts on your Windows desktop machine, then upload them to a *-nix server unchanged, you may want to steer clear of this type of command in Swift-Script, since virtually all shell commands are different between the two operating systems.

```
INPUT "../swt/directory.swt"
```

```
OUTPUT -cgi "-"

SUBSTITUTE TEXTFIELD 2 {
   STRING [..\mysql\bin\mysqlshow]
}
```

   This command shows the output from mysqlshow in the dynamic text field identified by *directory.swt* as "TEXTFIELD 2." If you try this, make sure that your MySQL server is running and that the path to mysqlshow inside the command square brackets is correct for your machine.

Other Parameters

There are lots of other useful parameters available in Swift-Script, including the length of time to cache the output, the referrers allowed, and on and on. Consult the manual for a comprehensive list and syntax.

Sticksville Star Classifieds Again!

We are going to brush the dust off the Sticksville Star one more time (two if you count the MP3 jukebox as separate). This example is part of a larger, imaginary application in which people upload their own pictures to go with their classified ads. (FTP like this is very easy to do with PHP, if you are interested.) The photos are put in a directory, renamed by serial numbers, which are grouped with their respective classified ads in one big XML file.

   This is the point at which we enter the picture. We have the resultant XML file, containing the same classifieds that we used in Chapter 18, only this time there is an element called picNum to link the correct photo to the listing. The challenge of this application is to dynamically load all sorts of JPEGs of different dimensions into our Flash application. These images all come from different sources and are not in any way specially prepared for Flash.

   The following code is from the timeline of classified MC. Much of this code is recycled from Chapter 18, which is a testimony to the flexibility of XML as a data source.

```
function showHeadlines(){
   // hide headlines
   ph._visible=true;
}
```

```
function hideHeadlines(){
   // hide headlines
   ph._visible=false;
}

function parser(branch){
   if(branch.nodeName == "category"){
      this.section = branch.attributes["name"];
   }else if(branch.nodeName == "headline"){
      this.ph.attachMovie("headline","headline"
   + HLCounter, HLCounter+5);
      with(this.ph["headline" + HLCounter]){
         _x=130;
         _y=215 + HLCounter * 30;
         headline=branch.firstChild.nodeValue;
      }
   }else if(branch.nodeName == "text"){
      this.ph["headline" + HLCounter].storyText=
   branch.firstChild.nodeValue;
   }else if(branch.nodeName == "picNum"){
      this.ph["headline" + HLCounter].picNum=
   branch.firstChild.nodeValue;
      HLCounter ++;
   }
treeClimber(branch);
}

//------------------------
function treeClimber(branch){
if(branch.nodeName != null){
   }
   if(branch.hasChildNodes()){
   branch = branch.firstChild;
   parser(branch);
   branch=branch.nextSibling;
   while(branch != null){
      parser(branch, tier+1);
      branch=branch.nextSibling;
   }
}
}
}
//------------------------
function myOnLoad(success){
```

```
    if(success){
        parser(xmlObj.firstChild);
    }
}
//------------------------
HLCounter=0;
this.attachMovie("ph","ph",10);
xmlObj=new XML();
xmlObj.ignoreWhite=true;
xmlObj.load("xml/Classified.xml");
xmlObj.onLoad=myOnLoad;
hideHeadlines();
```

In addition to the headline and storyText variables, we pull the value that becomes picNum from the picNum element in the XML document for each listing. Now each instance of the headline Movie clip contains the picNum that corresponds to its text content.

Next in the logical flow is the button in the headlines MC. This clip is dynamically pulled from library in the preceding code.

```
on(release, releaseOutside){
    _root.picGetter(this.picNum);
    _root.output=this.storyText;
    _root.headline=this.headline;
    _parent._parent.hideHeadlines();
}
```

You could just as easily place the call to Swift-Generator within this button handler. I chose to put the call in a function on the main timeline. This function, which is shown below, is picGetter().

```
function picGetter (picNum) {
    loadMovie
("http://localhost/cgi-bin/swiftgen?sws=../sws/pix.sws&picNum="+
picNum, _root.ph);
}
```

The loadMovie() action calls Swift-Generator, using the Swift-Script *pix.sws*, as seen in the next code example. The value of the variable picNum is given in the URL string. This name-value pair is appended with ".jpg" in the Swift-Script, and the proper image is retrieved and placed into the SWF output, properly scaled and sized.

```
INPUT "../swt/pix.swt"

OUTPUT -cgi "-"

DEFINE IMAGE "myPic.jpg" {
   FILE "../images/" + $picNum + ".jpg"
   QUALITY 60
   WIDTH 400
   HEIGHT 300
   KEEPRATIO
}
```

This output is loaded into the placeholder defined as _root.ph. This is a plain, white MC, as you can see here:

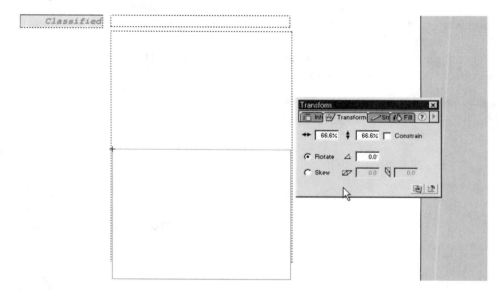

An interesting thing about this MC instance is that I have broken one of the hallowed rules of Flash bitmaps, namely, I have scaled a bitmap image down. This is an exception because 100% of the incoming bitmaps are likely to be scaled anyway. By starting with a slightly larger scale that was originally needed, you can easily change the size of the output without having to muck around with the source FLA again.

Sticksville Star Jukebox
SwiftGen-Jukebox.fla, SwiftMP3-Jukebox.fla

At present, everyone from clueless network news anchors to the pimple-faced teen who has hot-swappable hard drives for his music collection is muttering something he thinks is profound about MP3s; and the Sticksville Star is not going to miss out on the action! This example, like the previous one, assumes that some unrelated back-end work has already been done: a utility that creates a directory for a user and allows him to upload MP3s to that directory.

This is where we take over. This example is an MP3 player that creates a list of all available songs, builds a scrolling menu, and plays any song in the list. The following code, from *SwiftGen-Jukebox.fla*, is attached to the hub MC instance.

```
onClipEvent (data) {
    for (name in this) {
        if(name != "HLCounter"){
            nameValPairs[name] = this[name];
            _root.deadSeaScroller.document.document
    .attachMovie("headline", "headline"+HLCounter, HLCounter+5);
            with
(_root.deadSeaScroller.document.document["headline"+HLCounter]) {
                _x = 0;
                _y = HLCounter*38;
                headline = this[name];
            }
            HLCounter++;
        }
    }
}

onClipEvent (load) {
    loadVariables("http://localhost/dir.php", this, "GET");
    HLCounter = 0;
}
```

The first thing that happens is loading variables from the simple PHP script *dir.php*. This is a simple routine that runs through the directory, performs a simple pattern match to see if each filename ends in ".mp3," and spits out the results in Flash-friendly form. The code for this file is listed below for interested parties. When the data is received—onClipEvent(data)—a menu is built deep within the deadSeaScroller Movie clip. This MC contains the scrolling logic. We will not cover this code. The only important function in all this is the variable called "headline" being passed to each instance of the headline MC. This variable name was chosen because it was already in place from the last time we used this method of menu building, which was in Chapter 14.

```php
<?php

$counter=0;
$d = dir("../mp3");
while($entry=$d->read()) {
   if (eregi("[[:alnum:]]*.mp3$", $entry)){
       echo "song" . $counter . "=" . rawurlencode($entry) . "&";
       $counter++;


   }
}
$d->close();

?>
```

The next stage is the code attached to the button inside the headline MC. This MC is dynamically pulled from library at run time. The code is as follows:

```
on (release, releaseOutside) {
   loadMovieNum ("http://localhost/cgi-bin/swiftgen
   ?sws=../sws/mp3.sws&song=../mp3/" + this.headline, 1);
   _root.info.currentSong=this.headline;
}
```

In terms of function, this is where the application culminates in musical output. The new version of *mp3.swt*, complete with dynamically inserted MP3 audio, is loaded into _level1. This target path is chosen simply because it is out of the way. There is no visual content in the output, so there is no need to worry about its location on the stage. No placeholder is required. The information for the sake of the user is sent to the info Movie clip, where the following code creates a display of the percentage loaded. This code is attached to the blank MC inside info.

```
onClipEvent(enterFrame){
   loadNum=Math.round(_level1._framesLoaded/
   _level1._totalFrames * 100);
   if(isNaN(loadNum)){
      _parent.percentLoaded=0;
   }else{
```

```
      _parent.percentLoaded=loadNum;
   }
}
```

This function is especially noteworthy when using Swift-Generator to compile the MP3s as SWF output. If you tried this application, you noticed that the sound in the SWT is an event sound, so nothing plays until the entire song is loaded. The percentage loaded jumps from 0 to 100 after a long wait; then the song starts playing. To avoid this constraint, use Swift-MP3 to generate an SWF from an MP3 dynamically.

In the next example, *SwiftMP3-Jukebox.fla*, everything is the same except the loadMovie action in the headline MC in the library. This code appears here:

```
on (release, releaseOutside) {
   loadMovieNum ("http://localhost/cgi-bin/swiftmp3
   ?mp3=../mp3/" + this.headline, 1);
   _root.info.currentSong=this.headline;
}
```

Swift-MP3 works like Swift-Generator, except that no template or script is required. Since the job is always the same—transform an MP3 file into SWF—only one argument is required: the location of the file to be converted.

Scripting Versus Dynamic SWF Generation

If you begin to use Swift-Generator or other tools with similar capabilities, you have to start choosing between dynamic SWF generation and plain old scripting for each job. Although Swift-Script is perfectly capable of making text substitutions, connecting with databases, reading text files, and performing all manner of data collection and content generation, it is limited when compared to full-fledged server-side languages like PHP and Perl—even compared to ActionScript. It is clear that Swift-Script is not intended to be the sole manipulator of the data you use in your Flash application.

This is why the ability to execute external scripts is included in Swift-Script. Another possibility that I haven't even mentioned is calling Swift-Generator from within a script. For instance, suppose you had a PHP script that pulled personalized information from a MySQL database and fed name-value pairs to Swift-Generator via the URL string in the <OBJECT> tag:

```
<PARAM NAME=movie VALUE="http://localhost/cgi-bin/swiftgen?
   sws=../sws/mySticksVille.sws&bgimage=
   <?php echo $myRow["image"]?>">
```

Another example of good division of labor is the script *dir.php*, which we discussed briefly in the MP3 jukebox example. Although you could get a directory listing by using a shell command directly from within Swift-Script, there would be no way to apply logic based on a regular expression, as we did in *dir.php*.

The best approach is to rely on Swift-Generator and other such tools for their specialties—dynamically defining bitmap images, sounds, fonts, or anything else that can not be easily manipulated with ActionScript or a more comprehensive server-side scripting language.

I have so far neglected one other consideration in this discussion: offline SWF generation. Suppose you want to build a small-town news site (like the Sticksville Star) with daily updates. You want to be able to enter your new content in a desktop ODBC-capable database, like MS Access, and have all of your Flash movies on your hard drive updated, so that you can simply upload a batch of static SWFs to your production server every day (or script your FTP client to do it automatically). Swift-Generator can do this for you. By saving an SQL query in your Swift-Script for each template, you can update your content by running Swift-Generator from the command line as a standalone application. This is a very attractive option, especially considering that this scenario allows you to publish data-driven Flash with no special server requirements.

Other Dynamic SWF Tools

Since Macromedia publishes the SWF file SDK shortly after the release of each new version of Flash, there are lots of tools around that output SWF content. This is a very good thing for Flash developers. There are a few other tools that dynamically create SWF content. The following is a list of some of the more popular tools available at the time of writing.

▶ **Macromedia Generator**   This is the big one—the preeminent tool for large-scale server-side Flash development. In addition to extended output capabilities, Generator offers developers tight integration between the authoring environment and the server component. Generator comes with authoring extensions that let you drop objects into your Flash movies, designating how the data source should populate the object at run time. The most attractive feature, however, is Generator's extensibility. Java developers can extend Generator's battery of objects with their own. The last big issue to ponder when considering Generator, especially for a client with a very busy site and a little money to spend, is support. Macromedia Generator is backed by a huge company that is likely to be around for a while.

▶ **ASP Flash Turbine, PHP Flash Turbine, and Direct Flash Turbine**   Another commercially available dynamic SWF generation tool is the Turbine family of products from Blue Pacific. I must confess that I haven't tried these products yet, but I have it on good authority that they are effective, feature-rich, relatively low-cost tools. You can learn more about them at http://www.blue-pac.com/products.

▶ **Ming**   If the name isn't cool enough for you, the utility will be. This was the first PHP library I can remember hearing about that creates SWF content. You can directly create vector objects by entering vector parameters, which seems very cool for things like digital art. It also includes image and sound replacement capabilities. Learn more at http://www.opaque.net/ming/.

▶ **LibSWF**   This is another module for PHP. Learn more at http://reality.sgi.com/grafica/flash/.

▶ **SGUI**   If you like Swift-Generator as much as I do, you will be interested in SGUI, a visual front for SG. It is currently only available for Windows, but the price is right (free). Read about and download SGUI at http://www.derijen.nl/Peerless/SGUI/SGUI.htm.

What to Take Away from This Chapter

One of the most exciting things about Flash is that the set of tools, including its internal set of tools in the authoring environment, is quickly expanding. At present, it doesn't seem too far-fetched to conceptualize SWF as a Web standard, complete with all the attendant home-grown tools and lots of forums with code being exchanged. Swift-Generator is one of the oldest third-party tools for creating dynamic SWF content, and one of the easiest to use. This is an extremely valuable tool to have in your toolbox.

Flash Peripheral Issues

OBJECTIVES

► Overview of the Different Areas of 3D
Animation

► Learn Basic Modeling By Example in Strata 3D

► Explore a Sensible Workflow Using Strata and
Swift 3D

► Learn the Rudiments of Swift 3D

► Create a Simplified Character Animation Using
a Strata Model in Swift 3D

► Rundown of Amorphium Pro

Overview of Flash 3D

IN THIS CHAPTER:

his chapter covers some specific techniques for building 3D symbols and animations in Flash, as well as a broad overview of the major areas of interest in the huge and fascinating world of 3D. This is intended as an *introduction* to 3D for experienced Flash developers who have little or no prior exposure to 3D proper.

General Overview of 3D Topics

From fine art still images to title sequences for TV news to electronic actors in films, 3D tools are used everywhere in our media-saturated world. The range of tools is unbelievably large, too, from freeware desktop applications to high-performance, multiprocessor, dedicated machines on a network that do nothing but render frames of animation, day and night.

Although it does take a long time to find your voice in 3D and learn one of the incredibly complex (and expensive) software packages, there are some basic concepts that tie together all tools, goals, and areas of 3D.

NOTE

The concept of materials and textures is conspicuously missing from our roundup of general 3D subjects. This is because it is currently not practical to render textures to a 3D object in SWF vectors. Besides, the general lack of tools that will render textured 3D models to SWF vectors, the file size, and the complexity of such an SWF would prohibit its practical use.

Modeling

Modeling is the electronic equivalent of sculpture. This is the area of 3D that makes celebrities of good 3D artists (within 3D communities, anyway). The idea is that you start with a shape—usually a simple 3D object like a cube—and manipulate the vertices of that object to create a new shape.

If you haven't ventured into 3D before, you may wonder how you can effectively manipulate the appearance of a geometric shape like a sphere by its individual vertices, since a sphere is by definition an infinite number of points equidistant from the center. This leads us to the one central verity that underlies all work in all areas of 3D: models are made of polygons.

3D objects are typically made up of lots of little polygons, which are subdivided diagonally. We are not going to worry about the diagonals in this chapter. You can see how the sphere in the following image is not really a perfect sphere, but a sphere-shaped group of rectangles.

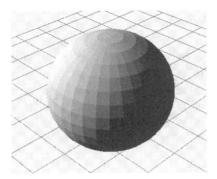

The array of techniques for manipulating these polygons is deep and wide. Some techniques are generally preferred for particular applications, such as low-polygon modeling by manually adding, subtracting, and moving vertices in a model with as few polygons as possible. This technique is preferred for artists who make models for 3D video games and other real-time rendering applications, because models with fewer polygons will take less brainpower for the game processor to render.

Other divergent methods of modeling are popular for different reasons, not the least of which are personal preference and artistic style. One family of modeling styles uses tangent handles to create 3D Bézier curves, which can give an object with few Bézier vertices a smooth, organic look. There are also tools-based approaches that deform the mesh of polygons for you based on parametric input, but these are a little outside the territory of hard-core 3D modeling. If you are interested in 3D, you could easily spend a month of focused, full-time study on the fine art of working directly on the polygon mesh to create models.

Another aspect of 3D that you should be aware of (though it will not be covered in this chapter) involves boning and skinning a model. This isn't as gruesome as it sounds. Boning a character is the process of building a skeleton for a model by drawing bones inside the character, while skinning is the process of attaching those bones to the mesh that makes up the model. You can even compose logic for the bones, giving them individual ranges of motion and particular bones that control others in a group—just like a real skeleton—using a technique and tool named, in 18th-century-birth-of-science fashion, *inverse kinematics*.

Animation

Any true Flash enthusiast will want to make a 3D model move. The particular workflow outlined in this chapter is limited to keyframes and tweening—just like those concepts work in Flash—because models will be built in one package and exported to another in a file format that does not support animation.

The larger world of 3D, by contrast, is anything but limited when it comes to animation. In addition to the control you gain over animated characters with a complex system of bones and skin, most packages have whole applications dedicated to the parametric manipulation of every aspect of animation. Most full-blown 3D packages have an electronic version of every camera and lighting apparatus used in cinema, plus some that exist only in the electronic world.

Rendering

All the parameters you define within a 3D model or scene, including the vertices of every polygon, the type, placement, and characteristics of lights, and so on, are all composed in the interest of generating visual output. Generating that output is called *rendering*, and it is a distinct interest in itself. We will be using Swift 3D to render our models and animations to SWF vectors, which means that the options for which details to render, as well as lighting, quality, and format options are much more limited than if we were rendering for video or still images. The process of rendering in Swift 3D is set in motion when you select File | Export.

Tools

Choosing tools to create 3D images or animation represents a larger risk than selecting tools for Web multimedia and graphic art. One daunting factor is the price of many of the high-quality 3D packages, which generally run in the same price range as a serviceable used car. Another factor is the number of tools offering different approaches to the same concepts and features. If you are interested in digging deeper into the 3D world than spinning logos, my recommendation is to start with free and low-cost tools, many of which embody the same concepts and even features of their high-cost siblings. The following is a short list of my favorite low-cost tools, with reasons for why I like each.

Strata 3D

This package is perfect for our purposes in this chapter. It is very easy to use, features an intuitive interface that should be easy for any Flash veteran to pick up, implements all the basic concepts of 3D we will talk about, and best of all, it is free. If you get bitten by the 3D bug and decide to dig deeper, you can easily and inexpensively extend the functionality of Strata with commercial plug-ins available from Strata at http://3d.com. The quality of Strata's rendering engine, even in the free version, is very good. Another feature of Strata is the active, fun, and open community of users. Many Strata users who participate in the Stratalist email discussion list are experienced 3D professionals who consider Strata to be a viable alternative the more expensive 3D packages. You can read more about Strata at http://3d.com.

Nendo

Nendo is a perfect tool to use as an introduction to modeling, and you may continue to use it for the remainder of your 3D career, regardless of the software package(s) you choose. Nendo is a masterpiece of desktop application GUI usability. I can hardly imagine a cleaner, more intuitive environment for traditional modeling techniques. If you entertain any fantasy of becoming a master 3D artist, you will have to learn to model at the polygon level. Nendo is a perfect place to start. There is a free, crippled demo of Nendo available at http://www.nichimen.com. At the time of writing, the full-blown pro version costs $100.

Blender

This is a curious package. Blender is freeware, and parts of the package are even open source, so there are multiple solutions available for some extensions. One of the most striking things about Blender is its interface, which provides every imaginable 3D tool within an elegant, nonclaustrophobic environment. However, since the interface is different from other 3D packages, and more complex, taking up Blender represents a larger initial investment of your time. Once you learn the interface, you will be able to access easily an amazing array of tools within an uncluttered environment. I had a very hard time picking which low-cost package to use in this chapter; the interface was the only reason I did not choose Blender. At the time of writing, there is a buzz in the Blender community about developing 3DS export, which would make it even more attractive to a very large number of Flash developers, since it would simplify a 3D-to-Swift 3D workflow. You can read more about Blender at http://www.blender.nl/.

Swift 3D

The primary strengths of Swift 3D are its well-thought-out, easy-to-use interface, the ability to import 3DS models and animations, parallel timelines for each object, its high-quality SWF rendering, and its popularity. Because Swift 3D is a successful product, it is likely to be around for a long time, and therefore likely to develop better features and interfaces with each version. Swift also includes the ability to group objects, which allows for more complex animation. Learn more about Swift 3D at http://www.swift3d.com.

Vecta 3D

At $60, you have little to lose by trying this product. Despite its low cost, the interface has a more *standard* feel to me than those of its direct competitors. It seems to include more controls that are familiar from my experience in other tools. For instance, in the "style" window alone, you have a selection scheme that is similar to 3D Studio Max, a distinction between outlines and fills similar to the Flash authoring environment, and a color selector that is common to a bazillion graphics applications, 2D and 3D alike. You also have the parametric object and world rotation dialog right in the main interface, as well as a simple tool to edit only the center of the object. Vecta will also import DXF models directly.

Crosswinds

At the time of writing, this useful little app is freeware. This tool can import and export a large number of 3D file formats, including 3DS, the preferred format for Swift 3D. Find out more about Crosswinds at http://home.europa.com/~keithr/crossroads/.

Amorphium Pro

This is a unique application, both in the arena of Flash tools and the 3D world in general. Since the chapter focuses on traditional 3D techniques and low-cost workflow for rendering 3D images and animation, a separate discussion of this tool is included at the end of the chapter. At an MSRP of $369 (though it is estimated that the street price will be less), Amorphium Pro is the most expensive tool to be covered in this chapter.

Animation: Master

If character animation is your cup of tea, proceed directly to Animation: Master. Its feature set for character animation is considered comparable to the big-name, big-money packages, yet it has a MSRP of only $300. The native modeling tools are certainly not as extensive as the big packages; but there are extremely low-cost modeling packages out there to make up the difference. Animation: Master is something of an industry phenomenon, creeping silently into use among professionals without any kind of advertising that I've seen. The only downside of Animation:

Master for Flashers is that you will not be able to translate your creations to
SWF in vectors, (not without tracing, anyway). Find out more about A:M at
http://www.hash.com.

Introduction to 3D Using Strata

Though different 3D packages vary in terms of the complexity of the working
environment, the common denominator among all of them is that they *are* complex.
There is no way of avoiding it. The challenge of all 3D art—and therefore of 3D
tools—is to represent three-dimensional objects in two-dimensional space. In
everyday life, this illusion is taken for granted. You see images in film and television
and you assume that they have depth, even though the depth is not explicitly visible.
Creating 3D models and animations, by contrast, requires that you be able to
explicitly define each point in a 3D scene. The first requisite for doing this is
understanding how you might represent 3D objects in three coordinate planes or
axes, and this is a matter of just having that part of the brain switched on. If you are
comfortable with the concept of points existing in a three-plane coordinate system,
all that remains is to figure out how your software package represents that system
and how to move around within that system. This part of the chapter attempts to
acquaint you with Strata's basic methods in this regard.

Primitives

Primitive shapes, or *primitives*, are the shapes that are built into the 3D software as
part of the toolset. There are different numbers of primitives available in each 3D
package. The free Strata 3D package includes six primitives, as shown in the next
illustration. They are, left to right, top to bottom: sphere, cube, cone, rounded
cube (called *chamfer cube* elsewhere), cylinder, and pyramid.

The easiest way to place one of these shapes is to click on the primitive on the toolbar
and then drag over the desired area on the stage. However, as with everything in 3D,

there are many options for how to do this. A primitive that has variable parameters, like the rounded cube, can be adjusted before you draw by double-clicking on its button in the toolbar before you place the primitive on the stage. Figure 20-1 shows a dialog for the rounded cube where the corner radius is set to 20% instead of the default 50%, with the resultant cube in the background.

Most people like to draw primitives one or two dimensions at a time. You can do this by selecting a primitive in the toolbar and then single-clicking on the stage to start drawing the base of the primitive object. After you click a second time, you will begin drawing the height of the object. The third click terminates the drawing at the current mouse position.

Another option you have with drawing primitives is the Constrain to Rectangle option. To constrain the primitive to equal dimensions in each direction, hold down SHIFT as you draw. This works exactly like it does in 2D graphic art software.

The last basic option for drawing primitives is drawing from the center point instead of the corner. Just as you would suspect from your experience in 2D art programs, the ALT key activates this option.

At this point, it is informative to note the exceptional level of precision and the number of options available for something so simple as drawing primitive shapes. In most 3D packages with a lot of features, there are many ways of performing any given task, each with its own advantages. Learning the exhaustive list of options for

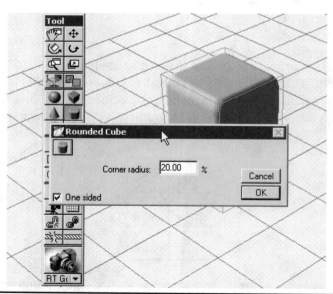

Figure 20.1   *Options for the Rounded Cube Tool*

each task is part of becoming proficient in a 3D tool. Precision is much more important in 3D art than in 2D, since everything is interrelated.

Views

Regardless of the software you are using, you will want to look at your 3D models and scenes from every angle, and you will want to be able to switch between views quickly. 3D software typically has a large set of tools just for manipulating your view of the objects you are building. Strata has a particularly good toolset for adjusting views.

The first thing you will want to do is to split the view window into multiple views. This makes your model accessible from many sides simultaneously and gives you an instant feel for where you are in 3D space at any time. Figure 20-2 shows my favorite view setup, with a window on the left that is rotated and moved around freely to see the results of manipulations done in the other windows, and two windows showing orthographic views (top, right, left, bottom, front, and back), where the manipulations are performed. I generally move between views frequently in the right two windows and frequently change the orientation of the perspective view on the left.

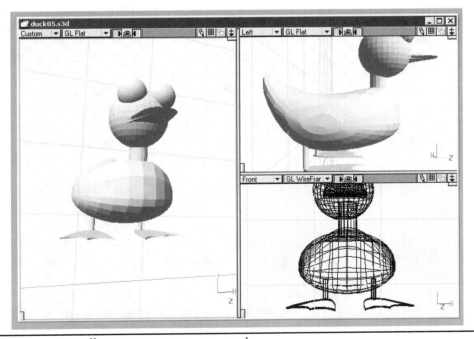

Figure 20.2   *An efficient view management scheme*

To split the window into multiple views, use the tiny options menu button with a little plus sign on it to get the drop-down menu for that window; then select Split View. To switch between the different views in each portion of the window, just click on the name of the current view (for example, Left or Front) in the upper-left corner of each section of the window to get the drop-down list of available views.

You can also maximize each view, so that it fills the entire window designated for viewports within Strata. To do this, click the little maximize button (it looks similar to the maximize button in Windows) just to the left of the options menu button. To go back to split views, click the button again.

The next button to the right of the view drop-down menu in each section of the window lets you select how the model will be rendered in that particular window. If you cycle through the different options with any shape showing in that window, you will immediately realize the meaning of each, so that a discussion of each option would be superfluous. I use the GL Flat option as much as possible. I like this option because it shows both the general shape of the model and the individual vertices. You can move between each type of rendering with the hot keys ALT-A (Point Cloud), ALT-S (Outline), ALT-D (Wire Frame), ALT-F (Flat), ALT-G (Shaded), and ALT-H (Hidden Line).

The next thing you will want to be able to do with your viewports is pan, rotate, and zoom. The three topmost tools in the left column of the toolbar perform these tasks for you. These tools are intuitive and can hardly be augmented by lengthy discussion on their operation. You should spend a little time getting acquainted with these tools before you go too much deeper into the software.

Finally, note the little slider that is in the middle of the menu bar on every viewport. It is supposed to be a little eye, but I thought it was a gear when I first opened Strata. This is a great tool. It lets you switch between a strictly orthographic view when the slider is in the left position (good for side, top, left, views), to a little bit of perspective in the center position (good for the so-called isometric view), to a wide perspective in the right position.

Selection

The importance of being able to select objects accurately increases as the complexity of your 3D creation increases. Strata has one method in particular that helps make accurate selection easier.

Create a few primitives in any view that are close enough together that they overlap in at least one view, naming each as you go. To name each primitive object, use the object palette, shown in Figure 20-3. Type in a name immediately after you create each primitive object, so that it is still selected. Another thing to notice in this image is the blue bounding box that shows an object as being selected.

Once you have several overlapping primitive objects in a particular view, switch to the move tool, shown in the next image. The hot key for the move tool is 1, and I suggest you use it. Using all available hot keys in complicated 3D software is all but an absolute necessity.

Move to the viewport where your primitives overlap and right-click on a spot where the objects overlap. You should see a context menu listing the objects that are in the direct line of view at this point, as in Figure 20-4.

In addition to this handy feature, you have all the same selection features you are accustomed to from 2D graphic art packages. For instance, you can drag a marquee around multiple objects to select them. You can also use SHIFT-select to add more objects to your selection.

You will want to remember the hot keys for grouping and ungrouping multiple objects. To group objects together, select them using a marquee drag or SHIFT-select and choose Modeling | Group or press CTRL-G. The blue bounding box expands to circumscribe all the objects in the group. To ungroup objects, choose Modeling | Ungroup or press CTRL-U.

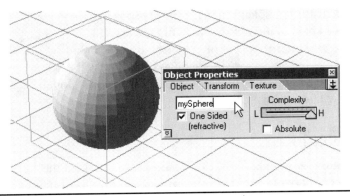

Figure 20.3   *Using the object palette to name primitive objects*

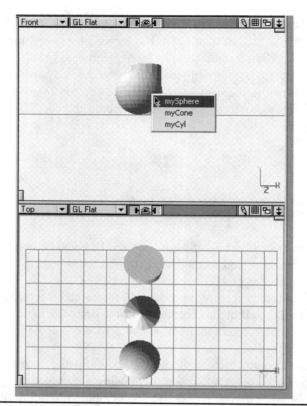

Figure 20.4   *Strata's selection tool*

Another tidy feature of selection is the ability to zoom in on a selection with CTRL+–. To zoom back out to show everything, use CTRL-=.

The last bare essential function of selecting objects is hiding the objects you don't want to work on. This is easily managed in Strata. To hide an object, go to Selection | Hide Selection or press CTRL-3. To reveal all hidden objects, go to Selection | Show Hidden or press CTRL-4.

Transformation Tools

The move, rotation, and scale tools, the topmost three tools in the right column of the toolbar, are collectively referred to as *transformation tools* in any 3D package. They perform similarly to their 2D counterparts, but, as with everything in 3D, the extra dimension compounds the complexity of the operations.

If you already tried the move tool, you may have discovered the key to its operation, or you may have been bewildered by the apparently inconsistent results of grabbing objects with this tool. The key to using this tool is taking note of the little handles Strata gives you to move an object in each direction. When you select an object with the move tool, little red dots show up on the plane of each side of the bounding box, as seen here:

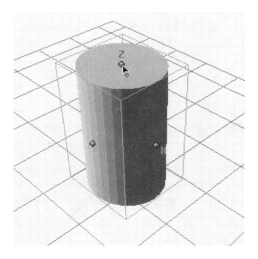

These are the handles by which you can move the object along a path constrained to a particular axis. For instance, if you want to move an object *only* vertically, grab it by the handle for the z-axis. If you grab an object at any point other than one of these handles, you can move it in two directions on the *active grid*.

The active grid is shown by the blue grid in each viewport. This is the plane that serves as your conceptual workspace. The y-plane is active by default, to reflect the real-world conception of the ground as the base to which matter "sticks," with structures extending upward from it. To change planes, go to Edit | Active Grid and choose the plane you want. The hot keys to change planes are X for the x-plane, Y for the y-plane, and Z for the z-plane. Once your mind has assimilated to the 3D world (this takes a while—at least it did for me), you will find it very helpful to be able to switch between active grids quickly in order to be able to constrain 2D translations (*translation* just means moving something) to the plane you choose.

TIP

You can toggle between the last transformation tool used and your current other tool (anything that is not a transformation tool) with the SPACEBAR. This is especially handy when you are trying to place something with the move tool and you need to keep adjusting your perspective view to see if you are getting the desired result.

Scale and rotate work the same way, with the same handles serving as constraints in their respective directions. The last remaining trick to master with the transformation tools is the keyboard modifiers. Don't worry—the concepts behind each modifier are the same as in 2D graphics tools you already know. The following list shows the most commonly used options.

► **ALT** As you would expect, holding down ALT while you move or rotate an object creates a copy of the original. ALT combined with the scale tool causes the object to be modified from the center instead of the opposite corner.

► **SHIFT** This modifier generally constrains the transformation tools. When you rotate along one axis using SHIFT, the rotation is constrained to multiples of 45 degrees. SHIFT used with the scale tool constrains the dimensions of the object to their original proportions (that is, scales each direction equally).

► **ALT-SHIFT** This modifier works the same as SHIFT with the scale tool, except that the object scales from its center. With the move tool, ALT-SHIFT moves the object along the axis that intersects the origin of the active grid (that is, moves the object up and down relative to the active grid, or moves the object closer to or farther away from the active grid).

At this point, you may well be thinking that all these permutations of the same tools aren't necessary, or that this kind of stuff is the domain of "advanced features"—whatever that is. As someone with a fair amount of experience in 3D as a hobby, I can assure you that you will cherish every option you have to view and transform parts of 3D models and scenes when they become complex.

Project—Build a Spaceship

The next logical step after learning the bare fundamentals of viewing, drawing primitives, and transforming them is building a fun, engaging model that we can use in an animation. We are going to build a spaceship (with guns, of course—why else would you go to space, except to shoot at things?). Feel free to compose your own, as you could hardly avoid improving on my design. This is just an exercise to demonstrate the concepts we have covered so far.

1. Start in front view, with the z-plane as the active grid (hot key Z).

2. Choose the pyramid primitive tool and click on the grid in the front view to start drawing the base. Click again when you are satisfied with the shape of the base, and once more when you are satisfied with the overall shape. Figure 20-5 shows my shape. I prefer to pull shapes out from the active grid, closer to myself, rather than away (the base of the primitive remains stationary and the volume of the shape gets closer). To make sure you are drawing with the base of the primitive on the active grid, just keep moving your mouse in the same direction that you used to draw the base.

3. Switch to the cylinder primitive and draw two cylinders, again in the front view. The larger one (shown in Figure 20-6) is supposed to represent the mouth of the rockets that will stick out the back of the spaceship. Because it needs to be either aligned with or sunk into the back of the pyramid, I drew it so that the

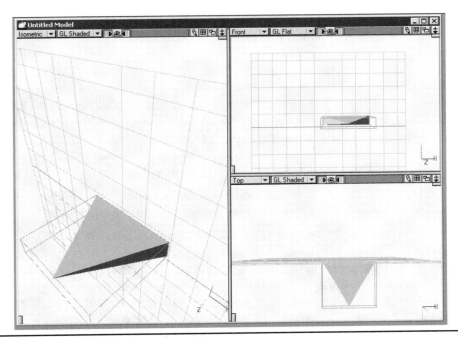

Figure 20.5   *The hull of a spaceship*

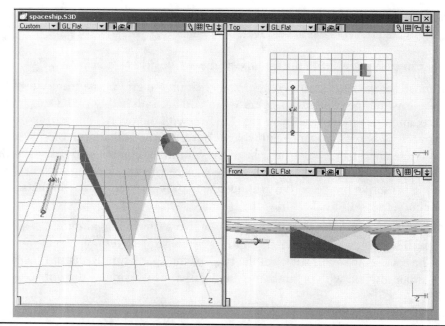

Figure 20.6 *Using the default alignment to draw spaceship components*

volume of the shape goes away from the active grid. To do this, drag your mouse the opposite direction for the volume as you did for drawing the base. If you want the base to be perfectly round, hold down the SHIFT key as you draw the base. Also draw a gun, as the infinite universe seems to be a hostile territory nowadays, filled with English-speaking hominids with funny prosthetics glued to their faces (this must be what makes them bad-natured).

4. Finally, draw a sphere. I made mine elongated to mimic small military aircraft, which seems to be the point of departure for spaceships in film and TV.

5. Your model should now be ready for assembly. First, position your rocket and gun at the correct vertical level. Then ALT-drag each of them on the x-axis to make a copy with the same y and z coordinates. Keep dragging until your new copy is where you want it and drop it. Place the originals by dragging with the x handle (you don't want to change the y or z coordinates at this point). Move your sphere into place, and you have a spaceship. My version is shown here.

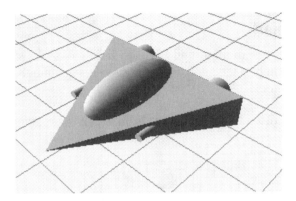

While 3D is definitely not a stronghold for instant gratification, a few notes are in order regarding the ratio of the difficulty of the work we have just done to the benefits of it. First of all, the exceedingly simple model we just created is impossible to create using a simple extrusion of a 2D image, which seems to be the most popular method of modeling for Flash at the time of writing. You can't make a pyramid or an elongated sphere by simple extrusion. (We will talk about better uses for extrusion in the next section.)

Another key observation at this point is that the model is more or less recognizable as a spaceship. This is a good lesson for beginning modelers: primitives can be used as a point of departure for any form. In fact, for the majority of known European art history, the idea of conceptualizing all objects as primitive shapes was a staple of 2D painting education. Even experienced modelers who create low-poly models for games point-by-point, manually adding, subtracting, and moving points, often start from a simple cube.

Modeling Basics Using Strata

This section uses the native tools within Strata as an introduction to the basic concepts of building a model in 3D. While its core modeling toolset is certainly complete enough to make good models using what it calls a Bézier Surface, Strata does skip over some of the tools for making basic, low-poly models, like the ability to split polygons in a mesh and extrude polygons within a mesh. If you are interested in this style of modeling, check out Nendo. You can easily import your Nendo models into Strata.

Extrude a 2D Object

Almost any 3D package can import an EPS file and extrude the shapes to give them depths, but we are going to take this opportunity to get acquainted with Strata's Bézier path creation tool.

1. First select the filled Bézier path tool from the flyout under the pen icon in the toolbar, as seen here:

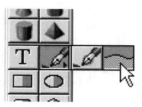

2. Using the same modifiers as you would in Flash, draw a path that looks like the outline of a piece of bread. To get the point in the middle with split tangent handles, first drag the regular tangent handle to where it looks about right; then hold down ALT to split the handles. You should get something like that shown in the next image. Notice that the way you draw the final point (over the original point, to close the path) is backward from the way most 2D graphics tools work—you drag back toward the last point you drew instead of following through.

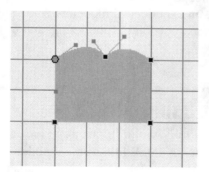

3. If you have trouble with your path, you edit it by selecting Modeling | Reshape or pressing CTRL-L. When you are done editing with the pointer tool in reshape mode (the point tool acts almost identically to a 2D subselection tool), you can exit back to object mode by selecting Modeling | End Reshape/Edit or pressing CTRL-E.

4. Next, select the extrude tool (just below scale on the toolbar) and drag the piece of bread to your desired thickness. You can enter the depth of the extrusion directly into the object palette, as shown below. This palette also gives you a number of options for the shape of the bevel.

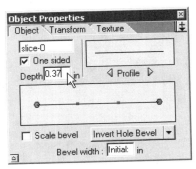

Lathe a 2D Object

A 3D bottle of something cold would be nice to go with our 3D bread.

1. Draw half of a profile of a bottle with the Bézier path tool, including the inner wall, as shown here:

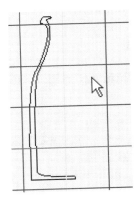

2. Next choose the lathe tool from the toolbar. It is just above the sphere primitive tool. The lathe acts just like its real-world namesake, cutting the shape of the 2D path into an imaginary piece of 3D material spinning on the axis you choose with the lathe tool.

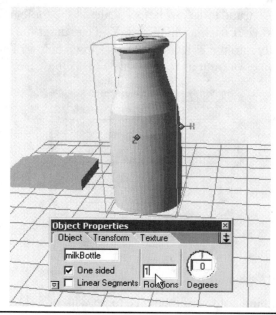

Figure 20.7 *Adjusting lathe parameters in the object dialog*

3. Drag the lathe tool on your outline to get the lathe process started; then enter 360 degrees or 1 rotation in the object palette to get the exact rotation you want, as shown in Figure 20-7.

You should now have an old-fashioned milk bottle.

Bézier Surface

This section describes how you might model a spoon using the Bézier surface reshape tools. Instead of using a tools-and-modifiers approach, we are going to directly edit the vertices and tangent handles that make up a Bézier surface. This is not for the weak-willed.

CAUTION

The following steps outline a process that requires a skill developed over time. Modeling using the vertices of an object, whether they be points on a 3D Bézier curve or the actual points that hold together the polygon mesh, is not easy. On the other hand, this is the essence of 3D modeling, and it is indescribably satisfying once it sinks into your brain.

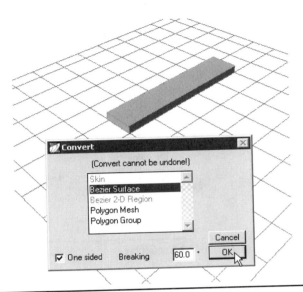

Figure 20.8   *Converting an object to a Bézier object*

1. Create a long flat cube, as shown in the following image.

2. Convert to Bézier surface and enter reshape mode (CTRL-L). The dialog for converting shapes is shown in Figure 20-8.

3. Use the add point tool to create three new points, as shown in Figure 20-9. These will be the tip of the spoon and the two rounded edges of the spoon.

4. Switch to the move point tool and delete the two corner points on the top and bottom. In other words, eliminate the square edges on either side of the tip of the spoon. This is where your selection skill, which depends greatly on your skill in manipulating views, comes into play. You will have to delete the corners on both sides of the thickness of the spoon, for a total of four vertices.

5. Create two more points for the shoulder of the spoon and bring them in to make the taper, as shown in Figure 20-10.

6. Move the ends of the handle toward each other, so that the handle is the same width throughout.

7. If you want to make it easier on yourself and give yourself fewer points to contend with, you can delete the bottom points on the handle end of the spoon and the points on the top surface where the dish of the spoon is. This will basically give you a *patch*—or a 2D mesh that wraps around 3D space. The effect is that the spoon looks like it is a single piece of flat material, stamped

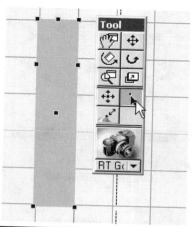

Figure 20.9 *The add point tool for Bézier objects*

into shape, like the plastic spoon they give you for some ice cream desserts at fast-food joints. This would look like Figure 20-11.

8. Keep working the tangent handles until you are satisfied with the shape of the spoon. Keep switching back and forth between views in each viewport, as well

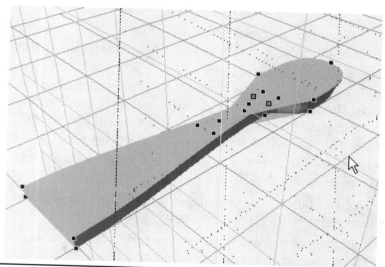

Figure 20.10 *The spoon beginning to take shape*

Figure 20.11   *The finished spoon*

as between rendering options. You should be able to view only the things you want to view at any time.

9. Finally, when you are done, don't forget to exit reshape mode by selecting Modeling | End Reshape/Edit or pressing CTRL-E. If you do forget, you will probably pull vertices to who-knows-where and get funny overlaps in your model. Be especially careful to save your models as you work because you have limited levels of undo.

Chances are you will make mistakes and have to start over several times in order to make a decent spoon. This is real 3D modeling. It's a little bit harder than drawing on a 2D plane. You should be starting to get a feel for how important it is to be able to manage your views and selections. As for adapting your mind to the way 3D programs represent space, that just takes time and practice.

Path Extrude

Now that I have a spoon, I feel like having a cup of coffee to stir. I made a cup using the lathe tool, just like the milk bottle. Now it's time to add a handle. I would like to have a basically cylindrical piece of material that forms the shape of a handle and is stuck onto the side of the cup, just like on a real handmade cup. You could extrude a square piece in the correct profile shape and try to bevel it to be round, but that method would be imprecise, time consuming, and worst of all, uncool.

The path extrude tool is better suited to this challenge. The idea of path extrude is that you take two components, a 2D shape and a path, and combine them. The goal is to extrude the shape along the path, so that it follows its curves, corners, and so on.

1. First make your coffee cup, using the same method as we used for the milk bottle.

2. Change the active grid to either the x- or z-axis, depending on which side of the cup you want to have a handle. (Figure 20-12 shows the z-axis as active.) Draw the circle to be extruded and the path.

3. Select the path extrude tool. This will be in the extensions palette, probably the first thing on the left in the Tools tab.

4. Drag from the circle to the path. When both of them are highlighted with a red bounding box, release the mouse button. Depending on your processor's speed, and other factors, your PC may have to think for a moment; but you will

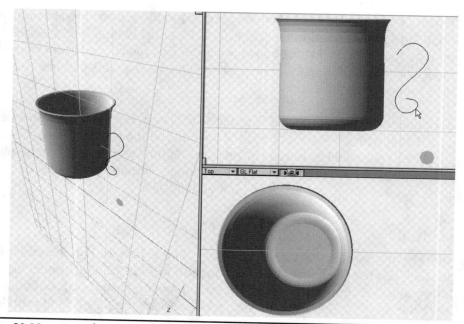

Figure 20.12   *Extruding a circle along a path to make a mug handle*

eventually get a cylinder that has been bent into the shape of our path. The following illustration shows what my first try looked like.

5. You can see that my handle isn't quite right. I really didn't do this on purpose—it's hard to imagine what a path-extruded shape is going to look like. The good thing is that you can still change the original path. If you select Modeling | Reshape (CTRL-L) with the cup handle selected, you can edit your path as if you never did the path extrude. When you end reshape mode, the cup handle will reflect your changes.

Polygon Mesh—Gravity

I made some eggs to go with our scene. Since eggs are made up of spheres in nature, it didn't take much imagination, as you can see here:

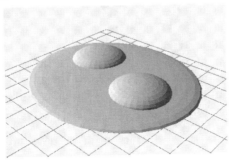

The problem with these eggs is that the whites make up a perfectly elliptical egg mass—not a likely scenario. You would have a hard time convincing anyone that these are eggs, even in a cartoon setting and even with good textures. The easy solution we are going to use is the gravity feature available with a polygon mesh in reshape mode.

1. Make some eggs using the sphere primitive, following the example of the egg image here.

2. Select the whites and convert to a gradient mesh by selecting Modeling | Convert.

3. Double-click on the point move tool to get the following dialog; then select Low.

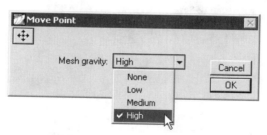

4. Select a point and move it to give the whites the shape you want. Surrounding vertices in the gradient mesh, responding to the gravity, move along with the point you selected. I indented the area between the yolks on either side to match my conception of ideal fried eggs, which you can see below. I also nudged up the bottom row of vertices, in case I decided to have the eggs lie flat on a plate.

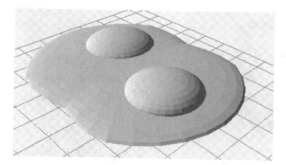

If you are low on time, patience, or even talent, the gravity feature can serve as an easy alternative to Bézier or polygon-level modeling. It will probably never get you the exact results you want, but it *is* easy and fast.

Meta Ball

handTrace.jpg

The final stop in our descent into cheap and easy shortcuts (everyone uses them) is the meta ball. The idea of the meta ball is that you place a bunch of spheres and then let the meta ball tool sort-of morph them all together, like the liquid metal guy in that *Terminator* movie. We are going to make a hand to go with our breakfast scene, to pick up the spoon, coffee cup, milk jar, toast. (The hand will probably also poke at the eggs to see if they are done—I don't know.)

1. The first thing we need to do is import a background image of a hand. Hands are hard to draw, and even harder to model in 3D space. Using a 2D image as a reference will give us a good head start. In the options menu for the top view, select Set Backdrop. In the dialog that pops up, select Load Backdrop and load *handTrace.jpg* from the examples folder on the CD. Accept the default parameters. You should get something like Figure 20-13.

2. Next start drawing spheres. Fill in the outline of the hand, putting elongated spheres where long bones go and rounder spheres where joints go. Your scene should look something like Figure 20-14.

3. Once you are satisfied with the quality of your hand parts, select everything (CTRL-A) and use the meta ball tool. This tool is in the extensions palette, on the Commands tab. This is one place where the parameters on the object palette are especially important. Adjust the slider to your liking. Figure 20-15 shows my final hand.

Using meta ball as a modeling method obviously has limitations. The first thing you will notice, especially if you have a slow machine, is that the complexity of this model is off the charts. My hand came out to about 14,000 polygons. A good professional 3D artist could easily make an expressive hand that gives you the

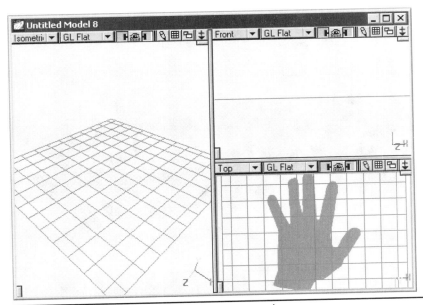

Figure 20.13 *An imported 2D image serving as a guide*

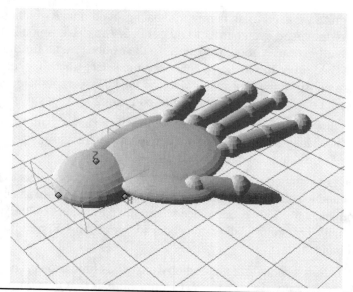

Figure 20.14 *The meta ball hand before smoothing*

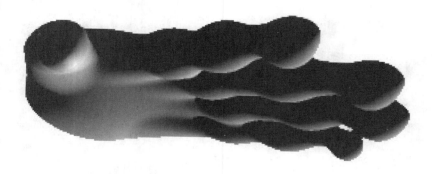

Figure 20.15 *The finished hand without texture*

impression of life with fewer than 1000 polygons. Since every polygon is considered when you render a model or scene, the more polygons you have, the longer rendering will take.

The other big drawback is that, like any modeling technique that does not operate directly on the polygon vertices or points on a Bézier surface, you don't really have *much* control over the shape. We did get a serviceable hand model from the exercise, which is no small feat for your first foray into 3D, but at the expense of efficiency and control. Use tools like this moderately.

Final Thoughts on Strata 3D

Strata 3D is the best tool I've seen to get started in 3D. It combines a sensible, easy-to-learn interface with a no-risk cost at entry level and amazing power. In addition, there is a wealth of information online, from free textures and models to tutorials, discussions, and galleries of work. A good place to start is the online Strata Manual, which can be found at http://works.3d.com/onlinemanuals/index.html.

Introduction to Swift 3D

spaceship.swf

It is no surprise that Swift 3D is very popular among Flash developers. It uses a familiar concept of timeline-based animation with keyframes and tweening, plus a few function-curve-style options for customizing the characteristics of keyframes. It offers superslick output for geometric solids and very good flat-color output for organically shaped models. Another great feature is the interface: it is designed to get work done. In a very short time from when I first installed Swift 3D, I felt comfortable performing every operation. The tools seem to be designed to require a minimum of interruptions to go to toolbars or menus. Finally, and not least of all, it is in such a price range that you might pick it up on an impulse while browsing your local office supply store on your lunch break. If you want to move models around, do some simple animation in an easy-to-learn and use environment, Swift is a good choice.

We are going to look at Swift 3D in the context of a project, the end result of which you can see in *spaceship.swf*. We are going to take the spaceship model we made in Strata and bring it into Swift 3D to animate it. Take a look at the finished movie to get an idea of what we are building.

NOTE

Strata has a complete animation toolset built in—even in the free version. We are importing models into Swift 3D because, at present, there aren't many 3D packages that have tools for models and animation, plus support plug-ins that will generate 3D output. The packages that do have these features are much more expensive than the tools covered in this chapter. You will know when you need them.

Conversion

The first thing you will have to do in order to animate your spaceship is to find a common file format between Strata and Swift 3D. Unfortunately, Swift 3D only supports incoming 3DS models, and Strata won't write to that format. The first bit of good news is that Strata *can* save your models in the DXF format, which is one of the most common media of exchange in the 3D world. The other good news is that there is no shortage of applications that will translate between these formats without losing any information that will matter to us for this type of project.

Find a conversion utility and use it to translate your DXF spaceship model (exported from Strata) into a 3DS model. If you already own any 3D applications, it is entirely likely that they can perform this chore for you. These are both very common file formats.

Materials

When you create a new Swift 3D movie from an existing 3DS model without any *material* (color) information, you will get the default gray color for the entire model. I still want to use a gray to start with, but a gray that better fits my conception of a Hollywood spaceship. Figure 20-16 shows the cursor dragging a material from the materials palette directly onto the spaceship.

If you exported your entire spaceship as one DXF and converted it automatically to a 3DS, you will not be able to ungroup the pieces of the spaceship to apply different colors to different parts. Fixing this is easy. You can either export your model from Strata one piece at a time or use modeling software that supports every aspect of 3DS.

Transformation, Selection, and Viewing

When I opened my version of the spaceship—possibly because of the conversion utility I used—the orientation of the model was off by 90 degrees. If you used my sample files to apply a material to the space ship, or if the tools you are using for

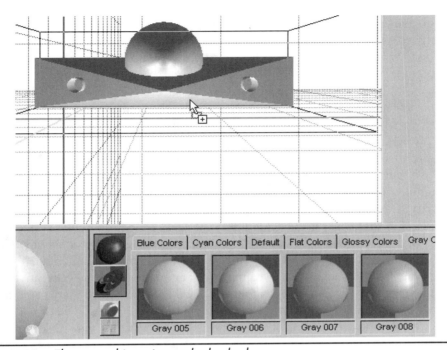

Figure 20.16   *The spaceship going to the body shop*

conversion produce similar results, you may have noticed that when the viewport says "Top-Active," you are really looking at the front of the spaceship. This is a good opportunity to get acquainted with the viewing, selection, and transformation tools in Swift 3D.

First things first: split the active viewport by either selecting View | Secondary Camera or by clicking on the little tool icon with two cameras in the main toolbar across the top of the screen. Some 3D applications make me literally claustrophobic, and the default view of Swift 3D is one of them. If you have multiple monitors, the best arrangement seems to be to undock the property tools palette and put it on another monitor. At this point, your two viewports should be nice and big. Notice that when you mouse-over any tool button in Swift 3D, you get a pretty good tooltip. Most of them say exactly what they do (as opposed to cryptic, mumbo-jumbo names).

The viewports work a little bit differently in Swift 3D than they do in Strata. Try clicking on an area in either viewport away from the model, and drag. The default action of the mouse in a viewport is to pan. That's a nice feature, and a good indication that ease of use was probably one of the top considerations when Swift 3D was designed.

The other built-in view feature works when you drag up and down with the right mouse button: you zoom in and out. These two features make changing your view to suit your moment-to-moment needs practically subconscious.

The basic nature of the viewports in Swift 3D is a little different from most 3D packages. In Strata, for instance, when you build an animation, you drop an actual camera into your scene, complete with all the controls that a real-world camera has. You can follow what the camera is seeing by opening a separate window for it and then toggle back to the regular viewports to move your objects around your scene in a familiar environment.

In Swift 3D, the viewports *are* the cameras, and vice versa. There are two main areas of impact where this is concerned. First, it is easier to keep track of simple animations, because you know exactly what you are getting. The second way this affects you is that you have to be very careful when you animate cameras. This is because you only get one camera to capture your animation. If you get creative, you can animate a standard view (top, bottom, etc.) and use it as a secondary camera, but then you lose your ability to view and select in that view.

Selecting and moving objects is also very easy. The first time you click in a viewport, you are activating that viewport. The next time you click, you are selecting the object you click on, or panning the viewport, depending on where you click.

Rotation is handled with Swift 3D's 100 percent unique transformation tools, which they call Crystal Trackball. The next step in the project is to correct the position of the spaceship, so that front is front and top is top. Select the spaceship in the front viewport and go to the rotation trackball. You can constrain the rotation of objects to a number of increments, which is especially handy if you are getting started with 3D concepts, have a small monitor or low resolution, or just have jittery hands. Click once on the constrain angle button to get the flyout menu as shown next and click on 90 Degrees.

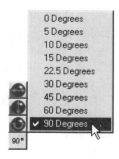

Next select the arrow that points up and down (above the constrain angle button). Pull the trackball down until it snaps 90 degrees. You should now have an orientation you can work with.

Finally, scaling follows the same concept as the easy zoom control: dragging toward the center of the object scales down, and dragging away from the center scales up. To enter scaling mode, select Edit | Scaling Mode or just click on the scaling mode button on the main toolbar. Following the guiding principle of ease of use and quick workflow that pervades Swift 3D, scaling mode automatically exits to the default move tool after every time you scale an object.

Animation in Swift 3D

Animation in this software is so easy that it is hardly worth mentioning the basics. We are going to incorporate a group of objects and a single object into the animation, each of which will move independently.

If you will recall the finished animation this project is intended to rebuild, there is a line of spaceships in the spaceship slow lane (moving slowly, all at the same pace) and one spaceship in the spaceship-pool lane going very fast. The first step is to lay out the ships as they will appear in the first frame of animation.

Using the copy and paste in top view, create an array of spaceships as shown in Figure 20-17. Notice that when you paste an object, it is in the same location as the copied object. This makes it easy to compose a line of objects with two sets of coordinates in common. Don't forget to apply a fast color to the fast spaceship.

SHIFT-select all the gray spaceships. You can't draw a marquee, since dragging in the open viewport causes it to pan. With all the gray ships highlighted, select Arrange | Group or press ALT-G. You now have a group of objects. This group will move as a single object when it is animated.

This is all the preparation that is required to produce the animation. With the group of gray spaceships selected, move the playhead on the timeline to frame 30, as shown in Figure 20-18.

You have to select the group of spaceships because each object has a parallel timeline. Selecting an object or group is how you tell Swift 3D that you want to edit the transformation of that object or group for that particular frame on the timeline. Right-click and drag your viewport to a very wide perspective and move the group of gray spaceships to where you think they should be at the end of the animation. This is easy to adjust if you don't like the result after you get the camera set up, so don't spend too much time worrying about it.

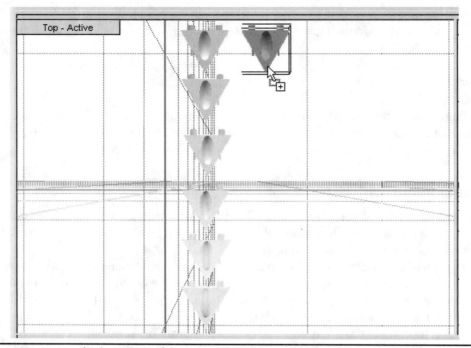

Figure 20.17   *Multiple copies of the spaceship object*

Next move the red ship to its position in frame 30. If it is going to go faster, it has to travel farther in the same amount of time, so move it far ahead of the group. Notice that the timeline automatically updates itself with keyframes and a green bar, representing a tweened parameter (location in this case). Figure 20-19 shows what your timeline should look like with either the red ship or the group of gray spaceships selected.

At this point, you should be able to play back the animation in one of the viewports and get a feel for how the action flows. Depending on your machine, you may need to switch to Outline display in the Layout portion of the property tools palette in order to keep up. Click Apply to make the change take effect.

Cameras

If you switch to rotating view in one of your viewports, the default view will be set to front, which is almost perfect for the starting point of our animated camera. Move

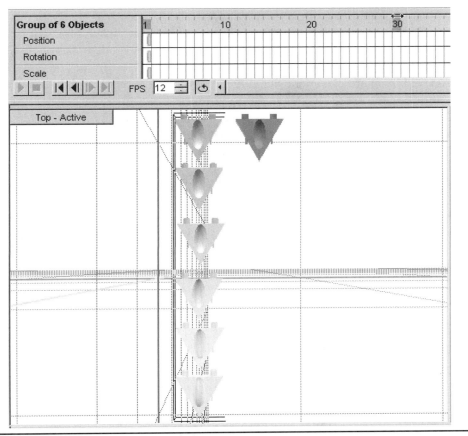

Figure 20.18   *Animating a group of objects*

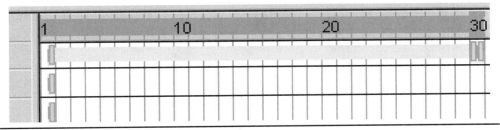

Figure 20.19   *A Swift 3D timeline with keyframes*

the playhead to frame 1 and drag the viewport so that you are looking down the center, between the two lanes of traffic, just above where the spaceships will pass. Switch to camera pan mode by selecting Edit | Camera Pan Mode or simply by clicking on that button on the main toolbar. If there are any keyframes on the timeline when you are in camera pan mode initially, delete them by right-clicking on the timeline and selecting Delete All Keyframes.

When in camera pan mode, every transformation you make applies to the camera instead of the models in the scene. Notice that the trackball now shows arrows, which represent the current orientation of the camera.

Move the playhead to frame 20 on the timeline. This is where the camera will stop following the fast spaceship because it has whooshed by too quickly to keep up. This is a cinematography trick that is approximately 12 years older than the hills—the closer you are to something when it goes by, the faster it appears to go.

Change the constrain angle measure on the trackball to 10 degrees and rotate it straight down until you have the red car in your camera in this frame. If you have to adjust the position of the red car at this point, be careful and *think* about what you are doing before you go grabbing things.

First of all, don't grab objects from within your camera view. Keep another viewport open for this. In this animation, the right view makes the most sense. Your camera should remain in camera pan mode, and the individual viewports will remember this state. In other words, at this point in the animation, you can activate the right view, and the camera pan button on the main toolbar will automatically toggle off. When you go back to the rotating view (your camera), the camera pan view button remembers its state and toggles back on until you turn it off.

Next, don't break up your tween without good reason. If you need to move the position of the red ship in frame 20, move its position in frame 30 in right view.

Finally, render your animation by selecting File | Export. The rendering engine is very efficient; you will probably have your finished SWF within a couple minutes. While it is rendering, you can't use the rest of the components of the Swift 3D package (you can't work on your animation or a model within it, but you can edit). Nor can you choose to render on a machine to which you are networked. This should be incentive enough for you to keep your movies small, which users at the end of a 28.8kbps line will appreciate.

Primitive Character Animation

swiftDuck.swf

If you look at the animation *swiftDuck.swf* in the Examples folder, you will see a terse, basic character animation: a duck who takes two steps (waddles), sits down as the camera moves, and finally, puts his head down. This movie is included as an example of another potential application of the combination of tools we have covered in this chapter.

This animation was made following this pattern:

1. Create the duck model in Strata using the techniques discussed in this chapter. The only primitives that were altered from their original shape were the body (lifted Bézier vertex on a sphere for the tail and tweaked one tangent handle for the chest) and the bill (tweaked one Bézier vertex of a pyramid for the upper lip and one on each side to round the top of the bill). The feet are extruded 2D paths drawing with the Bézier tool.

2. Export the model in pieces. To do this, select everything you don't want to export and hide it (CTRL-3); then save as DXF. Repeat until you have exported all the parts.

3. Paste all the DXF files into one 3DS file (if you have a modeling application that directly supports a 3DS), or into individual 3DS files otherwise.

4. Import the 3DS scene or individual 3DS files into Swift 3D. Now you will be able to color the pieces individually.

5. You have a few options for how to make the body parts move together. The most logical way would be to animate the points that are connected; then group them, animate the superset, and so on, until you are moving the entire duck. Or you could do it the lazy way, like I did—moving each part individually, more or less frame-by-frame.

While this particular animation definitely goes into the reject bin, I think this workflow has some potential to liven up the current spinning-logos-only world of Flash 3D. You could easily make some engaging character animation with a little talent, skill, and careful planning. For instance, when you are building the model in

Strata, you could make the axis at which the legs intersect the pelvis (or whatever a duck has that is like a pelvis) the center of the model, so that the legs automatically rotate around the correct origin.

If you are interested in 3D character animation, there are a few subjects to dig deeper into. You will want to get Strata's powerModule1, which gives you two big requisites for high-quality character animation, IK and Mirror. (You typically construct just half of the model and mirror it across an axis.) You should also check out Tomas Landgreen, the undisputed heavyweight champion of Flash 3D character animation. His site, http://www.titoonic.dk/, contains a number of characters that are extremely entertaining and engaging, regardless of the medium.

At the time of writing, it seems that there are a lot of Flash developers who do character animation in 2D cartoon style; but when it comes to 3D, they do spinning logos and solid objects flying in and out. I hope this overview of 3D will spur you to explore at least some of the easier possibilities in 3D.

Faking Real-Time 3D with Scripting
clothespin.fla

There are several big, obvious drawbacks to the current state of Flash 3D, but many of these can be solved with the simple trick of using a series of photographs instead of going through the mess of modeling, converting, animating, and rendering to SWF. Some of these problems are as follows:

▶   One of the Internet applications that is supposed to be a growing outlet for 3D art is e-commerce. The idea is that consumers like to look at products and touch them—somehow interact with them—before they buy anything. There are actually several problems with modeling a product for real-time 3D manipulation in a Web browser, including the cost of 3D production and plug-in compatibility.

▶   Moving models in real time in 3D space requires processor power and a plug-in with native support for 3D.

▶   A typical Flash 3D animation is not interactive in any way. It might as well be a QuickTime movie, or, more accurately, it would be much better off as a QuickTime movie.

▶   A level of detail in 3D Flash *vector* animations that rivals raster rendering is much heavier and requires exponentially greater processing power than a bitmap equivalent. Clearly, this is not what Flash is meant for.

The example *clothespin.fla* on the CD illustrates one way you can do interactive 3D without the 3D. It addresses the issues above and provides an easy solution to both interactivity and photo-realism within Flash. The movie is nothing more than a series of photographs (composed with high-quality equipment) and a little logic to move between the photographs. The object that rotates in this example was bisected with a thumbtack on the bottom side, which in turn was run through a white piece of paper marked with the rotations. If you try this type of fake 3D, you will need some kind of similar system to measure the rotations and position of the object exactly. You don't have a prayer if you try to eyeball it.

You can also fake real-time 3D with scripting by merely adjusting the horizontal and vertical scale of the object as it moves across a static 3D backdrop.

Real 3D with Scripting

At present, there is widespread interest in building real-time 3D rendering engines within Flash ActionScript. This area is very interesting to anyone who might be into 3D gaming programming, or even those who are just interested in a challenge in ActionScript.

There seems to be a well-defined, very low limit on the complexity of the models you can manipulate within Flash (less than 100 polygons), so you will not see a Flash port of Quake 3 Arena any time soon. This is one of those areas that, while it may develop into something of far-reaching utility someday, is currently in a theoretical stage. Some of the most promising experiments I have seen in this area are by Brandon Williams and Ethan Kennedy. You can see their work at http://www.homepages.go.com/~ahab_flash/exper/index.htm.

If you are interested in building real-time 3D for a well-established platform, you might want to check out Macromedia Director. Besides being one of *the* defining tools in multimedia, with all kinds of support for audio, video, and necessities for CD-distributed projects, Director also supports real-time 3D. In fact, there are multiple *Xtras* (third-party extensions) for Director that each do a tidy job of real-time 3D.

Amorphium Pro—A Different Approach

There are several reasons Amorphium Pro is listed separately from the main discussion of 3D. One is that the product was released within a week or so of the deadline for this book, and it took a few days to acquire it, so I didn't have much time to think about it. More importantly, though, Amorphium Pro is so completely divergent from conventional 3D packages in so many ways that it really creates its own category. Amorphium Pro is also a little more expensive than other tools in our roundup (about $370 retail).

At the highest level of overview, Amorphium is a professional 3D tool that happens to export directly to SWF using its native tools. If being used in big Hollywood films is a yardstick of success, Amorphium Pro is very successful. In short, it is recognized by 3D professionals in media outside of Flash. This is a valuable indicator for people coming from a non-3D background into a market filled with tools of all levels of quality.

The most striking thing about Amorphium Pro is its comprehensive set of tools for modifying a polygon mesh interactively with brushlike tools. Most of the tools are for deforming the mesh. I hesitate to call it "modeling," because it is so different from what I am used to, but that's what it really is—modeling with brushes.

The tools to modify texture mapping are even interactive, using the brush model. There are some tools that modify the mesh in ways that serve the interest of traditional 3D, such as the MeshMan set of tools shown in Figure 20-20.

This set of tools is a comprehensive set of solutions to the problems created by Amorphium's unique brand of modeling. The tooltip in the image labels the decimate tool, which reduces the number of polygons in an object, analogous to Flash's optimize curves function. What is even more amazing about this smart tool is that you can apply it to sections of the polygon that you select with a mask tool, which also uses a paint-on, interactive brush approach. These tools will also patch up ripped or torn polygon meshes, a common symptom of trying to automatically weld objects together into a single model.

At first the polygon deformation tools in the Tools section of Amorphium Pro struck me as gimmicky and not very useful for modeling. However, they grew on me fast. As you can see in Figure 20-21, the number of parameters and options available for each tool does give more control than the basic concept would suggest.

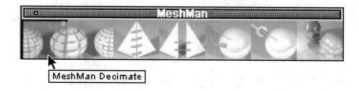

Figure 20.20   *Amorphium Pro's Mesh-Man toolset*

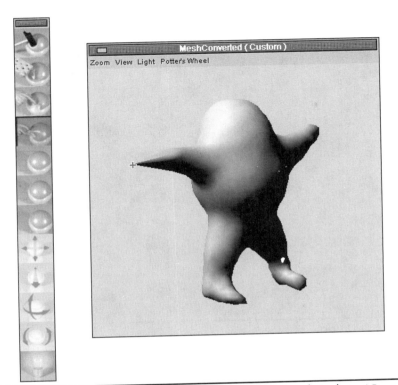

Figure 20.21   *The obligatory space creature, drawn with brush tools in AP*

The basic concept of the mesh deformation tools is that you have a brush—there is a built-in palette, plus you can edit the brushes or build your own—and this brush is used in conjunction with a number of tools to either push or pull on the mesh.

The most striking toolset in Amorphium Pro is called Wax. The idea behind the wax tools is that you add, subtract, or smooth a mass of wax with brushlike tools. Using this set of tools takes some getting used to. After spending a couple of hours with the software, I still found the results of my brush strokes to be less than 100% predictable. That said, I should point out that I was able to create a recognizable model within minutes, and people who have used the tool seem to operate effortlessly in this style of modeling. If you are interested in getting some quick gratification in 3D modeling, I can't think of a faster way than wax. Figure 20-22 shows an extruded appendage made with a single brush stroke.

There are plenty of other tools in Amorphium Pro for building, coloring, and texturing your model. Some of the more novel features include an Effects toolset,

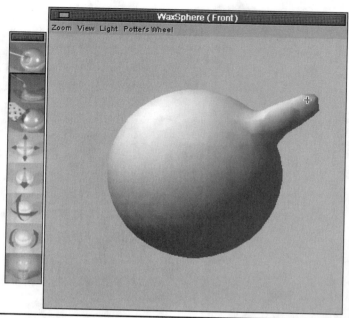

Figure 20.22   *An extrusion made with wax*

pictured in Figure 20-23, a "Potter's Wheel," which spins the model on an axis to allow you to get at every angle uniformly with the brushlike tools. I used the Potter's Wheel to paint the head of the character I created, which I estimate saved me at least 20 or 30 seconds on that simple job alone. It would have been hard to select the head with a marquee since it is not exactly symmetrical. The concept of the Paint toolset is one of the more orthodox interactive brush-type tools in Amorphium Pro.

While I personally wouldn't use Amorphium Pro as my *sole* application for modeling, it does have a surprising range of features for a tool in this price range, even before you consider SWF output. There are a number of tools that are typically found in very expensive 3D packages, such as HeightShop, which uses the light and dark areas of an imported image to deform a mesh. This type of tool is often used to assist in modeling complex shapes, like the surface of a lake.

I especially like the texture mapping functions because they are so easy and intuitive to use and produce good results. This function is of little consequence

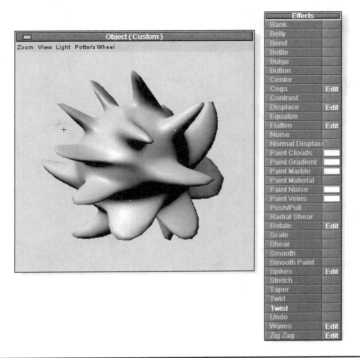

Figure 20.23   *Space mace made with drag-and-drop parametric Effects*

for Flash output, but if you are interested in 3D for any other medium, this feature is worth a look. You can import models of many varieties, including 3DS and DXF.

Amorphium Pro has a good set of standard features for viewing, selection, and animation. Figure 20-24 shows a context menu for a mesh sphere, which has a large number of options arranged in a sensible hierarchy. This is another feature reminiscent of much more expensive 3D packages.

Amorphium does a good job at rendering in any medium. Figure 20-25 took a matter of seconds to render at full size and full color. It is worth mentioning that this is the very first model I made, while still disoriented and skeptical. It still only took about 5 to 10 minutes to make, and came out with satisfactory results.

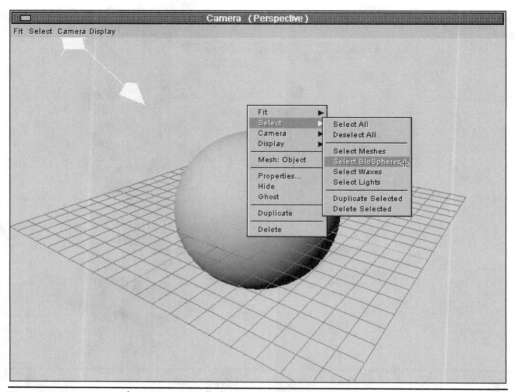

Figure 20.24 *Amorphium Pro's well-designed context menu*

The cool thing about rendering SWF is that Amorphium Pro will composite all shadows and render them on any surface, just like a regular raytracing renderer for bitmap output. This gives an added depth to SWF stills and animations that you might prefer to plain gradients or flat colors. Amorphium Pro has more parameters for rendering SWF than any other application I've seen so far.

While a professional 3D artist is not going to throw away his polygon modeling tools for Amorphium Pro, the application definitely lives up to the promise of providing an intuitive, easy-to-use modeling paradigm for 2D artists. There is no reason you couldn't start creating interesting, organically shaped 3D right out of the box.

Another way to look at Amorphium Pro is that the interactive tools are a great addition to your 3D toolbox. I can imagine a lot of applications for using Amorphium Pro as a last stop to touch up, paint, and texture a model. In addition,

Figure 20.25   *Final render of a rough-and dirty space man*

it is a great tool for assembling, painting, animating, and rendering models
that you build in another application like Nendo and Strata. If you want to produce
high-quality SWF 3D in an environment with lots of features, and you can afford to
spend a *little* bit of money on a 3D tool, Amorphium Pro is definitely worth a look.

What to Take Away from This Chapter

A survey of the current state of Flash 3D is worth its own section of a book, so I
won't pretend to cover it comprehensively in the closing notes of this chapter. I do
want to point out, however, that we are still at the very dawn of time concerning
Web 3D. In addition, Flash is not the only medium to convey 3D on the Web.

The aspiring Flash 3D artist could easily be discouraged by the astronomical gap in
function and price between established SWF-native tools like Swift 3D and the next-best
workflow. At present, the next-best workflow seems to be industrial-strength tools that

support SWF output plug-ins, like 3D Studio Max. If you haven't priced this class of tools, think "six months' mortgage."

The good news is that the gap is filling in slowly, and a smooth gradient of price ranges and functionality for the Flash developer is on the distant horizon. You can now export SWF directly from Poser using the Poser Pro Pack, which is far from low cost, but it does represent grown-up 3D functionality closer to the price range I like. Between the first draft and the first revision of this chapter, I got my first look at Amorphium Pro, which is, to my knowledge, the first real 3D modeling and animation package with native support for SWF output.

As a parting shot on 3D, I have assembled a list of big issues in Flash 3D to think about as you decide whether to plunge headfirst into this world.

▶ This chapter doesn't scratch the surface of the huge collection of topics in 3D; it merely points to a few places where you might like to start scratching.

▶ While 2D animation in Flash has its roots in traditional ink-and-cell animation, 3D is more closely linked to film. The sets of ideas that govern the two are more different than they are alike.

▶ You have probably heard Flash developers talk about how important it is to start with a storyboard for an animation, and this is, in fact, necessary to create coherent animations. This is exponentially more important in 3D. Starting a 3D animation within the 3D software package is roughly equivalent to starting production of a motion picture by rounding up 150 movie union employees on a multimillion dollar soundstage and saying, "I dunno…what do *you* feel like making a movie about? Who should we call to star?"

▶ The development of 3D for Flash is in a peculiar place right now. There definitely is no standard workflow or standard toolset. There is not even unanimous agreement that 3D content in Flash should be vectors and not raster movies. There will be more development before the dust settles.

▶ A lot of Flashers waste a lot of energy talking about expensive 3D packages. Expensive tools don't offer any advantage to 3D artists who aren't so well versed in the basics of modeling, animation, texturing, and so on, that they acutely feel the limitations of low- and no-cost tools like Strata, Nendo, and Blender.

▶ Finally, 3D tools are a means to an end. Good 3D animation (the film *Toy Story*, for example) begins with clear reasoning for why 3D is an advantageous medium for the story or user task. All 3D doesn't need to be superslick character animation with a brilliant story, but all 3D does have to present an advantage in order to be useful.

CHAPTER 7

Maximizing the Development Environment

IN THIS CHAPTER:

Making the most of the tools you use in any vocation is a matter of efficiency, and there are many compelling reasons to try to maximize your efficiency in working with any tool. For one, all people tend to value time more as they grow older. It seems that the more cognizant you are of a finite nature of your body's timeline, the more you realize the potential of each unit of time. In addition, the more efficiently you work, the better your work tends to be. If you spend less time worrying about the same nuts and bolts issues over and over, your mind is free to take on bigger tasks.

Basic Principles of Efficient Work

Without getting too philosophical or building enumerated lists, a few generalizations can safely be made about efficient work in the context of Flash development, and Web development in general. The overarching principle that holds together all of the ideas we will talk about is really centered on the nature of the modern desktop PC, a class of machine that includes both platforms for which the Flash development environment is available.

This machine has been conceived, designed, and developed over decades as a replacement for the old mainframe computer. At any point in computer history before the advent of the personal computer, most people probably would have guessed that the majority of the world's computing would be done by a huge central machine of ever-increasing complexity, maintained by professionals, while the majority of users would work at dumb terminals on a network, with smaller, self-contained machines being extremely specialized for individual applications. As you know, this is not what happened, and this central verity of the machine you use for Flash development is one of the keys to fostering good work habits.

Because the modern PC is designed to be able to do anything and everything—all at once—you are not limited to using a single tool at a time. You are also not limited to using tools exactly as they were designed. Many combinations of tools, especially in any kind of development that involves graphic arts, can work together in ways that are more efficient than other combinations. Another factor is the ability of some tools to be extended by the user.

Your PC is your own in every sense. There is nothing in the world that holds you to the default installation of anything on your computer, from hardware to software—even the operating system. Everything is up to you.

Never Do the Same Work Twice

Even though you would think that the idea has fallen out of fashion in recent years, any *successful* business owner will tell you that the only way to make money is not to spend it. If you have a sensible budget, it is typically a lot easier to make your top line than it is to make your bottom line.

The same is true of budgeting time, but to an even greater extent. You have a fixed number of hours in the day; that never changes. The only way to make the most of your time spent in any endeavor is to minimize the amount of time spent on the least valuable activities. In terms of working within Flash, this means reducing the number of steps required to perform any task, from coding to backing up data. Most of this chapter focuses on the idea of creating shortcuts for yourself for the tasks that you are ready do.

Keeping a Tidy (Electronic) Work Area

If you ever have to go *looking* for a file in a project—you navigate to one directory, find that it's not there, then remember where you *did* put it—you probably don't have a clear conception of how to organize files. The most helpful thing you can do to avoid wasting time organizing the files for your projects is to pick one model and stick with it. It doesn't matter what the model is.

Directory Structure

The first thing I do when I start any project, even a chapter of a book, is build the directory structure. The structure is pretty much the same for any project, whether it is a chapter in this book, an entire Web site, or a specific application that is part of a larger project. The following list is a summary of my personal guidelines.

▶   No two unrelated projects share any folders.

▶   Different types of media are grouped in different directories within each project.

▶   The same generic names (such as "images," "SWF," "workingFiles") are used on every single project. This way, I automatically know where a particular file is on any project, because there's only one logical place for it.

▶   Each application within a project resides in its own folder, but the media used by each application that are common to the whole project still go in the respective media folders. For instance, a Web site with a bulletin board done in PHP will have a folder specifically for the bulletin board. If that bulletin board uses static images, those images will still be located in the same directory that every other page in the site uses as a repository for images.

▶   All projects in progress get backed up on some kind of removable storage daily. With CDs and CD burning hardware so cheap nowadays, there is no excuse not to back up data. Backing up your project ensures that you will always be able to find it.

You don't have to follow my system. In fact, I recommend that you don't; there are probably better conventions invented by *real* programmers that you could find if you did some digging. These are just conventions that I have arrived at after making lots of mistakes. The point is that however you organize a project, you should do it the same way every time, as much as it is in your control.

Version Control
homepage01.fla, homepage02.fla, homepage03.fla

Flash doesn't have a history palette, and publishing to a directory different from the one in which the FLA is saved is a little clumsy. This leaves the developer in a dilemma regarding version control. If you are building just one FLA, with the output being embedded in one of the template HTML pages, it is easy to simply move to a new folder whenever you make a significant change. However, this scenario probably doesn't describe your typical needs.

The easiest way to maintain distinct, progressive versions is to designate the output directory explicitly in the Publish Settings (CTRL-SHIFT-F12), as shown in the following image. That way, you can rename your FLA, save it as a successive version number, or otherwise alter it, and the output directory and filename remain the same. If you enter the name of a directory that does not exist, Flash will give you a friendly error message to let you know that the publish function failed.

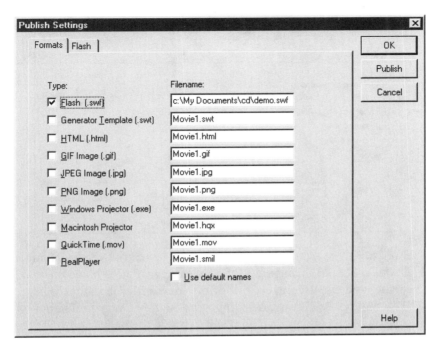

You can also move your FLA to successive version folders in a directory for working files, as you would if it were the only file in the project. When it comes time to test the SWF output with the other files in the project, instead of using Publish (SHIFT-F12), Test Movie (CTRL-ENTER), or any of the default methods that produce a SWF in the same directory, you can use Export (CTRL-ALT-SHIFT-S) to compile the SWF in the folder where it needs to be to work with the project. This keeps you in the Flash authoring environment, as you can see in the next image. The time you save here is in either moving files around between folders manually or renaming files for the sake of version control.

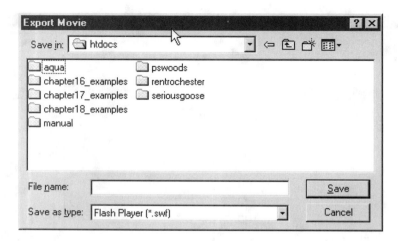

Another possibility is naming the FLA itself by sequential version numbers, for instance, *homepage01.fla, homepage02.fla, homepage03.fla*, and so on. Using this naming scheme, you can keep every one of the source files in the directory where the final SWF will reside. To avoid having to constantly change references to the SWF because of its changing name, you can override the name of the SWF in Publish Settings (CTRL-SHIFT-F12).

Every time you are about to try to add a new feature to your Flash movie, save the FLA as a new version. The new version will retain the publish settings from the previous version. When you're done with the final version, move all of the FLAs to a directory for source files.

When saving subsequent versions, keep an informal version history in the form of scribbled notes on a scratch pad. That way, when you want to backtrack, you can easily find the point where you went astray without having to open each version and poke around. If you use Dreamweaver in conjunction with Flash, a good place to keep your version history for all parts of you project is in the Design Notes palette that exists for every file.

Building for the Production Server

If you find more than a few problems with your project the first time you move it to the production server, chances are you haven't done a good job of modeling the server on your development machine.

Mirroring the Production Server on Your Desktop Machine

Chapter 15 described how to install the Apache Web server on a Windows desktop PC. If you use any kind of server-side application in your project, this is a bare necessity. By mirroring the server's directory structure on your development machine, you minimize the possibility of pointing to the wrong location throughout the project.

When I'm developing any kind of project that involves server-side functionality, I leave the Apache running the entire time I'm working. In addition, I use the project management feature in the text editor EditPlus to keep all files in the project easily accessible. Since EditPlus allows you to view files through your local server, it becomes very easy to view any application with live data, even with a Flash front end. I typically settle on an HTML page to frame the Flash content early on, then disable the HTML publish feature in Publish Settings (CTRL-SHIFT-F12), as seen here:

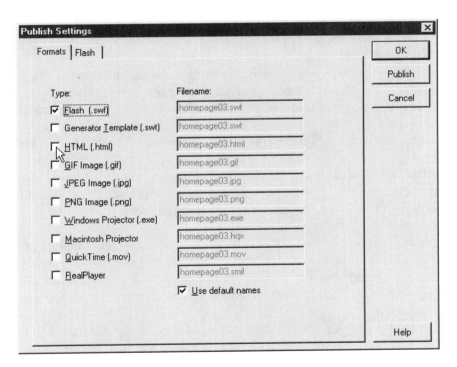

Using this scenario, it is fast and easy to see exactly how the application will behave on the production server, with the only variable being the difference between the operating systems. It is as simple as pressing ALT-TAB (to switch to EditPlus), then CTRL-B (to preview the selected file served from http://localhost...).

Hopefully, Flash will have a similar feature someday in the future. For now, you must come up with some way to emulate your production server on your development machine. If you use ASP, JSP, or ColdFusion, you can emulate server behavior within Macromedia's Dreamweaver UltraDev.

Changing Your Homepage

Another quick solution to Flash's lack of the integration with local servers is to change the homepage in your browser to the homepage of your project on your local server. Changing this is a matter of a few button clicks; then it can potentially save you from typing "http://localhost/community/myFlashChatteroo.php?threadID=frontPage" 65 times manually. Some of the better browsers offer you the ability to have multiple homepages, one for each window.

Using Relative Addresses

Another thing to watch as you try to build a project that will translate to the production server without changes, especially if you use a visual HTML editor, is paths. If you're not careful, some editors will add absolute addresses to links. You can do this manually if it seems easier at the time—for instance, if you want to point to a resource that is much higher in the directory structure. In other words, you may be tempted to type **http://localhost/login.php** instead of **../../../../login.php**.

Avoid this temptation. If you are using the same directory structure on your local machine, and you use relative addresses throughout the project, there's no reason that everything shouldn't work immediately when you move your project to the production server.

Of course, if you are working on-site or on an in-house project for your employer, the best scenario is to build your application where it will live. In other words, make an .htaccess protected directory where you want the final application to be, then move your source files and remove the password protection when the application is ready to go live.

Experienced Webmasters have lots of different tricks for this type of scenario. The main point is to build the application such that you won't have to move it when it goes live. If you do have to move it, build it so that you won't have to change anything.

Testing Different Browsers in Publish Preview

You should always test your applications on every browser you wish to target. To do this effectively, you really need to keep disk images of different browser, version, and plug-in combinations on CDs, loading them onto your test machine and trying your project with each combination. This should be one of the last things you do before you go live with your project.

If you use any client-side scripting in your project, such as the JavaScript/Flash applications we built in Chapter 8, you will want to test your project in each major browser at each stage of development. This can be a real drag, especially if you're having trouble finding where a function breaks down. If you just open the published HTML page in a browser and reload it as you update your Flash movie, you will probably have to clear the browser's cache each time you reload in order to get the updated version of the Flash movie.

On the other hand, using the Publish Preview (F12) function is much quicker. The problem is that at present, this function is designed to work with your default browser or a single other browser designated by a shortcut in the directory named "browser" in the Flash 5 installation folder. The problem with each means of changing browsers is that it takes several steps, and steps take time.

If you haven't discovered it already, look at the browser directory inside the Flash installation directory. If you want to use a different browser for Publish Preview and for the help pages, you simply copy a shortcut to that browser into this folder. (Mac users also have to change the name of the shortcut to "Default Browser.") A full description of this process can be found at http://www.macromedia.com/support/ flash/ts/documents/browser_pref.htm.

Another reason this feature is handy is that some browsers besides your default browser might be better suited to viewing the help pages. For instance, Opera has a tabbed interface that lets you jump between pages within the same window. On the other hand, the process of moving shortcuts using Windows Explorer is too slow if you want to change browsers quickly, trying each one after you make a change in your JavaScript/Flash application.

I came up with an extremely primitive but effective solution to this problem. First, I created three browser shortcuts in a folder inside the Flash installation, as shown next.

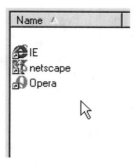

Each of these batch files contains two DOS commands. The first one deletes anything that exists in the browser directory. The second copies one of the shortcuts to the browser directory, switching the default preview. The code for these batch files follows.

```
del ..\Browser\*.*
copy ..\WTPD\Opera.lnk ..\Browser\Opera.lnk
```

CAUTION

These types of commands should be used with extreme caution. If you don't know DOS, it would be wise to do a little reading before using the potentially disastrous del command. If you hear your hard drive churning and nothing is happening on your monitor, you are probably erasing your entire drive.

Now I just have to run each batch file to change Flash's default browser. You will want to make the batch files easily accessible if you want to genuinely improve your overall usability. In other words, using batch files instead of manually moving the shortcut files is only beneficial if you can get to the batch files instantly. You may want to use a Windows Quicklaunch shortcut to their directory, or some other kind of shortcut.

This solution is the most primitive kind of application imaginable. Any experienced desktop application developer could come up with a better solution for a specific machine in a matter of minutes. The point is that you need to arrive at some means of performing common tasks with a button click or two. Since there is no way to extend the executable portion of the Flash development environment, you have to search for ways to create shortcuts to the tools you need.

The Permanent Library Feature

In contrast to hacking primitive batch files, the permanent library feature in Flash is an easy and reliable way of extending Flash. Saving reusable elements in your library is a classic example of not doing the same work twice.

You add a movie's library to your permanent library by saving it in the Libraries folder inside the Flash 5 installation directory. To use items in a permanent library, select Window | Common Libraries | [Name of the Library].

Shapes

There are many shapes that you may want to use often that are not convenient to draw within Flash. Even if you do use a vector illustration tool, like Illustrator or Freehand, putting reusable shapes into a permanent library will save you time. The reason for this may not be obvious; consider the steps you go through to bring a shape into Flash from another application:

1. Import the shape by either copying and pasting or choosing File | Import.
2. Ungroup the shape, possibly multiple times.
3. Convert the shape to a graphic symbol.
4. Open the symbol in order to edit it.
5. Select the shape within the symbol.
6. Use the info palette to position the shape at 0,0.
7. Exit the symbol editing mode to the main movie or parent Movie clip.
8. Position the symbol.

The funny thing is that this really doesn't *seem* cumbersome when you are doing it. For some reason, people just get used to doing mindless repetitive tasks, but the contrast between this list of steps and the steps required to bring in the same shape from a permanent library is striking. You simply position the symbol as you drag it onto the stage from the library palette. The ratio of steps required is literally 8:1.

The same concept applies to buttons. Most Flash developers use some kind of invisible button in every single application they build, but most do not keep an invisible button in a permanent library. This is just crazy. There's absolutely no comparison between the number of steps required to create an invisible button from scratch and the number of steps required to resize an invisible button from a permanent library. I keep two invisible buttons in my permanent library: one is perfectly round and one is perfectly square, each with a registration point in the upper-left corner, so that the defining shape starts at 0,0. These two buttons cover almost every situation that calls for an invisible button.

SmartClips

Chapter 10 covered using and building SmartClips. SmartClips are, without a doubt, the single easiest way to build reusable code objects and extend the Flash authoring environment.

Preloader

A preloader is one of the more obvious, and more useful, SmartClips you can put in your permanent library. First of all, every situation that requires a preloader is basically the same. You load a movie into a location (possibly _level0), and you need to show the user that something is loading, possibly showing progress. The logic for this type of application is exactly the same every time, so there is no need to build it from scratch for each project.

You can make a preloader SmartClip that takes as a variable the target path of the object being loaded. There are many preloader SmartClips like this available from independent Flash community sites like Flashkit and from Macromedia Exchange (http://macromedia.com/exchange).

Standard GUI

One thing that is lacking in most Flash Web applications at the time of writing is any kind of user-recognizable GUI elements. Take scroll bars, for example. While there is exactly one accepted standard (not counting middle mouse button or fingerwheel functions) for scroll bar functions outside of Flash in all applications on all platforms, I have yet to see a single Flash Web site that conforms to this most basic user control. Without going off on a usability tirade, suffice it to say that your Flash projects would not suffer from a standard set of controls, contained in SmartClips and reused in each application where appropriate. At the time of writing, one such SmartClip comes preinstalled with Flash 5: a drop-down menu.

Hot Keys

Having a good strategy for using hot keys is another way to reduce both the number of keystrokes required for any given task and the amount of brainpower you spend on mundane tasks. The amount of time and energy you can save is well worth taking a little time to really think through your strategy.

Reusing a Scenario from an Application You Know Well

Using hot keys in professional-quality applications is not simply a matter of memorizing the default assignments. Nowadays, just about any application worth its salt will give you the option of assigning hot keys yourself. This is especially true in applications relating to graphic arts.

The ultimate goal is to use the same set of hot keys for every single application you use. Software developers have long been mindful of the value of familiarity concerning hot keys, as witnessed by the standardization of the hot keys CTRL-S for save, CTRL-C for copy, and so on.

Different applications have different sets of tools, so you are never going to have the same set of hot keys, but you can use the same hot keys for similar tools between applications. For instance, many graphic artists–*cum*–Flash developers have a strong preference for Adobe imaging tools, namely, Photoshop and Illustrator. These two tools recently began consciously sharing hot keys as much as possible, which makes standardizing hot keys in every application used in the same production cycle all the more attractive.

Flash allows you to save your hot keys to any scheme you prefer. There are even predefined sets, including one that closely mirrors the default hot keys for Adobe Illustrator. Whatever scheme you choose, try to standardize the hot keys used for similar tools between applications as much as possible. This reduces the number of things you have to think about when you switch between applications.

Using Simple Keys for Things You Use Often

Anyone who has done a video tracing project like we did in Chapter 3, or a frame-by-frame, hand-drawn application, has probably grown weary of pressing four keys simultaneously to invoke the Optimize Curves (CTRL-ALT-SHIFT-C) function.

This is a prime example of a default hot key that would probably be better assigned to a simpler combination of keys. A few criteria for a good key combination for frequently used functions follow.

The keys should be close together. You should be able to find the key combination with your fingers (without having to look at the keyboard).

▶ The fewer keys in the combination, the better.

▶ If you can make any symbolic sense out of the letter combination, it helps you remember (such as CTRL-C for copy because *c* stands for "copy").

Making the best of these criteria and the existing array of hot keys I already use for Flash and Illustrator, I chose CTRL-Q for Optimize Curves in Flash. This hot key is used by default to quit most applications, but this is redundant for the Windows universal ALT-F4 to shut down an application. I also changed the hot key in Illustrator to CTRL-Q for Object | Path | Simplify. This is Illustrator's closest parallel to Optimize Curves.

Code

In general, good code is reusable code, and vice versa. Hopefully, you have learned a few good coding practices over the course of the book, and will continue to study programming proper. The next few sections will look at a few general considerations concerning how you write code, followed by the best options for storing reusable code.

Keeping It Tidy

One of the most effective and easiest things you can do to make your code easy to use in the future—either for yourself or for the next developer who works on the project—is to keep your code neat and organized. The following list shows just a few criteria for well-organized code.

▶ Indentation is uniform throughout.

▶ Naming conventions are consistent throughout (for example, either dot syntax or slash syntax for object paths, but not both; either underscore or capital letters between words in variable identities, but not both).

▶ Code is thoroughly commented.

▶ Each job is done in its own function, Movie clip, or other discrete container.

If you keep your code organized, you will save time the next time you use it. If the meaning of a block of code is clear at a glance, you can spend more time solving new problems and less time going over old ones.

Keeping It Modular

The last item in the list above is especially important to writing reusable code. If each function specializes in a particular task, you can easily copy it into a new application that requires a similar task. If, on the other hand, you follow the temptation to slug through an application with one block of spaghetti code, you are less likely to be able to reuse that code.

Keeping It

Regardless of where you keep it, you should always keep any code that you are pleased with and that you think you can use again. You should keep it in a place where you can easily find it and incorporate it into a new application. The old-fashioned way is to simply make a directory on your hard drive for each language you use, keeping each snippet in a separate text file. Different ways to save and organize code snippets are covered in the next sections on text editors.

Using the Best Tool for the Job

As wonderful as Flash is, it is not the only tool available for any given job. It's not even the only tool designed to be the primary authoring application for SWF output. When you become frustrated with a native tool in the Flash authoring environment, a little bit of research and asking around will usually point you toward a tool that is better suited to what you're trying to do.

Text Editor

The native text editor in Flash, the ActionScript panel, was a great advancement over the previous version, which offered just a tiny window with absolutely no formatting options whatsoever. That said, the ActionScript panel still has a long journey to becoming a full-featured text editor. If you do a lot of coding in ActionScript, you will want to choose an external editor with a fuller range of functions. I have already mentioned at least a half-dozen times in this book that I prefer derivatives of the NoteTab-style text editor, especially EditPlus.

Choosing an Editor with the Functions You Want

When you get to the point of becoming frustrated with the ActionScript panel, it will probably be easy to select an external editor because you will know which features you want. For example, some developers like to try alternative versions of the same function by commenting out one function while they try the other. When the first function you try doesn't work, you can add the comment notation "//" to each line of that function, then uncomment the other function. This is just one of many standard coding practices that a good text editor will automate for you. The following list shows some of the key features that I value in EditPlus that make my everyday work easier.

- ▶ Search and replace
- ▶ Search and replace using regular expressions
- ▶ Project management
- ▶ Clip text (snippets) library

Using an External Editor as Your Flash ActionScript Panel

If you use an external text editor as your primary tool for creating and maintaining ActionScript, you will run into the dilemma of wasting the time you saved by using a superior tool on the task of copying and pasting between applications. There's an easy solution.

A special syntax in ActionScript, #include "filename.as", allows you to pull in external files and evaluate them as ActionScript at the time the move is compiled to SWF output. This works approximately the same way as the PHP require() function.

My preference is to use an #include statement as a placeholder for the ActionScript that is developed as an external file and then copy the script into the ActionScript panel once it is complete.

The file extension .as was conceived for Flash 5 to denote an external ActionScript file, but it is not necessary to use this extension. You can just as easily use a text file with a .txt extension, or no extension at all.

Spending a Little Time Customizing Your Editor

The single most attractive feature of any good text editor is its extensibility. The most obvious form of this feature is the way in which a text editor can store and organize snippets of code for you. The time you invest in customizing your text editor typically pays off well if you do a lot of coding.

Specialized Image Editors

Since the time before Flash was even called "Flash," the basic concepts of the Flash native drawing tools have remained more or less unchanged, and during all those years, this set of tools has not had a single rival in the area of Web animation tools for hand-drawn cartoons.

On the other hand, at some point, a serious designer has to acknowledge that hand-drawn cartoons are not the only graphic art style available. Sometimes it makes more sense to compose your visual media in another application and then put it all together in Flash.

Vector Illustration

Despite Flash's obvious advantages in vector illustration, there are other vector illustration tools, most of which have been around a lot longer than the Internet as we know it, and therefore offer a lot of sophistication and range. The following list shows just a small sample of tasks that are easy to do in old-school vector illustration packages like Illustrator, Freehand, and CorelDraw, and not so easy to do in Flash.

▶ Combine paths according to parameters you specify.

▶ Attach text and objects to a path.

▶ Blend smoothly from one shape to another (like the Sticksville Star logo).

▶ Choose from multiple options for combining translucent objects.

▶ Perform multiple, independent transformations on an object (scale, rotate, skew).

▶ Use raster filters on vector objects. (Most filters can be used with the option of being nondestructive.)

Many of these functions can be mimicked in Flash, but they are less like useful functions and more like contrived, labor-intensive work-arounds. If you are responsible for composing vector art for Flash projects, you will have to buy a professional-quality vector illustration tool at some point. Don't worry, though; this will be less painful than it sounds. Macromedia practically *gives* you Freehand if you buy it as a package with Flash, and the upgrades are cheap once you own the current version. Adobe also has attractively priced bundles, especially their various collections. CorelDraw has always been less expensive than its competitors, and it is definitely a full-featured, professional-quality vector illustration tool. If you still aren't convinced, look for an older version of one of these tools. At present, each of these tools is in either version 9 (Freehand and Illustrator) or version 10 (CorelDraw), but the older versions can still be serviceable for a Flash developer. Computer shows and online auctions are good places to find legitimate, legal old-version software like this.

Raster Images

If you use raster images at all in your Flash applications, you should have a good bitmap editor. Even if you work with a graphic artist who works with the source and gives you the finished output, you can't have a good workflow if you rely on someone else for simple things like cropping, converting between file formats, and resizing. You can pick up the top-notch editor Paint Shop Pro for about $100.

Hardware

Hardware can make a big difference in how efficiently you can work in Flash. Having the right tools is a matter of nuts and bolts as well as zeros and ones.

Drawing Pad

Having a decent drawing pad does a lot of things for you—some obvious and some not. Obviously, the pad gives you greater control over illustrations by allowing you to draw naturally, recording your tip pressure, angle, and movement. The following list shows a few other, less obvious advantages of using a pad.

▶ Most designers use some type of pen for tasks other than drawing because they find it more natural and intuitive than a standard mouse.

▶ Most pads have hot spots at one edge that can be programmed to mimic hot keys, functions, or even macros. I use a Wacom Intuos 9 × 12 pad that has more than 20 hot spots.

▶ Some pads are compatible with a special mouse that has additional functions. I use the Wacom Intuos 4D mouse, which can trigger the hot spots on the pad, plus it has five mouse buttons and a fingerwheel. Each button (including the fingerwheel) can be programmed to mimic any hot key or function, just like the hot spots. In addition, combinations of mouse button clicks can be programmed. You can save a complete list of preferences for each individual application you use. I can hardly overstate how useful this little gadget is—it really saves me a lot of time.

NOTE

I don't get compensated in any way for pushing Wacom drawing pads—I just really like them.

Video Card and Additional Monitors

Even though vector illustration is designed for its file size efficiency, it can be taxing on systems to render complex vector art. In addition, developers need to have access to high color depth and good color reproduction. Another display consideration for developers is the ever-increasing complexity of IDE interfaces. The jump from the relatively simple Flash 4 interface to the Flash 5 palette-oriented interface is enough to make you scream for more screen real estate. Finally, if you get interested in 3D, a professional-quality card is all but an absolute requirement if you want to be able to see what you are working on. Redrawing your models— even as wireframes—can be too intense for standard consumer display hardware, especially if you use multiple views.

The solution to all these problems is having a decent graphics card. Obviously, developers who design strictly for the Web are under less of a burden to reproduce colors accurately than a print designer, but the rest of the considerations are the same. One particular type of card, the "Dual Head" cards made by Matrox, offers exceptional quality in 2D and 3D video output to two monitors from a single card. These cards are available in every possible price range.

Extra RAM

Being able to work without interruption using multiple imaging applications depends primarily on the amount of RAM available. In addition to buying more and/or faster RAM for your PC, you can install tray applications that help you manage allocation and free up unused memory. My personal favorite application of this kind for windows is MemTurbo (http://memturbo.com). If you have an application that is leaking memory, you can use MemTurbo to "scrub" all memory—physical and virtual—instead of rebooting. This is a great time-saver.

Keyboard

Now that you are fully converted to the gospel of shortcuts, you may want to reexamine the hardware you use to get to those shortcuts. There are keyboards made especially for people who write code, keyboards that are sized smaller so that all the keys are easier to reach, and even a one-handed keyboard that lets you input all the characters from a regular keyboard (http://halfkeyboard.com). This product is perfect for developers who work in drawing applications all day, because you can reach every hot key combination with one hand without straining or looking, while the other hand is free for the drawing pad.

What to Take Away from This Chapter

This has been a discussion of a few specific things that I do to make my work in Flash run more efficiently. Some of these things may be helpful; some may not. The most important practice you can develop regarding efficient use of your software is to think about efficiency. By simply being mindful of these issues, you are sure to find your own solutions as you work.

Tips and Tricks for Illustrator and Freehand

A t present, there aren't many tools to choose from for creating profoundly interactive SWF content. Although software companies are rapidly jumping on the bandwagon, adding SWF export ability to their tools and even creating tools designed for SWF output, you still have a choice of *one* IDE in which to put everything together with a complex underlying logic: Macromedia Flash.

Fortunately, choosing an illustration tool is not so easy. The big three vector illustration tools, Adobe Illustrator, Macromedia Freehand, and CorelDraw, have been around since "The Karate Kid" trilogy was a booming franchise. Over the decades, each tool has developed a deep, characteristic sensibility about how it creates vector images and how it presents its tools to the artist. The fact that there is enough demand to support the innovation of three similar tools over nine versions should tell you something about how powerful and specialized these tools are. You can find an interesting article on the history of Freehand at http://www.freehandsource.com/_frames/_news/_spotlight/_fh1/fh1_00.html.

This chapter is as much an admonition to acquire and begin using a vector illustration tool as it is an examination of specific techniques. My goal for this chapter is to encourage Flash developers who haven't yet tried a professional-quality vector illustration tool to give one a try and grow a little bit as an illustrator. The focus of the following tips is on things that are hard to do in Flash but fast and easy to do in any of the big three vector illustration tools.

Organizing Illustrations

One of the benefits of using a vector illustration tool that I value most is simply moving away from the Flash development environment to do purely creative work. In other words, sometimes it's nice to have one place in which to do the programming, tidying, and fussing over details (the Flash file), and another place in which to go wild and not worry about versions or cleaning up after yourself (the illustration software).

In addition to this psychological benefit, every professional vector illustration tool provides a few tangible features that are designed to help you organize your work. Some features are explicitly designed for organizing your work, while others simply lend themselves to organizational techniques.

Multipage Illustrations

If you have only used Flash for illustration in the past, multiple pages in an illustration may not seem like a big deal, but this feature was developed years after the basic toolset. In fact, Illustrator *still* doesn't support multiple pages with a special menu item or palette like Freehand and CorelDraw do.

It *is* possible to take advantage of multiple pages in Adobe Illustrator. There are two basic options: tiling and a third-party plug-in. To tile multiple pages, you simply expand the size of the artboard to accommodate the number of pages you want, then select Tile Full Pages in the Document Setup dialog (CTRL-ALT-P). The following image shows an artboard that is five letter-sized pages wide (42.5 inches) by three pages tall (33 inches).

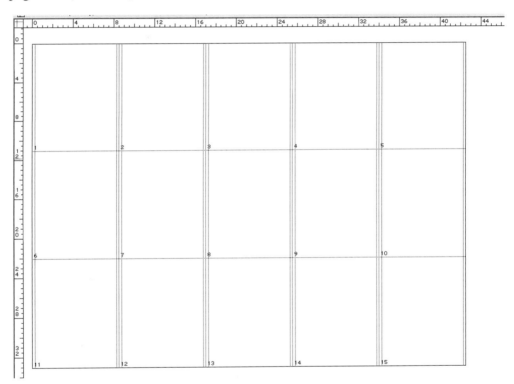

This is the perfect option for layout artists who are designing for print, or for anyone who conceptualizes an individual file as a single artboard, upon which all the relevant art is laid out. I personally prefer to be able to have many independent pages within a storyboard, with random access to each and the ability to delete individual pages. This is where the third-party plug-in MultiPage comes in. Figure 22-1 shows the interface. As you can see, MultiPage supports master pages, which is handy for composing an intricate illustration.

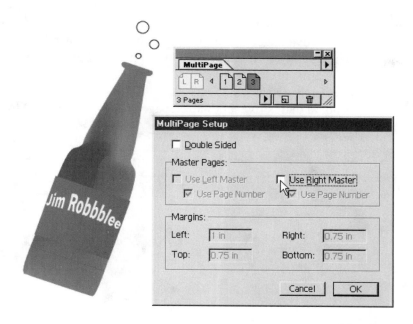

Figure 22.1 *MultiPage, a third-party plug-in, supporting master pages*

MultiPage gives you functionality similar to the multiple-page tools in Freehand and CorelDraw. Mileage will vary for artists in other media, but I believe this is an essential feature for Flash developers who do their own artwork in Illustrator. The following list shows a few of the benefits of creating art for Flash in a multiple page document in a vector illustration tool.

▶ Organization is easier. You can worry less about cleaning up your document and more about the creative side of the design task.

▶ You can use one idea per page. This helps isolate good ideas that might otherwise get lost and gives you space to develop them.

▶ Preparation of artwork for direct import into Flash is easier.

▶ You can use a custom page size for each page (such as 640px × 480px), instead of the printer's default page size. Freehand will even let you have different sizes for each page.

▶ Translation of your storyboards/proofs/whatever to most other media can be automated.

The only real drawback to MultiPage is that it uses layers to separate the individual pages. If you rely heavily on layers in your illustration style, you may not like that aspect. Plus, you have to print each page manually if you want a hard copy.

Freehand has a built-in palette to manage pages. To add another page to your file, choose Add Pages from the Options drop-down on the pages palette:

Within the palette you have three zoom levels for viewing the layout of the pages relative to each other. The more pages you have in a composition, the smaller you will want to make them in the palette. You can navigate between the pages by clicking on them in this palette, and the artboard will immediately update with the contents of that page. Finally, you can rearrange your pages in Freehand by simply dragging them in the pages palette. The order in which you place the pages in the pages palette will be the order of the pages for all other purposes, including printing and Flash import. The order goes from left to right, top to bottom. Some of the page view features are also available in the status toolbar:

Templates

Another handy way to easily organize your sketches, doodles, fizzled ideas, and your final artwork is templates. Templates in the major vector illustration tools are similar to the Movie Properties dialog in Flash, only with more options. In Illustrator, you have your choice between two templates, based on the two color modes. When you create a new file with the default method (CTRL-N or File | New), you get the following dialog. You can also create a new file using the last template and settings you used with CTRL-ALT-N.

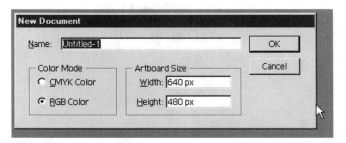

Illustrator templates save your brush sets, swatches, and patterns, so you can save yourself a lot of time in the long run by customizing your templates with the things you use often. This saves you from having to set up your work area from scratch each time you create a new file.

Freehand works similarly, with the added bonus of a symbols palette like Flash's. By using a template with design elements in a symbols library, you can start a new file without having to migrate the work you know you want to keep. When you are sketching for a new project, simply drop the keepers into the symbols palette (literally drag them to the palette and drop them in). For instance, you might devise a logo and color scheme and get them approved by your client. At that point, you can drop the logo an any other commonly reused design elements into your symbols library, clear the artboard, and save the file as a template. The following image shows the Dr. Ezekiel's Snake Oil design elements in a Freehand template.

To save a template in Freehand, simply go to the File | Save As dialog, as seen in the following image, and navigate to the place where your templates are stored in the Freehand application directory. Choose Freehand Template in the Save as Type drop-down menu and give it a name, as shown next. To use this template as the default for every new file, go to the Document tab in File | Preferences and type in the name of your template. In Illustrator, you just overwrite the *Adobe Illustrator Startup_RGB.ai* file in the Plug-ins directory.

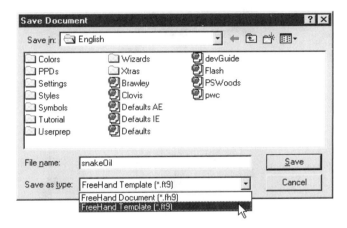

Hide and Lock

Compositions can become crowded, and the more methods you have to deal with the clutter, the better. Flash does implement a lock feature within the development environment (Modify | Arrange | Lock), but it is limited to symbols. This does not lend itself to the kind of smooth working processes you can achieve in Freehand and Illustrator using the hide and lock features.

In Illustrator, you can hide an object or group of objects by selecting them and using CTRL-3 (Object | Hide Selection). To show all objects, use CTRL-ALT-3. Currently, you cannot select which hidden objects to unhide, which would be a nice feature. Locking and unlocking objects in place works the same way, using CTRL-2 and CTRL-ALT-2, respectively.

In Freehand, the hide and show functions are in the View menu. They are not assigned a keyboard shortcut by default, but you can add them in File | Customize | Shortcuts. The Lock (CTRL-L) and Unlock (CTRL-SHIFT-L) features are found in the Modify menu.

Hide and show are especially useful when you are working with individual vertices. For instance, if you have a path made with a pen tool directly over a complicated brush stroke (which also contains PostScript path vertices), you have a much easier time if you select the brush stroke and either hide it or lock it before you begin working on the path on top.

Layers

The concept of layers plays out about the same in Flash as it does in the major vector illustration tools, but a few points are worth mentioning. In Illustrator, each layer can contain its own stack of layers:

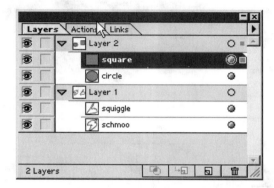

This is, in fact, the same scenario as in Flash, with two exceptions. Flash doesn't show you the order of the layers within each layer. The other difference is that when you overlap paths and fills in Flash, they automatically combine, whereas with Illustrator (and Freehand), you choose from a great number of ways to combine overlapping paths. More on this later.

The Freehand layers palette is a little different. Instead of the usual symbols for New Layer, Delete Layer, and so on, that you find at the bottom of a layers palette, all the functions are combined in the Options menu. The most confusing thing you will run into in the Freehand layers palette is moving an object between layers. To do this you have to select the object, select the destination layer, and select Move Selection to This Layer from the Options menu:

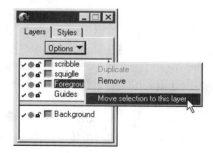

Color Selection

Illustrator and Freehand were designed and developed for print media, so it comes as no surprise that they both have comprehensive sets of tools for managing every aspect of color in a composition. Many of these tools focus on the fundamental challenge of getting your creation onto paper in exactly the right colors, which is of little consequence to us Flash developers. There is, however, one tool that is worth dwelling on for a moment: Freehand's color selection tool, aka the mixer.

The problem with most computer software that is supposed to help artists mix colors is that it focuses on everything but the one thing that matters: the visual perception of colors. While RGB or CYMK values are accurate ways for one machine to describe colors to another machine numerically, they don't say much about how the colors appear to the human eye. To illustrate, ask any nonartist to describe any randomly chosen color. The first component of the color's description you will get in every case, without exception, will be the hue of the color. "Reddish brown" or "green" or "bluish gray" would be typical answers. The next thing people notice about colors is the cumulative effect of their saturation and brightness.

While all art software does let you pick colors this way, I particularly like the way Freehand graphically represents this reality. As you can see in the following image, the *color wheel* is the selection tool for colors in the mixer palette. The color wheel, at least at some level, is the basis for most color theories, so however you conceptualize colors and their interaction, the color wheel in Freehand's mixer palette gives you a familiar and intuitive way to pick colors.

All of the operations involving color in Freehand can be executed by dragging and dropping color chips, as shown in the next illustration. Here you see a custom color being dragged from the mixer to the color list, which serves as a sort of custom color palette for your composition. The list starts off blank by default, except for three universal swatches.

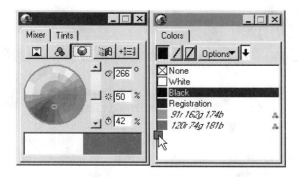

I like this color system a lot because every step in choosing the colors themselves and combining those colors in a composition has a direct analogy in the GUI. When you pick a color, you find your preferred hue and saturation on the wheel and then use the slider to control the brightness. When you decide on colors you like, you can save them in the color list, so that you are looking only at your choices for this composition. There is even a special palette to show you a smoothly graduated array of tints for the selected color. I find it easier to create harmonious color in Freehand than in any other vector illustration tool I have tried.

CorelDraw also deserves special mention for its color picking tools. While it doesn't strike me as being as intuitive as Freehand's, it is based on HSB by default and features a little flyout display of many closely related colors for each swatch in the selected palette, as seen here:

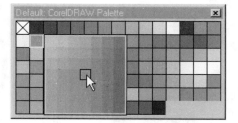

Incorporating Raster Plug-in Effects

Not surprisingly, Adobe Illustrator has a great system for applying bitmap filters within a vector illustration. The best part is that many bitmap filters can be applied nondestructively as what Illustrator calls Effects. Effects can be applied, kept while other transformations are made, then discarded later without losing any of the transformations. Consider Figure 22-2.

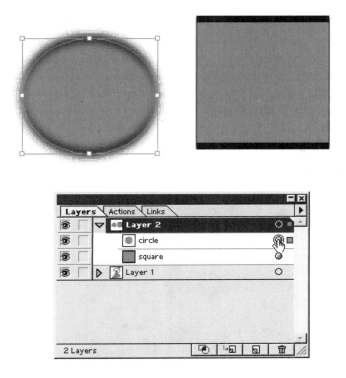

Figure 22.2   *The ellipse showing that a Gaussian blur has been applied to it*

A Gaussian blur has been applied to an ellipse. The little circle in the layer palette indicates that *some* appearance attributes have been applied to this object. If the circle were empty, that would mean that the object has no appearance attributes. At this point, you can either drag the circle to the trash can to remove the effect without changing the shape of the ellipse, or drag the circle to another layer to apply the same appearance attributes to the object(s) on that layer.

CAUTION

Raster filters are cool and fun, but they will invariably cause the objects they affect to be exported as bitmap elements when you bring them into Flash. These filters are best used only when vectors will not do the job effectively, as in rendering a convincing, natural texture.

Path Combination Functions

Way back in Chapter 1 we did a project where we combined several circles to make a single outline in the shape of a snake. This particular shape was easier to do in Flash than it would have been in most vector illustration tools. This is because Flash combines overlapping paths on the same layer using the same logic, no matter what your goals are for the particular shapes. This works out well in some cases, such as the snake, but in other cases you want to have more control over the way you combine paths. Look at Figure 22-3.

You could combine the paths shown on the left to produce the single path shown on the right, but this would require both your attention to tedious details and a lot of mindless work. In Illustrator, you just select the Unite button in the pathfinder palette, and it's done. Freehand uses a similar set of tools in what it calls Xtras. CorelDraw will also do these types of path operations, but from a dialog-style interface.

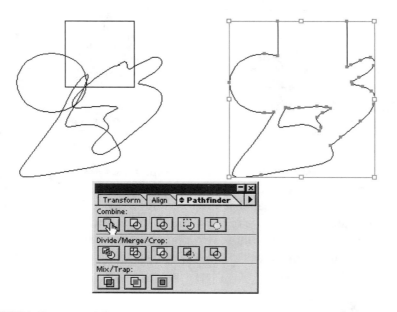

Figure 22.3   *Combining paths in Flash or Illustrator, which is much simpler*

A Better Bézier Toolset

The Bézier toolsets you find in each of the big three vector illustration tools are much more versatile and powerful than the simpler implementation in Flash. Table 22-1 shows the modifier keys for each of these applications' main Bézier tool. If you don't already know these, you should learn them. Having total control over the Bézier tool at a very low level of brain activity is essential—not only to vector illustration, but also to making paths for selection, masks, and so on, in raster imaging.

Each illustration package has its own extra additions to the standard Bézier tool. Freehand has an especially cool freeform tool. This tool incorporates behavior similar to the selection tool in Flash, so you can shape lines by pushing and pulling

Modifier	Freehand	Illustrator	CorelDraw
ALT	Makes the point being drawn a corner point. The first tangent handle is frozen in its current point when you first press ALT.	Makes the point being drawn a corner point. The first tangent handle is frozen in its current point when you first press ALT.	Makes the current point draggable.
SHIFT	Constrains angle of tangent handles to 15 degrees.	Constrains angle of tangent handles to 15 degrees.	(none)
CTRL	Makes the current point draggable.	Switches to most recently used selection tool.	Constrains angle of tangent handles to 15 degrees.
C	(none)	(none)	Converts the current point to a corner point.
S	(none)	(none)	Converts the current point to a smooth (curve) point.
SPACEBAR	(none)	Makes the current point draggable.	Ends path on current node.
Double-click	Ends path on current node.	(none)	(none)

Table 22.1   *Modifiers for the Bézier Tool in Illustrator, Freehand, and CorelDraw*

on them in any old place. In addition, you can click inside the path and push it outward, like painting with a brush, as seen in the following image. The resultant path is combined with the original to make one new, modified path.

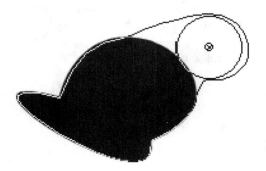

Cool Typography

As long as there have been mass media, typography has been one of the primary elements of design. Conveying meaning on multiple levels in type is a mark of a good designer. Each of the big three vector illustration tools is built with a set of tools worthy of the challenge faced by designers in creating compositions with engaging typography, from font management to horizontal spacing. One positive consequence of this emphasis on letters is the array of built-in tricks and gimmicks in each tool.

One class of function that is especially useful and easy is attaching a block of text to a path. This type of operation is next to impossible in Flash, but so easy in a good vector illustration program that it is hardly worth mentioning. For instance, Figure 22-4 shows the simple method by which text is attached to a circle in Freehand.

The text at the top and the black circle are simultaneously selected, and the Attach to Path button will run the text around the course of the path. You can also make an existing block of text conform to the inside of a path with the flow inside path tool, as shown in Figure 22-5. This example also uses the path combine tools discussed earlier in the chapter.

Adobe Illustrator has an especially cool tool for doing publishing-style layout in a graphics application: you can link text blocks so that one flows into the other. If you often need to prepare brochures and such for Web printing, this is a handy tool to

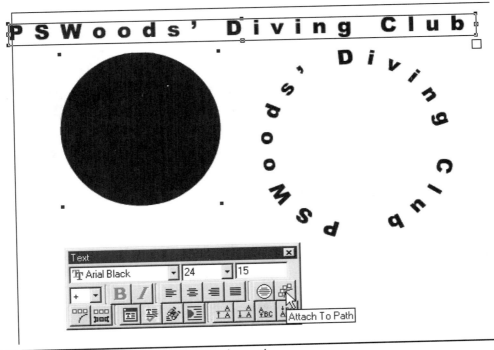

Figure 22.4   *Running text around a circular path*

have. You can prepare a single document and export one copy to SWF in order to use the Flash native printing capability, plus use the same document to publish a PDF document. The following image shows this function in progress.

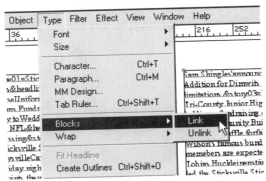

Figure 22.5   *Filling a path with the selected text*

To make text flow from one text area to another, first create a new text area by dragging the text tool. Next use the group selection tool (the other tool in the flyout with the subselection tool) and select both the new box and the box where the text starts. Finally, select Type | Blocks | Link.

What to Take Away from This Chapter

If you don't already own one of the tools discussed in this chapter, I hope it whets your appetite for a more powerful toolset for doing vector illustrations. If you already use Freehand, Illustrator, or CorelDraw, I hope you have found at least one little nugget you didn't know before.

The Appendixes

► Examples of Problematic Actions

► Online Resources for Flash-Related Topics

Examples of Problematic Actions

M any actions are easily forgotten or have a nonintuitive syntax. Although the Flash manual does an excellent job of explaining each action, this appendix is intended to provide you with a cheat sheet of those actions that most often seem to foster forgetfulness or mistakes.

This appendix is organized by ActionScript object, where possible. The first group of actions listed fall in the category of syntax, after which objects are listed alphabetically.

break

Example

```
for(keys in hugeArray){
    if(hugeArray[keys].indexOf("secretKey") != -1){
        output=hugeArray[keys];
        break;
    }
}
```

Comment

If an element in the array hugeArray is found to contain the substring "secretKey", the loop exits. Using break inside a loop saves you from performing meaningless operations after you have found what you are looking for. This is especially useful for functions that seem to move relatively slowly in Flash, like matching strings.

continue

Example

```
for(i=0;i<hugeArray.length; i++){
    if(hugeArray[i].indexOf("goodOne") == -1){
        continue;
    }...
```

Comment

If the current element in hugeArray does not contain the substring "goodOne", the loop exits to the top. This is different from break, in that you continue to loop through the control structure. continue is a handy action when you have a condition that you can test early in the loop and a whole bunch of operations after that test (like a complicated string manipulation) that you can skip if the condition tests a certain way.

delete

Example

```
delete myObj;
delete myList;
delete myXML;
```

Comment

The object myObj, the array myList, and the XML object myXML are cleared out of memory. This is something that doesn't seem to get done often enough in common Flash coding practice. When you know you have finished using an object, free up some memory by deleting it.

isNaN

Example

```
if(isNaN(loadNum)){
    loadNum = 0;
}
```

Comment

This evaluates whether the value of the variable loadNum is NaN (not a number). If this condition is true, loadNum is set to 0. This is a common scenario when you are evaluating the progress of something—in this case a MC preloader—where the initial value will return NaN.

print

Example

```
print(ph,"bmovie");
```

Comment

The MC instance ph is printed, using the bounding box located in the frame labeled "#b" in ph's timeline. This is probably the most common scenario for printing from Flash. You can also target a level of a movie.

printAsBitmap

Example

```
printAsBitmap(ph,"bmovie");
```

Comment

Prints the MC instance ph as a bitmap instead of vectors, using the bounding box located in the frame labeled "#b" in ph's timeline. This action is used to take advantage of transparent objects in the printable material. This method is remarkably slower on the hardware side (not the execution of the action) than the print method, so use it only when you need it.

return

Example

```
fullName=myNameIs("joe", "smith");
///------
function myNameIs(firstName, lastName){
    return firstName + " " + lastName;
}
```

Comment

The function myNameIs takes two arguments, concatenates them into a single string, and returns the string. The variable fullName will receive the value of the evaluated expression after return.

updateAfterEvent()

Example

```
onClipEvent (mouseMove) {
    _root.bugX=this._x;
    _root.bugY=this._y;
    updateAfterEvent;
}
```

Comment

The variables _root.bugX and _root.bugY are updated independent of the timeline (meaning that the loop doesn't wait for the playhead to enter a new frame to execute). The combination of this type of handler and updateAfterEvent() is superior to an onClipEvent(enterFrame) handler when you want to execute code to coincide precisely with user events, independent of the movie's frame rate, and stop executing the code when the user event ceases.

var

Example

```
var myVar=5;
```

Comment

The scope of the variable myVar is defined as the level on which the code executes. When you use var with an object within a self-contained block of code, such as a function, the object (usually a variable) is wiped from memory after the function finishes. In the first example in the "Date" section later in this appendix, var is used to ensure that a new Date object is used each time the code executes.

Array

An array is the easiest way to structure data within ActionScript. The following actions are ones that don't have a descriptive name, have a tricky syntax, or are otherwise tricky.

concat

Example

```
myDog=new Array("fleas","burrs");
symptoms=new Array("gas","aggressive behavior");
anotherDog=myDog.concat("ticks","dandruff");
worstDog=anotherDog.concat(symptoms);
```

Comment

First the arrays myDog and symptoms are created. Then the values "ticks" and "dandruff" are added to the array myDog to make the new array anotherDog. Finally, the array worstDog is a combination of the two previous arrays.

join

Example

```
myString = myList.join("|");
```

Comment

The variable myString now contains a long string, with a pipe character separating the values from myList. You might want to use this method when you want to save multiple values in your Flash movie as a cookie on the user's machine. You can then use the String.split("|") method to reconstruct your original array.

length

Example

```
numValue = myList.length
//echo each element in an array
for(i=0;i<myList.length;i++){
    trace ("element number " + (i + 1) + " is " + myList[i]);
}
```

Comment

The variable numValue gets the number of elements in the array myList.

slice

Example

```
newList=myList.slice(0,3);
```

Comment

The array newList is made up of the first four elements of myList, which remains unchanged.

splice

Example

```
myList.splice(0,3,"newVal1","newVal2","newVal3");
```

Comment

The first three elements of myList are deleted, then replaced with "newVal1","newVal2", and "newVal3".

toString

Example

```
myList=new Array("milk", "cheese","bacon");
commaDel=myList.toString();
```

Comment

The variable commaDel receives the string value of all the elements in myList, in order, delimited by a comma. This is the same thing you would get with String.join(",");.

unshift

Example

```
myList.unshift("newVal1","newVal2","newVal3");
```

Comment

The values "newVal1","newVal2", and "newVal3" are added to the beginning of the array.

Date

The date object has a large number of methods, but the meaning of most is so transparent that these methods can hardly be expounded upon in text. The following two examples show a couple of practical uses for the date object.

Clock.fla from Chapter 11:

```
onClipEvent(enterFrame){
var myDate=new Date();
mySeconds=myDate.getSeconds();
myMinutes=myDate.getMinutes();
myHours=myDate.getHours();

//you know how the hour hand doesn't jump all at once? - it just creeps?
hourAdjustment=myMinutes/2;

_root.minutos._rotation = myMinutes*6+180;
_root.secondas._rotation = mySeconds*6;
_root.horas._rotation  = myHours*30 + hourAdjustment + 180;
}
```

Excerpt from *Postcard.fla* in Chapter 17:

```
// create a unique ID
elDato = new Date();
hub.id = elDato.getTime()+hub.sender.substring( 0, 2);
```

Key

The key object gives you built-in access to important user events relating to the keyboard. These actions are especially handy for games.

DOWN

Example

```
down.diffX=0;
down.diffY= -5;
down.keyVal=Key.DOWN;
```

Comment

This code is from the example *itemAction.fla* in Chapter 11. This is one of four definitions for Movie clips that control the motion of a character in the game.

getAscii

Example

```
onClipEvent(keyDown){
    keyboardMap.currentKey=Key.getAscii();
}
```

Comment

Each time the user presses a key, the variable currentKey in the MC keyboardMap is updated to the ASCII code of the last key pressed.

getCode

Example

```
onClipEvent(keyDown){
    keyboardMap.currentKey=Key.getCode();
}
```

Comment

Each time the user presses a key, the variable currentKey in the MC keyboardMap is updated to the key code of the last key pressed.

isDown

Example

```
if(Key.isDown(Key.ESCAPE) {...
```

Comment

Tests to see whether the keyboard ESCAPE key is pressed.

isToggled

Example

```
if(Key.isToggled(20)){
    output="Release your caps lock, please.";
}
```

Comment

Returns true if the CAPS LOCK (key code 20) is toggled (CAPS LOCK is on).

LEFT

Example

```
left.diffX=5;
left.diffY=0;
left.keyVal=Key.LEFT;
```

Comment

This code is from the example *itemAction.fla* in Chapter 11. This is one of four definitions for Movie clips that control the motion of a character in the game.

RIGHT

Example

```
right.diffX= -5;
right.diffY=0;
right.keyVal=Key.RIGHT;
```

Comment

This code is from the example *itemAction.fla* in Chapter 11. This is one of four definitions for Movie clips that control the motion of a character in the game.

UP

Example

```
up.diffX=0;
up.diffY=5;
up.keyVal=Key.UP;
```

Comment

This code is from the example *itemAction.fla* in Chapter 11. This is one of four definitions for Movie clips that control the motion of a character in the game.

Math

The math object solves many problems that were previously solved with long, inefficient kludges. The ActionScript math object is a faithful implementation of the ECMAScript math object. Therefore, you may want to use http://www.devguru.com as your default reference for this object.

abs

Example

```
theTangent=Math.abs(yDistance)/Math.abs(xDistance);
```

Comment

This piece of code is from an old-fashioned way of tracking the angle between two objects. The quadrant of the angle is figured in a different section of code, so Math.abs is used here to get the absolute value of each distance.

atan2

Example

```
onClipEvent (enterFrame) {
    xDistance=_root._xmouse-_x;
    yDistance=_root._ymouse-_y;
    correctRotation =
Math.atan2(yDistance,xDistance)*180/(Math.PI)+90;
    this._rotation = correctRotation;
}
```

Comment

The method atan2 is the easiest way to calculate the angle between two objects. This is so because you can use two arguments, the vertical and horizontal distance between the objects, to figure the angle on an absolute scale. The scale is –PI to PI.

ceil

Example

```
roundUp=Math.ceil(rawNum);
```

Comment

The number rawNum is rounded up to the next nearest whole number that is greater than or equal to rawNum.

floor

Example

```
roundDown=Math.floor(rawNum);
```

Comment

The number rawNum is rounded down to the next nearest whole number that is less than or equal to rawNum.

pow

Example

```
//Do not use this method!
```

Comment

At the time of writing, this method produces unexpected results. Several Flash developers have written their own custom objects to replace Math.pow and posted them in discussion groups. I would recommend that you either obtain one of these or write one yourself (it's not brain surgery).

random

Example

```
with(_root["arrow" +i]){
_x=Math.random()*600 +10;
_y=Math.random()*760 +10;
_rotation=Math.random()*360;
scaleFactor=Math.random()*50;
_xscale=scaleFactor+50;
_yscale=scaleFactor+50;
}
```

Comment

The Movie clip instance defined by _root["arrow" + i] is placed, rotated, and scaled according to various multiples of random numbers.

round

Example

```
var myWholeNum=Math.round(myNum);
```

Comment

The number contained in the variable myNum is rounded to the nearest whole number and assigned to myWholeNum.

sin

Example

```
mySin=Math.sin(myAngle);
```

Comment

The variable mySin gets the value of the sine of myAngle.

sqrt

Example

```
_root.distance=Math.round(Math.sqrt((xDistance)*(xDistance)+(yDistance)
 *(yDistance)));
```

Comment

The Pythagorean theorem. The variable _root.distance is the square root of the sum of the squares of the respective horizontal and vertical distances.

Movie Clip

As the name suggests, the Movie clip object gives you access to methods and properties of movie clips. There are several new additions in Flash 5.

attachMovie

Example

```
document.attachMovie("headline","headline" + HLCounter, HLCounter+5);
```

Comment

The MC exported from the library as "headline" is attached to the MC instance called "document," given an instance name defined by ("headline" + HLCounter), then placed on the level defined by (HLCounter + 5). The position of attached Movie clips is 0,0 by default, so if you need to repeatedly attach an MC and put it in the same place, it makes the most sense to use a static placeholder in that place. A placeholder can be as simple as a blank Movie clip.

duplicateMovieClip

Example

```
bugMC.duplicateMovieClip("bugMC" + counter, counter);
```

Comment

The instance bugMC is duplicated, given an instance name described by ("bugMC" + counter) and placed at a depth described by the variable counter.

getBytesTotal and getBytesLoaded

Example

```
onClipEvent(enterFrame){
    loader.outputText=Math.round(ph.getBytesLoaded()/ph.getBytesTotal) * 100;
}
```

Comment

The text field outputText is continuously updated with the percentage of bytes loaded in the ph MC instance.

getURL

Example

```
//open a page in a new browser window
getURL (this.storyURL, "_blank");
//trigger a JavaScript event
getURL ("javascript:alert('hey');");
```

Comment

See the comment in the code example.

globalToLocal

Example

```
onClipEvent(mouseMove) {
    coords = new object();
    coords.horiz = _root._xmouse;
    coords.vert = _root._ymouse;
    globalToLocal(coords);
}
```

Comment

The object coords tracks the mouse position on the stage in the properties horiz and vert, which are subsequently converted to reflect the mouse position relative to the MC local coordinates. This is handy when you want to track the position of the mouse relative to a Movie clip. Instead of subtracting to find the difference in position on each axis, the converted coordinates *are* the difference on each respective axis.

hitTest

Example

```
if(this.hitTest(_root.memo)){
    _root.killor();
    }

//or
if(_root.memo.hitTest(this._x,this._y, true){
    _root.killor();
}
```

Comment

Tests whether the current Movie clip (this) overlaps the instance _root.memo. The second half of the example is another iteration of the same idea, only the shape of _root.memo is taken into consideration. It seems that the second method is more accurate for irregularly shaped objects, but this example only tests the registration point of the current Movie clip. If the current MC were very large, you would perceive an inaccuracy when it hits _root.memo on the side opposite its registration point.

loadMovie

Example

```
loadMovie (mc + ".swf", _root.ph);
   _root.ph._alpha=40;
```

Comment

The external SWF described by (mc + ".swf") will be loaded into the instance _root.ph.

loadVariables

Example

```
loadVariables ("postcard.php", this, "GET");
```

Comment

The Flash Player sends an HTTP GET request to postcard.php. The returned variables will be loaded into the MC in which the code resides ("this"). When you are having trouble with the action, try leaving off the HTTP request method argument. In the Flash IDE, this is represented as "Don't Send."

removeMovieClip

Example

```
for(MC in _root){
   if(MC.indexOf("menuItem") != -1){
      _root[MC].removeMovieClip();
   }
}
```

Comment

This loop removes any MC in the _root level that is named anything containing "menuItem". RemoveMovieClip() only works for MCs that have been placed on the stage dynamically. This is another good argument for less hard-coding and timeline-based Flash and more single-frame, ActionScript-driven movies.

startDrag

Example

```
draggerMC.startDrag(true, 0,640,0,480);
```

Comment

The center of the MC instance draggerMC becomes locked to the mouse and can be dragged from the upper-left corner of the stage (0,0) to the lower-right corner (640,480).

swapDepths

Example

```
player.swapDepths(2);
player.swapDepths(otherPlayer);
```

Comment

The MC instance called "player" is moved first to a depth of 2, then swapped with the instance called "otherPlayer." For some reason this method is often presented as an advanced ActionScripting technique, but nothing could be simpler.

Selection

There are still several caveats to using the selection object effectively in a Flash movie that is embedded within an HTML page. However, the Flash 5 implementation of this object is a good start, and a good sign that Flash is rapidly becoming a comprehensive multimedia tool.

getBeginIndex

Example

```
onClipEvent (mouseMove) {
   _root.output01=_root.output02.substring(Selection.getBeginIndex(),
Selection.getEndIndex());
```

```
    updateAfterEvent;
}
```

Comment

This action copies the selection in the text field _root.output02 to the other text field, _root.output03.

getEndIndex

Example

```
onClipEvent (mouseMove) {
    _root.output01=_root.output02.substring(Selection.getBeginIndex(),
Selection.getEndIndex());
    updateAfterEvent;
}
```

Comment

This action copies the selection in the text field _root.output02 to the other text field, _root.output03.

getFocus

Example

```
currentField=Selection.getFocus();
```

Comment

The variable currentField gets name of the currently focused text field.

setFocus

Example

```
selection.setFocus("_root.lastName");
```

Comment

This method moves the cursor to the text field _root.lastName.

setSelection

Example

```
Selection.setFocus("output02");
Selection.setSelection( 0, output02.length-1 );
```

Comment

This code selects the entire contents of the text field output02.

Sound

Use the sound object when you want to dynamically control audio within your Flash movie. Chapter 11 includes a cool example that implements the sound object in a mixing-board styled application.

attachSound

Example

```
channel1.attachSound("crickets");
```

Comment

The sound symbol in the library that is exported as "crickets" is pulled from the library and associated with the sound object channel1. You can have multiple sound objects simultaneously, as in the CampsiteMixer example in Chapter 10.

start

Example

```
channel1.start( 0, 999 );
```

Comment

The sound associated with channel1 is started and set to loop 999 times.

String

There has been a lot of talk about the performance of Flash's string methods. While Flash will never perform as well as languages like C++, ActionScript's string object is perfectly suitable for small jobs. The following examples show some of the less obvious string methods.

charAt

Example

```
lastLetter=myString.charAt(myString.length-1);
```

Comment

The variable lastLetter gets the value of the last letter in the string myString.

fromCharCode

Example

```
values=new Array();
values=bigHunkaText.split(String.fromCharCode(124));
```

Comment

The array values is created and then populated. The values of the array are derived from the characters between the pipe (|) delimiter in the string bigHunkaText.

indexOf

Example

```
if(element.indexOf("headline") != -1){
```

Comment

Tests whether the variable called "element" contains the substring "headline".

lastIndexOf

Example

```
lastMention=storyText.lastIndexOf(myName);
```

Comment

The variable lastMention receives the value of the index of the string contained in myName, where it occurs last in the string variable storyText.

split

Example

```
values=new Array();
values=bigHunkaText.split(String.fromCharCode(09));
```

Comment

The array values is created and then populated. The values of the array are derived from the characters between the tab delimiter in the string bigHunkaText.

substr

Example

```
mySub=myString.substr(0, inputNum);
```

Comment

The variable mySub receives a substring of the variable myString. The length of the substring is designated by the user input inputNum.

substring

Example

```
articleID=element.substring( 8, 10 );
```

Comment

The variable articleID gets a substring of the variable called "element," starting at the character with an index of 8 and ending with the 10th character (the character with an index of 9). It helps me to think of substring() as follows. The first argument is the index where you want to start, and the difference between the second argument and the first is the number of characters you want to get.

XML

I had to figure out some of the XML methods for myself, since there was little existing documentation or examples. Hopefully you will have an easier time by following these examples.

appendChild

Example

```
myXML2.appendChild(myXML1.firstChild.firstChild.cloneNode());
```

Comment

A node from the XML object myXML1 is copied into the top level of the XML object myXML2.

attributes

Example

```
this.section = branch.attributes["name"];
```

Comment

The name attribute of the node described by the variable called "branch" is assigned to the variable called "section" in the current movie.

createElement

Example

```
newNode = new XML();
newElement = newNode.createElement("anotherNode");
myXML.firstChild.appendChild(newElement);
```

Comment

The newNode XML object is created using the necessary constructor. Then, a new XML element is created called "anotherNode", which is appended to the tree in the XML object myXML. You have to use appendChild (or another method of appending a node to the XML tree) with newElement. When you create a new element, it is not linked to anything; it will show in your debugger as a variable, not as part of your XML object.

createTextNode

Example

```
newNode = new XML();
newElement = newNode.createElement("anotherNode");
textElement = newNode.createTextNode("node value");
myXML.firstChild.appendChild(newElement);
myXML.firstChild.firstChild.appendChild(textElement);
```

Comment

The text node defined by the variable textElement is assigned to the child node below the node defined by the variable newElement. This yields the XML structure <anotherNode>node value</anotherNode> within the first child of the myXML tree. The structure is built with the appendChild() methods; the elements created by the createElement() method aren't nodes on any XML tree until you place them.

insertBefore

Example

```
newNode = new XML();
newElement2 = newNode.createElement("yetAnotherNode");
myXML.insertBefore(newElement2, myXML.firstChild.firstChild);
```

Comment

The node defined by the variable newElement2 is inserted before the first child node of the first child in myXML.

nodeName

Example

```
if(branch.nodeName == "url"){
    displayMC.url=branch.firstChild.nodeValue.
}
```

Comment

This tests whether the current node, denoted by the variable named "branch," is called "url". This is the most common way to find the data you are looking for inside an XML tree. When the example matches a node that is named "url", it looks for the value of the node inside it, which it assumes is a text node (for example, <url>http://pswoods.com</url>).

nodeType

Example

```
if(branch.nodeType == 3){...
```

Comment

This tests whether the branch referred to by the variable called "branch" is a text node. A text node is the content between the opening and closing tags in an XML document. You can use this as an extra precaution when you are moving through an XML tree, looking for a particular nodeValue (XML nodes do not have a node value) or as a way to extract all text elements from an unknown structure.

nodeValue

Example

```
if(branch.nodeName == "url"){
   displayMC.url=branch.firstChild.nodeValue.
}
```

Comment

The variable displayMC.url gets the value of the first child node within the current node. This is an easy way to get the values of text elements when you know the structure of the XML tree.

onLoad

Example

```
xmlObj=new XML();
xmlObj.ignoreWhite=true;
xmlObj.load("xml/Classified.xml");
xmlObj.onLoad=myOnLoad;
//------------------------
function myOnLoad(success){
   if(success){
      parser(xmlObj.firstChild);
   }else{
      output="Something went wrong. Sorry.";
   }
}
```

Comment

The default handler onLoad is extended with the function myOnLoad to evaluate the success of the load operation and set the function called "parser" in motion if the document is successfully loaded. This block of code is so standard that you will probably want to have it in your snippets library. Once you settle on a way you like to load an XML document, handle errors, and move through the tree, you can use the same code on every project.

parseXML

Example

```
xmlString="<message user=\"" + user + "\">" + input + "</message>";
newXMLObj=new XML();
newXMLObj.parseXML(xmlString);
```

Comment

The variable xmlString is parsed to create a new XML object called "newXMLObj."

sendAndLoad

Example

```
incomingXML=new XML();
myXML.sendAndLoad(input.php, incomingXML);
```

Comment

The XML object myXML is sent to the script input.php, and the script response is loaded into the object incomingXML. If there is no XML object to receive the incoming data, the data will simply evaporate.

XMLSocket

The XMLSocket object is used to create, manage, and send information across an open socket connection. The classic application for this type of data transfer is chats but the possibilities are limited only by your imagination.

onConnect

Example

```
mySock = new XMLSocket();
mySock.onConnect=myOnConnect;
mySock.onXML=myOnXML;
mySock.connect("localhost", 1998);
```

```
///--------------------
function myOnConnect(success){
   if(success){
       chatMC.output="connected\n";
   }else{
       chatMC.output="connection failed...\n";
   }
}
```

Comment

The necessary constructor for the XMLSocket object is used to create the mySock object. The standard handlers onConnect and onXML are extended to include events for each possible outcome of sending and receiving data. Finally, the Flash Player connects. This is another standard piece of code you will want to add to your snippets. There is hardly a way or a reason to do these tasks differently.

onXML

Example

```
mySock = new XMLSocket();
mySock.onConnect=myOnConnect;
mySock.onXML=myOnXML;
mySock.connect("localhost", 1998);
///--------------------
function myOnXML(doc){
   tempVar="";
   message = doc.firstChild.firstChild.nodeValue;
   userName = doc.firstChild.attributes["user"];
   tempVar= userName + ">>>" + message;
   chatMC.output=tempVar + "\n" + chatMC.output;
}
```

Comment

The necessary constructor for the XMLSocket object is used to create the mySock object. The standard handlers onConnect and onXML are extended to include events for each possible outcome of sending and receiving data. Finally, the Flash Player connects. This code is from the example *leChat.fla* in Chapter 18.

Online Resources for Flash-Related Topics

IN THIS APPENDIX:

3D

ActionScripting

Audio Tools

Flash Third-Party Tools

Text Editors

T his appendix points to a few off-the-beaten-path online resources. Some are the commercial sites of companies that make products related to Flash development, while other sites are intellectual resources.

3D

3D art is popular right now, to the point of being glamorous. An increasing demand for 3D art and animation in entertainment media has generated a whole new wave of 3D artists and a fresh batch of applications to meet their needs. One of the most frustrating things about getting started in 3D is that you almost have to make a decision about which expensive tools to buy before you can even get started. To aid in this respect, I have included a list of my favorite tools and where to find them online.

Swift3D

http://www.swift3d.com   Swift3D is one of the oldest and certainly one of the best established 3D tools made specifically for Flash. Swift3D gets a lot of attention in the Flash community, so you will be able to find lots of tutorials and community support. Swift 3D tools are simple, easy to use, and powerful enough to realize just about any noncharacter animation.

Amorphium

http://www.amorphium.com   To my knowledge, Amorphium Pro is the first full 3D package to include native support for SWF output. Its engine for SWF output is top quality, rendering shadows on all planes. While it is definitely not a standard 3D product, using a 100 percent unique approach to modeling, it is a good option for Flashers who want to create high-quality 3D without spending months learning how to model at the polygon level. Amorphium Pro also has a lot of features that make it attractive for traditional 3D artists, such as Morph, selective interactive smoothing with a brush tool, and Decimate, an intelligent function to reduce the polygon count in selected portions of the model.

Strata Software

http://www.3d.com/   When you consider the base price (free), you can hardly argue against Strata as being the best way to break into serious 3D. The base package does not include some tools I like for editing models at the polygon level, but this shortcoming is easily overcome. Strata can import your low-poly models built in other packages. Strata's rendering tools—even the ones that come with the free version—are top-notch.

Blender

http://www.blender.nl/   Blender demands, and gets, a lot of respect. The interface requires a little time to learn, but it is worth it. The tools built into Blender at present could probably get you through an entire career in 3D; and the functionality is ever increasing, thanks to the work of both open source community contributors and NaN.

Webreference 3D—Rob Polevoi

http://www.webreference.com/3d/   Rob Polevoi wrote the book on modern 3D—just search for his name at Amazon.com. His biweekly column covers three main areas: tutorials in a wide array of software packages, overviews of new tools, and trends and comparisons in the larger world of 3D. I have been doing 3D as a hobby for some time, and this has been one of my most valued resources for getting my bearings in a big subject.

Titoonic—Tomas Landgreen

http://www.titoonic.dk   This site contains the most adorable 3D characters you will find in Flash. This is a good source of inspiration for anyone aspiring to do 3D animation in SWF format. Landgreen does the only 3D work for SWF that I have seen so far that I would call "professional" or "real 3D."

Crossroads Conversion Tool

http://home.europa.com/~keithr/crossroads/   Crossroads is a freeware 3D model format conversion tool. If you want to exchange models between applications, but they don't support a common file type, this will probably work for you. There are many conversion tools of this type available commercially.

Curious Labs—Poser

http://www.curiouslabs.com/   Character animation is all the rage nowadays; and Poser is intensely focused on providing professional-quality 3D output for character animation with the easiest possible interface. You can sit down with the manual on a long and clear-minded afternoon and learn the basics of 3D character animation in Poser in one sitting, which is nothing short of amazing, when you consider your alternatives. With the recent introduction of the Pro Pack, you can now export your characteristic creations directly to SWF. The price tag (about $400 with the Pro Pack) may seem steep compared with some tools designed specifically for Flash, but this price compares favorably with other packages capable of both high quality character animation and SWF output. Such packages start in the thousands of dollars.

Winged Edge Technologies—Nendo

http://www.nichimen.com/nendo/   Nendo is good, old-fashioned polygonal modeling, at a price that is next to free ($100). If you want a comfortable environment in which to do precise modeling with total control, Nendo is perfect.

Martin Hash's Animation: Master

http://www.hash.com   If you get interested in 3D, you will probably start getting the urge to do some character animation. It's only natural. Animation: Master is simultaneously one of the best character animation packages available for any price and one of the least expensive 3D packages in any class. The quality of the rendered output is excellent. There are several small annoyances with A:M, such as the manual (apparently, the page layout was done by a software engineer), having to boot the program from a CD every time, and instability on machines with hardware that is incompatible or just set up wrong (most software is tolerant of that kind of thing). However, for the $2,000 to tens of thousands you will save by avoiding the high-end packages that Animation: Master seems to rival, you may be willing to make a few sacrifices. Animation: Master also features a thriving, open community, which produces a fun list (Animaster), free plugins for A:M, and a lot of entertaining animation.

Photomodeler Lite

http://www.photomodeler.com/Lite/   More and more, lately, there seem to be a lot of this type of tool popping up. The idea behind Photomodeler and the many similar applications is making a 3D model from photographs of real-life objects. This particular tool offers the advantage of being free.

ActionScripting

Flash is one of the most vibrant, open, and fun communities online. There are lots of resources for Flashers to share ideas and code, and even some devoted specifically to ActionScript. Here are few of my favorites.

Actionscripts.org Flash Tutorials

http://www.actionscripts.org/   This is a good resource for tutorials, FLAs, and news.

Figleaf Software's Flashcoders Mailing List

http://chattyfig.figleaf.com/   This is an amazing resource. The people on this list are all talented, accomplished Flash developers, and the discussion stays on topic like no other list I've subscribed to. Topics are limited to Flash coding issues *only*. The site is moderated by Flash guru Branden Hall.

Flasher Mailing List

http://www.chinwag.com/flasher/   This is another hangout for advanced Flashers. Unlike Flashcoders, the range of topics is not limited to coding.

Ultrashock.com

http://ultrashock.com/   Many FLAs from popular designers and Flash coders can be found here.

Audio Tools

The dilemma of choosing audio tools is similar to choosing 3D tools—you stand to spend a lot of money just to get started. There are many low cost, high-quality tools with which you can get a solid start. Here are some favorites.

FASOFT-n-Track Studio

http://www.fasoft.com/   This tool is a high-quality, no-frills multitrack recording studio for your PC. It supports many plug-ins.

Sonic Foundry Products

http://www.sonicfoundry.com/products/   Sonic Foundry makes Sound Forge and Acid. You can buy them directly from their site.

Syntrillium—Cool Edit

http://www.syntrillium.com/   Syntrillium makes Cool Edit and Cool Edit Pro, my favorite multitrack recording package.

Flash Third-Party Tools

Because the SWF file format has a freely available SDK, third-party tools for creating and editing Flash content are always popping up. Many of them are free. The following is a short list of some of the best values in the bang-for-the-buck category.

Action Script Viewer

http://www.buraks.com/asv/   Have you ever entrusted the safekeeping of FLAs to the client for whom you produced them? If you have, you have probably had to reconstruct those FLAs from scratch. This tool will extract your ActionScript from the SWF. ActionScript Viewer is also a nice alternative to the Movie Explorer and ActionScript panels when you are debugging a movie with a lot of code, especially since you can change the font in which the code is displayed.

Adobe LiveMotion 1.0

http://www.adobe.com/products/livemotion/   Poor LiveMotion doesn't get the attention it deserves in the Flash community. Part of the reason is that when it was first released, it was compared side by side with Flash. (I fell into this trap, myself.) If you look deeply into LiveMotion, however, you will discover a fundamentally different approach and a different set of goals. A few features that really stand out are importing and animating Photoshop layers, visually editable motion paths for all tweens, and drag-and-drop textures and styles. LiveMotion is at least worth checking out, especially if you do a lot of raster work.

BluePacific Software Flash Turbine

http://www.blue-pac.com/   BluePacific makes various versions of Flash Turbine, a server-side component that dynamically creates SWFs.

FlashJester

http://www.flashjester.com/index.htm   FlashJester makes many SWF tools, mostly for projectors. If you want to make a projector for a CD project in Flash, they may have a product that will help you.

Flashtool

http://www.flashtool.de/   Links to many third-party tools, including lots of clever little freeware apps.

SwiffTOOLS

http://swifftools.com/stools/   You'll find commercial tools for Flash developers, including projector applications for making CDs and screen savers.

Swift-Tools Swift-Generator and Swift-MP3

http://www.swift-tools.com/   Oliver Debon is the developer of Swift-Generator and Swift-MP3. See Chapter 19 for more information.

Wildform Flix and SWfX

http://www.wildform.com/   Wildform makes two important tools: Flix, which converts conventional video files to SWF, and SWfX, which creates hundreds of text effects. There are some other interests at the Wildform site, including tutorials.

Text Editors

A good text editor is kind of like a dog: It is always there with you. You either love it to death or you are vaguely sorry for ever getting it and secretly wish it would go away. In general, a good one makes your life a lot better, regardless of your former quality of life.

EditPlus

http://editplus.com/   This is my current favorite. Best features include previewing work via http://localhost and snippets libraries.

NoteTab—Text Editor

http://notetab.com/   The original and still one of the best text editors.

Ultra Edit—Text Editor

http://www.ultraedit.com/   This is another very popular programmer's text editor.

EvrSoft—1stPage2000

http://www.evrsoft.com/   This is a great IDE for HTML/JavaScript.

Miscellaneous

These two are not directly related to anything covered in the book. However, I feel that these tools are necessary for any serious Flash developer—if not these exact tools, then at least something similar.

WebSpeed Optimizer

http://www.xat.com/wo/index.html   This is a handy tool for checking the performance of your projects from any location. This tool simulates different transfer rates, so you can easily get a feel for the download times that different users will experience, even if you are testing on a local network.

Wacom Drawing Pads

http://www.wacom.com If you do visual art on a computer, you need some kind of drawing device. You might as well get the best. Many software manufacturers who produce visual art tools design applications with Wacom products specifically in mind. In other words, you can use any input device; but you will experience tighter integration with your software with a Wacom drawing pad.

Index

INTERNATIONAL CONTACT INFORMATION

AUSTRALIA
McGraw-Hill Book Company Australia Pty. Ltd.
TEL +61-2-9417-9899
FAX +61-2-9417-5687
http://www.mcgraw-hill.com.au
books-it_sydney@mcgraw-hill.com

CANADA
McGraw-Hill Ryerson Ltd.
TEL +905-430-5000
FAX +905-430-5020
http://www.mcgrawhill.ca

GREECE, MIDDLE EAST,
NORTHERN AFRICA
McGraw-Hill Hellas
TEL +30-1-656-0990-3-4
FAX +30-1-654-5525

MEXICO (Also serving Latin America)
McGraw-Hill Interamericana Editores S.A. de C.V.
TEL +525-117-1583
FAX +525-117-1589
http://www.mcgraw-hill.com.mx
fernando_castellanos@mcgraw-hill.com

SINGAPORE (Serving Asia)
McGraw-Hill Book Company
TEL +65-863-1580
FAX +65-862-3354
http://www.mcgraw-hill.com.sg
mghasia@mcgraw-hill.com

SOUTH AFRICA
McGraw-Hill South Africa
TEL +27-11-622-7512
FAX +27-11-622-9045
robyn_swanepoel@mcgraw-hill.com

UNITED KINGDOM & EUROPE
(Excluding Southern Europe)
McGraw-Hill Education Europe
TEL +44-1-628-502500
FAX +44-1-628-770224
http://www.mcgraw-hill.co.uk
computing_neurope@mcgraw-hill.com

ALL OTHER INQUIRIES Contact:
Osborne/McGraw-Hill
TEL +1-510-549-6600
FAX +1-510-883-7600
http://www.osborne.com
omg_international@mcgraw-hill.com

On the CD-ROM

The CD-ROM contains a large number of examples, primarily FLA. It is organized by chapter, with one chapter per subdirectory. The chapters that contain a large number of examples, or variations on the same example, or both, contain subdirectories within each chapter folder.

In the web connectivity section, some of the examples must either be moved to specific locations on your local web server or edited to reflect their actual location. Read the notes and cautions carefully in that section to get the examples working. All the examples have been tested at the time of writing and found to work properly. However, if you do find a mistake or bug, don't hesitate to tell me about it at the forum for this book located at http://pswoods.com/devguide.

WARNING: BEFORE OPENING THE DISC PACKAGE, CAREFULLY READ THE TERMS AND CONDITIONS OF THE FOLLOWING COPYRIGHT STATEMENT AND LIMITED CD-ROM WARRANTY.

Copyright Statement

This software is protected by both United States copyright law and international copyright treaty provision. Except as noted in the contents of the CD-ROM, you must treat this software just like a book. However, you may copy it into a computer to be used and you may make archival copies of the software for the sole purpose of backing up the software and protecting your investment from loss. By saying, "just like a book," The McGraw-Hill Companies, Inc. ("Osborne/McGraw-Hill") means, for example, that this software may be used by any number of people and may be freely moved from one computer location to another, so long as there is no possibility of its being used at one location or on one computer while it is being used at another. Just as a book cannot be read by two different people in two different places at the same time, neither can the software be used by two different people in two different places at the same time.

Limited Warranty

Osborne/McGraw-Hill warrants the physical compact disc enclosed herein to be free of defects in materials and workmanship for a period of sixty days from the purchase date. If you live in the U.S. and the CD included in your book has defects in materials or workmanship, please call McGraw-Hill at 1-800-217-0059, 9 A.M. to 5 P.M., Monday through Friday, Eastern Standard Time, and McGraw-Hill will replace the defective disc. If you live outside the U.S., please contact your local McGraw-Hill office. You can find contact information for most offices on the International Contact Information page immediately following the index of this book, or send an e-mail to omg_international@mcgraw-hill.com.

The entire and exclusive liability and remedy for breach of this Limited Warranty shall be limited to replacement of the defective disc, and shall not include or extend to any claim for or right to cover any other damages, including but not limited to, loss of profit, data, or use of the software, or special incidental, or consequential damages or other similar claims, even if Osborne/McGraw-Hill has been specifically advised of the possibility of such damages. In no event will Osborne/McGraw-Hill's liability for any damages to you or any other person ever exceed the lower of the suggested list price or actual price paid for the license to use the software, regardless of any form of the claim.

OSBORNE/McGRAW-HILL SPECIFICALLY DISCLAIMS ALL OTHER WARRANTIES, EXPRESS OR IMPLIED, INCLUDING BUT NOT LIMITED TO, ANY IMPLIED WARRANTY OF MERCHANTABILITY OR FITNESS FOR A PARTICULAR PURPOSE. Specifically, Osborne/McGraw-Hill makes no representation or warranty that the software is fit for any particular purpose, and any implied warranty of merchantability is limited to the sixty-day duration of the Limited Warranty covering the physical disc only (and not the software), and is otherwise expressly and specifically disclaimed.

This limited warranty gives you specific legal rights; you may have others which may vary from state to state. Some states do not allow the exclusion of incidental or consequential damages, or the limitation on how long an implied warranty lasts, so some of the above may not apply to you.

This agreement constitutes the entire agreement between the parties relating to use of the Product. The terms of any purchase order shall have no effect on the terms of this Agreement. Failure of Osborne/McGraw-Hill to insist at any time on strict compliance with this Agreement shall not constitute a waiver of any rights under this Agreement. This Agreement shall be construed and governed in accordance with the laws of New York. If any provision of this Agreement is held to be contrary to law, that provision will be enforced to the maximum extent permissible, and the remaining provisions will remain in force and effect.

NO TECHNICAL SUPPORT IS PROVIDED WITH THIS CD-ROM.